1987

Self-Knowledge in Plato's *Phaedrus*

Self-Knowledge
in Plato's *Phaedrus*

CHARLES L. GRISWOLD, JR.

YALE UNIVERSITY PRESS
New Haven and London

Designed by Susan P. Fillion
and set in Garamond #3 type by David E. Seham
Associates, Inc.
Printed in the United States of America by The
Alpine Press, Inc., Stoughton, Mass.

Library of Congress Cataloging-in-Publication Data

Griswold, Charles L., 1951–
    Self-knowledge in Plato's Phaedrus.

    Bibliography: p.
    Includes index.
    1. Plato. Phaedrus.   2. Self-knowledge, Theory of.
3. Socrates.   4. Lysias.   5. Rhetoric, Ancient.
6. Love.   7. Soul.   I. Title.
B380.G75 1986 184 86–5506
ISBN 0–300–03594–2 (alk. paper)

*The paper in this book meets the guidelines for
permanence and durability of the Committee on
Production Guidelines for Book Longevity of the
Council on Library Resources.*

10   9   8   7   6   5   4   3   2   1

For S.R., D.H., K.F.G.,
and my parents

ψυχῆς πείρατα ἰὼν οὐκ ἂν ἐξεύροιο,
πᾶσαν ἐπιπορευόμενος ὁδόν·
οὕτω βαθὺν λόγον ἔχει.

You would not find out the boundaries of soul,
even by travelling along every path:
so deep a logos does it have.

ἐδιζησάμην ἐμεωυτόν

I searched out myself.

HERACLITUS

Contents

Acknowledgments

This book first saw the light of day some years ago in the form of a doctoral dissertation presented to the philosophy faculty at the Pennsylvania State University. Articles drawn from the dissertation have been published in the *Monist, Revue de métaphysique et de morale,* and *The Classical Bulletin.* However, my thinking about the *Phaedrus* has changed substantially over the years, and at virtually every important juncture the interpretation presented below bears little resemblance to the dissertation.

In order to make the path through this book easier for the Greekless reader, most of the Greek terms have been transliterated (almost always with the accents omitted) and the quotations from the Greek translated. The translation of the quotations from Heraclitus on the epigraph page (frs. 45 and 101, respectively) and at the start of the Introduction (fr. 93), and from Xenophanes at the start of chapter 5 (fr. 34) are taken from Kirk and Raven's *The PreSocratic Philosophers.* I have, however, left the word *logos* untranslated. The text and numbering of these fragments, as well as of fr. 115 of Heraclitus with which the Epilogue begins, are those of Diels, *Die Fragmente der Vorsokratiker* (7th ed. rev. W. Kranz).

A project so long in the making as this one owes much to many. I would especially like to thank Edward Regis and David Levy for their comments on the Introduction, Dale Sinos for his suggestions about chapter

4, Kenneth M. Sayre for his comments on chapter 5, and Nicholas Rescher and Jim Lesher for their remarks on an early draft of the Epilogue. I am deeply grateful to Rémi Brague, Drew Hyland, Mitchell Miller, Robert Pippin, and Stanley Rosen for reading the entire MS and for supplying me with many penetrating criticisms. While they saved me from countless errors, none of these fine philosophers can be held responsible for whatever defects may remain. I am also much indebted to Jeanne Ferris, my editor at Yale University Press, who did so much to make this book possible, and to Cecile R. Watters for her judicious editing of the final version of the manuscript. Katie Heines did a commendable job in preparing part of the Index.

I acknowledge with gratitude the two Summer Research Fellowships awarded me by the Earhart Foundation for work on this book, as well as a sabbatical granted by Howard University. The technical assistance extended to me by Howard's Graduate School of Arts and Sciences during the preparation of the final version of the MS was extremely helpful. I would also like to thank Bernard M. W. Knox for permission to use the invaluable library at the Center for Hellenic Studies.

Finally, I owe a great debt to my wife, Katie, who not only mastered the intricacies of word processing (a friend of Plato must cringe at the phrase) and put the whole MS on magnetic disk, but who tolerated, indeed contributed to, endless discussions about Phaedrus and his walk with Socrates to the banks of the Ilissus on that hot summer's day.

Introduction

The lord whose oracle is in Delphi neither speaks out nor
conceals, but gives a sign.
HERACLITUS

The *Phaedrus* presents the appearance of a tapestry that has come partially unraveled into a tangled skein of themes and images. The warp and woof are Socrates and Phaedrus, a pair so ill matched that their relationship strikes us as comic. Their exchanges seem thoroughly permeated by irony and playfulness, and composed of little more than storytelling and wishful thinking. So recondite is the *Phaedrus'* design that the dialogue, like a colorful but poorly patched quilt, has been considered too thin to warm the interest of the serious scholar. Schleiermacher judged that the *Phaedrus* must be Plato's earliest dialogue, intended by its author as a sort of compendium of his favorite philosophical theses, theses that are explored separately and more deeply in the later dialogues. In Schleiermacher's view, the compendium is a good advertisement of Plato's ideas, but it is not a coherent or especially profound treatment of them.[1]

In spite of his false conclusion about the date of the *Phaedrus'* composition, and in spite of the false premises that led to this conclusion (the most important of which is the judgment that the *Phaedrus* is an essentially incoherent and superficial work), Schleiermacher did point out the significance of a dimension of Plato's dialogues crucial to my own study of the *Phaedrus*. This dimension is the dialogue form itself, including all the literary qualities that enrich it (the drama, images, myths, metaphors,

1

and the like). The maxim governing my interpretation of the *Phaedrus* is that the form of the dialogue is as intrinsic to its meaning as the content. The text's content is not truly intelligible independent of its form, and vice versa. In general, this approach to interpreting Plato is now widely accepted. Nevertheless, a certain latitude in the use of the maxim is possible, and in a moment I will spell out further the reasons for applying it as I have done here. I would like to begin with a brief and compact synopsis of some of the main issues and questions to be discussed in this book. Most of my positions on these issues and answers to these questions, and all my arguments in favor of them, are reserved for the text itself.

THE SELF-KNOWLEDGE THEME

Toward the start of the *Phaedrus* Socrates declares in extremely strong terms that he cares only about knowing himself, every other pursuit being "laughable" to him so long as self-knowledge is lacking (229e4 ff.).[2] A major thesis of this book is that when the *Phaedrus* is interpreted with the form-and-content maxim in mind, the dialogue comes to light as a whole unified by the theme of self-knowledge.[3] The problem of self-knowledge must be approached with some care. There is a Greek word for "self" in Plato, but the word is used as a pronoun, not as a substantive. The word "psyche" functions as the noun corresponding to our "self." In the *Phaedrus,* however, "soul" does not necessarily have the connotation of "substance" that came, during the history of philosophy, to be associated with "self." In this dialogue the "soul" is fundamentally different from Descartes's *res cogitans,* as well as from Kant's "transcendental ego" and the "soul-substance" Kant attacks in the *Critique of Pure Reason.* Still further, "soul" in the *Phaedrus* is not what we call "mind," and "self-knowledge" is not our "philosophy of mind." Thus the sort of thing Plato is talking about in the *Phaedrus* and the sort of thing Shoemaker is talking about in *Self-knowledge and Self-Identity,* for example, differ fundamentally.[4] This accounts for the almost complete absence from the *Phaedrus* of issues we would expect to see discussed in connection with "self-knowledge" (such as the "other minds," "mind/body," and numerous other epistemological problems) and, conversely, the presence of issues (such as those of the Ideas, eros, and dialogue) we might not expect to see in this context.

The *Phaedrus'* account of "self-knowledge" begins not with a technical interpretation of the notion but with an ordinary one. Socrates wants to know what he in particular—as an individual person—is. At the end of the dialogue he returns to this commonsensical level in his famous prayer to Pan: he prays that (among other things) he in particular might lead a harmonious sort of life. In the intervening discussion, however, the meaning of "self-knowledge" changes from "understanding myself as a whole person" to "understanding my soul" and then to "understanding *the* soul"—possibly even the "cosmic soul." A central issue to be discussed below concerns the reasons for these extensions of the meaning of "self-knowledge," and particularly for the introduction of the term "soul." Still further, at the start of the dialogue "self-knowledge" is an ethically charged term, as Socrates' comparison of himself with Typhon makes clear (see below). That is, Socrates wants to connect self-knowledge with leading a morally right life. In what sense does the *Phaedrus* explain this connection, if at all?

The extension of the meaning of self-knowledge does not end with talk about the soul. In the palinode Socrates suggests that in order to know the soul one must know the soul's function in a "cosmos" or "Whole," a crucial element of which are the Ideas. It is not obvious how self-knowledge and knowledge of Ideas are to be connected. At the very least it is clear that the picture of self-knowledge Socrates wants to argue for is fundamentally different from that to which our own culture has become accustomed. Crudely put, for Socrates, self-knowledge is not primarily a matter of what we would call "psychology," above all because of the "metaphysical" connection between self-knowledge and knowledge of Ideas he wants to draw. This connection involves, in part, a relationship between theorizing (in the literal sense of the term; 247c1) and practice (the soul's experiences in the world); between the soul as that which mirrors "what *is*" and the soul as that which chooses to live out its embodied life in a certain way; between the thematic of objectivity and eternity on the one side and the complex hermeneutic of human existence on the other. Understanding oneself as a being which is imperfect and incomplete because it is no longer nourished by Truth introduces, needless to say, a number of other issues. We are entitled to ask why the imperfection exists in the first place, how it can be overcome, and to what extent that process of overcoming, referred to in the *Phaedrus* as "recollection" *(anamnesis)* and as "divine madness," is a rational one.

Although the *Phaedrus* suggests that self-knowledge includes understanding one's character, it rather oddly describes that process of understanding as a kind of remembering. Consequently I shall also discuss the connections among character, recollection, and self-knowledge. Some very important issues surface in relation to the matter of character. Certain types of characters are persuaded of certain types of propositions about human beings and the world; character and intellect, the *Phaedrus* tells us, influence each other. This point immediately raises the specters of (roughly speaking) solipsism and subjectivism, since it threatens the objectivity of knowledge (including self-knowledge). It threatens to reduce self-knowledge to nothing more than the analysis of what each person is persuaded of and why—the question of the truth of what one is persuaded of being otiose (every answer to that question just constituting evidence, once again, of what a particular person is persuaded). The phenomenon of disagreement (which shows that people are *persuaded* of different things) adds fuel to the fire. As it turns out, in the second half of the dialogue Socrates founds an art of rhetoric, devoted in part to the sort of analysis just mentioned, and also discusses the phenomenon of disagreement. The issue of character, then, seems closely connected with the problem of rhetoric. This helps explain why a lover of wisdom should take an interest in rhetoric, even though he is concerned primarily with self-knowledge rather than with pedagogy, political power, and the like. For reasons to be explored below, dialectic suggests itself as the sort of rhetoric best suited to counteracting the drug of mere persuasion, mere opinion, and unreflective character.

The definition of the "soul" that Socrates offers in the *Phaedrus* complicates things further, in particular the puzzling definition of soul as "self-motion." How is this psychic kinesis to be related to the famous simile of the soul as a winged charioteer and horses, and still further to the phenomenon of eros about which Socrates also has much to say in the *Phaedrus?* At the end of the palinode, indeed, Socrates makes his familiar claim to possession of a special knowledge about eros. Is self-knowledge the understanding of what the soul "really" desires and so wishes to move toward?

At first glance the notion of self-motion seems to contradict the idea that the soul is erotically attracted to the Ideas, for to be so attracted is to be moved by something other than oneself. This apparent contradiction requires discussion. A preliminary connection between soul and Ideas is suggested at the start of the great myth in the *Phaedrus* (246a3–4), namely in the reference to an "ἰδέα" of the soul. This term might be understood in its metaphysical sense, in which case the *Phaedrus* speaks of an Idea of the soul, or it might not be so understood. Which interpretation of the term is correct? Clearly the answer will have critical consequences for our understanding of the meaning of self-knowledge. If there is such an Idea, for example, then to know oneself will include knowing oneself qua eternal "essence," and the latter process is referred to in the *Phaedrus* as anamnesis. To know oneself would thus be to recollect oneself in a way analogous to that in which one recollects Justice, Beauty, *Sophrosyne,* and the other Ideas (a process about which Socrates has something to say in the *Phaedrus*).

If this passage does not advert to an Idea of the soul, on the other hand, self-knowledge might seem reduced to a matter of opinion. Alternatively, it may be possible for an entity such as "soul" to have a nature *(ousia, physis)* but not an Idea. Yet if there is no Idea of the soul, the soul seems reduced to amorphous material to be molded by rhetoric. As already mentioned, Socrates attempts at great length in the second half of the *Phaedrus* to define the art of rhetoric and to show how it might exert the maximum influence on souls. We may therefore wonder whether by the end of the *Phaedrus* we are still meant to distinguish between self-knowledge and ignorance of oneself in a sense that is not entirely relative to rhetorical conventions. How to do so if the soul lacks an Idea?

As I have indicated, Socrates wants somehow to connect self-knowledge with eros. At the same time, a good part of the *Phaedrus* is about rhetoric. Correspondingly, the problem of the unity of the dialogue has often been taken to be the problem of the unity of eros and rhetoric, or more broadly, desire and speech (Socrates will virtually equate rhetoric and discourse). Self-knowledge is connected not only to eros but also (since for Socrates it is at least in part a discursive enterprise) to speech. The *Phaedrus* presents us with an extremely odd, but very rich, description of how eros and logos are connected to each other in the desire to give a discursive description of oneself, that is, to self-knowledge. The *Phaedrus* links two themes to the issue of self-knowledge in an intricate and valuable way, namely, the themes of what we want and how we talk about ourselves. The description begins with the two speeches ostensibly composed by an uninspiring character called the "nonlover." This frequently maligned character combines discourse and desire in a way that exhibits a low level of self-knowledge. We must therefore determine what the two speeches in question tell us about desire, speech, and self-knowledge, and indeed why the nonlover is present at all in the *Phaedrus.*

Brief reflection on the claims of the nonlover brings us very quickly to the matter of knowledge, for the nonlover claims to possess knowledge of a certain sort (namely, knowledge of what he wants and how to get it, as well as of the general nature of eros). Socrates' term for "knowledge" in the phrase "self-knowledge" derives not from *epistasthai* but from *gignoskein.* Of course, the Delphic command was traditionally formulated in this way.[5] In the *Phaedrus* the use of the one term instead of the other is philosophically important. In his second speech (the palinode), Socrates refers to an Idea called *"Episteme* Itself" (247c8 ff.). True Episteme is of,

or about, the other Ideas. We are given to understand that this perfect
Episteme (that is, the perfect vision of the Ideas) is the province of the
godly souls. Now, if the soul has no Idea, then there is in principle no
Episteme of the soul, no self-knowledge in the highest sense. And in the
discussion of rhetoric in the second half of the *Phaedrus*, Socrates repeatedly
outlines a methodological episteme that can be applied to the soul or
anything else (270c9–271a2, 271a4–b5, 271c10–272b4, 273d2–274a5,
277b5–c6). This episteme is a quasi-mathematical *techne*, specified in terms
of its rule-governed means of operation. The means consist in part of
cutting up, counting up, defining the forms, causes, and the like of the
things *(onta)* in question. The goal is always an exact analysis of the object.
To understand the soul through the mediation of this "method" (269d8,
270c4, d9) is to arrive at a notion of self-knowledge that differs significantly from the sense usually associated with Socrates' self-knowledge.
This sort of episteme is teachable, it is not associated with anamnesis,
and it has nothing particularly divine or godlike about it. Its objects are
not said to be Ideas, and it is closely tied by Socrates to artful rhetoric.
An important issue for this study is whether self-knowledge is to be
understood as an "episteme" in either of these two senses or whether there
is a third sense of self-knowledge signaled by the term "gignoskein," a
sense somehow related to Socrates' characteristic "knowledge of ignorance"
(also referred to in the *Phaedrus*) and worked out in the existential context
of dialogue. Is there a sense of self-knowledge that tells us "what it is to
be human" without transforming the soul into a special type of abstract
object (whether an Idea or a complex of forms and causes)?

These issues are of decisive importance for the interpretation not just
of the *Phaedrus* but of Plato's philosophy as such. The notion of "Episteme"
is closely tied to various theses about the Ideas, the immortality of the
soul, and anamnesis. The other sense of "episteme" is closely tied to the
techne of division and collection. Thus the *Phaedrus* offers us an occasion,
unparalleled in the Platonic corpus, for studying the relationship between,
roughly, the metaphysical and methodological approaches to knowledge.
Since the two kinds of episteme at issue are widely thought to characterize
the middle and late Platonic dialogues, respectively, the *Phaedrus'* demonstration of the relationship between the two may shed some light on
the connection between these two groups of dialogues. Still further, the
Phaedrus invites reflection on the connection between the two senses of
episteme and the knowledge-of-ignorance thesis which is, as just indicated,
tied to dialogue. That is, it invites reflection on the connection between
the knowledge of the Ideas, "dialectic" understood as "division and collection" (266c1 and context) and "dialectic" understood as the "erotic art"

of conversation (276e5–6 and context). The problem of how these notions are related pervades the corpus, but only in the *Phaedrus* are they all discussed explicitly. The very comprehensiveness and complexity of the *Phaedrus* from which Schleiermacher deduced its "youthfulness" may in fact be evidence of the dialogue's importance.

The *Phaedrus* is famous for its criticisms of writing and its praise of spoken dialogue. The issue is (as one can see in hindsight) hinted at near the beginning of the *Phaedrus*. The Oracle's command "Know Thyself!" is engraved on the temple at Delphi, and so is an instance of writing (*gramma;* 229e6). Socrates responds to the inscription by dedicating himself to spoken dialogue. Moreover, Lysias' written treatise is read aloud with enthusiasm by Phaedrus at the start, and it sits quietly throughout the remainder of the dialogue.[6] The content, the form, the fact that it is written, and Phaedrus' infatuation with this mere "phantom" of the truth are all criticized in the *Phaedrus*. Are there any interesting philosophical reasons for Socrates' own infatuation with spoken dialogue? His criticisms of writing do not seem, prima facie, terribly powerful and require deeper analysis. We must also evaluate the fact that these criticisms are after all written down by Plato. Plato too shows himself in his written works to be dedicated to dialogue. The criticisms of writing offered in the *Phaedrus* (and only in detail in the *Phaedrus*) might therefore be of help in understanding why Plato wrote dialogues. If so, the *Phaedrus* once again proves to be critical to an understanding of the corpus as a whole. If the *Phaedrus'* discussion of rhetoric (of which the criticism of writing is a part) helps explain Plato's decision to write dialogues, then in a peculiar sense the *Phaedrus* comments on itself, that is, on its form as written dialogue. Might not this self-commentary be a special case of self-knowledge?

Several interesting issues arise in connection with the notion that dialogue is the appropriate medium for philosophizing. One of these concerns the question of completeness. As we shall see, the *Phaedrus* suggests that philosophical dialogue (whether spoken or written) is not completable; philosophizing will remain the love of wisdom and will never yield wisdom, which is the province of the gods. Does this mean that philosophical dialogue ultimately becomes a Sisyphean enterprise? Many philosophers have said as much, and the familiar search for a system founded on indubitable first principles often seems motivated by the belief that if wisdom is unattainable skepticism and related doctrines will have won the day. I discuss this fundamental issue in some detail in the Epilogue, partly by means of a comparison between the notion of "dialogue" to which the *Phaedrus* points and the surprisingly similar notion of "conversation" advanced recently by Richard Rorty. As it happens, Rorty's position (if one may so refer to it) is very close to that of Jacques Derrida; and since Derrida has written a justly well-known essay on the *Phaedrus,* I shall also have something to say in the Epilogue about him.

The *Phaedrus* suggests, for example, that if philosophical dialogue is to get us anywhere, it must somehow proceed in conjunction with anamnesis. Thus much hinges on the meaning of anamnesis and so on our understanding of how Socrates thinks in the *Phaedrus* that Ideas and particulars, or originals and images, are connected. His account of the matter is not unambiguous. He seems to suggest that recollection is a making explicit of what is, until then, implicit in opinion. That is, the suggestion is that recollection is the coming to understand explicitly what we have always known obscurely, but known nevertheless. Correspondingly, it appears that the Ideas are present to us as informing and illumining the icons of the things that in *doxa* we (mistakenly) trust to be primarily real. If so, then Socrates is committed to holding that opinion is not entirely separated from the Truth; human beings do generally know, though through a glass darkly, what is the case. The existence of dialogue would thus have ontological consequences. A Socratic or Platonic criticism of Rortean conversation would have to show that this is true for every dialogue, even for the conversation premised on the view that "the Truth" is a fiction of the philosophers.

The issue about the meaningfulness of never-ending dialogue grows out of the *Phaedrus* in a number of intriguing ways. One of the peculiarities of the Platonic dialogues, and especially of the *Phaedrus,* concerns the choice of dialogue partners—Socrates' choice of interlocutor here is very odd. Why does Socrates talk to Phaedrus, and at such length? It is not clear how discussion with such a person could possibly help Socrates to know himself. Since Socrates is by far Phaedrus' superior, their "friendship" is very poorly balanced. Phaedrus exhibits in an interesting way the lack of self-knowledge, but it is not evident why this fact should attract Socrates to him. Indeed, the prologue to the *Phaedrus* is one of the strangest in the Platonic corpus. Socrates presents himself as half-crazed with the desire to listen to a manifestly absurd seduction speech written by a popular rhetorician, and then as willing to discuss the matter at length with the rhetorician's manifestly mediocre disciple. An elderly Socrates, who claims to still not know himself, produces lengthy disquisitions about the soul, all for the benefit of someone who does not know himself and is not aware of it. The *Phaedrus* would seem to be a species of comedy.

Not just Socrates' interlocutor but the place where the dialogue occurs is puzzling. Alone among the dialogues in which Socrates participates, the *Phaedrus* takes place outside the walls of the city, away from all human habitation. From the dramatic standpoint, the *Phaedrus* is a return to nature. Away from the technical and rhetorical sophistications of the city, Socrates emphasizes his devotion to self-knowledge. This suggests that the devotion to self-knowledge, indeed self-knowledge itself, transcends in a metaphorical sense the limits of convention and polis. Is self-knowledge in some sense suprapolitical? Socrates' subsequent joining of self-knowledge with divine erotic madness points to an affirmative answer, whereas his commitment to dialogue inevitably involves him with the political. The complexity of the situation is alluded to in the drama of the *Phaedrus*, about which I will have a good deal to say in chapter 1.

The countryside is rife with reminders of gods (such as Pan) and nymphs (such as Oreithuia). The setting naturally breeds myths as well as discussion about myths. Even a superficial glance at the *Phaedrus* shows how pervasive myths and talk about myths are in the dialogue. Indeed, Socrates calls his two speeches *mythoi* as well as *logoi*. The issue of myth also demands our attention. Are there any interesting philosophical reasons for Socrates' use of myth in the *Phaedrus* and in particular for his use of myth to talk about the soul? Socrates cares only about self-knowledge. But it is far from obvious what myths have to do with a philosopher's pursuit of self-knowledge, and so whether there is any reason we would want to say what the soul *is* by saying what it is *like*. We shall also ask in what sense Socrates' philosophical myths can be said to be "true" and how, correspondingly, we are to interpret them. These questions arise at the start of the *Phaedrus;* Phaedrus, in fact, explicitly inquires whether Socrates thinks the Boreas/Oreithuia myth is true. I shall discuss the matter in detail in chapter 4, "Excursus."

The *Phaedrus* is, as should already be clear, typhonic in its complexity. My efforts to make sense of it assume certain principles about the interpretation of a Platonic dialogue. Before turning to the text I would like to discuss these principles further.

THE QUESTION OF INTERPRETATION

I have mentioned that the maxim governing my approach to the *Phaedrus* is that the text's content and form are both intrinsic to its meaning. In the present instance, this signifies that the text's drama, along with all the associated literary dimensions (myths, images, and the like), are integral to our understanding of what the text means. This maxim is, of course, extremely general and seems crushingly obvious. It is a matter of record, however, that some interpreters of Plato pay little or no attention to it in practice and that others apply it in a variety of ways. In the main

I share an interpretation of the maxim with a number of other Plato scholars.[7] Since they have developed and defended it at great length, and since this type of interpretation of the maxim has gone virtually unchallenged in print, I will limit myself to several brief comments about this complicated issue.[8]

Interpreters do make assumptions when they read a text. Frequently readers do not share an interpreter's assumptions but are unaware of this fact (possibly because they do not understand themselves as making assumptions). The result is that they may criticize his interpretation of a given passage by appealing to details of the text when they should be specifying the assumptions that lead them to see the text in a certain light. The interpreter, who is looking at the same text, sees something else there, thanks to his own assumptions. The critic's criticisms thus miss their mark, and dialogue between interpreter and critic quickly grinds to a halt. Not all disputes in the area of textual analysis are so intimately related to interpretive assumptions, but many are.[9]

For example, interpreters who reject from the start the notion that irony can play a significant role in the rhetoric of a Platonic dialogue, and who believe that inconsistencies in the text should be explained by reference to Plato's putative development, limited knowledge of logic, carelessness, or "Greekness," will find it difficult to accept critical sections of my interpretation of the *Phaedrus*. To take two illustrations of the matter: Hackforth believes that the plan of the *Phaedrus* is centered on the discussion of the method of division and collection at 265c–266c.[10] In this discussion the results of the first half of the dialogue are ostensibly recapitulated in the idiom and format of the method. Unfortunately, the recapitulation is seriously inaccurate, as Hackforth recognizes.[11] He explains that "a writer with more concern for exact statement than Plato had" would have summarized his own words accurately. Hackforth's guiding assumption is obvious: Plato did not follow the advice that he puts in Socrates' mouth in the *Phaedrus* itself, namely, that a written text should be composed with "logographic necessity" (264c). Moreover, Hackforth is also forced to conclude that, relative to the formal plan of the *Phaedrus*, the palinode "is both too magnificent and too long; the balance of the dialogue is upset and the structural plan at least partially obscured."[12] To Hackforth, it is clear that the *Phaedrus* is, from the formal standpoint, botched. He nevertheless goes on to praise the content of the palinode, thus attributing a disjointedness of form and content to the *Phaedrus*, one that is supposedly symptomatic of a disjointedness between the "mystic" and "rationalist" "halves" of Plato.[13] Crude psychological speculations about Plato's inner psyche and the assumption that he is less than fully competent thus permit Hackforth simply to affirm that the inconsistencies are in the text and to forgo the search for an underlying meaning.

I will argue, by contrast, that the inaccuracy in the illustration of the method of division and collection is *intended* by Plato to tell us something about the limitations of the method, and that the jarring transition from the great palinode to the discussion of method is also designed to teach us about the limitations of the palinode (the limitations are very different from the ones Hackforth detects). Plato's pedagogy in these cases relies heavily on irony; views are initially advanced with great seriousness, but in a context relative to which they can be seen to undermine themselves. I maintain that my reading of the dialogue produces a truer (as well as richer and more fruitful) interpretation of the *Phaedrus* than does Hackforth's, one that also shows how the dialogue is coherent. Although this claim (if true) goes a considerable way toward vindicating my interpretive assumptions, something more must be said about the general assumption that warrants the introduction of references to irony, among other rhetorical devices.

Roughly put, the main assumption supporting the hypothesis that a text is coherent is that the author knows precisely what he is doing and so that he means to write both what and how he does write.[14] The assumption is not intended to be of the sort that can be verified or falsified on the basis of a biographical study of the author. The point concerns not the causal factors (if any) that may surround the author's psyche, the author's motives, or what was going through his mind as he wrote but the logical precondition of the thesis that a text is coherent and possesses a unified meaning.[15] The assumption is warranted at the very least on heuristic grounds, that is, relative to the reader's desire to be instructed. To deny the assumption is to begin study of the text with the prejudice that from a philosophical standpoint it is not worth the most serious study. Differently put, it is essential to begin serious study of a philosophical text by granting the claim, definitive of philosophers, that the text articulates the truth and does so in the most precise manner allowed by the subject matter and by the level of the readers to whom the author wishes to address himself.[16]

One might respond that to take this approach is to divinize the author. Could we not just assume that Plato too makes mistakes from time to time, and discuss the matter on a case-by-case basis? But how will one go about adjudicating the first case (and in the *Phaedrus,* as in many other dialogues, the first case arises very quickly)? The question of interpretation is only postponed momentarily by this response. When we reach the first problem area in the text, we should, I am arguing, give Plato the benefit of the doubt and treat the problem as Plato's challenge to the reader to look deeper. If we are unable to find a reasonable interpretation of a passage or text, *then* we are justified in concluding that for now, at least, it seems to us that Plato nodded there. Should we fail to implement this sort of hermeneutical strategy, we risk denying ourselves the opportunity of learning everything an author wants to teach us. Indeed, in our own capacity as authors we normally hope our readers will adopt this approach to our own texts.[17] None of this excludes the possibility, moreover, that a given text may turn out to be deeply aporetic in the sense that it defines a problem and shows that there are no available solutions to it. A Platonic dialogue may be designed to establish with great consistency that there is an irresolvable inconsistency in our accounts of how things are, even if none of the characters in the dialogue explicitly recognizes it. I am arguing that in such a case we should begin by assuming that the aporia is part of the author's design and therefore that he understands it.

Finally, I note that this approach to interpretation seems especially reasonable relative to the *Phaedrus*. For in this dialogue Socrates himself stipulates, as already mentioned, that written compositions must meet the strictest requirements. Moreover, Socrates insists in the *Phaedrus*, against the popular rhetoricians, that truth is accessible and worthy of our care. Thus the approach to Plato I am advocating is Platonic in spirit. I am aware that some interpreters (such as Derrida and Rorty) are in every way opponents of Platonism; for them, consequently, the entire discussion about true and false interpretations is beside the point.[18] But for reasons that will emerge in the course of this study (particularly in the Epilogue), I do not find that sort of objection persuasive.

If one accepts my interpretive maxim, several features of the Platonic dialogues become very important, starting with the fact that Plato does not actively contribute to his dialogues as a dramatis persona.[19] We must begin by assuming that Plato cannot be identified with any character in his dialogues.[20] Indeed, the *Phaedrus* shows that with respect to the crucial issue of rhetoric or communication, Socrates does not speak for Plato. Socrates declined for philosophical reasons (*Phr.* 274c ff.) to write philosophy, but Plato did write philosophy; indeed he wrote Socrates' reasons for not writing, a fact that "Socrates" is unaware of. Plato's distance from his characters supplies the basis for Platonic irony.[21] Platonic irony is not, therefore, simply equivalent to the "esotericism" which, as Hegel remarks, is endemic to all philosophical texts, thanks to their intrinsic difficulty.[22] There is a tension in the dialogues between the surface of the text and its context, a tension that points to an underlying meaning. In general,

Platonic irony depends on the difference between the fact that the dialogue is written and the fact that what is written is supposed to be a nonwritten spoken dialogue. Differently put, it depends on the difference between the dialogue that the reader conducts with Plato's text and the dialogue that is conducted by the interlocutors within the text. Hence it is necessary to distinguish between Socratic (or simply intradialogical) irony and Platonic irony and, more generally, between the apparent significance of a particular passage and the significance it possesses as part of a larger whole.[23]

Platonic irony, like Socratic irony, is not a stratagem for creating an inaccessible "esoteric doctrine" or "secret teaching." Platonic irony is certainly a kind of dissimulation, but one that, as René Schaerer notes in his excellent discussion of the matter, is designed to be understood *as* dissimulation.[24] It does not follow from this that the irony can be understood or penetrated in such a way that it becomes dispensable, that is, that an underlying stratum of meaning can be disengaged from the way in which it is presented and then grasped as a self-sufficient teaching. Part of the ironist's teaching may consist in the thesis that the irony itself, and so the different levels of meaning and the relationship between them, is inseparable from the teaching in question. I shall argue that such is indeed the case with respect to the *Phaedrus* and, thus, that there are philosophical reasons underlying Plato's use of the dialogue form. Platonic irony is not a function of political and pedagogical considerations alone. A study of the *Phaedrus*, of course, is the ideal context in which to develop this argument.

I have indicated that the meaning of Platonic irony is accessible in the whole of the text, a text that is held together by the bonds of logographic necessity. The whole here explicitly communicates itself on at least two levels, namely, those of logoi and of *erga*. This duality constitutes another important feature of Plato's dialogues. The "deeds" in the *Phaedrus* are in one sense obvious: they include the trip into the countryside, Phaedrus' effort to hide Lysias' text under his cloak (228d6–e5), and Socrates' effort to conceal his (presumably) ashamed face (237a). The words or speeches can themselves, furthermore, be viewed as verbal deeds. Still more broadly, how the interlocutors say what they say and how they fail to say other things are "deeds" that show us something about their characters and intentions. According to Socrates, Phaedrus virtually glows with delight as he reads Lysias' text (234d); and after hearing Socrates' magnificent palinode, Phaedrus fails to raise a single question about its meaning. To insist on the necessity of interpreting the whole of the text is to insist that the various levels of words and deeds be integrated into the interpretation. For example, a crucial "deed" of the *Phaedrus* consists in the fact that Socrates talks to Phaedrus at all. An issue is explicitly made out of this fact, for Phaedrus is on his way out of the city walls which Socrates (so Phaedrus supposes) never leaves (230c6–e4). Moreover Socrates threatens at one point to terminate the dialogue and to return to the city (241e). Thus an important question for the interpreter is, as I have already intimated, why does Socrates talk to Phaedrus?

Yet the issue of interpretation may still seem vague. I do not believe that a defensible canon of specific rules for interpretation (comparable, say, to detailed instructions concerning the proper use of a topographical map) exists, but I do think that the plausibility of a given interpretive framework hinges in part on its ability to yield an illuminating explanation of the text. What will count as illuminating will in turn depend partly on one's philosophical orientation. At this point hermeneutical considerations become questions about the philosophical enterprise as such. In this essay I shall have something to say about that enterprise, and so I shall postpone discussion of it for now. For the time being, I shall try to elaborate on what my interpretive approach entails.

First, it entails that the reader must assume, at least initially, that any gap, inconsistency, fallacy, or contradiction in the text is present for a reason and that the author is fully conscious of it. Second, the dialogues cannot be read as transcripts of the author's life or beliefs. If, for example, homosexuality is praised by a character in the dialogues, we cannot infer from this that Plato was a homosexual.[25] To make an inference of this sort is to transform the interpretation of the text into speculation about the author's psychohistory and so to deny that the text is a self-consciously crafted whole. Third, as already stated, Platonic irony governs every Platonic dialogue insofar as the irony is an expression of the ever-present Platonic anonymity. Hence variation within a dialogue, or from dialogue to dialogue, in a character's statements of his opinions is not per se evidence that the author's views have also changed (indeed, given the possibility that the character is speaking ironically at times, it is not evidence that even his views have changed). Before speculating about changes in the author's views, we should seek contextual reasons for the variations. These reasons may warrant references to a character's irony, but may not; in a dialogue, the interlocutors are permitted to revise their views as the discussion progresses. So too with variation in the choice of subject matter. Finally, it follows from our maxim that if a character in a dialogue is speaking ironically, there must be reasons in the context that would explain why he is so speaking. The purpose of this maxim, after all, is not to encourage the arbitrary invocation of irony to resolve all textual difficulties but rather to prevent arbitrariness of interpretation.[26]

Nevertheless it may be objected that once references to irony are permitted to serve as explanations of a text, interpretation will inevitably become capricious and nonfalsifiable, since the interpreter might appeal to irony to resolve any difficulty whatever. Granted that any type of explanation can be abused, it seems to me that this objection rests on a straw-man argument. An appeal to irony in any specific case must satisfy the same requirements to which any other explanation of the text is subject. A good deal of work has, moreover, been done on the various characteristics and forms of irony; an appeal to irony can be faulted on the basis that it confuses different types of irony, for example.[27] Once it has been agreed that, unless all else fails, we are not to appeal to an author's ostensible carelessness, Greekness, stage of mental development (all of which are far more conducive to arbitrary interpretation than is the appeal to irony), the basic criterion for adjudicating an interpretation remains what it has always been, namely, the context. If the interpretation, whether it appeals to irony or not, produces a coherent explanation of all the details of the passage and avoids speculative references to the author's putative mental development and the like, then until a better explanation is formulated it is to be accepted.

I would like to mention a final assumption of my interpretation. Each dialogue, I hold, is the primary whole relative to which the parts of the dialogue are to be judged. This assumption is not a trivial one. I have already said why I do not think that the culture of Plato's time, or Plato's psychological history, are the relevant wholes. Some interpreters believe, however, that the Platonic corpus is the relevant whole. Thus, in analyzing a specific passage in one dialogue, they appeal to evidence from another dialogue as a basis (and not just as correlative evidence) for their interpretation. That approach is implausible, in my view, because the corpus simply does not possess the degree of organic unity each dialogue possesses.

It does not in the least follow from this that one ought not refer to other members of the corpus in interpreting a given dialogue. For example, Plato has ordered most of the dialogues in terms of a fictive chronology (the *Parmenides* being, in this sense, the earliest dialogue and the *Phaedo* the latest, though the *Laws* is difficult to date dramatically and may take place still later). He has also made the life of Socrates a theme in almost all the dialogues. In doing so Plato has provided some unity to the corpus and so a basis for defensible use of one dialogue in interpreting another. Seeing a dialogue in the larger context of the corpus may help highlight certain peculiarities of the dialogue and so formulate the problems the reader is to solve. The setting of the *Phaedrus*, for instance, is remarkable relative to the rest of the dialogues in which Socrates participates, for only here does he exit the city in pursuit of a philosophical conversation (the uniqueness of this event, to be sure, is also called to our attention in the prologue to the *Phaedrus*). But we must look primarily to the *Phaedrus* to understand the significance of this fact, and in this sense the *Phaedrus* is the primary whole relative to which an interpretation is to be formulated. The fictive chronology prevents us from using a (fictively) later dialogue in order to interpret an earlier one, even if the historical order of the dialogues' composition is the reverse. For example, it would be a mistake to interpret Socrates' reference to Simmias at *Phaedrus* 242b in terms of the *Phaedo* (though the reverse is possible). On the other hand, a brief examination of the *Symposium* will help us establish the significance of Phaedrus' reappearance in the "later" *Phaedrus*.

Interpreters who appeal to the corpus, Plato's culture, Plato's ostensible state of mind, the date of the dialogue's composition, or the like as the whole on the basis of which a dialogue is to be explained usually ignore the given dialogue's singular drama, as well as its dramatic connection to other dialogues. They thus fail to do justice to the empirical fact of the dialogue form itself.[28] Consequently I will not appeal to passages of other dialogues as a *basis* for my interpretation of the *Phaedrus*, though I will discuss the relationship between the *Phaedrus* and other dialogues to which it is linked dramatically by Plato. Similarly, I do not regard citations from other dialogues as possible refutations of an interpretation of the *Phaedrus*. If, for example, we were to conclude that the *Phaedrus* teaches that the soul has four parts and all the other dialogues teach that it has three, we are free to note the difference but not to infer that Plato changed his mind, matured, or made a mistake, or that the four simply must be reducible somehow to three. We must first uncover a particular dialogue's teaching primarily with reference to that dialogue, and only then decide whether it is an anomaly.

1

The Dramatic Scene
and the Prologue

Everything in Socrates is exaggerated, buffo, *a caricature;*
everything is at the same time concealed, ulterior,
subterranean.
NIETZSCHE[1]

In this chapter I consider a number of the dramatic aspects of the *Phaedrus* and their connection with the self-knowledge theme. I begin first with the title of the dialogue and the character to whom it refers, and then turn to Socrates' relationship to Phaedrus and his reasons for talking to him. In the third section I consider the time and especially the place of the *Phaedrus* and, in the final section, the references in the prologue to Boreas, Typhon, and the Delphic Imperative. The comments in this chapter about Phaedrus, the prologue, and the dramatic scene generally are not exhaustive, since some of the commentary on these matters naturally falls into other chapters.

The dramatic structure of the *Phaedrus* should not be classified as background information. That structure contains the various matrices (the characters, the time and place, and so on) that mold the development of the dialogue. At its own level it articulates the dialogue's questions and answers. The drama gives the dialogue a strongly allusive, illustrative, and analogical character, but in a way that is important to our understanding of the whole conversation. The drama represents the everyday context in which philosophizing begins and never really leaves, and thus guides (rather than merely prepares) the conversation, to the point of determining what sorts of questions we ought to be asking and with whom.

PHAEDRUS

In a sense the title of our dialogue is uninformative, since it does not tell us what the subject matter is (as does the *Republic*) or even the occasion for the discussion (as does the *Symposium*). The title names one of the two interlocutors present. Why should Plato have named the dialogue after Phaedrus and not, as one might expect, after Socrates? By means of the title Plato draws the reader's attention to Phaedrus and so suggests that Phaedrus is of central importance to the dialogue. Since Phaedrus is manifestly Socrates' inferior in all important respects, the title of our dialogue is puzzling, and we are entitled to wonder what its significance might be. Why should a serious student of the dialogue pay much attention to the mediocre Phaedrus? But if Phaedrus is so uninteresting, why did Plato not only include him in the dialogue but name it after him?

I shall argue that Phaedrus' very shortcomings make him an ideal character for the development of what I take to be the central theme of the dialogue. To state the point in a preliminary way, everything about Phaedrus points to the necessity for self-knowledge. By showing us what it means to lack self-knowledge, Plato is able to show us both why the philosophic life is superior to the Phaedran and what would be required to achieve it. A successful demonstration of these points would be no mean feat. Further, since Plato has Socrates address the demonstration to Phaedrus, and so suit his words to the level represented by Phaedrus' soul, it is reasonable to expect that Phaedrus will exert considerable influence on the dialogue. I hope to show that this is indeed the case.

That is, Plato chose to say something about self-knowledge by constructing dialogue between someone who possesses a knowledge of his own ignorance and someone who is ignorant of even his own ignorance. The context is one in which we observe the emergence of self-knowledge, or at least the necessity for it. Among the advantages of a setting of this sort is its ability to depict the obstacles and objections to the pursuit of self-knowledge, as well as the ways in which this pursuit is both connected and distanced from ordinary experience. As we shall see, a number of further elements in Phaedrus' character make him a suitable interlocutor for a fruitful description of both the virtues of self-knowledge and the vices that follow from self-ignorance. That the *Phaedrus* does revolve around its eponym in important ways is already clear from the dialogue's prologue. It is Phaedrus who introduces the themes of eros, rhetoric, writing, remembering, the nonlover. It is Phaedrus who takes the discussion, and Socrates, out into the countryside. Thus Phaedrus virtually sets the stage on which the self-knowledge theme will be developed. We must, therefore, understand who Phaedrus is and what he represents.

Not just the theme of eros but Phaedrus himself supply us with links to the *Symposium,* a dialogue that precedes the *Phaedrus* in dramatic chronology (the fictive date of the former being 416). In the *Symposium,* Doctor Eryximachus calls Phaedrus the "father of the logos" (177d5). Phaedrus had complained repeatedly to Eryximachus that too little praise of eros has been sung. At Eryximachus' bidding, in fact, Phaedrus delivered the first round of the *Symposium*'s logos about eros. Thus the title of our dialogue takes us back to the start of the logos about eros. Phaedrus once again delivers the initial speech and so initiates another contest of speeches. Although this time Phaedrus' speech is composed by Lysias, Phaedrus identifies himself very closely with it.[2] Is a return to the beginning in our understanding of eros required by some shortcoming of the *Symposium*'s treatment of the matter? The answer is certainly affirmative.

Of course the *Symposium* is incomplete in the sense that it is transmitted to us by persons whose memories are imperfect (*Symp.* 178a, 223c–d); indeed, several of the speeches that followed Phaedrus' are omitted altogether (180c). Everything is presented to us indirectly through Socrates' disciples. These facts are inseparable from the fact that the *Symposium* is a narrated dialogue. By contrast, the *Phaedrus* is a performed dialogue and is given to us in its entirety and without mediation. The directness of the *Phaedrus* is visible in the fact that it occurs in broad daylight, in the steady glare of the bright sun. The *Symposium* takes place inside and at night, in the flickering light of torches (perhaps the *Symposium* and the *Phaedrus,* then, together form a complete cycle). Still further, the *Phaedrus* takes place in an atmosphere devoid of inebriation; in the *Symposium* the issue is raised at the start (since a number of the symposiasts are suffering the consequences of the previous night's drinking), and with the entrance of Alcibiades the drinking begins anew.

Moreover, unlike the *Symposium,* the *Phaedrus* praises spiritual madness and criticizes physical license explicitly (in the *Symposium* only Alcibiades mentions madness; 218b). The *Phaedrus* also deals much more directly and at greater length with the soul (especially the soul as detached from the body), the gods, the Ideas. And in the *Phaedrus* Socrates proclaims his devotion to self-knowledge, but self-knowledge is not mentioned at all in the *Symposium.* Still further, anamnesis, dialectic, and writing—all ways of transcending one's finitude—are treated briefly or not at all in the *Symposium* but in considerable detail in the *Phaedrus.* So too with the themes of rhetoric and of the method of *diairesis.* The prominence of method and techne in the *Phaedrus* again points to the dialogue's abstractness relative to the *Symposium,* in which the conceptual art of division and collection is not discussed. Correspondingly, the *Phaedrus* is much more explicitly devoted to reflection on our discourse about eros than is the *Symposium* and so manifests a curious detachment from eros (particularly eros that is concerned with bodily satisfaction), even as it describes and recommends the desire for logos (more on this in a moment). On both dramatic and discursive levels, then, the *Symposium* is more closely related than is the *Phaedrus* to the this-worldly context of generation and decay as well as to the eroticism of the body. In the *Phaedrus* the rhetorical symposia of mortals are seen as poor imitations of the intellectual banquet of the gods.[3]

Another notion that is prominent in the *Phaedrus* but seems missing from the *Symposium* is that of the nonlover. However, a defense of the nonlover is implicit in Phaedrus' praise in the *Symposium* of nongenerative eros.[4] In the *Symposium,* Phaedrus describes how a lover would do anything rather than be found acting shamefully by the beloved, and vice versa (178d1 ff.), but he soon restricts the phenomenon of shame to the lovers. The beloved controls the lover, for the latter would rather die than undergo this shame. This does not mean that the lovers are noble; their seemingly brave deeds are produced by a desire to be held in favor, not by an understanding of noble principle. Hence Phaedrus' famous "army of lovers" illustrates the *utility* of eros (as well as, I add, the harmony between eros and the polis). The beloved in particular *uses* the lover by means of the latter's desire. Phaedrus cites the deeds of heroes as examples of the kind of eros he has in mind. In fact, his account of the motivation of these deeds reduces them to fairly ordinary pseudoheroes (their motivation is simply *philotimia;* cf. *Symp.* 178d2); Phaedrus' theory of eros is in that sense "democratic." Similarly, Socrates immediately labels the thesis of Lysias' speech "urbane and useful to the people" (227d1–2; cf. 242e5). Neither Phaedrus' nor Lysias' account of eros is based on a particularly edifying vision of human excellence.

In short, Lysias' notion of the nonlover is implicit in Phaedrus' *Symposium* speech, though it ignores altogether other elements of the speech. That is, Lysias' nonlover is a Phaedran beloved who needs more than he is needed. The nonlover is like an impoverished beloved; the beloved (in both Lysias' and Phaedrus' speeches) is a wealthy nonlover. Lysias' speech explicitly condemns the sort of lover who is implicitly criticized in Phaedrus' speech. The lover is too selfless, too passionate; he destroys himself. He is transformed (at least in the discourse of a clever sophist) into his negation, the nonlover, who in turn imitates the Phaedran beloved by forgoing further slavishness and espousing selfishness and utility. Lysias' speech turns the lover into a self-consciously selfish businessman who appeals to a similarly disposed beloved. Lysias carries out, generalizes, and improves upon the logic of this aspect of Phaedrus' conception of eros. This is why Phaedrus raves about Lysias' speech and identifies so strongly with the position articulated by the nonlover. Phaedrus, then, serves as a bridge between the start of the *Symposium* and the start of the *Phaedrus*. We begin another discussion about eros by making explicit, and initially concentrating exclusively on, one strand of Phaedrus' *Symposium* speech, namely, that of the nonlover. It will turn out that an appreciation of the nonlover is necessary in order to complete our understanding of eros and that development of the nonlover theme does help formulate the self-knowledge problem.

While Phaedrus is interested in eros, he is even more interested in speech about eros. The themes of eros and rhetoric are already combined in the persona of Phaedrus. Phaedrus goes so far as to say that life without the pleasures of conversation is scarcely worth living (258e1–5; cf. 276e1–4). He loves to talk about love, and in that crucial respect he resembles Socrates. His ultimate threat against Socrates is to refuse to deliver to him any other logos ever again (236e). Socrates calls Phaedrus "godlike about discourses" (242a7) and says he is a person who has caused an almost unparalleled number of speeches to be delivered, whether by delivering them himself or compelling others to do so (242c8–b2; this surely is a reference, in part, to the *Symposium*). Phaedrus, however, is not really a dedicated composer of speeches himself. Thus he is content to spend the entire morning sitting (along with unnamed others; 227b7) at the feet of Lysias and has no thought of entering into a speech-giving contest with him. Indeed, Phaedrus shines with delight as he reads aloud not his own but Lysias' speech (234d) and has been trying to commit it to memory. At 228a3–4 Phaedrus says that he would rather have the capacity to memorize Lysias' speech perfectly than to have much gold. He manifests no desire to become a popular rhetorician, sophist, or *logographos* himself. Phaedrus seems to be an eternal student and disciple (though at the dramatic date of the dialogue he would be about forty years of age).[5] This accounts for the great difference between Phaedrus and other students of sophists, such as Meno and Callicles.

Equally revealing is his extraordinary lack of response to Socrates' palinode. Phaedrus only compliments Socrates on the style and wonders whether Lysias will be able to match the performance (257c); he fails to raise a single question about the palinode! Phaedrus certainly is not naturally inclined to Socratic cross-examination. In the *Symposium*, in fact, he puts a stop to Socrates' questioning of Agathon; Phaedrus says he enjoys listening to Socrates question other people, but for now the speech-giving contest must go on (*Symp.* 194d).

Phaedrus' love of speeches springs not from a love of the truth but from a love of their form, their shape or appearance. He loves "beautiful" or "rhetorical" speeches, though of course he has a poor understanding of these terms. He thus accepts the popular conception of rhetoric and is very impressed with the power of rhetoric in the assemblies (259e–260a, 268a5–6, 273a).[6] Correspondingly, Phaedrus is interested in the question of the techne of rhetoric, that is, of the power of speech to appear beautiful. Thus in the first half of the dialogue Socrates attempts to woo Phaedrus by presenting him with beautiful speeches, and in the second half, with an analysis of their artfulness (the importance of Phaedrus to the development of the dialogue is once again clear). Phaedrus eagerly interrupts Socrates as he summarizes the results of the conversation about the art of rhetoric, results that are to be conveyed to Tisias (273c–d). As already suggested, however, Phaedrus' interest in rhetoric seems unpolitical (hence the setting of the dialogue outside the city walls is appropriate for the way in which rhetoric is approached here). His interest tends more to the aesthetic, if I may hazard the term; he is interested in beautifully composed speeches (granted that he has a rather uninspired perspective on the nature of beauty). Thus Socrates does not emphasize here the connection between rhetoric and justice (as he does, for example, in the *Gorgias*).

All this would seem to make Phaedrus a singularly poor interlocutor for Socrates, especially given Socrates' enthusiasm for self-knowledge. Yet it is precisely Phaedrus' passive and formalistic love of speeches that makes him congenial to Socrates. Socrates too advocates a nonpolitical love of speeches directed to their manifestation of beauty. He loves not so much to create speeches (in the *Phaedrus* Socrates pretends, as usual, that he has heard his speeches from someone else) as to discuss them. Neither Phaedrus nor Socrates engages in the writing of speeches. Phaedrus says that he is an "amateur" or "private man" (*idiotes;* 228a2), a term applicable to Socrates as well. Phaedrus' love of the beauty and artfulness of speeches will allow him to transcend his fondness for the low conception of eros espoused in Lysias' speech as well as in his own *Symposium* encomium.

Consequently Phaedrus' love of speeches already exhibits the dialectic between lover and nonlover that soon becomes an explicit theme in the *Phaedrus*. Phaedrus is not a polymorphous erotic in the way that Alcibiades, for example, is; unlike him, Phaedrus possesses a crucial detachment from eros. Alcibiades is fascinating because, in part, the nature of his remarkable eros prevents him from turning to philosophy. The last section of the *Symposium* documents Socrates' inability to get Alcibiades to understand

and control his eros. For all his mediocrity, Phaedrus is in a way closer
to philosophy than is Alcibiades, and at the end of the dialogue Phaedrus
agrees to represent the claims of philosophy to his former beloved (Lysias).
Socrates has, to that extent, succeeded with Phaedrus.

It is important that the eros Phaedrus practices remains unrequited:
the oral and written monologues he finds so attractive do not repay him
in the way that the polis can repay an Alcibiades. The monologues are
"dead," like the "hyperuranian beings," but unlike the soul of one's beloved
in which one's admiring gaze is recognized and returned. The written
word may especially be said to lack life or soul, as Phaedrus exclaims at
the end of the dialogue (276a8–9). And of course Lysias' text is not just
written, it is also a praise of the detached, unmoving, and relatively unanimated nonlover. In these respects the particular monologue Phaedrus
loves so much is paradigmatically lifeless and unresponsive. The odd unity
in Phaedrus of attraction and detachment, or of lover and nonlover, is
thereby illustrated in a particularly stark way. Finally, I repeat that Phaedrus does not love speeches the way Callicles or Lysias loves them—as a
means of satisfying the desire for power or money. In iis respect Phaedrus
is detached from his love of speeches, even though his love of speeches
for their own sake is in a way immoderate (hence Phaedrus' love of rhetoric
must be regulated by his doctor's prescriptions lest it damage his health).

In short, Phaedrus manifests at his own level the strange dialectic of
desire and discourse, lover and nonlover, attraction and detachment, or
madness and sophrosyne, which eventually becomes an explicit theme in
the dialogue. This dialectic has something philosophic about it, and this
helps explain the sense in which middleman Phaedrus "wavers back and
forth" between Lysias and Socrates (257b). Phaedrus is not simply an
unredeemable or boringly unphilosophic person—which makes more understandable Socrates' desire to converse with him. Before turning to that
issue, however, several more observations about Phaedrus are necessary.

Phaedrus loves others out of a sense of utility. It soon becomes clear
that he decided to talk to Socrates in order to exercise his capacity to
memorize Lysias' speech (228e4), and that he was willing to deceive Socrates (by concealing Lysias' text from him) in order to achieve his purpose.
Eryximachus is of course eminently useful to him, as is Eryximachus'
father Acumenus.[7] His love of doctors seems to spring from his effeteness
and effeminacy.[8] In the *Symposium* he and Eryximachus leave early, no
doubt because late nights and drink are bad for you (see the doctor's
comments at *Symp.* 177c–d), and here he sets out on doctor's orders for
a gentle stroll in the fresh air. Today Phaedrus has his shoes off (as Socrates
almost always does) but only because of the heat (229a3–6) to which he,
unlike Socrates, is very sensitive (242a3–6; 279b4–5; cf. *Symp.* 220c–d).

Yet the entire *Phaedrus* countermands Acumenus' orders; Phaedrus' over-powering love of speeches leads him to sit down again for the rest of the day. Care for the soul's health replaces concern for the body's.

Phaedrus is also very interested in the sophist's reduction of myths to materialistic terms (229c). In the *Protagoras* he is presented as a student of the sophist Hippias; Hippias' disciples are asking him questions about natural science, especially astronomy (*Prot.* 315c; see also Hippias' words at 337d–338a). Phaedrus has a propensity, it seems, for materialistic physics (consider also the thesis about eros that Phaedrus' mentor Eryxi-machus presents in the *Symposium*). He certainly has no great respect for tradition, the opinions of the ancients, and the like (as the deeds of the historical Phaedrus also attest).[9]

If we allow ourselves a metaphorical reading of the first line of the dialogue, it is clear that Phaedrus cannot answer Socrates' question, as is also shown by Phaedrus' comic infatuation with Lysias' speech. He has come from listening to the speech and he is going to recite it to himself. Phaedrus does not ask himself whether these comings and goings are good or not. He does not naturally reflect on the significance of his own in-fatuation, that is, on himself. Had Socrates not interfered with him, Phaedrus would have circulated in the countryside, absorbed in reciting aloud for no one else's hearing the nonlover's address, answered only by the numbing humming of the cicadas—a comic scene indeed. The speech of solitary Phaedrus would resemble not the reflective soliloquy of a dreamer but the self-forgetful chatter of a sleepwalker. Thus Lysias' speech is "not healthy" (242e5) for Phaedrus; it is a *pharmakon* in the sense of "poison," not "remedy." Phaedrus' desire to memorize a text illustrates perfectly Thamus' critique of the written word (275a). To be sure, by attempting to commit the text to memory Phaedrus in one sense counteracts the debilitating effects of writing on memory. But in the sense of "remem-bering" that is at play in Thamus' critique, Phaedrus' mnemonic efforts illustrate the dangers of the written word, for they deprive him of true recollection as well as of dialectic (more below on the connection between these two terms). Thus the theme discussed at the end of the dialogue is already implicit in the beginning and especially in Phaedrus' character. Here again Phaedrus exerts his influence on the dialogue named after him. The theme of writing is appropriately discussed in the natural setting (and we are taken outside the city's walls, moreover, as a consequence of Phae-drus' intentions, not of Socrates'), for that setting removes Phaedrus from the scrutiny of other men. The silence both of Lysias' written text and of nature is dangerously conducive to Phaedran thoughtlessness. Unaware of the sense in which he needs other men, Phaedrus lacks self-knowledge;

and without the right companions, as we learn later in the *Phaedrus*, he lacks the means for coming to know himself. Phaedrus must be induced to sit down and talk with someone else if he is to give some sense to his comings and goings. This is precisely what Socrates brings about.

In sum, Phaedrus is a somewhat effete and self-indulgent "lover of the Muses" (259b5), a cultured dabbler in rhetoric, materialistic physics, and medicine. He has a fondness for avant-garde literary movements (he certainly has no aversion to the written word), for cleverness and novelty, for hedonism, utilitarianism (in a loose and ordinary sense of the term), and materialism. His morals are undoubtedly very permissive. I imagine him as a devotee of health fads and gatherings of fashionable literati. A more self-conscious Phaedrus might well resemble today's urbane, bohemian, leisured "intellectual" (the "cultured" representative of the "beautiful people," as they are now called). Next to him, Socrates looks like a rustic, tradition-loving, and rather uninformed individual (for example, he did not know that Lysias was in town), a man with a propensity for citing wise sayings of the ancients and of the Egyptians, and especially for criticizing the lifeline of the intellectuals, the written word. Of course, Socrates' conservatism is in fact much more radical than Phaedrus' superficial radicalism; and unlike Phaedrus, Socrates understands that he nevertheless needs the polis and what it can teach him about himself (230c5–d5). Hence Socrates, unlike Phaedrus, is unwilling to dissect and destroy customary beliefs as they are expressed in myths (see below).

For the reasons I have already mentioned, however, Phaedrus does serve as a suitable interlocutor for a conversation in which the self-knowledge theme is developed. Phaedrus' character already suggests many of the themes (eros and the nonlover, enthusiasm and moderation, rhetoric, writing, utility, memory, the health and sickness of body and soul, and so on) that subsequently become explicit in the dialogue and that are key to Plato's presentation of the self-knowledge issue. Thanks to the particular way in which he loves speeches, there is even some potential for changing Phaedrus for the better. Phaedrus is also suitable because he nonetheless lacks certain qualities *conspicuously*, in particular a concern for questioning and, finally, for self-knowledge. Having said this, however, we still need to explain Socrates' odd relationship to him, and it is to this which I now turn.

SOCRATES AND PHAEDRUS

The dialogue begins with a question posed by Socrates; he thereby engages in the discussion with Phaedrus voluntarily. Why does Socrates initiate the discussion? He refers here to Phaedrus as *phile*, a gesture that Phaedrus does not return in his reply. In the *Phaedrus*, Socrates repeatedly addresses Phaedrus as *phile* or *philotes* (227a1, 228d6, 229e5, 230c5, 235e2, 238c5, 243a3, 264a8, 271b7, 275b5, 276e4, 279a9), as *hetaire* (227b2, 230a6, 234d1, 262c1, 270c6, 273c9), and by other friendly terms.[10] In contrast, Phaedrus addresses Socrates as *phile* just twice (236b9, 259e7); at 279c6 (his last utterance of the dialogue) Phaedrus implies that he and Socrates are friends (cf. also 234e2), and at 227d6, 230c6, 235d4, and 257c5 he addresses Socrates as *beltiste, thaumasie* and *atopotatos, gennaiotate,* and *thaumasie,* respectively. In short, Socrates seems to extend the hand of friendship far more enthusiastically than does Phaedrus. Phaedrus' addresses suggest that he does not so much feel friendship for Socrates as he does a kind of wonder at Socrates' strangeness. Indeed Socrates seems to court Phaedrus as though he were a beloved. Socrates looks rather like the "lover" criticized in Lysias' speech (compare 228b6 with 231d). It is Socrates who wants to know about Phaedrus' comings and goings (not vice versa); it is Socrates who will follow Phaedrus around Attica (not vice versa). By contrast, Phaedrus' motive in inviting Socrates to walk with him is to have a chance to exercise his mnemonic powers.

At least initially Socrates takes a great interest in Phaedrus because Phaedrus can tell him about the "feast of discourses" served up that morning by Lysias. Socrates declares (before he learns of the specific thesis about eros that Lysias had advanced) that he places hearing about this "above all lack of leisure," in Pindar's phrase (227b9–10).[11] Phaedrus then remarks that Lysias' speech is appropriate for Socrates to hear, for in "I know not what way" (227c4–5; Phaedrus' confusion is understandable) the speech concerned eros (presumably Phaedrus recalls Socrates' interest in the matter from the *Symposium*). Although Socrates immediately mocks Lysias' clever *(kekompseutai)* thesis, he says that he desires to hear it so badly that he will walk to Megara and back (as recommended by yet another doctor, Herodicus)—quite a long distance—if necessary.[12] His enthusiasm is still greater now that he knows what the topic and thesis were. And once Socrates divines that Phaedrus actually has Lysias' text with him, he draws a picture of himself as almost out of his mind with desire to hear this "citified" *(asteios,* 227d2; cf. 242e5) speech. Socrates is now not just "sick concerning the listening to discourses" (228b6) and a "lover of discourses" (228c1–2), he is also willing to be led out of the city and all around Attica like a "hungry animal" who is "driven by dangling a young shoot or a bit of produce in front of it" (230d7–8; the foodstuff being Lysias' "discourse in a book"). The image is that of a stupid creature, such as an ass. In an amusing way it captures the sense of the soul's self-motion discussed in the palinode. The animal moves itself by desiring, and so valuing, what it deems nourishing, a value it carries wherever it goes. The type of creature alluded to anticipates the obstinate black horse of the palinode—the symbol of Lysias' conception of eros. Thus we already suspect that Lysias' logos cannot satisfy the whole soul.

At the beginning, then, Socrates needs Phaedrus because he needs to hear the logos about eros which is in Phaedrus' possession. Evidently Socrates does not have access to Lysias himself; at least, he treats Phaedrus as the conduit between Lysias and himself. But then Phaedrus would be entirely dispensable once he had delivered the speech; and yet that delivery is only the first step of the *Phaedrus.*

Socrates' desire to continue with Phaedrus after the speech has been read may be partially accounted for by Socrates' explicit effort to turn Phaedrus into his own emissary to Lysias (see 243d3–e1, 257b–c, 278b–c). Still further, Phaedrus is to deliver the results of *part* of the dialogue to all composers of discourse, to Homer and all the poets, and to Solon and all composers of laws. A good deal is omitted from Socrates' list at 278b–c of the results to be publicized. All of the metaphysical doctrines of the *Phaedrus* concerning the soul, eros, Ideas, anamnesis, and the like are omitted from the message. The message is therefore, if I may put it this way, a politically accessible and so partial summary of the *Phaedrus.* That is, Phaedrus is to serve as an intermediary between Socrates and the "opinion makers" of the city.[13] Phaedrus must therefore be educated and equipped with the proper teaching to take back with him. Socrates would wish to upgrade the rhetoric of the opinion makers in order to save philosophy (and so himself) from condemnation by the city. By not writing and by limiting his direct involvement in politics (cf. *Apol.* 31c–e), however, he has abandoned the most obvious means for doing so. Philosophical rhetoric, as outlined in the *Phaedrus,* is effective only when the speaker can know the soul of his interlocutor(s), an impossibility when a large group is being addressed (at least if the truth is to be conveyed). Hence Socrates does not have a dialogue with the many (*Gorg.* 474a–b; cf. *Apol.* 37b); and yet he wishes to present them with a defense of philosophy. Socrates thus requires intermediaries who can convey something of his views in the form of a message, that is, a teaching or doctrine. On this interpretation, in sum, a strong political undercurrent prevails in the *Phaedrus;* Phaedrus is useful to Socrates as a conveyor to the city of a partial, politically useful defense of philosophy. Presumably the reason that Socrates does not himself go at least to Lysias is that he thinks that

Lysias will listen more closely to the words when they come from the lips of his "lover" Phaedrus.

This explanation of Socrates' desire to converse with Phaedrus even after Lysias' speech has been read does not take us quite far enough. It does not account for the fantastic length to which Socrates goes both to educate Phaedrus and to formulate a superior account of eros. Nor does it integrate Socrates' desire to converse with Phaedrus with his professed interest in nothing but self-knowledge. In order to account for all this adequately, it is important to see that the low thesis of Lysias' speech, as well as Phaedrus and everything he represents, constitute an extremely serious challenge to Socrates in a number of ways and further that the speech does articulate something true about eros. Since in subsequent chapters I will be saying a good deal about these points, I will postpone comment on them. Let us assume for now that Socrates has good reason to be intrigued by Lysias' thesis and to want to refute it and so to meet head on the pedagogic challenge posed by Phaedrus. Understanding and articulating the positive and negative aspects of the thesis—and doing so in the face of one enamored of the thesis—really does contribute to Socrates' understanding of himself. This approach to the "Phaedrus problem" anticipates a much larger issue I shall discuss below, namely, the connection between Socrates' desire for self-knowledge and his avid commitment to dialogue. I have, in sum, suggested three reasons for Socrates' desire to talk to Phaedrus. The first is that Phaedrus is in possession of Lysias' text, and Socrates naturally takes an interest in the topics of eros and soul. Second, Phaedrus serves as a conduit between Lysias and Socrates and so as one means by which Socrates can propagate a defense of the philosopher's vision of rhetoric, truth, and kindred topics. Third, Lysias' discourse does pose a real challenge to Socrates' conception of the love of wisdom. The fit between Lysias' thesis and Phaedrus' character, along with Phaedrus' other attributes, also makes Phaedrus himself the sort of challenge to which the dialectical Socrates is attracted.

I would like to turn now to another dimension of the *Phaedrus'* drama. Socrates' remarkably intense professions of desire to hear Phaedrus read Lysias' speech are made shortly after Socrates has sarcastically commented on the speech. We are justified for this and other reasons (see below) in suspecting that Socrates' professions are not entirely serious. Might not some of Socrates' enthusiasm be mimetic in character? That is, does not Socrates imitate Phaedrus in such a way as to both hold the mirror up to Phaedrus and show Phaedrus what he (Phaedrus) should look like? The image of the ass led about by some foodstuff dangled in front of it, after all, fits Phaedrus better than Socrates. It is Phaedrus who unthinkingly allows himself to be led out of the city by a book, his eyes focused on it alone, in the mistaken belief that it will nourish him well. Moreover, when Socrates has consumed the speech, he pronounces it "not healthy" (243a1) and purifies his system with another speech. Socrates thus enacts the *periagoge* that Phaedrus should follow. Socrates' mimetic irony is fully in accordance, in fact, with the rules for philosophical rhetoric described later in the *Phaedrus*. Its goal is to lead the auditor to self-knowledge.

Socrates begins, that is, by characterizing himself in such a way as to make himself resemble Phaedrus' disposition toward Lysias' speech; hence he is able to characterize them both as "synkorubantic" (228b7). This Socrates achieves by concealing himself in the prologue as Phaedrus' lover. Phaedrus himself responds by casting himself as a hard-to-get beloved. Phaedrus said that he would be willing to tell Socrates what was discussed that morning (227b8); then he pretends not to be able to remember accurately what was discussed (228a1–4), though he intended if necessary to compel Socrates to listen to him try to recite it from memory (228c1–3). Socrates reveals Phaedrus' deception by constructing a drama in speech in which Phaedrus is referred to in the third person and is asked to make himself do now what he will soon do anyway (228a5–c5). This drama functions as a mirror in which Phaedrus is made to detach himself from himself and so observe himself. He can become self-conscious only when his love of speech becomes reflective, that is, itself an object of speech. Socrates enters into a comedy of imitation and deception with Phaedrus in order to lead Phaedrus to self-knowledge. Even after Socrates' third-person drama Phaedrus tries to prolong the deception by hiding Lysias' text, which he holds with his left hand, under his cloak.[14] He claims that he has not gotten all the words by heart, but that he can sketch out the meaning *(dianoia)* of each of them from the beginning to the end.[15] Phaedrus' deceptions speak volumes about him, revealing far more about him than he might wish—an example of Platonic irony at work.

Although in the prologue Phaedrus plays the part of a beloved, and Socrates, of the lover, their relationship undergoes a number of transformations in the *Phaedrus*.[16] Phaedrus begins by playing or concealing himself as a beloved, and Socrates, as a concealed lover. When Phaedrus reads Lysias' speech, he plays the part of a nonlover, and Socrates, the part of the boy being courted, a part that I shall correspondingly refer to as the "nonbeloved" (a term I shall explain in chap. 2). In the interlude after the reading of Lysias' speech, the relationship between Phaedrus and Socrates explicitly becomes the inversion of the one that held in the prologue. Phaedrus refers to his assuming Socrates' former role and Socrates assuming Phaedrus' former role as an affair of "poor comedians" (236c2). Phaedrus now plays the lover, and Socrates, the hard-to-get beloved; it is Phaedrus who must "compel" Socrates to deliver his speech (236d2–3, d6–e5, 242d4–5). Then in his first speech Socrates plays the part of a lover concealed as a nonlover, and Phaedrus, of the "boy" (237b7) he attempts to seduce. That is, while reciting this speech Socrates hides himself under his cloak in shame, even though he seems to wax enthusiastically while speaking. He is actually only concealed as a lover who in turn is pretending to be a nonlover. Phaedrus is playing the role of the addressee of the speech, and so of a nonbeloved. Thus far we have:

	Prologue	*Lysias' Speech*	*First Interlude*	*Socrates' First Speech*
Phaedrus	Concealed as a beloved (B)	Concealed as a nonlover (~L)	Concealed as a lover (L)	Concealed as a nonbeloved (~B)
Socrates	Concealed as a lover (L)	Concealed as a nonbeloved (~B)	Concealed as a beloved (B)	Concealed as a nonlover (~L)

While Socrates and Phaedrus begin by playing different parts, the sequence of parts remains the same (that is, the sequence is always B – ~L – L – ~B – B, and so on). Socrates and Phaedrus merely join it at different points.

Our problem is not only to understand the "logic" of these transformations, but also to understand how to break out of the cycle and so ascend to a higher level.[17] That the sequence of roles and role reversals tied to the thesis of the first two speeches of the dialogue is a dead-end may be one reason Socrates interrupts his first speech halfway through, abandons the whole mad play, and threatens to return to Athens. This is in effect the problem of the transition from the level of the first two speeches of the *Phaedrus* to that of the palinode. A number of clues to its solution are to be found in the interlude between Socrates' two speeches. So as not to run ahead of myself, for now I note only that in that interlude Socrates again casts Phaedrus in the part of the lover. Socrates ironically asserts that Phaedrus is compelling him to deliver another speech (see 242a–b and context) and so to play again the role of the beloved. The two thus appear to slide back to the status they held in the previous interlude.

Thankfully the sequence of steps is not simply resumed when Socrates recites the palinode. At the start of the palinode Socrates refers to Phaedrus as the *pai* who is the auditor of the speech (243e4–8). However playful the reference, it distinguishes this speech from the previous ones in which the identification of Phaedrus (or Socrates) as the auditor was implicit and quite formal. In the earlier speeches Socrates and Phaedrus were compelled to play roles in order to fulfill the formal requirements of the rhetorical situation described above. But in the palinode Phaedrus is being addressed much more directly, as is shown by the concluding paragraph in which Socrates prays that Phaedrus may be turned to philosophy as a consequence of the speech (see also 243e9, 252b2, and 256e3 where the boy is addressed directly). And whereas Socrates begins by attributing his palinode to Stesichorus, in the concluding paragraph he takes responsibility for it himself. The palinode is meant to turn boy Phaedrus to philosophy and to the worship of Eros rather than to the gratification of any person (257b). Phaedrus in effect is treated as a potential philosopher who joins his dialectician-teacher (Socrates) in a shared love of wisdom. This arrangement reflects a potentiality in both men for a relationship they ought to possess, one they would possess if they realized themselves as they would be at their best. Best is the relationship of friendship (philia) between lovers of wisdom described in edifying terms toward the end of the palinode. Phaedrus and Socrates do not attain friendship in that sense. Nevertheless Socrates holds it up to them as an ideal and certainly as an improvement over the result aimed at by the previous speeches and reflected in that sequence of roles Socrates and Phaedrus played before recanting. No longer objectified as material entities whose worth is fixed on the open market (see chapter 2), lover and beloved—as well as Socrates and Phaedrus— begin to enact their true substance. In ways examined in subsequent chapters, we shall see that the meaning of "self-knowledge" changes accordingly.

This relationship between Socrates and Phaedrus is preserved in the second half of the *Phaedrus,* where Phaedrus is still addressed as the boy who is learning from the dialectician Socrates (257c8, 267c6). That Phaedrus fails to lift himself up to Socrates' level means that, in performing the function of the potential philosopher as he—boy Phaedrus—listens to the palinode, he is playing a role he cannot fully live up to. Likewise, we shall see that Socrates too cannot sustain the role of the divine poet which he claims to possess in the palinode. In that sense the comedy of the *Phaedrus* is not yet over. But since the roles Phaedrus and Socrates play in the palinode and in the remainder of the dialogue do reflect human potentialities they ought to strive to fulfill, the comedy of deception and concealment, which characterizes the prepalinodic speeches of the dialogue, is virtually absent from the palinode as well as from the second half of the *Phaedrus*. The termination of the comic exchange of roles between Socrates and Phaedrus is connected to the fact that in the palinode the lover/nonlover dichotomy is dropped and that an effort is made to fuse them in the character of the philosopher.

I would like to hazard an observation about the logic of the sequence of roles outlined above. Each character becomes his own negation by first becoming the negation of the other character (Socrates the lover becomes nonbeloved), then negating that negation (Socrates becomes the beloved, that is, Phaedrus), and finally becoming the negation of his initial character (Socrates becomes a nonlover). The logic of the sequence is bipolar or dialectical, essentially dependent on the asymmetrical relationship between the lover/leader and beloved/follower. Each becomes his own negation only by first incorporating the other character in his negation. It seems that who a person is and how he positions himself vis-à-vis another person are inseparable. This suggests that dialectic and rhetoric are inseparable in the context of self-knowledge and that self-knowledge possesses an irremediably "social" or (in the broadest sense) "political" character. Hence Socrates' statement at 228a5–6: "Oh Phaedrus, if I do not know Phaedrus, I have forgotten myself." When their roles are reversed, Phaedrus mimics this same phrase (236c4–5). In doing so he says more than he thinks. These points about the social character of self-knowledge are developed in the palinode and borne out in the remainder of the *Phaedrus*.

The bizarre comedy of the first half of the *Phaedrus* illustrates how the self-understanding of a soul, which is mediated by its understanding of how it is related to the desires and thought of others, causes the soul to move itself. The central suggestion seems to be that the soul cannot know itself directly without the mirrorlike presence of another soul. The problem, of course, is to find or construct (both terms are used in the palinode in this connection) a reflection that will somehow cause one to move in the direction of self-knowledge rather than a reflection that will simply mirror what one is already or what one would vainly like to think of oneself as already being. What combination in two people of lover, nonlover, beloved, and nonbeloved provides the right mix for self-knowledge? How to bring about that mix? For Socrates, a good friend is one who helps him to question himself. *Dialegesthai* turns out to be the sort of discourse appropriate to friendship so understood.

The strange comedy we have been examining illustrates, in part, Socrates' mimetic irony vis-à-vis Phaedrus. But it is not only Phaedrus who can see himself and his own defects and potentialities in Socrates' mirror. Socrates too can learn something about himself by observing Phaedrus. It is not just that Phaedrus resembles Socrates in the ways I have specified above. More important, by looking at a degraded image of eros Socrates can challenge himself to think through again the nature of eros. To pursue anything other than self-knowledge is laughable in Socrates' eyes (229e–230a), and the day's conversation with Phaedrus is not laughable in that sense. Thus when Socrates repeatedly refers to Phaedrus as his "friend," he is not simply joking. I grant that the force of this interpretation depends partly on the views that Lysias' speech, along with everything Phaedrus represents, really does present a philosophical challenge to Socrates and that dialogue is the indispensable route to self-knowledge. The *Phaedrus* will provide us with extended opportunities for considering these controversial views. But the *Phaedrus* has a time and place, and it is these I shall consider next.

THE TIME AND THE PLACE

Socrates' opening question concerns Phaedrus' destination and the origins of his walk. The immediate focus is on place, and most of my comments will center on the setting of the *Phaedrus* rather than on its chronology (I have said a bit about the latter above by way of comparison with the *Symposium*). As I have already pointed out, the *Phaedrus* is the only Platonic dialogue in which Socrates participates that takes place in nature, outside the shelter of the city. The setting is thus unusual in the extreme. It is also the dialogue in which Socrates proclaims with unparalleled forcefulness his dedication to self-knowledge. In what sense is nature a suitable context for this proclamation? How is self-knowledge connected with the extrapolitical (in a metaphorical sense of the term)?

The topology of the *Phaedrus* is carefully marked for us, and it recurs in the spacing of the universe described in Socrates' palinode. The palinode's transposition of the dramatic setting to a mythic context suggests that "this" world is an "image" of another, "higher" world. That suggestion is itself in keeping with the palinode's teaching. The dramatic setting thus possesses a double significance, as is particularly appropriate in a dialogue so permeated by allusion, irony, metaphor, imagery, and myth.[18] Socrates' and Phaedrus' sedentary tour through the discourses on love is analogous to the *periphora* that carries the gods around the outer edge of the cosmos so that they might gaze upon and be nourished by the Ideas. Athens thus corresponds to the interior of the palinode's universe, an interior that is home for even the gods (247e4). The palinode teaches, however, that unlike the gods men cannot entirely leave home when partaking of truth. In order to present his "feast of speeches" (227b6–7), Lysias has come up to Athens and is staying with Epicrates in Morychus' old house (near the temple of Olympian Zeus).[19] Just as much as them, Socrates and Phaedrus must feast on *discourses,* a fact that bears testimony not only to their desire to rejoin the gods but to their fundamental separation from them. The banquet of the gods is a feast of theory (of *theoria* in the literal sense), not of discourses (more on this below). Does the conjunction of the discourses (both spoken and written) and the natural setting thus suggest that every effort to leave the polis is stymied from the start by the means required, and so that every ascent from the polis both bespeaks a prior descent and promises a reenactment thereof? At least this much seems clear: the unique return to nature with which the *Phaedrus* begins signals that self-knowledge is a transcendence of the city, while the confinement of this sortie to a mere day suggests that for men the transcendence cannot but be temporary.

That our movement to the palinode's description of the ascent is itself a temporary ascent is suggested symbolically by the carefully noted ascending and descending movement of the sun (consider 228b3, 242a4, 259a1–6, d8, 279b4–5). The sun's zenith occurs at the conclusion of the palinode. Thus the palinode immediately precedes, but also leads to, that moment when the sun is at its brightest and most blinding. This is the moment when the eyes are in the greatest danger, when a "darkness at noon" (*Laws* 897d) threatens. Not coincidentally, it is precisely at this moment that Socrates recounts a story about the cicadas overhead, a story about death as well as the passionate love for beautiful odes. This story is the turning point of the dialogue, and after it the tone and in a way the substance of the conversation are more down to earth. I shall discuss it in chapter 5, where I will make some further comments about the chronology of the *Phaedrus.*

The symbolism of the *Phaedrus'* setting requires further comment still. Socrates explains with the following words why he does not leave Athens: "I am a lover of learning; the open country and the trees do not wish to teach me, but the men in the city do." Socrates silently accepts Phaedrus' false assertion that he never leaves the city (230d1–2; cf. *Crito* 52b). Indeed, Socrates knows precisely where Boreas is said to have taken Oreithuia and that there is an altar to Boreas near it (229c1–3). He knows the Ilissus and that quiet resting spots are to be found on its banks. He is able to identify the statuettes and images surrounding the place where he and Phaedrus sit (230b7–8). Clearly, Socrates has been in this area before. Yet unlike Phaedrus, Socrates is remarkably sensitive to the beauty (230b2) of the spot, as his encomium of it indicates.[20] He does indeed react to it as though it were new to him. Phaedrus finds this so odd that he infers that Socrates really is a stranger to the countryside (230c6–d2)! Socrates' sensitivity to the magic of the place contrasts sharply with Phaedrus' perception of it solely in terms of physical comfort. Socrates is not so drugged by the thought of hearing Lysias' text that he is insensitive to nature's beauty. The edifying and salubrious setting seems to hint at a cure for the "sickness" Lysias' text has caused.

Even if Socrates does not learn anything from the setting, we may wonder whether his capacity to appreciate it is indicative of philosophical character. In the palinode the lover of beauty is at the very top of the hierarchical list of souls, along with the lover of wisdom (248d3). We are also told there that of all the "really real beings" Beauty alone is visible to the senses and so is the most desirable of them. In the palinode (as in Socrates' speech in the *Symposium*), sensitivity to earthly beauty is a prerequisite (though not a sufficient condition for) remembrance of Beauty itself. Socrates fully appreciates the nonsexual and nondiscursive beauty manifested through the nonhuman shapes around him. Perhaps the place does not "wish to teach" Socrates as men in the city do, for the beauty of the place is not discursive. Socrates is not just a lover of learning (*philomathes*) but also a lover of discourse (*philologos*, 236e5) and of divisions and collections (266b). Above all, he loves dialogue. But dialogue, we will soon learn, cannot flourish in the absence of both the soul's recollection of a natural order and other human beings. The complex relationship between recollective vision and discourse, which will be pivotal in the palinode, is anticipated in the *Phaedrus'* setting (so too with blindness to Beauty). Socrates, who loves self-knowledge and professes knowledge of ignorance, is eminently sensitive to natural beauty, whereas Phaedrus, who loves a written discourse about the nonlover and who is ignorant of his ignorance, is insensitive to the same beauty. Is there not a connection between these phenomena? The *Phaedrus'* unique setting forces the question on us. The remainder of the dialogue responds with answers.

Phaedrus' insensitivity to the beauty and magic of the spot is deeply symptomatic of him and of the type of person he instantiates. Phaedrus walks outside the city, but his soul is owned by it. Hence the symbolic power of Phaedrus' possession of Lysias' written text outside the walls of the city. I refer not only to the thesis of the discourse but also to the fact that it is contained in a book, that is, in a product of the polis' techne which in spite of its lifelessness animates the city's urbane Phaedrus. Socrates dislikes leaving the city, but only because he *chooses* to remain in it; he is in, not of, the polis. Hence the aptness of Phaedrus' reference here to Socrates as "atopotatos" (230c6); Socrates is always "most out of place."

He both needs and must transcend the men in the polis; he must both desire and avoid the nature that resides "outside" the polis. In this duality, which is as it were inscribed in the *Phaedrus'* setting, resides much of the difficulty of the palinode's teaching. Nature is not good without qualification; indeed, we are warned repeatedly about the potentially destructive powers of the local gods (especially Pan), the soporific power of the cicadas, even the multiple dangers of the sun's heat. Close proximity to nature can engender recollection *or* forgetfulness. The remedy easily becomes the poison. If not in a simple return to nature, or in immersion in the polis, wherein lies the path to spiritual health?

This question is analogous to our previous question concerning the unity of lover and nonlover. The desire of an Alcibiades to attract other men into his orbit closes him off from the detachment necessary for theory. His eros is, so to speak, almost exclusively political. But the nonlover is debased by his ostensible transcendence of the erotic bonds that tie lovers to what is beloved to them. His eros is, roughly speaking, almost exclusively apolitical. The problem is to articulate a unity of, in effect, theoria and eros in a way that recalls "human nature." At least in part, self-knowledge is this articulation. My remarks so far about the dramatic setting of the *Phaedrus* may suggest that in some way an almost Phaedran love of speeches will be necessary to this self-knowledge—but a love measured by nature, not just other speeches, books, or the applause of one's admirers. We will require a form of rhetoric that humanizes.

This brings us to a further question to be discussed below, one central to the self-knowledge theme. Socrates does not try to persuade Phaedrus that the place actually is beautiful (no doubt Phaedrus thinks that Socrates' experience is subjective and peculiar). Does this constitute an acknowledgment of the incommunicability of the experience, of an unbridgeable gap between the philosopher's vision and the nonphilosopher's lack of it and so of a limitation on the power of philosophical rhetoric to humanize?

Socrates is, enigmatically, both most out of place and quite at home in the *Phaedrus'* remarkable setting. At this point it is not clear where *he* has come from and is headed. Socrates does give us some further clues a few moments before Phaedrus begins to read.

BOREAS, TYPHON, AND THE DELPHIC IMPERATIVE

Phaedrus observes that this is a perfect place for girls to be playing and is reminded of the story about Boreas' rape of the nymph Oreithuia (229b4–9). In fact, it all happened farther downstream while Pharmakeia was present (229c ff.).[21] The violence of eros is a central theme in the first two speeches of our dialogue, as is the theme of possession by outside forces. The story (Phaedrus calls it a *mythologema;* 229c5) might well be interpreted as a rudimentary allegory about human nature as it is defined in these two speeches. But when Phaedrus excitedly asks whether Socrates is "persuaded" by its "truth,"[22] he evidently has something else in mind. By "truth" he means (or so Socrates assumes) the reduction of the allegory to a causal explanation of natural phenomena.[23] This notion of truth suggests that popular myths are nothing but imaginative interpretations of the perceptible world in terms of chimerical entities. That is, from the view that myths are generated from nonmythic origins, it would be easy to claim that the myths are false in that the beings they depict do not in fact exist. Socrates himself makes up such a logos (229d2): the north wind Boreas blew the maiden down onto the rocks, where she was killed (229c7–9). A violent and "accidental" death is the truth of a story about violent desire. In reality and in fiction, Oreithuia is subjected to an act that dissolves her as a person, just as (according to Socrates' nonlover) does the "love" a wolf has for a lamb (241d1).[24] Socrates does not say that such clever or sophistical accounts are either impossible to formulate or wrong. Rather, he pities the poor fellow whose job it is to produce them (229d). Since the throng of mythic figures is gigantic, the work of the "unbeliever" (229e2) is endless. Socrates has no time for any of this: all his time is devoted to knowing himself. The clever are referred to again at the start of the palinode's demonstration of the soul's immortality and the myth about the soul (245c2). This reference ties Socrates' partially mythic talk about the soul to the issues discussed in the prologue to the *Phaedrus.*

Lack of time seems to be an oddly weak reason for not engaging in the reductionist enterprise, particularly since it is clear that Socrates does not want to give a reductionist account of myths about the *soul.* Ought he not reject such reductionist accounts as false and not just as a waste of time? In reply I suggest that in the present passage Socrates is referring to popular myths that are not (at least not explicitly) about the soul. There is no reason for Socrates not to agree that these myths might have had their genesis in the way the reductionists suggest and still to think that there is such a thing as immaterial soul. Nor would it be inconsistent of him also to put popular myths to work as images of the soul (and so as aids to self-knowledge) in spite of their origins in people's imaginations. There is more to be said than this, however, about Socrates' odd remarks about reductionist translation.

The reductionist's "wisdom" is "boorish" or "rustic" (*agroikos;* cf. *Theae.* 146a5–8 on Socrates' own "boorish" love of dialegesthai) because his accounts disregard the terms in which the polis articulates itself. The polis's written doxai are expressed in myths about its founders, the gods, and so forth. By just "being persuaded by the customary belief" about these myths (230a2) Socrates does not directly threaten the city by attempting to debunk the stories through which it understands itself. This is one reason, in addition to lack of time, that Socrates is not interested in re-ductionist interpretation. Phaedrus, by contrast, loves rhetoric but does not understand its deeply political function. Socrates knows how to get out of the city's confines and look at what is natural, but also knows that he needs the city in order to learn about himself. Phaedrus has reflected on neither of these things.

Furthermore, Socrates' proposed demythologization of the Oreithuia story robs it of its human significance, replacing eros with death caused by natural factors, and so renders the story useless for self-knowledge. The conclusion follows if the experience and opinions men have of them-selves as persons are not to be disregarded. The clever reductionists in-terpret the mythic in terms foreign to the context of ordinary human experience, and specifically they interpret the human in terms of the sub-human. Such interpretation dissolves the prescientific world of human experience into "scientific," causal, or naturalistic categories. And *that* is unacceptable because the prescientific sense of what we are does contain something of the truth. Socrates says here that he is not interested in "correcting" (*epanorthousthai*) the mythic "look" or "appearance" (*eidos*, 229d6; this is the first occurrence of the term in the *Phaedrus*) of the Centaurs, Chimaera, Gorgons, Pegasuses, and so on. The references to Centaurs and Pegasuses cannot but help remind the reader of Socrates' subsequent image of the soul. That famous image is at odds neither with the way that we look at ourselves nor with the way we would like ourselves to look. In spite of the fact that Socrates may think that many of the popular myths are fictionalized interpretations of nature and that the beings of which they speak do not exist, his own use of myth shares something very important with the popular use of it: an acceptance of our everyday self-understanding as beings who live in a world in some sense animated by incorporeal beings (that is, for Socrates, by souls). It seems inevitable that the reductionists will ultimately want to translate reductively all self-descriptions that rest on ordinary opinions. Socrates must reject the re-ductionists' position (when it is comprehensively formulated) as wrong and not just a waste of scarce time. The groundwork for the stronger position has not yet been laid, however, and Socrates reserves his statement of it for the palinode.

Although it is true that Socrates tends not to offer interpretations of his own myths about the soul, he never says that *every* kind of interpretation of myths is a waste of time. He excludes only the kind of interpretation that does not help him know himself and that, by implication, is reductionistic in the sense described above.[25] Indeed, in the very process of explaining that he only "inquires about himself," Socrates calls upon yet another monster, namely, Typhon. Socrates plainly views the Typhon story allegorically. Accepting the difference between what a story literally says and its truth, we are called upon to think nonreductively about Typhon as an *image* that is somehow useful for self-knowledge. Our approach to the subsequent image of the winged charioteer and horses must follow similar lines. In asking whether or not he is typhonic, Socrates is comparing himself with this monster and so is "translating" it into terms applicable to himself. He "sees" Typhon as an image of himself; or rather, since Socrates' goal is to discover what he is, he both understands himself in terms of a myth and translates a myth into psychic terms. Socrates' hermeneutic activity is not reductionistic; he preserves the truth of the story (Typhon really is arrogant and complex) in order to elicit the truth about himself. He neither interprets the Typhon story literally nor understands the "truth" of the story in materialistic terms.

None of this explains, to be sure, why Socrates needs to use any sort of image in order to know himself. He could make his objections against reductionist interpretations, agree that there is something essentially right about our prescientific way of describing ourselves, but deny that we must describe the way we are by describing what we look like. This is another difficult puzzle posed by the *Phaedrus'* prologue, but I shall postpone discussion of it until I examine the palinode in chapter 3 and myth in chapter 4, "Excursus." For now I would like to look more closely at the mythic monster Socrates uses here as an image of himself.

Typhon is monstrous in part because he is an unnatural synthesis of distinct species. At least in Apollodorus' version, Typhon is (among other things) part man (from head to thighs) and part beast (*therion,* from thighs down), and is winged all over (*katepteroto,* or "feathered").[26] In wondering whether he is typhonic, Socrates is (among other things) asking whether he is monstrous in the sense of being unnatural when judged by the standard of corporeal nature. In one sense the answer given in the palinode's Pegasus-like image of the soul is affirmative; every soul is like a winged charioteer and winged horses. In that image, man, horse, and bird are combined—an unnatural creature, though one very different from Typhon in other respects. By contrast, in the epistemic analysis of the soul described in the second half of the *Phaedrus,* the issue of the monstrosity of the soul is dropped entirely.

The fact that a plurality of descriptions of the soul are possible (the soul is like Typhon, it is like a winged charioteer, and so on) points to the following issue implicit in the Typhon comparison itself. Apollodorus mentions that Typhon had a hundred dragons' heads projecting from his hands, which, in combination with the huge coils of vipers, emitted terrifying shouts and hissings. Hesiod says that the hundred heads of a snake growing from Typhon's shoulders, and the many tongues of a dragon, spoke in many voices (*phonai*) which at times made sounds of the different animals and at times, sounds the gods could understand (*Theogony* 825–35). Typhon's complexity also consists in his many voices. One wonders whether the theme of rhetoric might not already be implied, then, in Socrates' use of this image. For Socrates too speaks with many voices, as his heterogeneous discourse in the *Phaedrus* and other dialogues shows. "Rhetoric" will have so broad a meaning in the *Phaedrus* as to include all the discourses with which we communicate with ourselves and others. Socrates seems implicitly to wonder, then, whether his rhetoric is as fantastically complex as the voices of Typhon.

At the present juncture Socrates sets out two alternatives (230a1–6): either (1) he is a beast (wild animal; therion) more much-braided (much-plaited, complex; *poluplokoteron*) and more puffed up with pride than Typhon, or (2) he is a living being (natural animal; *zoion*) who is tamer (more civilized, gentler; *emeroteron*) and simpler than Typhon, one whose nature participates in some divine lot (measure, destiny; *moira*) and who is untyphonic (not vain or arrogant; *atuphos*).[27] In this passage, Typhon is actually the mean between the two extreme alternatives. The contrasts, then, are between (a) wild beast/natural animal; (b) more complex than Typhon/simpler; and (c) more arrogant than Typhon/tamer; and (d) Socrates also says in the second alternative that the sort of being described has a nature participating in a divine lot and that it is untyphonic, but the qualities contrary to these are not made explicit. I note too that Socrates drops the comparatives in (d) and just says that such an animal would be untyphonic (rather than just less typhonic).

The first alternative is hyperbolic; how could anything be more typhonic, as it were, than Typhon? Typhon is already a representative of disorder and destruction. Socrates envisions an unnatural creature of perplexing complexity and of unbridled hubris. Both self and knowledge would seem impossible under these conditions, given the almost complete absence of pattern, structure, shape, and stability that would characterize a hypertyphonic soul. Indeed, one wonders whether such a beast could be said to have a "soul."[28] This is why, I think, Socrates does not use the word "physis" in reference to this first alternative (see [d] in the previous paragraph). The extreme hubris of such a beast must be equivalent to an irrational desire (cf. 238a1–2 and context, where eros is a species of hubris)

to be master of the universe—a radical version of Typhon's desire to dominate the gods, including the god who issues the Delphian command, and
so to recognize no natural limits. In the context of the *Phaedrus* I think
that we can say that this alternative represents the absolute tyranny of
eros deprived of intelligence.

The other alternative refers to a zoion—a quite natural sort of being.
As zoion Socrates would not be essentially different from anyone else or
perhaps from other living animals. The tameness would seem to be a
result of domestication, of an acquired recognition of *nomos* and *doxa* (cf.
237d8–9), and so of an acceptance of one's limits. The reference to "divine
lot" suggests both that such a nature (unlike Typhon) lives in harmony
with the divine and that its character (being untyphonic) is bestowed
upon it from without, as befits a "simpler" animal.

Neither of these alternatives alone describes Socrates, a fact which suggests that neither sort of animal is philosophic. This point seems obvious
enough in terms of the hypertyphonic creature. A being characterized
solely by the first alternative would not desire self-knowledge. One characterized by the second, however, might regard it as impious or unnec-
essary. The tame nature would seem to lack the eros and dialectically
generated knowledge of ignorance characteristic of the philosopher. Its
nature would seem to be too simple to do justice to the soul, as Socrates'
own subsequent image of the soul indicates. If this tame nature's "participation" in a divine lot can be classified as a kind of mania at all, it
would probably be of the poetic, not the philosophic, sort (consider the
reference at 245a2 to the Muse-sent madness that seizes a "simple and
chaste soul"). It would seem more accurate, however, to just associate
this tame animal with undiluted sophrosyne.

That is, when we reflect on Socrates' reflections about himself, we are
drawn to the suggestion that the truth lies somewhere in between the
two alternatives he sets out here. The ability to ask questions about oneself,
or indeed to "participate" (*metechein*) in a divine lot, already seems to
indicate that one has a complex nature; in this sense perhaps only a monstrous being could say what Socrates does here. And yet the desire to ask
these questions also signals a relatively untyphonic desire to find one's
boundaries. The fact that Socrates sets out the alternatives in the first
place and so wants both to know himself and to formulate intelligible
questions with the hope of finding intelligible answers indicates that Socrates is neither simply untyphonic nor hypertyphonic. Might not Socrates
be tame *and* complex? Or even complex and *both* tame and hubristic? At
the start of the dialogue Socrates behaves in a hypertyphonic manner for
the benefit of Phaedrus' relatively simple soul.[29] And in the palinode's

image the soul is a complex beast, part of which is naturally hubristic (253e3) and part self-controlled (253d6; *sophron*); a third part is neither. While the human soul aspires to the divine, its highest achievement (in the persona of a philosopher) is to follow Zeus, not to usurp him. This desire is, admittedly, thought by nonphilosophers to be mad and arrogant. Even in Socrates' first speech, the two ideas represented by these alternatives are said to reside in each of us (237d–e). In both of Socrates' speeches the soul is complex. Still further, in the palinode the soul seems, complexly enough, to be in one way complex (in the sense of having an articulated structure, symbolized by the winged charioteer and horses) and in another way simple (its ousia being just self-motion). This initial formulation of the matter, then, is valuable but itself oversimplified, as befits initial formulations.

Socrates' use of the Typhon image, in sum, implicitly raises the problem of the relationship between complex hubristic madness on the one side, and simplistic sophrosyne on the other; between unintelligible and ungovernable eros and law-abiding reasonableness; between the lover and nonlover, attraction and detachment, desire and discourse. In short, the reference to Typhon articulates the self-knowledge problem in terms that we have already detected in the *Phaedrus* and that are subsequently discussed at length.

Socrates' way of putting things in this passage provides us with the terms of subsequent formulations in still other ways. For example, Socrates' use of the Typhon image implies that his character, whatever it is, will have to be understood relative to some larger context of which he is one part. It implies that self-knowledge is not knowledge of oneself as an entity isolated from a "world." Socrates' two alternatives also describe, in part, ways in which one might be related to beings higher than oneself (as an enemy or as the recipient of a lot determined by them). Of course, in the palinode this context is the cosmos, or Whole, and the divine beings are both the gods and Ideas. Hence the contrast between what is "within" and what is "without" the soul is also anticipated by the Typhon image. The contrast is important in the palinode (at 245e it is tied to the body/soul distinction), in the criticism of writing (275a), and at the end of the *Phaedrus* (Socrates prays to Pan for a harmony between the inner and outer). Finally, as I noted, the Typhon example points to the issue of rhetoric not only because of Typhon's many voices (especially in Hesiod's version) but because the discussion of myth and reductionism compels us to reflect on the use of a mythic figure as a form of speech and so of rhetoric.

Socrates says that he does not *yet* know himself. Is full self-knowledge still a possibility? But how could the famous Socrates, who at the dramatic time of this dialogue (if a time can be fixed) would be about sixty years old, *still* not know himself or at least not know what he has been thus far in life? Part of the answer, which will become evident in the palinode, concerns the view that a person can always become something more, or different, than he presently is. A philosopher can become wiser or can degenerate into a sophist. The possibility of becoming different seems to entail that self-knowledge is not terminable so long as one lives. Another part of the answer will be that the soul is genuinely difficult to know, for it seems to be, among other things, both simple and complex. That Socrates does not yet know himself reflects the inability of any human being to know himself perfectly.

The kinds of things Socrates is asking here about himself seem to have nothing to do with "epistemology" or "philosophy of mind." At this stage "self-knowledge" means understanding oneself as "this particular person" in a very general, quite everyday, and prescientific sense. Although this may include understanding oneself relative to a larger context, Socrates has not yet suggested that self-knowledge entails knowledge of human nature as such. Indeed, he has not yet mentioned the word "soul" (even though the figures of the hyper- and nontyphonic do, as possible types of character, possess a degree of universality). Why does Socrates begin by formulating the self-knowledge issue on such an "personal" level?

This question might be pursued by asking another: why does Socrates wish to know himself? Socrates does not provide us an explicit answer in the prologue of the *Phaedrus*. As ethically charged, however, the Typhon story and Socrates' corresponding formulation of his desire to know himself implicitly point to the answer developed later in the dialogue. The formulation is at least in part about what sort of person one is and would want to be. The hypertyphonic beast is, for example, scarcely admirable or noble.[30] Socrates wishes to know himself in particular (and not just "the soul" or "human nature") in order that he may lead the life that is best. The centrality of leading one's life in the best possible way supplies a clue as to why self-knowledge must ultimately return to the level of an individual's knowledge of himself in particular. Such knowledge may extend so far as to include knowledge of one's soul and its place in the cosmos, but it is desirable so that a person might live out his own life in a certain manner. That is not something someone else can do for you. Of course, the connection between knowing oneself and leading the best life calls for explanation. Once again the *Phaedrus'* prologue sets out in an adumbrated and allusive way the puzzles to be discussed later in the dialogue.

As we glance back at the prologue to the *Phaedrus,* three themes seem pervasive: eros (in contrast with the nonerotic), discourse (in contrast with nondiscursive vision), and rhetoric (in contrast with truth). In particular, we have noted the prominence of rhetoric about eros and of eros for discourses. In ways that we have only just begun to specify, these themes are connected with one another through the controlling theme of self-knowledge. With the basic issues and questions set out, Plato next presents us, by means of the nonlover's speech, with a specific combination of these themes.

2

Lysias' Speech, Socrates' First Speech, and Interludes

Self-knowledge is useful for all men.
MENANDER[1]

LYSIAS' SPEECH

Lysias' speech represents a singularly odd effort by a nonlover to seduce a young boy with whom he seems already to be acquainted (consider the opening of the speech, and 233a1–2). The nonlover argues that the boy should gratify him sexually *because* he does *not* love the boy. The addressee says nothing; the speech is a monologue. The nonlover, who is the speaker, is clearly associated with discursivity (as the speech itself testifies) and calculation (*hypologizesthai;* 231b4). That is, the nonlover can articulate what he wants, what he does not want, and how to get the one and avoid the other. The nonlover can talk reasonably because he has mastered his eros (we are not told how he achieved this). By contrast, the converse between lover and beloved (232a8–b2) is essentially irrational and so equivalent, from the "reasonable" standpoint of the nonlover, to the silence of overpowering desire. So confident is the speaker that in his last sentence he rhetorically instructs his listener to feel free to bring up any points that were left out (but not, presumably, to question or reject any of those that were included)—as though the boy is to contribute to his own seduction! The boy is put in the position of an impartial judge, the lover in the position of the defendant, and the nonlover in that of both the prosecution and plaintiff. The speech reads like a very sober legal brief, enumerating in an ostensibly logical manner the pros and cons of satisfying the nonlover and lover, respectively.[2] Thus it is lacking in flattery, poetry, imagery—in short, in the rhetoric of love. Of course the boy's name is never mentioned; there are, in fact, no addresses in the speech. The nonlover thereby ignores the rules for artful rhetoric outlined later in the *Phaedrus,* for his speech contains no ad hominem qualities.

The purpose of Lysias' speech is to solicit a ruling that will gratify the nonlover sexually. Yet the speech cannot, in reality, function as a love speech, although it is meant to have the same effect. The absence of any talk about the speaker's or auditor's beauty turns their sexual desire into a mute fact (only Phaedrus alludes to the beauty of the boy; 227c6). In this consists much of the absurdity of the speech. All this indicates that this speech could only exist in a *written* form. It would make no sense as spoken in a real situation. Yet however absurd in its form and however base in its content, it represents in a rough way what has become a very common phenomenon. As the point might be put today, liberation from moral constraints is justified in the name of controlled satisfaction of subjective preferences. If both parties are cognizant of the risks and participate willingly in a joint business venture whose profits (maximization of satisfaction consistent with preservation of reputation and so on) greatly outweigh the losses, are not their actions reasonable? Lysias' speech represents a libertarianism of the spirit entailed by the generalization of free market economics to the realm of the erotic. Calculation, frankness, privacy, selfishness, a freedom to choose a life-style based on the primacy of the physiological are some of its essential ingredients.[3]

Just as nothing about the boy in particular is mentioned, so the speaker says nothing about his own personal qualities. Although the soul is not mentioned in the speech, it is obvious that the speaker is assuming either a dichotomy between body and soul or the nonexistence of the soul. Presumably one nonlover or one boy is basically as good as the next; their individuality is not important. This is a sense in which the speech is democratic or, as Socrates called it, "useful to the people" (227d2). No doubt if many nonlovers exist (as the speaker suggests at 231d6–e2) they would have to distinguish themselves from one another in increasingly trivial but novel ways, always hoping to catch the eye of a "disinterested" boy, while never behaving in a way that fails to conform to social expectations (nonconformism of the sort that is not chic characterizes the lover). The problem of whether to gratify every available nonlover is referred to at the conclusion of the speech (234b6–7). The speaker suggests that it is more economical to restrict one's involvements, but he does not explain why *he* should be gratified. Of course, a ranking of nonlovers might be established on the basis of wealth or social connections, thus reproducing the deleterious situation said to hold in the case of lovers

(232c4–d4)—a difficulty not resolved by the speaker's reference to the nonlover's "virtue" (*arete*, 232d5). Indeed, would not a crafty beloved prefer to control an enraptured but wealthy lover rather than an independent-minded and poor nonlover?

The law of supply and demand renders the relationship between nonlover and beloved unequal. In a labor-saturated market, the beloved controls the capital, and the proletarian nonlover must secure wages by an unusual sales pitch. The nonlover needs rhetoric to survive; Lysias' nonlover even makes a virtue out of his poverty, all the while negotiating in a way that suggests a rough parity between himself and the beloved. In a strange sense, the parity does exist; for while the nonlover is a slave of the master beloved, a beloved who is not desired is worthless. His capital lies in the eyes of his beholders. Thus the beloved is a slave of those who need him even as he masters them. The entire debasing dialectic results from the self-understanding of the nonlover and boy, which Socrates will soon clarify and reject.

The nonlover's speech begins, ends, and is interspersed with references to the importance of being self-interested and of watching out for one's own benefit. The value of enlightened self-interest is emphasized throughout the speech (for example, see 232d3). The goods, which it is in one's interest to obtain, are satisfaction of physical needs, maximization of pleasure of all sorts, minimization over a length of time of all pain, preservation of reputation and of good standing with family and friends. Implied in the nonlover's speech is thus a distinction between needs and desires (consider 231a1); he admits to the former, but not the latter. Socrates implicitly rejects the distinction in his speeches.

For the Lysian nonlover, pursuit of the end of need or desire is enlightened only if passion collaborates with reason and vice versa. He negates eros only in this specific sense: he wants the identical goods the lover does, but has acquired different means for attaining them. The ends are assumed as constants dictated by universally recognized needs. The nonlover mentions (with reference to himself) "not being a slave to eros, but being master of myself" (233c1–2; and 232a4–5, d3), in contrast with the lovers who "agree that they are more sick than self-controlled, and know that they consider poorly, but are not able to master themselves" (231d2–4). Although the nonlover is still a slave to eros, he has achieved a certain detachment from it, and so a kind of freedom (*hekontes*, 231a5) with respect to his satisfaction. Reason, that is, is an instrument for the satisfaction of desire; the virtue of intelligence is efficiency. This is a very widespread and very powerful conception of reason, perhaps far more today than ever before (given the mathematization of reason and the infusion of this notion into culture through technology). I do not mean to say that Lysias' speech articulates the full phenomenon of what is now called "technicism." But it does seem to me that Lysias' speech sets out, in a rough way, some of the basic assumptions of the phenomenon. Socrates must also challenge these assumptions in order to progress beyond the speech, and so must show that it is possible to reason about ends as well as means and that such reasoning can affect desire.

Socrates will try to show, to state the matter in an abbreviated and preliminary way, that the rather base irrationality of the nonlover's position is a result both of its restriction of reason to techne and of the corresponding antithesis of reason and desire. Socrates will also try another strategy for showing that reason and desire are not separable in the way that the nonlover pretends. Socrates does this in exposing the nonlover as a concealed lover. That is, the nonlover's reason is not really detached from his desire in the way he claims. The value of reason is dependent on its being a means for achieving the ends set by desire. The formulation of the means is not value neutral. Indeed, the nonlover desires reason; that is, he is attached to his detachment. He values reason because he also holds a number of other values (such as good reputation). There are many candidates for the status of "means"; the nonlover argues in favor of one of them (reason qua instrument), but his own argument shows that the means are not value neutral. The detachment of reason from desire is untrue in this respect, too. To demonstrate all this, however, is no small task. Lysias' speech thus presents a serious challenge.

We ought not infer that Lysias' assumptions about eros and reason are simply false. Even in the palinode, satisfaction of some desires does depend on control of others; and there *is* a level at which reason and desire collide. Sexual desire is not necessarily harmonious with other desires. It is also the case that reason and desire must collaborate if a person is to be satisfied. Further, the detachment from sexual desire represented by the nonlover is a necessary ingredient of philosophical knowing. The nonlover represents an effort to attain objectivity. In the palinode, this notion finds its highest expression in the gods' noetic contemplation of the eternal Ideas. But that contemplation is also erotic. The nonlover's rationality, elevated to the level of *nous,* turns out to be the proper satisfaction of eros. Philia does indeed depend on intelligence and on the pursuit of the steadfast.[4]

Let me turn now to the difficulties internal to Lysias' speech that require its revision. The nonlover presents himself in a way that is self-contradictory. As is evident from Socrates' first speech, the nonlover is actually a concealed lover. There is in fact an inconsistency between the word and deed of Lysias' nonlover. Whenever the lover and beloved talk, everyone assumes that they are planning to have sex (232a6–b2), whereas they will not assume this if they see a nonlover talking to a boy, since the nonlover "acts normal" when he is with the boy. In fact, however, the nonlover is (in Lysias' speech) talking to the beloved in order to obtain sex. But after everything the nonlover says about the defects of the lover, how can he admit to the fact that he wants the same things the lover does? At 233b the speaker attacks eros directly and claims that unlike the lover he will care about the boy even when the sexual affair is over (which will occur, apparently, when the boy's hour is past; 234a). It is a crucial thesis of the nonlover's pitch that he is capable of friendship with the boy before and after sexual involvement. That this thesis is groundless becomes evident when we remember that the nonlover is really a concealed lover. The nonlover's motives and interest in the boy are the same as the lover's; there is no reason to believe that the former is more capable of long-term friendship with the boy than is the latter. Indeed, such behavior would be unprofitable, for once he has what he wants, the nonlover has achieved a satisfactory return on his investment and has no reason to concern himself further with this boy. The nonlover's pledges of fidelity are empty. The nonlover's self-interest is in fact as poor a basis for friendship as the lover's lust, and this because the nonlover is, underneath it all, a clever lover. But the nonlover cannot admit any of these things.

The entire speech is incoherent on other grounds as well. The nonlover assumes from the start that the boy is similarly self-interested, passionless, and calculating. The lack of reason the nonlover attributes to eros would also characterize a beloved (even if in subdued form; cf. 255d–256a), who would thus by definition be unmoved by the speech. Thus the speaker urges the boy not to allow himself to be infected by eros, but rather to "look to your own interest" (232d3). A beloved who did so would be a sort of nonlover. Since he is the counterpart of the nonlover, we might better refer to the self-interested boy as a "nonbeloved," even though initially "nonbeloved" does not seem to designate a stance in the way that "nonlover" does. The meaning of the term will become clearer when we turn to Socrates' first speech (though the blame for the absurdity of the term ultimately rests with Lysias). What reason would a nonbeloved have to gratify a nonlover? Presumably the former too has needs, such as the need for money, social standing, and the like. Such a nonbeloved would look rather like a prostitute, though a prostitute does not require a seduction speech. Perhaps in this speech the nonlover is trying to transform a beloved into a nonbeloved. Yet a nonbeloved would immediately see that much of the speech is groundless. Hence in producing this transformation the nonlover would be achieving a result antithetical to the one he desires. Still further, a nonbeloved who accepted the nonlover's argument would (in a twist analogous to that just described with reference to the nonlover) actually be a concealed beloved, with all the difficulties that accompany this stance.

The nonlover assumes that his self-knowledge does not require the discursive mediation of another person. He mentions the "necessity of dialogue because of friendship or some other sort of pleasure" (232b4–5), but obviously he does not envision Socratic dialogue. The nonlover thinks himself satisfied with who he is; he does not approach the boy in order to learn about himself. This situation stands in vivid contrast with the lover-beloved relationship described in the palinode. The nonlover's self-certainty might be shattered by asking him to "define his terms," and this is precisely what Socrates advocates doing in his first speech.

Lysias' speech lacks a beginning; it starts partway through and only alludes to remarks previously made by the nonlover to the boy. Yet the speech itself alludes to the circumstances (230e6) of the nonlover as well as his intentions. Hence, as Phaedrus subsequently admits, the beginning of the speech is really a peroration (264b1–2). The speech moves in a circle; that is, it has no real beginning. This I take as another indication of the speech's existential and practical incoherence. At the same time, this circularity illustrates the repeatability of the written word; even the utter impersonality of Lysias' speech (it is addressed to no one in particular by no one in particular) seems to epitomize writing as such. Lysias' text is paradigmatically "dead" (cf. 276a), a fact that blends nicely with Lysias' vocation as a logographos. As I have already noted, as "speech writer" he did not deliver his own speeches and so, in an obvious sense, could not himself enliven them in the way Socrates recommends in the second half of the *Phaedrus*. Plato thereby begins to prepare us for the final section of the dialogue in which writing itself is criticized for possessing just these sorts of defects.

No doubt someone could try to live out, however incoherently, the nonlover's position. Yet in order to do so, he would necessarily ignore the potentially elevating effect of his rhetoric of seduction. Even so base a speech as the one we have been examining implicitly appeals to what is good for lover and beloved and therefore makes a claim about what is good. For the speech to succeed with anyone but the most jaded nonbeloved, the appeal must be made explicit and more edifying. The boy must be flattered, and the nonlover must at least pretend to be interested in the beloved as individual. Socrates takes this step in his first speech when he introduces the notion of "divine philosophy" (239b4). Carnal desire is transfigured by speech about the beautiful. However base his intentions, the nonlover must conceal himself as a lover and so transcend

in his own rhetoric the level of his intentions. And this, for similar pragmatic reasons, must lead to a change of his behavior, and possibly of his
intentions.

That is, a sort of invisible hand reshapes the nonlover's position when
that position is articulated in an erotic context. Eros and the desire for
edification seem inseparable; together (perhaps with the assistance of the
sensibility to shame; see below) they possess an uplifting energy. They
seem based, as Socrates might put it, on a glimmer of anamnesis. The
nonlover who ignores the implications of his own rhetoric is refusing to
know himself. Just as Socrates refused to interpret myths in terms of the
subhuman, so he will soon refuse to interpret the desire to be desired in
simply sexual terms. Self-knowledge must "save the phenomena," and
this includes saving the ordinary perception that there is a difference between the noble and the base, the beautiful and the ugly, the person and
his body. Rejection of self-knowledge in this sense leads to the reduction
of the human to the bestial, as the first two speeches of the *Phaedrus*
suggest. In order to nourish our humanity, we must talk about what it
means to be human. Such talk is implicit in the language of love. It is
explicit in the therapeutic language of philosophy. We begin to see, then,
why Socrates should care so much about self-knowledge. It is not the sort
of knowledge he can live, or love, without.

The nonlover's praise of self-control assumes, as we have seen, inadequate
conceptions of reason and desire. Admittedly, the nonlover exhibits a
certain self-consciousness precisely in his self-control. But he has not yet
reflected on himself philosophically and so has not asked himself questions
such as "what am I?" or questions about the nature of desire and reason.
Lysias' nonlover takes his notions of self, desire, and reason uncritically,
as they are given to him, and then manipulates them in a way that suits
his "self-interest." We have examined the resulting defects in detail. What
Lysias' speech helps us see is the necessity for self-knowledge in a philosophical sense, and so for talk about human nature. Socrates introduces
the requisite vocabulary in his first speech, and that is one reason even
his first speech represents an advance over Lysias'.

THE INTERLUDE BETWEEN LYSIAS' SPEECH
AND SOCRATES' FIRST SPEECH

This interlude is probably the most consistently playful and ironic section of the *Phaedrus*. As noted in the previous chapter, Phaedrus himself
suggests that he and Socrates are behaving like poor comedians in mim-
icking each other and exchanging roles (236c). The miming is even carried

into some small details; for example, just as Socrates quoted from Pindar, so now Phaedrus does the same (236d2). The playfulness engenders a forward movement in the dialogue by recasting (in a way that the logic of Lysias' speech makes predictable) the roles played by the interlocutors. Progress is not engendered by a frontal criticism of Lysias' speech. Initially, Socrates' criticisms are, in fact, fairly superficial, touching only on the formal, the technical, or what he calls the "rhetorical" (235a1) aspects of the speech. The explicit issue at this point is not whether the speech was noble or base, or even whether it was persuasive or not. This first use of the word "rhetoric" in the *Phaedrus* thus takes the term at its ordinary, Phaedran level. Socrates challenges Phaedrus' estimation of the speech on Phaedrus' own level, for Phaedrus thinks that the speech overlooked not a single important aspect of the subject and that no one else could possibly do better (235b1–5). Hence he promises a more comprehensive and better arranged speech, not a truer or nobler one. As Socrates puts it, with respect to "necessary" features of the topic, the only issue is their "arrangement," not the "invention" of new ones (see 234e–236a). Since Socrates does not complete his speech, he breaks his promise. He does, moreover, add new points not mentioned in Lysias' speech. At this stage he seems bent on showing that he is superior to Lysias even on Lysias' own grounds.

Socrates not only listened to the speech; he watched Phaedrus read it and was "struck" by the speech by virtue of the delight Phaedrus took in reading it (234d1–6). Socrates claims he vicariously reveled in the logos of Lysias by looking at Phaedrus' "divine head" (234d6). In a comment that echoes the earlier reference at 228b7 to Socrates and Phaedrus being "syncorybantic" in their love of speeches, Socrates says that they have now become "synbacchic" (234d5). Socrates thus attempts to mirror or mimic Phaedrus.

Phaedrus shines (*ganusthai;* 234d3) while reading, perhaps putting quite a bit of expression into his voice. In (re)reading this speech Phaedrus is in an important sense talking to himself. He is in a world of his own, or rather, in the world of the text with which he identifies. As is evident from my discussion of Phaedrus' character in the previous chapter, and my discussion of Lysias' speech above, Phaedrus' delight is an egocentric revelry in the repetition of "truths" he unreflectively holds dear. Once again, the perfect harmony between the thesis of Lysias' speech, its form, and its status as a written work and the character "Phaedrus" is evident. That is, the anonymity, circularity, repetitiveness, and lifelessness of Lysias' speech and of its thesis are nicely reflected in its status as a written, nondialogical text, while Phaedrus' disinclination for dialogue and inclination for memorizing makes him a natural disciple of texts and especially of this particular text. Nothing in this written monologue questions Phaedrus. And, as already noted, Phaedrus' own affection for the standpoint of the beloved as it emerges in his *Symposium* speech makes the thesis of Lysias' speech very attractive to him. When Socrates criticizes the thesis of Lysias' speech, therefore, he in effect criticizes all the just mentioned phenomena with which it interlocks. Phaedrus rightly senses that he himself is being critized as well, and Socrates rightly tries to turn around Phaedrus' character by reorienting his desires. The argument against Lysias ends up being a wide-ranging argument against a way of writing (if not writing as such), a certain form of character, and a thesis about eros and its connection to reason.

"Wise men and women of old who in past ages have spoken and written on these themes" would refute the contention that it is impossible to surpass Lysias' treatment of the topic. Socrates vaguely cites the "beautiful Sappho," the "wise Anacreon," and "some prose writer" as his source for a better speech, and then says he cannot remember the "external source" from which he heard it (235c–d).[5] We are then told that the Muses (237a), a divine being (238c9–d1), the nymphs (241e), and even Phaedrus (237a9–10, 244a1) are responsible for Socrates' capacity to recite his first speech with such enthusiasm. That is, Socrates claims no responsibility for what he says (it derives from another author), how he says it (the divinities are the cause), or why he says it (he is compelled to do so). All these sources are external to Socrates, in obvious contrast with the nature of true anamnesis. In this way the speech he is about to deliver is devalued from the start. Hence Socrates' statement that the speech has been poured into him as if into a vessel from an outside source is literally false but metaphorically true. Moreover, he thereby pretends that he is very much like Phaedrus into whom Lysias' speech was poured. Yet the source is ostensibly higher than that by which Phaedrus is inspired. Through that conceit Socrates seeks to evoke in Phaedrus a sense that there is some nobler ground of discourses.

Socrates cites an odd reason for supposing that he did *not* make up this speech. He claims that he "senses" that there is in his breast something to say, and adds "that I have conceived none of these things from myself, I know well, knowing the ignorance in me" (235c5–8). Socrates affirms his famous "knowledge of ignorance" in the middle of a thoroughly playful and ironic context. Since Socrates *does* in fact make up the speech on his own, his "I know my own ignorance," which is meant to explain at least part of his ostensible lack of "creativity" in speech making, is itself tinged with irony (an irony that is visible to the reader, though it is missed by

Phaedrus). Socrates' reference to his knowledge of ignorance invites us to consider these speeches in connection with the notion of self-knowledge, that goal to which Socrates declared himself entirely dedicated.

Phaedrus himself invokes Delphi in the course of his offer to set up the golden "isometric icons" of Socrates and of himself should Socrates succeed in his speech. Phaedrus mentions the nine archons; they took an oath that if they broke any of the laws they would set up a golden statue of a man.[6] The deed is a form of punishment; yet the offer of a statue of Socrates, at least, seems more like a prize to the winner of a competition or possibly a bribe. Socrates' success will signal Phaedrus' transgression. Phaedrus does not believe, after all, that anyone in Greece could outdo Lysias. If Socrates succeeds, he will have shown that he was correct in thinking that he had a better speech in him, that is, that he did know himself. Can this law, which Phaedrus will transgress, be anything other than the Delphic "know thyself"?[7]

In response to Phaedrus' offer, Socrates compliments him on being "truly golden" (235e2), that is, inwardly rich. The compliment is an ironic one, of course, but not without point. At the very end of the *Phaedrus* Socrates prays that he may possess an appropriate amount of "gold"; the term needs to be taken metaphorically (279c2). That Phaedrus is not entirely without inner wealth is signaled by his proclaimed preference for the ability to memorize perfectly Lysias' speech to the possession of much gold (228a2–4). Yet in the realm of speeches Phaedrus does not yet understand the difference between fool's gold and the true. At 236a8–b4 Phaedrus offers to move Socrates' golden statue (but not his own) to Olympia, beside the offering to the Cypselids. Socrates' statue would be at the temple of Zeus, perhaps, the god who, in the *Phaedrus*, is patron of the philosophers. Possibly Plato wishes us to infer that if Socrates knows himself, he is a philosopher, and his statue ought not to be associated with that of Phaedrus, breaker of the Delphic command.

Socrates knows his ignorance, but pretends that while delivering the speech he is losing control of himself, that he forgets himself. The inspiration that generated the speech is subsequently linked to forgetfulness (263d1–3). Indeed, given the content of the speech, Socrates does seem to forget what a really good and true treatment of eros should be. Of course, Socrates manages to interrupt himself partway through his first speech in order to secure Phaedrus' assent to the view that he really is getting quite inspired and to do so at just the right place (between the part of the speech that defines eros and the part that evaluates it). Thus Socrates suggests by his very deed that he is well in control of himself, so signaling the irony of his words about his lack of self-control.[8]

Phaedrus feels compelled to try to compel Socrates to give the speech he so mysteriously has inside him. Having tried bribes, Phaedrus threatens physical force (236d1–3), and then, swearing an oath by the plane tree, he threatens never again to convey any other speech to Socrates (236e1–3). Socrates and Phaedrus have power over each other because each possesses what the other desires, namely a logos. Having aroused Phaedrus' desire to hear him instead of Lysias, Socrates does something neither Lysias nor Phaedrus would dream of doing; he pulls his cloak over his head while delivering the speech. He makes this gesture so that "I can rush through my speech at top speed, without looking at you and breaking down for shame" (237a4–5).[9] Socrates is concealed as he speaks—a visible icon of his irony. His speech can be heard but its source cannot be seen directly. The disembodied voice seems to represent the mysterious origin of the speeches. Since Socrates cannot see, the speech could not arise from the reading of a book. The gesture thus underlines the difference between the source of Phaedrus' speech and that of Socrates.

Socrates, however, is also imitating Phaedrus here. Both of them begin by attempting to conceal, under their cloaks as it were, the sources of their speeches. Just as Lysias "speaks" through the dramatic fiction of the nonlover, and to that extent conceals himself in that character, so Socrates conceals himself as a nonlover who is pretending to be a lover. And by concealing himself Socrates acts out the anonymity that characterizes the dramatic speaker of Lysias' text (the impersonal nonlover) and, more explicitly, the concealed lover of his own speech. Socrates enacts here the impersonality of these seduction speeches in this sense, too: with the persons unable to see or to be seen, their mutual look of recognition generated by desire so elegantly described in the palinode is impossible. Like Phaedrus, Socrates is in an important sense talking to himself as he speaks. Indeed, Socrates' gesture even detaches him from Phaedrus in a way that Phaedrus did not achieve relative to Socrates: while Socrates (ostensibly) became "synbacchic" while watching Phaedrus' "divine head" as he read Lysias' speech, Phaedrus will not have the privilege of participating in Socrates' expression. Phaedrus will have to concentrate on the logos alone. And that, Phaedrus says, is fine with him: Socrates can do whatever he likes so long as he delivers the logos (237a6).

Phaedrus has shown some awareness of the whole mimetic irony of his relationship to Socrates, and in spite of the remark just adverted to, one wonders whether Phaedrus can be completely ignorant of the significance of Socrates' elaborate mirroring of him. At the very least, Phaedrus could not fail to be impressed by the bizarre sight of the elderly Socrates sitting in the brilliant heat of the countryside he ostensibly never visits and criticizing eros with a cloak covering his eyes. Whether or not Phaedrus understands it all, it should be clear by now that Socrates' self-concealment is actually a rather complicated gesture. It serves, on the one hand, to hold up to Phaedrus a mirror of a special sort, one that both shows Phaedrus what he is and shows him that he ought to be different. For the explicit motive for self-concealment is that the speech is shameful. When Socrates delivers the palinode, he unmasks himself; Phaedrus is thereby offered the opportunity for self-recognition, for the realization that *he* was the person who said the shameful things. Indeed, Socrates even says that his own first speech was "by Phaedrus" (244a1). And, on the other hand, the gesture does enact or reflect in dramatic terms critical elements of the content of the speeches in question. Thus the gesture is molded by both what is being said and the person to whom it is being said—the two ingredients that are later found to constitute good rhetoric. In the interlude that follows the speech, Phaedrus' deficiencies as well as those of the content of the speeches are again exhibited in deed and in word. As Socrates speaks, he is blind and thus enacts symbolically the fate of Stesichorus (243a–b). The speech does lack insight into the whole truth about eros.

One of the most intriguing aspects of Socrates' self-concealment concerns "shame," a phenomenon that is crucial in the *Phaedrus*. Phaedrus is meant to learn that even a speech technically superior to that of Lysias should be judged in terms of moral categories as well. Shame is a kind of self-consciousness, mediated by one's consciousness of how someone else would evaluate one's deeds. It combines the immediacy of a perception of what one is doing, awareness of moral categories, and awareness of another's awareness of how these categories apply to one's actions. It seems to exemplify a sense of the *nous* which is praised in the palinode (although shame is here associated with sophrosyne rather than mania). Shame is a good paradigm, in these respects, of the complex reflexive nature of self-knowledge. It seems that Socrates is trying to teach Phaedrus the need to become self-conscious about his love of discourses (Phaedrus is not the only interlocutor Socrates tries to imbue with a sense of shame).[10] However, although through shame one becomes aware of oneself, one does not normally become aware of oneself as an object, that is, as a "soul." The experience of shame is not yet a knowledge of one's nature or ousia. Self-knowledge in that sense gets introduced in Socrates' first speech. Yet shame does involve objectifying oneself in that one views oneself as one imagines that others view one. Shame is an ethically charged example of (literally) reflection. It is thus a suitable preparation for Socrates' first speech.

Phaedrus may not initially understand the complex significance of the shamefulness of the two speeches. He probably begins by assuming that the cause of Socrates' shame is his inability to better Lysias in their competition. Phaedrus does seem, however, to have a particular sensitivity to shame. In the *Symposium,* he is emphatic in his association of eros with shame (*Symp.* 178d), and here he is quite struck by Socrates' reference to the opinion of the man of generous and humane character, a man who would be sensitive to the shamefulness of the first two speeches of the *Phaedrus* (243c).

It may seem strange that Socrates could, as he himself says, feel shame in looking at himself through the eyes of Phaedrus, in that Phaedrus finds nothing wrong morally in what Socrates is saying.[11] Indeed, Socrates is not ashamed to be heard making this speech. Is not the calculated avoidance of shame itself shameful? In the present case the answer is negative. Socrates' motives for reciting the speech are good ones, namely, to educate Phaedrus and to prepare the way for a superior conception of eros and reason. The speech is in fact superior in ways that allow us to see why the whole Lysian standpoint is defective. And understanding that is a valuable contribution to our effort to understand ourselves.

SOCRATES' FIRST SPEECH

Socrates begins his tale (*mythos;* 237a9) in propria persona, by supplying a dramatic setting for it. He thus momentarily steps back from the speech and provides some context. The "very beautiful" youth (who is a bit older than the boy of Lysias' speech) is said to have many lovers. The suitor is identified as "wily"; when faced with competition, he disguises himself as a nonlover. The real nature of Lysias' nonlover is thus revealed, and a motive for the deception is established from outside the speech (the only way it could be established)—thus supplying us with an explicit contrast between the concealed lover's ergon and his logos. This contrast will nevertheless destroy the speech's plausibility, for it shows that the whole speech is a lie. Indeed, if the concealed lover succeeds in persuading the boy, he must remain concealed and so cannot satisfy his desire in the manner he would prefer. The concealed lover cannot admit his deception without confessing that he is a liar. Indeed, if the youth is persuaded by the speech condemning eros, he will become a nonbeloved (ruled by reason rather than by desire) and so may decide not to satisfy the concealed lover's desires. One wonders whether he might even decide to conceal himself as an innocent beloved so as to better attract useful (that is, rich) nonlovers. In any event, if he is not persuaded, he remains a beloved, and the concealed lover remains unsatisfied. Thus whether the concealed lover succeeds or fails rhetorically, he very probably fails in practice to satisfy his desire.

The speech is impersonal (devoid of flattery, it terminates with a line of unflattering poetry) and is highly technical and sober. Unlike the nonlover in Lysias' speech, the concealed lover never says explicitly that the boy should satisfy him in particular (consider 237c5–d3), all of which helps abstract from the lover's base self-interest. The context Socrates supplies for the speech lies outside it; in the speech itself the speaker's intentions are more concealed than was the case in Lysias' speech. The extreme impersonality of Socrates' first discourse reflects the importance it places on an abstract method of analysis. The speech actually begins with a sort of lecture as to how one should proceed if one wishes to know what one is talking about. It sounds as though it is addressed to an impartial auditor, not to the boy. As before, this speech is a monologue, one in which the boy's response is in no way articulated (though a response is called for by the talk of "mutual agreement" at the start of the speech).

Even though a number of practical as well as theoretical difficulties (see below for the latter) plague Socrates' first speech, it does represent an improvement over Lysias' speech, as is evident from its very un-Lysian beginning and organization. The speaker starts by enunciating a comprehensive rule applying to every act of deliberation. That is, he starts by reflecting on the procedure or method for proceeding. This step back to second-level talk about talk is unmistakably similar to the turn to the analysis of techne in the second half of the *Phaedrus*. The present reflections on how reason is to be rightly conducted are also metaphilosophical. This constitutes an advance over Lysias' speech. The self-consciousness it entails is necessary, even if the procedure advocated is not persuasive. This is also an advance in the sense that it takes us from the level of particularity to that of universality. In order to know what (or whom) I want, I must know something about eros as such and, still further, must reflect on how anyone could *know* what eros is. The speaker justifies the call for metaphilosophical reflection on the basis that failure to undertake it will result in disagreement both with oneself (a point that should be compared with 262a5–7, b7) and with others (237c5). The basis is a pragmatic one; we need a theoretical account of how to proceed in understanding ourselves and (in the present case) of what eros is if we are to find constancy in our actions. That is, to desire properly we need something steadfast, and steadfastness is found through discourse.

One must, we are told, first know *(eidenai)* what one is deliberating about, that is, one must know and define the "ousia of each thing" (or "what sort of thing it is"; 237c8). Second, having done that, one can go on to deliberate about whether the thing is advantageous or harmful. This step-by-step procedure seems perfectly reasonable. Indeed, the knowing/ deliberating and ousia/utility distinctions sound a bit like our theory/ practice and fact/value distinctions. Evidently values (utilities) are not ousiai and so are not known in the way ousiai are known. As in the present speech's discussion of eros, it seems that what a thing is must be agreed upon at the start with the help of some analysis (including, in this case, some etymological analysis), whereas its utility is to be established dia- lectically by enumerating pros and cons, refuting objections, and so forth. What a thing is may be "clear to all" (237d4); it is something people can "see" *(noesai;* 237d6) if they stop and take a careful look. In spite of 239e2–3, this sort of clarity seems unavailable with respect to a thing's utility. The concealed lover does not explain why this is so. Indeed, the diairesis between a thing's nature and its value, though commonsensical, is philosophically very difficult. The speaker says nothing at all here to justify it.

Socrates' concealed lover defends his procedure by pointing out that most people begin by believing that they know what they are talking about, even though their belief is usually not based on knowledge (237c2– 3). The term "boule" helps suggest that the rule (first analyze the thing, and then debate its qualities) applies to any situation in which a choice must be made concerning action. Theory is necessary for successful de- liberation; else *hamartanein* is unavoidable (237c1–2). Let us note that Socrates subsequently refers to the premise of this same speech as a ha- martema (242c3, c6, d2; cf. 243a3). Even as he recommends the proper procedure for knowing, Socrates fails to know truly. And this raises a question: does the procedure, as it is outlined in this speech, fail in this particular case because it is misused, or is this procedure not sufficient to "know the ousia of each thing"? A way must be found of distinguishing between situations in which we know and those in which we (erroneously) think we know; that is, we must know our own ignorance and our own knowledge. This aspect of the problem of self-knowledge lies just beneath the surface of this discussion. Indeed, what the speaker proceeds to analyze is human nature.

Unfortunately, the speaker does not succeed in distinguishing ade- quately between the two situations just mentioned. The ousia is known if its nature is agreed upon at the start. We are told, as I have already noted, that failure to do this leads to disagreement both with oneself and with others. Theoretical knowledge of ousia is in fact measured by a pragmatic criterion. Hence, it seems there is no reason an agreed upon "definition" (horos, 237d1) should not also lead to subsequent disagreement as the result of contradictions or inconsistencies. Many a Platonic dialogue includes mutually agreed to definitions that are subsequently found to be incoherent.

Moreover, the concealed lover's procedure, by equating knowing with agreeing, reduces knowledge to doxa, or truth to convention. Since the concealed lover's speech is meant to exhibit the procedure, it has the status of agreed upon opinion. We can mutually agree upon false premises and construct through valid reasoning perfectly coherent definitions. The reflexive problem concerning the status of the concealed lover's speech becomes especially clear once the division between the "idea" of "acquired opinion which aims at what is best" and the "idea" of "natural desire for pleasures" is made. All forms of reasoning must fall under the former, and this would include both the theoretical and the deliberative kinds. This speech must therefore be an example of acquired doxa. What is best in the matter of theory as well as in the matter of deliberation is a matter of opinion. True enough, no thinking can proceed without agreement at some level. But this point together with the just noted defects of the concealed lover's procedure bring us to a question that is fundamental to understanding the Phaedrus: how are we to distinguish, in any given situation, between intelligent and unfounded agreement?

The arbitrariness of the concealed lover's technique of conceptual analysis (if I may so dignify it) is visible in the emphasis he places on the need for mutual agreement, that is, for definition, at the start (arche; 237c4) of deliberation. How does one define where deliberation is to begin? In order to define "eros," the concealed lover avails himself at crucial junctures of some philosophical sounding terms, such as "ousia," "idea," "meros." Do not these terms, however, fall into the class of "disputed words" (263a–c)? Must these terms not also be defined? Must there not be a still prior start to deliberation?

For example, the speaker does not say formally what his diairesis between the two "ideas" in us is a division of. That is, the ousia we are meant to understand is eros, which we get to by dividing a still prior entity, namely, human nature. The speaker just refers to this nature indirectly as "us" or "each of us," but not explicitly as an "ousia." The whole account rests on this unanalyzed "us." Since our understanding of the whole of which these "ideas" are divisions is preanalytical or a matter of opinion, the speaker's account clearly rests on doxa. He does refer to "soul" later on, but only in the evaluative part of the speech and only as a way of edifying the beloved (in the palinode, of course, "soul" is introduced as the name of that of which the various parts of oneself are parts of).

Of course, one might reject the premise that philosophical deliberation should *begin* with definitions precisely because such a procedure seems to rest on arbitrary stipulation, leaps into mystical intuition or religious faith, or is easily made to lead to an infinite regress of definitions of terms. Knowledge might be arrived at in a nonarbitrary way if deliberation has an immanent logic of progress, one that can certify the validity of its own development as it progresses. Such a logic is usually referred to as dialectic. Its greatest modern proponent is undoubtedly Hegel.[12] Is not its greatest ancient proponent Plato? Of course, Platonic and Hegelian dialectic differ in important ways. But Plato's claim to such a title seems to me to be secured not so much from the intermittent discussions in various dialogues (including the *Phaedrus*) about a dialectical art as from Plato's unbroken reliance on dialogue (dialegesthai) as the comprehensive and indispensable medium of philosophizing. The progress of the *Phaedrus* itself, which exhibits the strange dialectical logic of dialogue, is different in kind from the procedure recommended in Socrates' first speech (and indeed from that recommended in sections of the second half of the *Phaedrus*). For example, the *Phaedrus* does not begin with definition or mutual agreement about an ousia. I shall say more in subsequent chapters about the philosophical significance of dialogue. For the time being, I am suggesting that the method of the concealed lover's speech is problematic in a way that will help shed light on why Socrates prefers dialogue to the method. The problems emerge when we reflect metaphilosophically both on how the concealed lover thinks we ought to proceed and on how Socrates does proceed even as he (as concealed lover) advocates an analytical procedure. As already indicated, the problem of agreement and dispute as well as that of knowing when we have got something right and when not are important to the whole issue of dialegesthai. And the problem of agreement is closely connected to the problem of rhetoric. But we are getting ahead of ourselves. Let us return to the concealed lover's speech.

The speaker now applies his rule-governed procedure to the disputed topic at hand. One must first show what sort of thing eros is and after that what its benefits and disadvantages are with respect to both body and soul. First off, "that eros is a sort [*tis*] of *epithumia* is clear {*delon*} to all; and further that nonlovers desire {*epithumousin*} what is beautiful, we know" (237d3–5).[13] It is equally clear that this assertion amounts to little more than an ordinary opinion that has been accepted uncritically. It also constitutes an admission that the nonlover has something in common with the lover. The speaker suggests that although eros is a species of desire, there is nonerotic desire (237d3–5). But if both kinds of desire (epithumia) are equivalent to strong attraction for bodily beauty (see the definition of "epithumia" below) and with the same intention, how do erotic and nonerotic desire differ? The speaker answers this question as follows. It is necessary to "perceive" (noesai) that in each of us there are two ruling "ideas." The visibility of these "ideas" amounts to a sort of elementary self-knowledge. Presumably one can perceive them in oneself or at least in one's actions. The "ideas" articulate the ways in which we ordinarily appear to ourselves. Certainly the whole framework here artic-ulates, in pseudotechnical language, a quite ordinary and common un-derstanding of inner moral conflict. This is an understanding Socrates will want to revise. I note that the distinction here between what is "in us" (237d6, d9) and what is not is also commonsensical. Socrates later calls upon this distinction at several important junctures.

The first "idea" is an innate desire (epithumia) for pleasures and the second is acquired opinion (doxa) that aims at what is best and so at sophrosyne. The latter is, roughly speaking, reason. The former is irrational (*alogōs;* 238a1), and when it rules a man it is called hubris, which is a multi-eidetic phenomenon. Hubristic desire for bodily beauty is eros. The concealed lover says that the forms of hubris are "neither something beau-tiful nor a credit to possess" (238a5–6). This remark occurs in the context of the analysis of an ousia, even though it is clearly an opinion about the thing's value. Although the nonlover too is interested in bodily beauty, the speaker argues that the nonlover is not interested *only* in bodily beauty (see below), and that his desire is not hubristic, that is, not unrestrained by that other "idea."

This other "idea" is acquired, whereas desire is natural. Man has become a synthesis of nature and, if I may risk the word, culture. Sophrosyne, which is a product of culture, is not natural; presumably it must be brought to be by the desire that precedes it, even though it also conflicts with desire. Since reason too must, according to this account, be acquired, there is a hint here of a unity between reason and desire: reason seems to be a permutation of, or at least acquisition of, desire. It is fairly clear that the "idea" of reason is acquired because nature unassisted by reason is not satisfying to either lover or beloved. Indeed, we learn that since eros is the tyrannical desire for power, the lover wishes to master the objects of his love and thus prefers weak rather than strong beloveds (238e2–5). The speaker simply asserts this as a bald fact and then infers that the "sick" lover tries to "make" (*apergazetai;* 239a2), "prepare" (*para-*

skeuazein; 239a6), and "construct" (*mechanasthai;* 239b6) the youth into a weak and stupid person. Eros is the narcissistic effort to annihilate its object by working it to death in the service of the master/lover. That the relationship between the lover and beloved is short-lived (thanks to the nature of eros) is repeatedly mentioned and implied by Lysias' nonlover and Socrates' concealed lover. Eros is the desire for bodily beauty, but the lover prefers a beloved who is unmanly, weak, and lacking in natural charm (239c–d). Eros is thus self-contradictory. Nature left to its own devices cancels itself out.

Even if acquired opinion becomes a sort of second nature, it cooperates with nature in decisive ways. The speaker says "the two ideas in us are sometimes of one mind (*homonoeiton*) and sometimes at odds; now one gains control, now the other" (237d9–e2). This formulation is ambiguous, since it seems to present four ways in which the two ideas might be related, namely: (1) of one mind, (2) at odds, (3) the one idea in control, (4) the other in control. Since in the remainder of the speech only (3) and (4) are discussed, presumably the speaker wants to exclude (1) and (2). Yet the collaboration of "ideas" exemplified by the nonlover requires that the "ideas" control each other and so requires a version of (1). That is, the best that reason pursues is, in the last analysis, what nature demands, namely, physical gratification. This is what is meant by saying that the nonlover's desire is a sort of epithumia (237d4–5). In this respect, nature (eros) rules doxa (reason). As in the case of Lysias' speech, reason is the instrument of nature, which in turn is conceived of on the level of the body. The natural is the bestial. But man distinguishes himself by acquiring techniques for becoming satisfied. Man is, as it were, the efficient animal. Nonerotic desire differs from erotic desire by virtue of being efficient. Thus there is a secondary sense of the good (as distinguished from pleasure; 239c4 et passim) which reason pursues, namely, efficiency in the pursuit of pleasure. To the extent to which reason has a separate goal of its own, that alone is it. In sum, reason is and ought to be the slave of desire, but to serve well reason must restrain desire.

A few more comments about the second, evaluative, part of this speech. In a significant move, the concealed lover links sophrosyne with nous, and eros with mania (241a3–4). This is the first occurrence of "nous" and "mania" in the *Phaedrus*—another step forward in developing a vocabulary of self-knowledge. This vocabulary, let us note, is introduced in the deliberative, not analytical, half of the concealed lover's speech and so in connection with considerations of utility. The horizon is, as it were, an ethical one; the terms carry their prescientific, value-laden connotations. This vocabulary becomes important in the palinode, where the connotations of the terms change somewhat but are not deprived of their ethical sense. We are told here that the lover suddenly acquires intelligence and self-control when it is time to fulfill his extravagant pledges to the boy, this being a switch from an old (erotic) self to a new one (241a–b). We see here, again, why the acquisition—or perhaps we should say reacquisition or recollection—of reason occurs at all; it is a matter of self-preservation.[14]

The speaker does repeatedly emphasize that the lover is under "necessity" and "compulsion" (anagke). The lover is "enslaved" to eros (238e3), although (as I have just remarked) he can control his eros when he thinks it beneficial to do so. It is equally clear that the lover is cunning in his effort to master the youth. His compulsion is inseparable from his opinion about what is in his best interest at the time. This suggests that, contrary to the concealed lover's initial sketch, lover and nonlover are inseparable and that reason is as natural, at this level, as desire. That is, even the lover is not utterly irrational, since even in him there exists a collaboration of reason and desire. And the nonlover, as we have seen, is rational only in a limited sense. He too is advocating a collaboration between reason and desire, but of a different sort than characterizes the lover. The nonlover is compelled to be reasonable in order to satisfy his eros. The nonlover is a concealed lover; and the lover is a concealed nonlover. The point of all this is, once again, that the separation between reason and desire as formulated in the theoretical portion of this speech is not adequate to the phenomena. Since this doctrine about the "ideas" of desire and reason is a doctrine about human nature, the deficiencies of this doctrine require nothing less than a rethinking of what man is. And this is what occurs next in the Phaedrus.

In order to formulate a better conception of human nature, Socrates will deny that reason is acquired, that eros is a species of epithumia, and that the ends of reason are epithumetic. That is, Socrates will argue that the hubris of reason which is philosophy is as natural as the striving for bodily beauty. Even the concealed lover refers to "divine philosophy" (239b4), professing to believe that the development of the "soul" (241c5; this is the first use of the term in the Phaedrus) is the greatest good. Such remarks are the basis for the rhetorical suggestion that nonerotic desire is not concerned only with bodily beauty. But the concealed lover cannot reconcile this suggestion with his analysis of the ousia of man. How can the concealed lover account for the acquisition of philosophy? or for its divine character? or for the (putative) epithumia which drives philosophy? (The speaker would at least have to distinguish between two kinds of epithumia, the one for corporeal, the other for incorporeal, beauty.) If philosophy were classified as a natural good or pleasure, then the schema would have to include not just revised meanings of these terms but also new concepts such as "natural logos" and perhaps "unnatural eros." By referring to "divine philosophy" the concealed lover suggests a notion he cannot account for. For the concealed lover's speech is, as I have already argued, bounded on all sides by opinion, according to the speech's own standards. Even the judgment as to whether opinion or nature should rule would seem to be a matter of opinion.

How, moreover, would the concealed lover account for soul? Would it be natural or acquired, erotic or reasonable? What would its unity be? What is the good proper to it? The concealed lover indicates that nurture of the soul is a serious matter; yet a serious account of it cannot remain at the level of the concealed lover's speech. For these reasons, as well as all the others I have discussed above, the concealed lover falls back, for all practical purposes, to the level of Lysias' nonlover, who in turn is really a concealed lover (see above). This circle between the rhetorically edifying speech of the concealed lover (edifying both in its recommendations concerning analytical procedure and in its concern for the beloved's welfare) and the unedified, businesslike position of the Lysian nonlover parallels the circular exchange of roles between Phaedrus and Socrates (chapter 1). Once again, we are faced with the problem of breaking out from the horizon of the first two speeches of the dialogue.

Yet the present speech is also placed in between the other two speeches and so would seem to mediate between them. Is there not a sense in which it represents a step in the ascent to the palinode? The answer is affirmative. The just mentioned circle is not, at least so far as the reader is concerned, merely a repetition. To understand that the circle exists and why it is defective is to understand that it is necessary to get beyond it and, roughly, what we need in order to do so. This is not something that is visible the first time around.

To begin with, the speech is a step forward in its rhetoric, and this furnishes grounds for the recantation of the speech. That is, the concealment of the lover's true intentions forces him to acquire noble words whose appeal is widespread, almost natural. Of course, this vocabulary is given a fresh significance in the palinode. For example, "nous" will play a crucial role, for it alone apprehends the hyperuranian beings (247c7). Recollection of noetic vision will replace the "mutual agreement" of the present speech. The step upward to the palinode is achieved by a kind of deception; tricked into conceiving of ourselves from the higher standpoint implied by words like "divine philosophy" and "education of the soul," and by the distinction between the good and the pleasurable, we are enabled to recollect ourselves at a level higher than that advocated by the theory of the concealed lover's speech. This is an example of the self-motion of dialectic. As I noted at the conclusion of my discussion of Lysias' speech, eros and the desire for edification seem inseparable; the latter helps to uplift the former, and the former generates the latter.

Differently put, the concealed lover is compelled to conceal his true intentions because he is, after all, a lover trying to devise a means for obtaining what he wants. He is moved by eros to acquire both a general theoretical procedure and a deliberative evaluation of what sort of thing eros is. This acquisition of logos by eros is also, of course, discussed in the speech itself. On both levels (that described within the speech and that exhibited by it as a speech spoken by one person to another) the desire for satisfaction leads to the acquisition of theory, which in turn expands our vocabulary and conception of eros. And this in turn sparks the desire to perfect our understanding of eros and related notions. This self-moving dialectic is, so to speak, the cunning of desire which propels us from Lysias' standpoint to that of the palinode (and beyond), as well as from Phaedrus' and Socrates' initial relationship (as beloved and lover) through several transformations to that of dialectician (or philosophical erotician) and potential philosopher.

Further, Socrates' first speech shows us in a number of ways that in order to understand our desire we have to do more than think about ourselves as particular individuals. The point is visible at the start of the speech. If we are going to praise or blame the lover, and so figure out who we should please and who not, we must first think about what is true of eros as such. And this requires saying something about what human nature is, and not just about what I am or you are. To know ourselves we must, that is, understand the whole of the phenomenon we find puzzling in ourselves, and this requires understanding something that is true of all persons. This enlargement of our discursive and conceptual horizon goes hand in hand, in Socrates' first speech, with the call for metaphilosophical reflection. In order to talk about oneself properly one must talk about talking in general, and this opens up a number of general issues. Thus the shift from "self-knowledge" as "understanding myself" to "self-knowledge" as "understanding general issues relevant to me and others of the same kind as myself" has already taken place in this speech. The introduction of terms such as "philosophy," "nous," and "soul" serves this purpose, too. They expand our vocabulary and get us describing ourselves in terms that relate us to some larger context. Or more precisely, they help us become self-conscious in a philosophical sense of the fact *that* an individual is somehow a part of such a context, and not just to talk unreflectively as though this were the case. Even the addition by Socrates of a dramatic context for the speech, along with the information that the nonlover is actually a concealed lover, expands the whole in terms of which we are to understand the nonlover.

The concealed lover's speech also anticipates several other substantive theses of the palinode. For example, the nonlover equates reason with freedom, as does the palinode. The concealed lover holds that the lover does not know what is good for him; the lover lacks self-knowledge. This accusation against a particular kind of lover is accurate and is repeated in the palinode. The concealed lover's two "ideas" prefigure the two horses (deprived of their wings, perhaps) of the palinode. Correspondingly, the reality of inner moral conflict is not called into question in the palinode, but instead receives a different interpretation. Both of Socrates' speeches suggest that we must understand who and what we are in order to desire properly.

This brings me to another crucial point, already noted above, which the defects of the first two speeches of the *Phaedrus* make evident. Eros and logos, attraction and detachment, or (speaking loosely) desire and reason are not separable in the way these speeches would pretend. Lysias' speech advocated the view that reason is the instrument of desire, and Socrates' first speech added that reason is an acquired faculty and is desirable. In Socrates' second speech reason will be organically connected with desire, and being as natural as desire, winged reason will have the capacity to motivate and control action. This is a crucial element in the palinode's view that at least at the highest level reason is erotic, or eros rational. This view in turn is key to a host of theses, such as the thesis that philosophy is divine erotic madness; that philosophical knowledge is the same as understanding what one desires, and so self-knowledge; that to lack such knowledge is to desire in a self-destructive way; that those who desire badly reason badly, though they necessarily lack the reason to see even that (they do what they *think* is good); and that knowledge of the highest truths (the Ideas) is not a simple negation of eros— a sort of asceticism—but a kind of eros. That is, the palinode will advocate the view that the lover and nonlover are the same. This is why, as I indicated in the previous chapter, the comic interchange of roles between Socrates and Phaedrus does not continue past the interlude between Socrates' two speeches. For that comic cycle turned on the dichotomy between lover and nonlover advocated by the first two speeches of the *Phaedrus,* and we are now about to recant them. With these still sketchy theses in mind, I would like to mention one more consequence suggested by the first two speeches of the *Phaedrus* and Socrates' first speech in particular.

That speech suggests that it is possible to desire something well only when one knows what one desires. The concealed lover understands this point in a fairly crude way. In a sense, one must already have what one desires in order to desire well. The nonlover "has" the object of his desire in speech. In the palinode, this "having already" becomes anamnesis. The object thus possessed, moreover, must be stable or steadfast; the concealed lover's knowledge of human beings, of the "ideas" in them, and of what he in particular wants gives him (or so he thinks) a constancy the lovers lack terribly. We cannot just let our desires run away with us; they need to be made reflective in a way that allows them to be measured by an answer about what it means to be human. The measures cannot themselves be further desires or other discourses about desires. In the concealed lover's language, they are "ideas in us." In the palinode's language, they are the "hyperuranian beings" (the Ideas). The concealed lover's theory of ideas is inadequate, as we have seen; hence, the palinode's alternative at least deserves to be considered.

Differently put, discourse and desire must be measured by standards that are detached from them, even as discourse must be attracted to articulate these standards. It is not just that reason and eros are closely related, but that both must be for the sake of ousiai. In the palinode, again, this thesis is portrayed on a much broader canvas. When we realize what we really want, or are really talking about, we see that it is something there. But the point is prefigured in these speeches (once one analyzes their various defects), indeed even in their use of terms such as "idea" and "ousia." The concealed lover's reason for reflecting on what we mean by eros and so forth is, as I have said, that failure to do so has deleterious consequences in practice, regardless of what we say or think. This is a sort of naive realism, one that is modified but not simply rejected in the palinode. Desire, human nature, ideas; these are there and have a way of working themselves out. Unless one understands them, they tend to work themselves out badly, as the fate of the irrational lover illustrates.

I have already noted that in delivering the first two speeches of the *Phaedrus,* Phaedrus and Socrates are playing the roles of the fictional speakers and auditors implied by the speeches. On the level of the fiction, the motivation of the two speeches is the non- or concealed lover's sexual desire (these are meant to be seduction speeches). On the level of the dialogue's dramatis personae, however, the motivation is Phaedrus' and Socrates' love of discourse (see chapter 1). The duality of levels is also implicit in the comic role playing and deceptions prominent in the sections of the *Phaedrus* examined thus far. This duality of logos and ergon will crop up again in the *Phaedrus* in more subtle ways. Stated in abstract terms, the duality provides us with an interplay between object- and metalevels of discourse. Neither of the first two speeches of the *Phaedrus* gives us an account of eros that explains the desire of Phaedrus and Socrates to listen to and deliver those very speeches. A comparison between what is said in the speeches (the logos), and the deed of pronouncing them (the ergon) reveals a tension between the two. As a metalevel discourse comments upon the relevant object-level, so the ergon comments on the shortcomings of the logos. But the logos, on the other hand, articulates the vocabulary and ideas required for a grasp and evaluation of the ergon. We shall return to this intricate interplay several times in succeeding chapters.

I conclude this section with the following observation. The concealed lover's position condemns passion for the sake of defending reason, but does so in a way that debases man, in whom passion and reason are combined, to the bestial. This is admirably conveyed by the verse that Socrates breaks into at the end of his speech: "as wolves love lambs, so lovers love beloveds." The lover and, as we know, thanks to the dramatic setting of the speech, the nonlover (the concealed lover) are basically intelligent wolves, animals whose appetite is enlightened. This position, however base it may seem, is not presented in the *Phaedrus* as a straw man set up only as a foil for the exposition of higher truths. Supplying a better account of eros and its relationship to reason is difficult. This point is critical to explaining Socrates' interest both in Lysias' speech and in continuing the conversation with Phaedrus (see chapter 1). Since Socrates accepted the challenge to state Lysias' position better than Lysias could, Socrates delivered a superior but shameful speech. Having articulated that side of the debate fully, Socrates now articulates the other side still more adequately; he thus feels compelled to refute himself. In its own rather structural way this is an excellent example of Socrates' adherence to dialogical thinking.

THE INTERLUDE BETWEEN SOCRATES' TWO SPEECHES

Although Socrates' speech possesses a much clearer structure than does that of Lysias, initially it seems difficult to tell whether it fulfills its promise of being more comprehensive as well (other than in the ways I have indicated above), since Socrates refuses to complete it by praising the nonlover.[15] At this juncture two questions arise immediately. Why did Socrates stop his speech partway through, and what would he have said had he continued with it? The answers are connected.

Socrates begins by claiming that if he had continued with the praise of the sober, self-controlled nonlover, he himself would have become enthusiastic and would have completely lost his self-control. I have already commented on the irony of this claim. Socrates adds that, to construct the end of the speech, one would follow the rule that for every bad characteristic in the lover there corresponds a good one in the nonlover. This would mean that the nonlover would (1) not be sick, but healthy, and so would not be offended by what is stronger than he; (2) gain pleasure from making the beloved stronger and more intelligent, better spoken, better in dianoia; (3) encourage the boy to consort with others and especially with divine philosophy; (4) in general try to make the boy an independent person; (5) prefer a strong tough boy, the type who is dependable in war; (6) not rob the boy of family friends or property; (7) be the most agreeable of men to be with and not be driven by necessity for physical pleasures; (8) not flatter the boy unduly or make extravagant pledges; (9) not suddenly become a new person, or at least not in a way that would cause the breaking of trust (yet, might not the nonlover suddenly become full of "eros and madness"?); and (10) benefit, in sum, the boy's body and psyche.[16] The nonlover is, as so described, strikingly similar to the philosopher described in the palinode. In a sense, then, the palinode is the missing half of the speech. Socrates implies as much at 265c ff., where *both* speeches are referred to as one (265c6; *ho logos*). However, the palinode incorporates the first speech only after revising it; Socrates' two speeches cannot be halves of a whole in an arithmetical sense. But then the nonlover could not be a concealed lover, given the meaning this speech attaches to *eros*. The present description of the nonlover is not incompatible with the view that divine philosophy (3 above) is doxa (even alethes doxa) rather than noesis, as in the palinode. If the nonlover is to be given a significance that goes beyond the concealed lover's speech, we need an account of these terms that is not present in Socrates' first speech.

For Socrates to enumerate the nonlover's good points as part of his first speech would be to perpetuate the rhetorical or practical contradictions already outlined. That is, the speaker is supposed to be a lover who is only concealed as a nonlover. For him to praise his disguise rather than the real thing would prevent him from achieving the goals for whose sake he adopted the disguise in the first place. Hence an effort to complete the concealed lover's speech would lead to progress beyond it. This is in fact what occurs next.

Socrates suddenly threatens to get up and leave rather than fulfill his promises (cf. 241a2 ff.). The threat elicits from Phaedrus a plea that he stay and discuss (dialegesthai; 242a6) what has been said (as *Symp.* 194d shows, Phaedrus is aware of Socrates' love of discussion). The suggestion is at least partly motivated by Phaedrus' feeling that it is too hot to venture away from the spot. Socrates' "you are godlike about discourses, Phaedrus"

(242a7) is thus partly ironic. Nevertheless, Socrates is once again able to cast Phaedrus as the lover who is "compelling" him to deliver another speech. I have already commented, in this and the previous chapter, on the significance of this reversion back to the dramatic level of the first interlude. The cycle of roles and speeches is not simply resumed at this point; it is here that Socrates breaks out of it. It is interesting that Socrates offers another speech, and not the dialogue Phaedrus has requested; certainly Phaedrus did not expect Socrates to deliver yet another speech. Socrates' explanation of why he must deliver another speech suggests that he is concerned more with his own spiritual well-being than with Phaedrus'. Moreover, Phaedrus is not yet ready, in Socrates' view, for dialogue about the complex themes already spoken about.

The threat to leave and the termination of the speech halfway through interrupt the course of the dialogue in a very sudden and unexpected way. The language in which Socrates goes on to articulate his reasons for not wanting to continue in the present vein is also unprecedented in the *Phaedrus*. Socrates states (with no apparent irony) that his "daimonic and customary sign" prevents him from leaving.[17] Unlike his previous speech, which was inspired by deities outside him (some residing in nature), the need for and the determination of the content of this speech derives from sources inside him. In addition to hearing his voice, Socrates claims he is a seer (*mantis;* 242c4) and so is able to determine clearly what the error (hamartema) consisted of and what the cure should be. This mantic capability seems presupposed by the daimonic voice, which tells him that the error must be corrected. Socrates' mantic capacity is merely an instance of the fact that "the soul is somehow prophetic" (*mantikon,* 242c7; this is the second reference to "psyche" in the *Phaedrus*). This power had warned him in advance that, as the poet Ibycus says, he might sin in the eyes of the gods for the sake of honor among men (242c6–d2).[18] The various inner sources that lead Socrates to the palinode contrast sharply with the external sources that produced his first speech, not to mention the external book Phaedrus read.

Phaedrus' soul seems to have forgotten its prophetic abilities. Thus Socrates conveys the knowledge that he, qua seer, possesses by reminding Phaedrus of the generally held opinion that eros is a god (or divine being; 242e2), a child of Aphrodite (242d9–10), and by inferring that eros cannot be evil (242e2–3; cf. *Rep.* II, 380a ff.).[19] Socrates feels a certain awe, indeed fear, before divine Eros (243d4). Hence at the end of the palinode Socrates prays to Eros that (among other things) he might not lose his "erotic art" (257c). Socrates has just given a speech about eros that betrays both what he knows about himself and the very project of self-knowledge.

The poet Stesichorus is called upon as an example of what needs to be done in such a situation, for he was "musical" and so understood the "cause" of his own plight (243a).

But since he wishes to educate Phaedrus, Socrates first cites an example based on another opinion: if a man of "noble and gentle character" who had experienced love of a similar person overheard the previous speeches, he would judge the speakers to be not "free" ("liberal"; *eleutheron*) and the speeches to be sailor's talk.[20] Hence he would never agree with such a description of eros (243c). As his oath indicates (243d2), Phaedrus is impressed by this point. The example, like the whole interlude itself, occupies an intermediate position between low and high, or nonphilosophical and philosophical, positions. The first three kinds of divine madness are represented dramatically in this interlude (see below), and they too are intermediate between Lysian sobriety and philosophical madness (see chapter 3). The gentleman's judgment about sailor talk is not philosophical in that it just expresses an opinion or true belief. But the example, along with the remainder of the interlude, also indicates that self-knowledge and an understanding of the noble are inseparable. The man of noble and gentle character understands this intuitively. According to the palinode, the philosopher possesses the sort of character expert in moral intuitions.

In sum, an inner voice, madness, the power of edifying opinion, the example of noble character, the sayings of the poets (some based on musical knowledge), respect for the divine, and the feeling of shame in the face of blasphemy are the pivots on which the transition from the low to the high discourses turns. This interlude articulates, that is, the rhetoric of moral insight that shows us that the circle of roles and speeches I described in the previous chapters must be left behind. Although the language of ordinary opinion, poetry, and religion is not that of argument and analysis, it is nevertheless appropriate to articulate the ascent of knowledge. The recognition of error (or sin) and the knowledge of what to do and say next does require insight and introspection. In order to desire a catharsis, Socrates must have a sense of what is good and what is bad for him. This sense, along with the inner phenomena and the vocabularies mentioned above, could not have been experienced by the lover or nonlover as defined thus far in the *Phaedrus*.

Socrates will atone for his sin with an "ancient purification," which was known to Stesichorus but not to Homer.[21] When Stesichorus was blinded for accusing Helen of adultery, he knew why, and wrote a recantation stating that actually Helen never did go to Troy. Socrates mentions in the *Republic* (586c) that Stesichorus accounted for Helen's ostensible presence in Troy (and so for the war) by saying that only her *eidolon* went there; through "ignorance of the truth," men fought the war. Having made his palinode, Stesichorus recovered his sight.[22] Socrates is still wiser, perhaps thanks to his practice of higher music (*Pho.* 60e–61a); he will recite his speech *before* he loses his sight (243b3–7). Indeed, with his head now uncovered, Socrates has already regained his sight. The palinode is both a remedy and an inoculation—the perfect pharmakon. Sight was restored to Stesichorus' eyes because he recognized that the poetic and popularly accepted description of Helen was a lie. Socrates will, presumably, also recollect what is truly beautiful. To do so *is* to have his sight restored; hence the appropriateness of his uncovering his eyes.

Socrates claims that his palinode is "by Stesichorus" (244a2–3). This conceit emphasizes the analogy between their two palinodes and therefore connects the original/image distinction with Socrates' two speeches. Socrates' first speech corresponds to Stesichorus' original ode (or the part of the ode in which Helen was slandered); as Helen was unjustifiably condemned, so too with eros. The war fought over Helen corresponds to the contest between Socrates and Lysias, a contest that we now see to have been over a mere image of the true thing. This point fits nicely with the just noted *Republic* passage in which base and warlike behavior is connected with the failure to distinguish between images and reality. Even as Helen's eidolon occupied the enemy's camp, so the eidolon of eros occupied Lysias' text from which Socrates tried to wrest it. Since neither side understood that the object of their contest was an image, both sides were in that respect on the same plane. Thus Socrates' speech was Lysian; he says, in fact, that Lysias was its father (257b2). As Stesichorus remedies his fault by claiming that only Helen's eidolon was immoral, so Socrates can claim that he did not slight the true Eros.

Strangely enough, Socrates' description of what eros really is turns out to be another image, itself woven into the fabric of a myth. One already wonders whether the palinode may not be an image in its own right, one sent out into the world by Socrates' eros. The connection between eros and image making is intimate, as the palinode itself will show. Men not only pursue images of what they find desirable (so moving themselves), these images are generated by eros. Poetry is the language suitable to articulating the fantasies of love, and Socrates' palinode is suitably poetic.

3

The Palinode

*True, we love life, not because we are used to living but
because we are used to loving. There is always some madness
in love. But there is also always some reason in madness.*
NIETZSCHE[1]

The palinode may be divided into two main sections: (1) 244a8–
245a8, the discussion of the three traditional forms of madness (243e9–
244a8 is introductory), and (2) 245c5–257b6, the *apodeixis* (a term better
translated here as "exposition" or "exhibition" than as "proof") defending
a fourth form of madness (245b1–c4 connects the two sections). The second
section is divisible into three main parts, namely (2a) 245c5–246a2, the
soul's self-motion and immortality, (2b) 246a3–257a2, the ἰδέα and image
of the soul, the divine banquet, recollection, and the workings of eros,
and (2c) 257a3–b6, the prayer to Eros and concluding words. As we shall
see, (2b) is itself divisible into three parts. As 253c7 makes clear, (2b)
is a myth, a fact that helps demarcate it from the other sections.[2] The
entire discourse is introduced with a formal sounding pretense; Socrates
conceals himself under the name Stesichorus in order to speak on behalf
of the lover, and he addresses a boy (243e4) who is played by Phaedrus.
Socrates is concealed as a poet and as an advocate of noble love, and Phaedrus as a potential philosopher. A new rhetorical framework is thereby
created for this speech.

Socrates introduces the palinode by stating what must be demonstrated:
it is false that one should gratify the nonlover rather than the lover. The

contrary view would hold only, he says, if the premises that (a) the lover is mad while the nonlover is sophron and (b) madness is invariably an evil were both true (244a3–8). Socrates accepts (a) but rejects (b). Hence, he proceeds in the first section to rehabilitate the notion of madness by showing that at least in three established cases heaven-sent madness is a good (though Socrates does not claim in the palinode that madness is invariably a good). Of course, this alone does not show that there is a divine sort of madness that benefits lover and beloved. This is what the apodeixis, the second section of the palinode, is supposed to show (245b1–c1). Before mentioning divine erotic madness, though, Socrates must discuss the soul in detail. As the sequence of topics in the palinode shows (traditional forms of madness—soul qua soul—erotic madness), the notion of soul is indispensable to Socrates' thesis about eros. In fact, the palinode as a whole is primarily about the soul; it is a psychology first and a cosmology second. In the apodeixis topics are introduced in order to explain something about the soul, and only to the extent that they do so. Hence little is said about the internal logic of the Ideas or about cosmological issues of the sort that are addressed in the *Timaeus*. It is already clear, however, that the palinode has a good deal of work to do if it is to supply an alternative to the earlier speeches on eros. The challenge posed by those speeches is a very difficult one to meet, as the length and breadth of the palinode testifies.

Each of the first three kinds of madness is sent by the gods. The overcoming of Lysias' standpoint seems to require a religious premise, a premise for which we have been prepared in the interlude between Socrates' two speeches. Yet the role of the gods in the fourth kind of madness is unconventional. Divine erotic madness is not so much sent from gods external to the individual as sparked from a source within him, as is suggested by its association with anamnesis.[3] This fact is closely related to the superiority of the fourth kind of madness to the others (see below).

It should be noted that Socrates does not mention at this point the complicated status of sophrosyne. Earlier it was assumed that sophrosyne, defined in a utilitarian way, was simply good. It turns out that *that* was just "mortal sophrosyne" (256b6, e5). There exists a higher sophrosyne (see the role of sophrosyne at 254b7, and the whole description of the lover learning self-control). Socrates does not give it a name, but it is fairly clear that divine sophrosyne would be appropriate. Indeed, the apodeixis teaches that divine erotic madness and divine sophrosyne are to be united in the successful experience of love. That is, the philosopher (= the erotic madman) is somehow the synthesis of lover and nonlover.

Sophrosyne is good *if* it is combined with erotic madness, and vice versa. This difficult thesis goes beyond even the three relatively traditional forms of madness in which there remains, more or less explicitly, a contrast between sophrosyne and madness, as was the case in the earlier speeches.

THE THREE TRADITIONAL FORMS OF MADNESS (244a8–245a8)

The first form of madness receives the longest explanation of the three; it can be labeled "prophetic madness" and is exhibited by (among others) the prophetesses at Delphi, the priestesses at Dodona, and the Sibyl. It is "clear to all" that such madness is beneficial, and further that sophrosyne does not produce such benefits. The *ad verecundiam* argument supporting the worth of madness is supplemented by humorous etymologies and word histories. The "ancients who gave things their names" understood the true value of madness and prophecy, whereas "men of today" do not, since they try to replace the prophetesses' mad "techne" with a "human" technique of interpreting nature by means of calculations and information gathering (for example, about "birds and signs"). The vain self-glorification by the moderns of their analytical powers reminds us of the self-praise of the nonlover; both are characterized by the kind of sophrosyne Socrates now wants to criticize. The ancients may have been unsophisticated, but they understood themselves to the extent of understanding their dependence on higher powers. The reference to Delphi here is the third and last in the *Phaedrus* and recalls the connection between Delphi and self-knowledge.

Socrates himself claimed a prophetic capacity (for the "soul is somehow prophetic"; 242c7) of which this very speech is a result. Socratic prophecy seems to combine the human techne of division or dissection with the divinely given techne of madness; that is, it somehow combines, as the rhetoric of the palinode itself suggests, ancient and modern arts, or madness and sophrosyne. I note that according to Socrates, the ancients felt no shame in praising madness (244b7); they would, presumably, be ashamed to condemn it, as the moderns do. The moderns feel no shame because they are *apeirokalos* (244c4), "ignorant of the beautiful."

The second kind of madness liberates the present and the future from the grip of the past (it too prophesizes about the course of action to be taken). It is fundamentally medicinal or psychiatric, curing ancient sicknesses through catharses and rites. This telistic madness reminds us of

Socrates' behavior in the previous interlude. Moreover, the language of telistic madness is used several times in the palinode in connection with erotic madness (249c7–8, 250b8, 253c3). The soul is primordially deficient; it has forgotten its true origins, a defect overcome only through the madness of recollection. Philosophy is true psychotherapy for the sickness that infects every human soul.[4]

The third kind of madness is that of the poets. Socrates specifies the source of this madness—the Muses. The poet teaches future generations by conveying to them edified *(kosmousa)* stories about the ancients. In the palinode, Socrates will himself claim that his myth is above earthly poetry and that it speaks the truth (247c3–6). The complexity of the status of poetry is also clear from the fact that the palinode is itself a kind of poetry; that Socrates in his first speech called upon the Muses for inspiration; that Socrates both places the poet (along with the other imitative artists) sixth in the ranking of lives (248e1) and puts the philosopher, the lover of beauty, and the musical person together at the top of the scale; that in the story about the cicadas the philosophers are said to have their own Muses (259d); and finally that Plato's own dialogues are themselves edifications of the wise men of old (for example, Socrates) for the instruction of posterity. Of the three forms of madness, the poetic sort seems to be the closest to Socratic-Platonic philosophizing and hence to be its most complex antagonist. I note that the opposition between reason and madness seems minimized here, but not entirely overcome (245a5–8). However, all three forms are inferior to erotic madness, as is indicated by the ranking they receive subsequently (at 248d7–e1; prophetic and telistic madness are ranked fifth). These examples of divine madness serve to bridge the gap between the defective modern understanding of the phenomenon and a more archaic and philosophical conception.

In introducing the apodeixis, Socrates says that it will be "unbelievable to the clever but believable to the wise" (245c1–2). The clever were mentioned at 229d4; they were the physicists, or the sophists with an inclination for demythologizing. Perhaps they are unpersuadable (and so unteachable) because they do not believe that soul exists, or at least they believe that it is reducible to the elements (the soul being a poetic-religious metaphor). And perhaps they are unpersuadable because they lack the requisite sense of shame, sensitivity to beauty, experience of eros, and understanding of the religious premise referred to above. We will note in a moment the point in the demonstration of immortality to which the clever might object. Socrates seems to be admitting here that his palinode does not possess the kind of demonstrative force required by the clever.

This does not mean that it has no rational force or that it is offered not as a truth claim but as a device for edification. The palinode is in part a phenomenology of love. Those who see nothing familiar in the phenomenology will feel quite unpersuaded. Phaedrus, in any event, is friendly to the reductionist position; and the sudden emphasis on soul, as well as the apparently rigorous demonstration of its nature and immortality, surely have as a purpose that of shaking Phaedrus' proclivity for that position.

I turn now to the apodeixis, which begins, without warning, with the nature of the soul. The air of logical rigor in the discussion of immortality contrasts with the reliance on convention in the discussion of the three types of madness and with the mythic character of the second part of the apodeixis. It is as though the self-sufficiency of human reason is being touted in the face of conventional beliefs and imaginative stories. Nevertheless, *both* parts of the apodeixis are needed to constitute the exposition in question. This suggests that the first part is not supposed to be a proof that can survive on its own. Perhaps the rhetoric of argumentation is no less rhetorical (in the sense outlined in the later part of the *Phaedrus*) than the rhetoric of myth.

THE APODEIXIS

The Soul's Self-Motion and Immortality (245c5–246a2)

One must approach this controversial passage with consternation. Not only is it difficult to formulate a satisfactory analysis of what this passage means; there are also problems of a philological nature (the manuscripts offer varying readings of crucial segments of the passage). Let me begin by reflecting on the purpose of the passage in the context, since understanding the context is crucial for appreciating this passage.

If the passage is extracted and treated as an independent venture into cosmology or physics, the prospects for finding much that is of interest in it are very slim.[5] At the very least, the passage asserts that the soul's ousia is self-motion. Why is the soul so forcefully brought to our attention now? Why is it characterized in terms of motion? The notion of soul, we recall, made its first appearance at the end of Socrates' first speech, in connection with the judgment that the boy ought not to be treated as merely a means to the lover's appetite. The soul is what ought to be the object of *paideusis;* there is "in truth nothing for men or for gods which is or ever will be of greater value" than the soul (241c5–6). The presence of soul in the boy entitles him to be treated as a person who is a being possessing the capacity for education and learning. Thus soul is first introduced, in the *Phaedrus*, within a practical or moral, not theoretical, perspective.

In the interlude between his two speeches, Socrates referred to "psyche" (242c7; "the soul is somehow mantic") by way of explaining how he knew that his previous speech was an error. Thus "soul" is that which possesses quasi-cognitive insight or judgment about the truth of human and divine phenomena (such as eros). Since in this instance the soul divines something about the true nature of man, "the soul" seems to make self-knowledge possible. The third and last reference to "soul" prior to our present passage occurs in connection with the third kind of divine madness, the poetic (245a2). Perhaps the reason for mentioning "soul" there is to suggest, once again, that it is thanks to its capacities and work that education (effected in this case through the interpretation of the past with an eye to recommending certain virtues to posterity) is created. Soul is the seat or origin of the creation of beautiful speeches as well. However, neither of the two references to psyche so far makes any claims about its structure, permanence, or origin. The references are, so to speak, metaphysically neutral. They describe the soul's functions and value, not its nature.

The intentions of the palinode as a whole continue to warrant the introduction of the notion of soul in at least a moral or practical sense. The palinode provides a very abstract statement of the conception of the erotic soul required to overcome the earlier and base conception of eros. The necessity for something like soul is also shown indirectly by the failure of the theoretical part of Socrates' first speech to account satisfactorily for the relation of the "two ideas in us" or, more pointedly, to account for that in which they are united. Furthermore, we saw in our discussion of Socrates' first speech that self-knowledge must extend to a knowledge of human nature, and not just remain a commentary on oneself as a particular individual. The first step in Socrates' refutation of his earlier, Lysian, view of eros consisted of rehabilitating the notion of madness. The next step up is the introduction of soul as an explicit theme in the new account of human nature. Whatever else may be required for the refutation of the earlier view of eros, the notion of soul is indispensable.

The introduction of soul as a theme and the identification of soul with a certain kind of ceaseless motion is accomplished with almost shocking suddenness. It would make sense to identify eros with motion; might "soul" and "eros" be different names for the same entity? Certainly the definition of soul in terms of motion seems to be the opposite of what Socrates should want at this stage. For it was precisely the irresponsible motion of eros that led to the nonlover's criticisms of it. Socrates now seems to be affirming a Heracliteanism of the spirit. Immediately preceding the present passage, Socrates says, "Thus let us not be frightened by this, and let us not be troubled by a logos which seeks to scare us into [the view that] it is necessary to prefer the friendship of the one who is sophron to that of one who is moved" (245b2–4; this is the first use of *kineo* or cognates in the *Phaedrus*). The kinesis of eros, in other words, is frightening. If Socrates is to argue that the soul is a sort of motion, he must do so in a way that calms the fears just referred to. He achieves this by defining the soul as *self*-motion and deducing that the soul is immortal. The motion of eros, we recall, seemed to lead to self-destruction. The definition of soul now suggests that self-annihilation is not possible.

The identification of soul with *self*-motion will have the further advantages of allowing Socrates not only to establish a categorical distinction between soul and body but also to point to the priority of the former (it possesses the sort of being that does not deteriorate, whereas body does since it always depends for its motion on something other than itself). In this way, another step beyond the level of Lysias' speech is taken (cf. *Laws* 891c–e and context, where materialist physics is linked with the denial of the primordiality of the soul and so with atheism). In sum, by generalizing the property of motion from eros to soul, and by guaranteeing that the motion is both internally sustained and immortal, Socrates both redeems an essential feature of eros (and the palinode is, after all, a defense of eros) and tries to quiet fears one may have about the consequences of kinesis. Having said all this, though, it still is not clear how eros and self-motion are to be connected, especially since erotic motion seems to be caused by the object of desire. At best, eros would seem to be only a type of self-motion; in itself, self-motion is a very broad notion.

In his final remarks before beginning the apodeixis, Socrates says, "First it is necessary to perceive (noesai) the truth of the soul's nature both divine and human, looking at its *pathe* and *erga*" (245c2–4; some translations of these terms in a moment). The perception required to state the essence of human and divine soul would seem to transcend human powers; indeed, to try to state the essence of the divine seems hubristic. Perhaps this is why so little is said in the passage about the soul beyond the assertion that soul is immortal self-motion. Further, describing the soul that is common to gods and men requires an abstraction from the body as well as from the familiar human world and the familiar human conception of the gods. Hence the immortality passage does not refer to mind or desire or imagination. This definition of soul as self-motion cannot, then, be more than programmatic; for it is scarcely the same as an account of human desire, self-consciousness, or divine madness. Indeed, no examples of soul moving itself are given in this section of the palinode.

Thus it might seem that in this passage we are trying to perceive the soul's nature *without* looking at its "experiences" (or "sufferings," "passions," "conditions," "states") and "doings" (or "deeds," "actions," "activities"). That looking takes up at least the mythic portion of the apodeixis, upon which we must therefore rely for help in understanding the meaning of self-motion and soul. All this leads us to the question: is soul as soul something over and above its experiences and doings, a tertium quid? And if this is true, is it not the case that by relying on the remainder of the apodeixis to explicate the meaning of "self-motion" in terms of its pathe and erga we are admitting that the essence of the soul must remain permanently beyond our grasp? Self-knowledge would then be limited to the manifestations of the soul, while the ousia of the soul remained knowable only to the extent that the bare label "self-motion" can be attached to it, the explanation of which refers to the soul's manifestations (pathe and erga). We do not know what the soul is, but we do know how it changes. If this is so, then Socrates will have a new cause for shame—his inability to know the soul in itself and so, perhaps, to decisively overcome the lower standpoint of the earlier speeches.

Or, alternatively, is it the case that the soul is not something other than its pathe and erga? A description of them would then be a description of the soul's self-motion. Although at this point it is not easy to say which alternative is correct, the reference to pathe and erga already suggests that it is the second. We are to start by looking at the nature of soul that is common to both gods and men, and to do this by looking at the soul's pathe and erga (245c2–4). That formulation suggests that we see the soul's self-motion by looking at its experiences and doings, the description of which does begin, however minimally, in the immortality passage. Moving bodies and moving oneself would seem to qualify as pathe and erga. The soul is not, in this reading, some third thing beyond its experiences and doings. This suggests that it would be a mistake to try to find some metaphysical description of the soul that somehow goes deeper and beyond the phenomenological description of its pathe and erga to some other inner essence.

If self-motion is (in whole or part) experiences and doings, then the soul is complex rather than simple. We have here an answer to one of Socrates' initial questions about himself (230a4–6). Indeed, the very notion of self-motion, though initially suggestive of a kind of simplicity, actually is internally complex since it requires a mover and a moved, and so a doer and a something that undergoes the doing. The soul's activity divides it. The soul is not a simple monad. Hence the problem of the unity of the soul arises immediately. We learn in a moment, not surprisingly, that the soul has a number of elements (represented by the winged charioteer and horses). Even if self-motion were simple, soul would be that *and* a complex of elements, the result being that it would be twofold and so complex. Hence the demonstration of the soul's immortality here will not rely on the view that the soul is incomposite.

Let me turn directly now to the passage in question. It seems to me that the central argument of the passage can be reconstructed in the form of a valid sorites (several of the premises are enthymematic), as follows:

Whatever cannot abandon its own nature *(ouk apoleipon heauto)* cannot cease moving *(oupote legei kinoumenon)* (see 245c7–8).
Whatever moves itself *(to auto kinoun)* cannot abandon its own nature.

So what moves itself cannot cease moving (245c7–8; explicit).

What cannot cease moving cannot come to be or be destroyed.

So what moves itself (= the *arche* and *pege* of all motion) cannot come to be or be destroyed (245d).
What cannot come to be or be destroyed is ever-moving *(aeikineton).*[6]

So whatever moves itself is ever-moving.
Whatever is ever-moving is immortal (245c5; explicit).[7]

So what moves itself is immortal (245e2–3; explicit).
The soul by nature moves itself (245e3–4).

All soul is immortal (245c5).

In the passage under discussion Socrates also identifies what moves itself with the arche and pege of *all* motion and then argues (a) that as arche, it cannot by definition come to be, since it would have to come to be from an arche, and so would be presupposing its own existence. Hence it would already have been in existence (or, alternatively, the entity that is coming to be would not be an arche but would still have to arise from a preexisting arche, which arche therefore did not come to be).[8] This point helps to support the second conclusion in the sorites. Further (b) Socrates also argues that the pege and arche of all motion cannot be destroyed. This conclusion does not follow from (a), and in support of it Socrates introduces a counterfactual: if the arche were to be destroyed, nothing else could come to be, and the "whole universe [*ouranos*] and all of genesis would collapse into immobility and would never find again another source of motion to bring it back into being" (245d7–e2).[9] This argument also serves to give additional support to the second premise ("whatever moves itself cannot abandon its own nature") and second conclusion ("what moves itself cannot come to be or be destroyed") of the sorites. Its force is not, however, logical, but moral. The prospect of the universe being irreversibly destroyed and bereft of all life is morally unacceptable.[10] The arguments (a) and (b) just outlined consume a significant portion of the passage in question and also interrupt the course of the sorites as outlined above.

The last premise in the sorities ("the soul by nature moves itself") is arrived at in an interesting way. "Soul" is mentioned only twice in the course of the argument (245c5–e4), once in its conclusion (which, however, is stated at the start of the whole argument) and once in this premise. The conclusion cannot be drawn unless soul can successfully be introduced in this premise. But what justification is offered for it?[11] As already noted, this premise is necessary if the base standpoint of the earlier speeches on eros is to be overcome. Socrates' point d'appui for his justification of this premise has a by now familiar ring: "And now that we have seen that that which is moved by itself is immortal, one who says that the ousia and logos of the soul are this very thing [self-motion] will not be ashamed [or: need not feel ashamed]" (245e2–4). It would be *shameful* to deny this, presumably because it would reduce the soul to something that is moved only by something else and so would reduce it to the level of a body. And this would return us to the level of Lysias' and Socrates' first speeches, which, as we have already seen, were a cause for shame.[12] No doubt this is one point the "clever" but not the "wise" will find "unbelievable." Indeed, a materialist might accept everything in the proof up to the identification of "self-motion" with "psyche"; he might construe the arche of self-motion as the "immortal" movement of atoms. He does not sense the shamefulness of a reductive account of human beings. He wants to avoid talk about soul and so avoid the entire myth about the soul and cosmos that Socrates elaborates. The apodeixis, after all, suggests that to understand the motion of a rock one must understand the motion of an invisible entity, soul. The apodeixis thus reinfuses nature with myth. Socrates' answer in the *Phaedrus* to the reductionist's shamelessness can only be to start over at the beginning of the *Phaedrus* and go through the two speeches, pointing out their defects and what is needed to overcome them. But Socrates does not have in this dialogue an ironclad proof that incorporeal soul exists. His appeals to moral intuition are not, however, defective substitutes for such a proof. He wants to claim, after all, that moral intuition does tell us something true about things.

In his peroration at 245e4–246a2, Socrates emphasizes once again that the essential quality of soul is self-motion, of which immortality is a consequence. The *pan soma* must mean "each and every body"; hence it seems that soul can be spoken of distributively, as either being or not

being in *a* body. But can "soul" also be spoken of collectively, in such a
way as to denote a "world soul"?

This question adverts, of course, to the famous ambiguity of *psyche pasa*
(245c5).[13] The phrase is used at 249e4–5 distributively. At 246b6–7 we
are told that "psyche pasa[14] has care of [*epimeleitai*] all the unsouled, and
traverses the whole universe [*panta ouranon*], though becoming different
in different forms." Although here Socrates might be taken to refer to
"soul" in a collective sense, the "forms" seem to be the individual gods
and their followers, who traverse heaven "ordering all things and taking
care [*epimeloumenos*] therefor" (246e5–6). The human souls "become different" in the way in which Socrates immediately proceeds to describe;
they shed their wings, regain them, and so forth. It seems to me that
246b6–7 is best taken as declaring something generally true of souls taken
as a group. Nowhere in the third section of the palinode, or indeed in
the *Phaedrus,* is anything like a "world soul" explicitly or unambiguously
mentioned; we hear only of the souls of gods, men, and beasts. One might
object that the movement of the periphora of the heaven (247c1–2) must
be caused by an impersonal world soul, one that keeps the whole of the
universe moving while the gods take care of the parts. This unlikely objection has little force given that there are so many references to the work
of individual souls and no unambiguous references to the work of a cosmic
soul. Possibly the function of Hestia (who "alone of the gods stays home";
247a1–2) is to care for the periphora (that *a* soul or several souls might
do this is also suggested in the *Laws*).[15] This leaves us with the ambiguous
"all soul" of 245c5, and I would again urge that the preponderance of
the evidence in the *Phaedrus* should inhibit us from postulating a world
soul that exists over and above the souls of gods, men, and beasts. General
truths about all individuals can be stated without entailing the existence
of separate entities over and above these individuals. The "all soul" at
245c5 is thus a mass term.

If this passage is to cohere with the rest of the apodeixis, then, it would
seem that what is said about all soul must apply to each and every soul.
Yet Socrates declares that "immortality" is frequently misunderstood to
mean the permanent unity of soul and body (246c5–d2), whereas in fact
it refers to the permanence of soul alone. It is thus difficult to imagine
that personal immortality is envisioned in the present passage, since it
seems difficult (though not impossible) to conceive of oneself as this particular person without conceiving of oneself as embodied. Or at least, it
seems that people "irrationally" (246c6) hold that the body and soul are
immortally joined because they sense that the compound of the two is
essential to preserving their particularity and this is what they fear to

lose. The nonphilosopher's fear of death is calmed by a misconception about immortality. Hence it seems that the palinode cannot ultimately extinguish the fear of the nonphilosophers, because it cannot (and does not) promise personal immortality. However, the notion of immortality is a component of the thesis that every human soul has by nature some understanding of the Truth. Intelligence does not inhabit an absurd world; there are eternal principles of intelligibility the understanding of which is an escape from our finitude. If something like that is true, then death is not "the only reality."[16] Whether this interpretation of "immortality" requires life before and after death is open for debate. I shall discuss the matter further in chapter 4, "Excursus."

Before bringing my discussion of this section of the *Phaedrus* to a close, several further comments about the meaning of self-motion are in order. First, given the way in which it is distinguished from the movement of body, it is plausible to infer that self-motion is incorporeal. Therefore it cannot in itself be, for example, locomotion through space or, more broadly, cannot be understood in the same way that bodily motion can be. Second, while it is not explicitly stated that soul causes every kind of bodily change, this seems implied by the sweeping universality of the passage. "Life" is mentioned once in this passage (245c7) and is connected with soul. This leads to the odd consequence that the growth *and* decay of organic body is somehow due to the action of soul, and so that death (the separation of soul and body) is the result of the principle of life. As a whole, indeed, the palinode abstracts from the possibility that the soul may produce evil or disorder—an abstraction that is in keeping with the edifying purpose of the speech.

The palinode does not explain just how a soul moves the body it occupies, or how it could move an object (such as a stone) without inhabiting it (cf. *Laws* 897a ff.). Presumably the category of life would help explain the way in which a soul and its body are united, since life seems to integrate consciousness (including self-awareness and purposiveness) with the functioning of the body. It is worth noting that the palinode's description of the experience of eros is cast in obviously sexual vocabulary, and that the description in no way suggests a metaphysical dichotomy between body and soul. Nevertheless, we are not given here anything like the sort of explanation Aristotle, for example, offers in the *De Anima*.

Just as it is unclear how soul and body are united, so it is unclear in what way they are separate. Indeed, it is very difficult to understand how that which makes a body a living body could be separate from body in the sense of being a different kind of substance (as the now famous soul/body problem shows). The myth pictures soul as existing incorporeally before and after death. If that picture is not taken literally, then the chief characteristic of soul that distinguishes it from body is its self-motion, and so its desire and thought. Although these are to be explained non-reductively, it does not follow that they can somehow exist in the absence of body. The notion of immortality means at the very least that we should not try to account for the soul in terms of material nature and that we ought not picture the universe as existing without soul, as though the universe were just a repository of directionless inorganic matter. These are not fruitful ways of looking at things when we are trying to explain, in a way that will overcome the low interpretations of eros offered earlier in the *Phaedrus,* what human nature is. Of course, much more needs to be said about all this. At this point, I just want to indicate that though the myth initially suggests a *chorismos* between soul and body, the matter is more complicated. And, to repeat, the myth never tells us that the soul is anything like a Cartesian substance or a Leibnizean monad.

Furthermore, the notion of rest is alluded to in this passage only in the development of the counterfactual argument, as a condition that would result universally if soul disappeared. It is unclear whether self-motion excludes the possibility that some parts of the soul can be at rest while others move. In the next part of the palinode we learn that the hyperuranian beings are at rest. If nous (which "alone" sees the beings: 247c7–8) is to see them accurately, it must not impart its motion to them or move itself in a way that distorts its vision (perhaps it must be internally at rest). One reason for placing the beings outside the heavens and the soul inside is to secure the stability of the former.

Finally, the notion of self-motion implies that of circularity and of self-relation. Like that of self-motion, they suggest self-sufficiency, a trait associated earlier in the *Phaedrus* with the nonlover. Possibly the emphasis on the soul's self-sufficiency accounts for the absence of the Good in the palinode (see below). However, Socrates must still explain how the soul's self-sufficiency is to be reconciled with its longing for the hyperuranian beings, not to mention other objects of desire. Indeed, the experience of eros is repeatedly described as a "pathos" in the soul (251d8, 252b2, c2, 254e1, 255d4); is the soul not moved, thanks to eros, by something outside itself (for example, the beauty of the beloved's form)?

Stated in a preliminary way, the palinode's answer to this question is the following. The workings of eros do explain how self-motion describes the soul, for in desiring X or Y and so in being affected by one or the other, the soul is deciding, choosing, valuing, or simply directing itself to X or Y. These choices are limited; desires are given naturally, and they have their goals. The palinode does not suggest the idea of an indeterminate desire; even eros has its natural fulfillment in contemplation of the Ideas.

Thus the choices are not "free" in the sense of "autonomous" or "creative." But a soul can choose to let some desires be fulfilled and others not, a process the palinode describes vividly. If the choice of the object desired is an ignorant choice, the soul's ignorance (not the object of desire) is in a sense what moves the soul. If the soul desires what appears to it to be good and beautiful, the appearance may be said to move the soul, but only because the soul values the appearance. In this very broad sense, then, the soul may be said to move itself.[17]

Of course, more needs to be said about the self-motion issue. In particular, it would seem that at least on the highest level, that of the soul's contemplation of the Ideas, the soul is attracted to Ideas because they are intrinsically desirable. Or are they desirable because they are good for the soul's nature? I shall argue that, in the final analysis, the palinode tells us that there is no priority involved between saying that something is truly desirable for the soul because it is good and that something is truly desirable because it is good for the soul. There is a natural fit between soul and Ideas, and both descriptions are true. There also seems to be a natural fit between the soul's lower desires (such as that represented by the black horse) and their objects. Self-motion is still a good description of Socrates' point that people choose in accordance with their nature, character, and recollection the images they desire. Correspondingly, *psychagogia* is possible because of the soul's self-motion; that self-motion is what allows the soul to be talked into desiring different things. Of course, substantiation of these sketchy points must await my interpretation of the myth. As I have said above, the significance of the self-motion passage should not be assessed independently of an interpretation of the remainder of the palinode. At this point, I am only adumbrating the general direction my interpretation will take.

With the reference to all soul the *Phaedrus* has brought us all the way from Socrates' questions about who he in particular is to questions about what human nature as such is. Self-knowledge has moved from the personal to the general and abstract plane. Socrates' first speech, as we saw, was instrumental in bringing about, and showing the necessity of, this transition. An individual's efforts to understand his own pathe and erga rapidly lead to a level of discourse that articulates truths about himself and other persons, as well as about the context in which they find themselves. The myth to which I now turn will emphasize this thesis all over again.

The Myth (246a3–257a2)

The palinode's myth is divisible into three sections, though in treating of each of them I have found it necessary to comment on others. The

sections are (1) 246a3–250c6, the ἰδέα and image of the soul, the divine
banquet, the soul's journeys, and the description of recollection; (2) 250c7–
253c6, the role of the gods in the experience of eros, and the lover's
pursuit of the beautiful beloved; and (3) 253c7–257a2, the description
"from inside" of the love affair, the process of self-control, and the standpoint of the beloved. The break between the first and second sections is
signaled by Socrates' "There let it rest then" phrase (250c7) and his turn
to an elaboration of a theme (Beauty) that had been mentioned only in
passing. The break between the second and third sections is clearly marked
by a return to the original division of the soul and by a turn to a new
theme (the "capture of the beloved").

The myth begins with the realm that is furthest from ordinary experience
and ends with a description of an experience that is fairly common.[18]
Roughly put, we move from the soul as disembodied to the embodied
soul's travails; from the nature of soul as such (both human and divine)
and of the hyperuranian beings to the intense feelings of a lover and a
beloved. The myth proceeds, in a sense, from high to low or universal
to particular, that is, from the divine to the all-too-human (the reverse
order from that of the *Phaedrus* up to now). The order of demonstration
suggests that to understand the relatively ordinary experience of desire
we must understand ourselves as part of (and dependent upon) a Whole
that is composed of both incorporeal and corporeal entities.

Section One: 246a3–250c6

The ἰδέα and Image of the Soul Divine and Human.   The term "ἰδέα" can
have the ordinary and somewhat indeterminate sense of "nature,"
"shape," "look," "articulation," or the "technical" sense of "Idea." In the
last of these what is being adverted to is the sort of entity that is called,
in the palinode, a "hyperuranian being" (247c–e; I shall capitalize "Idea"
when the term has the sense of "hyperuranian being").[19] The Beings named
here (Justice Itself, Sophrosyne, Episteme; and later on in the palinode,
Beauty and *Phronesis*) are not referred to in the palinode as "ἰδέαι" or
"εἴδη." Socrates assiduously avoids applying such terminology to them
(not even referring to them as "ones"). On the other hand, "ἰδέα" (and
"εἶδος"; the two are synonymous terms in the *Phaedrus*) is used in a
variety of ordinary senses, but only once in a context that might suggest
a more technical connotation. This context occurs at the very start of the
myth. It runs as follows: "Concerning [the soul's] immortality, let this
be sufficient; but concerning its ἰδέα, this must be said. What sort of
thing it [the "idea"] is in all ways would be an entirely divine and long
narrative [*diegesis*], but what it [the "idea"] resembles is both human and

shorter; in this way let us speak."[20] This reference to the ἰδέα of the soul
has received scant attention in the secondary literature.[21]

What is at stake in the interpretation of the word at issue? I put aside
as uncontroversial the view that the soul cannot be identical with an Idea
(the soul being in motion and the Ideas motionless). The issue is, rather,
whether there is an Idea *of* the soul. According to the *Phaedrus,* there is
true Episteme only of Beings.[22] These Beings are pictured as immutable,
stable in every way, eternal, soulless, and separate from the spheres of
genesis, motion, and life (hence they are "above the heavens" and "outside"
the cosmos cared for by soul). We are given to understand that the Beings
are incorporeal, colorless, shapeless, and untouchable. They are distinct
from each other and can be contemplated separately. Each is fully intelligible in itself and is the "original" of an "image" in our world. Each is
a principle of intelligibility of this image. Every incarnate soul has seen
something of these Beings (249b5–6, e4–5) and yearns to know them
again; in this life, however, the best one can do is to recollect them.

If there is no Idea of the soul, then there does not exist a comprehensive
and divine Episteme of the soul; not even the gods could know the soul
in the highest sense of the term.[23] Hence self-knowledge is not, *in principle,*
perfectible. If there is no Idea of the soul, then there is no anamnesis of
the soul qua soul, and self-knowledge cannot in principle be recollective
in that sense. Human souls are not intelligible as images of an original
principle of Soul, and the world is populated not by images of Soul but
by souls. No one has ever had the experience of gazing directly into the
immutable essence of man, for such an essence does not exist if there is
no Idea of the soul.[24] If self-knowledge nevertheless requires knowledge
of the Beings, at least two kinds of knowledge, the one Epistemic (knowledge in the highest sense of the term) and the other non-Epistemic are,
in principle, required for self-knowledge. The question of the existence
of an Idea of the soul, then, is by no means an insignificant one.[25] Does
the *Phaedrus* support an interpretation of "ἰδέα" as "Idea"? Although the
evidence in the *Phaedrus* is not conclusive either way, on balance it points
to a negative answer. Of course, this answer is compatible with the possibility that other dialogues provide arguments for or against the existence
of such an Idea.

I begin by repeating that the term "idea" is not uncommon in the
Phaedrus (or throughout Plato's dialogues for that matter). However, this
is the only occurrence of the term in the *Phaedrus* that one might want
to understand as referring to an Idea. The word's ordinary meaning is,
as already mentioned, "look," "form," "articulation," "nature." The
"technical" meaning of the term is a minority meaning in this dialogue

as well as, I think, in the other dialogues. The mere occurrence of the word proves nothing in favor of the technical meaning, while it naturally suggests its nontechnical meaning. As a general rule, then, it seems that the burden of proof is on those who think that the term has a technical meaning rather than on those who think that it has its ordinary and usual meaning. This is a fortiori the case since interpreters usually assume that the term does not mean "Idea" here. The announcement that an Idea of the soul exists would be an event of some importance in the Platonic corpus as well as in the *Phaedrus*. One would therefore expect that such an announcement would be reasonably unambiguous. What evidence, then, is there that "ἰδέα" at 246a3 means "Idea"?

The references in the lines quoted above to the difficulty of knowing the soul's ἰδέα, to the fact that discourse about it would be long and divine, and to the likeness of the soul's idea constitute, so far as I can see, the only evidence in favor of the technical meaning. This is rather weak evidence. For it may be quite difficult to know the soul if it lacks an Idea (indeed, perhaps it is more difficult to know it if it has no Idea); discourse about what the soul is might be long and divine even though (or even because) it has no Idea; and it is possible for something to have a likeness even though it is not an Idea. Within the myth, for example, we hear of persons' souls being images of the gods, but these god-originals are not Ideas.

What evidence is there that "ἰδέα" here should be taken in its ordinary and less specialized sense? As I have already noted, to begin with, the entities about whose status as "really real beings" the *Phaedrus* is un-ambiguous (Justice, Episteme, Sophrosyne, Beauty, Phronesis) are *not* called "ideas" in this dialogue. Reference to an idea of the soul not only proves nothing in favor of the inclusion of soul among the Beings, it seems to militate against it. If the "really real beings" are not called "ideas," while something of an ambiguous status is said to have an "idea," it is natural to assume that that ambiguous entity is not to be included among the Beings. Moreover, none of the pleonastic terms that are used to describe the Beings ("ousia ontos ousa," and so on) is applied to the soul. So, the use of the term "idea" for it seems, in this context, to distinguish the nature of the soul—whatever it may be—from the nature of those truly real Beings. Moreover, there is not the slightest hint any-where in the *Phaedrus* that there is a "hyperuranian being" called "Soul." Given the tremendous importance that an "Idea of the Soul" would have for the palinode, as well as for the *Phaedrus'* development of the self-knowledge theme, one would expect that such a (putative) Idea would at least be hinted at. The text contains no confirmation at all of the suggestion that "ἰδέα" at 246a3 means "Idea."

Still further, in the present passage the soul is said to be immortal. This characteristic distinguishes the soul from the other sorts of things said, in the *Phaedrus* and many other dialogues, to participate in the Beings. These participants are characterized not by immortality but by its opposite, namely, their subjection to the process of coming to be and passing away. Immortal self-moved soul could be neither a "participant" in the sense assumed just a few lines further on in the *Phaedrus* nor an Idea. Thus if there were an Idea of the Soul we would have a startlingly new view of the whole Idea/instance schema—a unique development in the *Phaedrus* of critical importance to the Platonic corpus. An interpreter would have to produce some very strong arguments, I think, to justify the assertion that such a development has taken place in this dialogue. But in the *Phaedrus* there is no evidence for such an argument. Other than the bare word "ἰδέα" at 246a3, *none* of the language that might even remotely suggest some sort of Idea/participation scheme is present. The soul is never characterized as an "image" in any sense that would suggest that it has an Idea. Nor is there any suggestion in the palinode that there exists anything like "recollection of oneself" in the sense of "recollection of an Idea of the Soul." Instead, we hear about souls remembering the gods they followed in heaven, and the gods are (among other things) character types, not Ideas.

Moreover, none of the Beings mentioned in the *Phaedrus* is given a description that goes beyond the general statements that apply to all the Beings ("really real being," and so on), the negative (without color or shape, untouchable), or the redundant (Episteme is not of that to which we commonly ascribe being, but is of what truly is). This pattern occurs in the other Platonic dialogues. But the soul's ousia does receive a specific, positive, and informative characterization here as self-motion. And the image of this "idea" is spelled out at great length. Assuming that the image tells us something about the "idea," we do get in this passage an impressive amount of information about the soul's "idea." All this suggests, again, that whatever the "idea" of the soul is, it is different from the Beings, known in a different way than they are, and spoken of differently. Those who think that Socrates is referring to an Idea of the soul are committed to saying that the passage is a unique and momentous event in the Platonic corpus. Again, there is no evidence to support an assertion of this sort. On the contrary, everything speaks against it. Finally, it is worth noting that it is possible for something to have an "idea" in the sense of ousia, and yet not have an Idea. In fact, there is a passage in the *Phaedo* (108d4–e2) that is remarkably similar to the present one and in which one would not be tempted to think that Ideas are adverted to.[26]

At 245c3 Socrates referred to the "physis" of the soul (soul divine and human), and the passage is summed up a moment later with the assertion that the "ousia and logos of the soul" is "self-motion" (245e3). A moment later, he refers to the soul's "idea." It seems to me that "physis," "ousia," and "idea" all mean the same here. They refer to the "look" of the "psyche" understood as "self-motion." Socrates cannot offer a narrative (diegesis) about what self-motion is; a complete description of the soul's internal articulation would be in every way an entirely divine and long narrative. Instead, he will offer a likeness of the soul's nature, which is the human and shorter path. And the likeness he proceeds to offer does, of course, represent the notion of self-motion nicely. The relevant contrast here is not between speaking about the soul's "idea" and speaking about something other than this "idea" but between speaking in the form of a narrative and speaking in the form of a likeness. That is, a narrative is being thought of here as a logos which dispenses with eikastic speech (more on the question of myth in chapter 4). Socrates' famous image of the soul's idea is the following:

> Let it be likened to a natural union of powers in winged horses and charioteer. The horses and charioteer of the gods are all good and from good stock, but those of the others are mixed. For us, first of all, the driver is charioteer of a pair of horses, and next, of those horses one is noble and good and descended from such, and the other is the opposite and of the opposite descent. Hence the task of our charioteer is necessarily difficult and troublesome. (246a6–b4)

This likeness is short indeed, but how long is the narrative about its meaning!

As already noted, Socrates starts the myth with a discussion of soul because the soul is the central topic of the myth. The simile is the foundation of the myth. Thus the apodeixis as a whole is primarily an exercise in psychology. That the Beings are also discussed on the way (though very sparsely, ontology not being Socrates' main concern here) is an indication that psychology is not to be understood here in the sense familiar to us (as an analysis of the structure of the mind, of character traits, or of the individual as an isolated entity). Part of the teaching of the palinode is that to know the soul is to understand its role in the cosmos. Hence Socrates goes on now to describe the role of "all soul" in caring for the cosmos, then the function of the soul's wings, then the nature of the god-souls, then the difference between godly and human souls, which in turn requires a (rather short and elliptical) description of the hyperuranian place—after which the embodied soul's fate is examined.

One sees immediately how Socrates' image of the soul's idea captures the sense not only of movement but of self-motion. In fact, two kinds of motion are indicated here, namely, that of the horses (the horizontal motion, as it were) and that of the wings (vertical motion)—hence the potentiality for internal discord; the desires may move in contrary directions at once. In human souls the potentiality for disharmony is further increased by the heterogeneity of the horses, as Socrates explicitly points out. The unity of the human soul will therefore present a special problem. The image indicates that this unity should be hierarchical; reason is needed to guide the soul, since without reason the wings are blind and the horses run amok. A charioteer fails in his duty if he is drawn by the horses in whatever direction they wish to go. Indeed, the direction of the whole contraption ought not to be dictated by the horses (as it is in Lysias' and Socrates' earlier speeches) but by the charioteer.

At the same time, the charioteer is dependent on the wings and horses if he is to move forward and upward. Indeed, the horses too are winged (any ambiguity about the wings belonging to every part of the soul is resolved by 251b7; cf. 248c1–2). Even the horses of a god must be nourished by his charioteer, though only after he has feasted (247e5–6). Unlike men, the gods are wise enough to know what and when to feed the horses. Reason and the desires are interdependent, as the myth makes abundantly clear.[27] The mind cannot contemplate the truth until it is brought within sight of the truth by the soul, and the mind's contemplation of the truth nourishes the whole soul, just as the incarnated soul's vision of the beautiful beloved powerfully affects the "whole soul" (253e5–6, 254c4–5, and context). Even in stating the image of the soul's idea, Socrates says that the charioteer and horses are "naturally united" to one another. This does not mean "naturally harmonious," but it does at least suggest "inseparable." The charioteer alone (reason isolated from desire) is no more human than is a pair of horses.

The strangeness of the soul's natural unity is made clear when we ask *by what* the soul's parts are unified. The easiest answer would be "by the chariot." But not only is a chariot not a natural being (unlike the charioteer, wings, and horses), it is not actually mentioned in the myth.[28] Indeed, Socrates says at the very start that the charioteer and horses are naturally united (*sumphuto,* 246a6). Now, only the horses and the charioteer are referred to in the myth as "forms" (253c7–8) of the soul; the wings are not counted as forms, perhaps because of their radical instability (they can flourish and then wither to a pulp) and because they are everywhere in the soul. Since the wings are nevertheless distinguishable from the remainder of the soul, we may say that in the palinode the soul is not tripartite but quadripartite (charioteer, two horses, and wings). Socrates' original question as to whether he is complex or simple (230a) has been answered: he is complex.[29] The soul is polyeidetic and noneidetic. And as my discussion of them will suggest, the various elements of the soul are better thought of as capacities or potentialities than as faculties.[30] Let us say that however strange these wings might be, they at least are united with each form of the soul naturally, in that they "grow" on each part. We are still left with the difficulty of specifying what connects the forms of the soul to each other.

The answer is, I think, that soul as such has the potentiality for either internal discord or harmony. The unity a soul possesses is functional and teleological; it derives from the successful pursuit of the goal desired by reason (the charioteer). This in turn requires a functioning hierarchy within the soul; as Socrates' image suggests immediately, the charioteer should control the horses, not vice versa. The wholeness of a soul yoked by reason is not achieved by satisfying every desire of the soul. Were that to happen, the soul would fly apart. Indeed, reason is to guide the horses in a direction that is, in a sense, not natural for them, namely upward (though since in Socrates' image they too have wings, the ascent is not entirely unnatural to them). All the parts of the soul are covered by the wings; the principle of unity is thus eros (this is, of course, precisely the opposite of the conception of eros proposed by the earlier speeches of the *Phaedrus*). But eros functions as this principle only when it is aroused by images in this world and recollective of the originals. The complexity of the *Phaedrus'* account of this process is due in part to the fact that it combines two sorts of accounts offered in other dialogues, namely, the notion of the soul as divisible into parts (as in the *Republic*) and of the soul as erotic (as in the *Symposium*). The latter, in turn, is connected with a number of the Socratic paradoxes (to desire something is to consider it good; no man does evil knowingly; and so on).

Indeed, there is something unnatural about the soul as it is represented here. Horses are not naturally yoked to the service of a charioteer, after all. This is brought about by an act of force applied with the help of skill and is sustained by training and habituation (although the chariot may not be mentioned in the myth, the reins, bit, and whip are). Nor are horses ultimately descended from domesticated teams.[31] One might respond that man's subjugation of nature is itself natural.[32] In this event, we are permitted to observe that human nature, as represented in the image of the soul's idea, is at one remove from brute nature; it is, as it were, a second nature and requires some use of artifice governed by an understanding of what is good for the whole soul. Still further, we should again note (without trying to push the image too far) that strictly speaking the soul is represented as being unnatural in a way that distinguishes it sharply from the nature of the body. For the soul results from a seemingly impossible grafting together of the human, the equine, and the avian. This synthesis of different species is characteristic of monstrous beings. I suggested in chapter 1 that Typhon (to whom Socrates compared himself) was one such monstrous being. Now we find a much more edifying and beautiful, but nonetheless equally monstrous and unnatural, image of the soul's idea.

Socrates' image of the soul's idea also suggests that the equine element is far stronger than the human. How then will this puny charioteer ever control these terrifically powerful horses, especially given the awesome power of the black horse? Will the charioteer require an artifice produced by his intelligence, comparable to the reins, bit, whip, and goad? It is worth noting here that the horses, however inferior to the charioteer, nevertheless possess a modicum of intelligence and a capacity to learn, acquire habits, and so on; like the charioteer, they can see the outside world (including the beauty of the beloved; 254b4). The wings lack all these characteristics, but have a goal to which they are directed. They symbolize, among other things, the potentiality for growth and fulfillment. Hence Socrates does not speak of the charioteer as having to persuade them to do X or Y, though the charioteer does converse with the horses (254c–e). While the wings powerfully influence the soul, they draw their life from the soul to which they are attached. They could not fly off on their own, as it were. It is with their help, as it turns out, that the charioteer is able to control the black horse. Since all parts of the soul are winged it is fair to say that the control of the black horse by the charioteer is the control of unreasonable desire by reasonable desire. Thus the horses' wings do not per se elevate the horse's desire; they actually cooperate with that desire until the charioteer remembers the Beings. The presence of eros everywhere in the soul is not an automatic guarantee of transcendence. Eros can, it seems, be reasonable (when the charioteer does his duty) or unreasonable.

So far as the "structure" of the soul is concerned, men and gods differ only with respect to *one* of their "forms," namely, the quality of one of the horses.[33] From this standpoint, the difference between the two types of souls seems small. Yet the black horse is enormously important in determining human nature; indeed, much more is said in the myth about it than about the white horse. That black and white horses are coprimordial in the human soul indicates that our soul is not per se either good or evil. Socrates does not present us with a romantic picture of human nature. Originally, structurally, the human soul has the potentiality for being either good or bad, hence the tremendous importance of self-knowledge and, later in the *Phaedrus*, of rhetoric (understood as education). Moreover, incarnation is not the cause of the presence of the evil horse but its effect (see below); to that extent the body is not in itself evil, however much of a hindrance it may be.[34] The charioteer represents reason, the black horse sexual desire (epithumia), the white horse spiritedness and sensitivity for honor and shame, and the wings eros (this last point clear from 252b inter alia). Thus in Socrates' image the soul has a certain number of basic desires that have their own goals (the wings, as Socrates is quick to say, also have a natural *dynamis* of their own; 246d6–e4). Man is not indeterminate, directionless desire. Socrates' image is an intelligible articulation of the soul's complex nature. This nature is teleological not just in the sense that the elements of the soul have goals toward which they naturally move themselves but also in the sense that these elements have (potentially) a hierarchical relationship to each other. This in turn allows Socrates to speak of the soul as a whole, and of what is naturally good or bad for it as a whole.

When the earlier speeches of the *Phaedrus* are seen in terms of the palinode's image of the soul's nature, it is clear that their notion of eros is represented by the black horse alone, and the nonlover by a charioteer that guides the black horse only to the extent of helping it to reach its natural goal. Missing from that interpretation of the soul are, of course, the wings, a hierarchy of ends, and the notion of reason as possessing a desire and a goal of its own, a goal to which it can motivate the soul. In Socrates' image the earlier view of the soul is not entirely suppressed; it is just seen as part of a more complex picture. Thus the two "ideas" of Socrates' first speech are now equally natural and are reorganized into four (the horses, the wings, and the charioteer). We also see now that the soul is, so to speak, by nature both a lover (by virtue of the wings and horses) and a nonlover (by virtue of the charioteer).

Socrates proceeds with a general outline of the way in which "all soul cares for all the unsouled" (246b6 ff.). "Care" would seem to be an intelligent, purposive activity. After distinguishing between embodied and nonembodied souls, Socrates focuses on the "natural power of the wing" (246d6 ff.) before describing the other parts of the soul. The wing's function is to raise the soul upward to the abode of the gods. The wings are "related to the body" (246d8);[35] thus the wings seem to have a function only for the fallen souls. These wings obviously represent the potentiality of an ascent from this-worldly goals to the higher goals of a life of recollection. But their association with the body, and the association of recollection with sense perception (see below), suggest that the ascent is impossible for a disembodied soul. Initial confirmation of this view exists in the fact that the gods' wings do not seem particularly important to them. Although we hear about the charioteer and horses of the gods, there is no mention of the functioning of their wings. This suggests that the eros of the gods is always satisfied. The feasting of the gods is cyclical and almost mechanical. Unperturbed by powerful desire and emotion, able to function without effort or conflict of any sort, the wings of the gods are always complete. Socrates even suggests that the gods are able to disconnect their reason from the horses (247e5–6). The gods have no need for madness, let alone erotic madness; hence the gods are not philosophers. It is not surprising, then, that the gods seem to have no need for logos (let alone for rhetoric).[36] Although there is a certain amount of noise in the heavens, there is no reference whatsoever to there being any discourse among the gods or between gods and men. The divine banquet consists of contemplation of the Beings, not of an effort to analyze them discursively. Logos, as we shall see, comes into play for fallen, embodied souls.

Since the symbolic function of the gods in the palinode is important to clarifying the human condition (in large part the description of the gods provides a useful contrast to the human condition and so aids in formulating what the latter is), a few more words about them are in order. The twelve gods are hierarchically organized, like an army. Zeus is the general, and each god is leader of a troop of daimons.[37] There is no jealousy among them—another sure sign that they virtually lack eros. Each god minds his or her own business. For this army there are no wars and no commands. These astral souls circulate through the heavens without paying any attention at all to human beings. Evidently their caring for the cosmos does not include caring for human souls. The myth teaches that we are on our own; we cannot beseech heaven for relief from our miseries, forgiveness for our sins, answers to our questions. Is the human soul really at home in the cosmos of the *Phaedrus?* (Socrates several times refers to the "home" of the gods, but never, in an unambiguous sense, to the "home" of men; 246d7, 247a2, e4.) As we shall see, an unqualifiedly affirmative answer to this question cannot be given.

The description of the wings not only serves as an occasion for describing the gods and pointing to their difference with men; it also introduces the account of the hyperuranian place. For the wings especially participate in "divine beauty, wisdom, goodness, and all such things." These qualities nourish and increase the soul's plumage (246d8–e2; 248b5–c2). There is a natural affinity between desire and the divine. Eros is essentially intentional and other-seeking. This is a statement of the palinode's crucial thesis that eros naturally possesses a goal, the same goal that reason possesses. Correspondingly, people who have "forgotten" themselves do not know what they want, that is, they do not know what is good for them. In the language of the *Symposium* and *Lysis,* they do not know what they *lack.* Unless they possess what they lack, they cannot be themselves. *The desire of the wings, and thereby of the whole soul, for "divine qualities" is in this way a desire for one's true self.* Since self-knowledge is the means for discovering what naturally satisfies desire, self-knowledge, the satisfaction of eros, and understanding one's soul as a whole all come to the same thing. To be oneself one must know oneself. This is the secret the philosopher understands. And since self-knowledge requires knowledge (recollection) of what is nourishing, self-knowledge will include knowledge of entities other than one's own particular soul. Hence the talk about the wings leads Socrates to talk about the vast cosmos. Knowing ourselves turns out to mean knowing ourselves as a part of a larger Whole, elements of which naturally attract and fulfill us when we understand them. Since understanding the divine is (in the best case) both to become a certain kind of person and to know what is naturally right and good, Socrates also will suggest that self-knowledge is the key to virtuous action.

Even in so sketchy a form, the ethics of the palinode can be seen to differ radically from that of the first two speeches of the *Phaedrus,* in which the ends of man were taken to be those values that are widely opined by the common run of mankind to be good (particularly if their deeds are taken as evidence of their beliefs). As Socrates suggested in his first speech, one could argue, presumably on the basis of observation, that the governing or natural desire of human beings is for (physical) pleasure, and that opinions about the good are secondary (acquired). What we *really* desire (so the argument runs) is precisely what people confess (independently of any recollection, or of any dialectical searching into oneself) they desire. Hence virtue is a skill or craft (perfected by the non-lover) for locating the most efficient means for the satisfaction of natural ends. From the standpoint of the palinode, however, virtue cannot be a skill or craft; it must instead be knowledge of the true ends of desire.[38]

From this standpoint, the ordinary endorsement of "normal" goals, such as that of physical gratification, is a partially mistaken opinion about nature. That is, the soul by nature does desire such goals, but only in part (the part being the dark horse). Hence the palinode requires a fairly

complicated thesis about the satisfaction of the whole soul if it is to overcome the position of the two earlier speeches, and this will include a thesis
about a hierarchy within the soul. What I "really" want is to be satisfied
as a whole, and this will include *not* allowing myself to be directed solely
to satisfying what a lower part of me naturally wants (hence the need to
tame the dark horse). It should be obvious once again that the challenge
posed by the first two speeches of the *Phaedrus* is an extremely difficult
one to meet satisfactorily. To do so Socrates must produce a comprehensive
description of the soul, its place in the cosmos, its desires, and the reasons
for which people fail to know themselves.

The Soul's Journeys and the Divine Banquet.   When the time comes for the
divine banquet, the souls of the gods easily drive their teams up to the
top of the heavens and proceed to stand on the constantly rotating surface
(or "back") of the heavens. It is as though the universe were a sphere
within which souls go about their business until it is time to find nourishment; then, if they are able, they make their way to the exterior of
the sphere and feed, as Socrates clearly says, on what is "outside" the
sphere (Socrates does not explicitly use the image of the sphere, but it
seems helpful in picturing the situation and not inconsistent with what
he does say). Now the structural differences between human and divine
souls become critical. Our evil horse upsets the ascent, and the consequence
for human souls is pathetic. Starved for nourishment, each of them tries
to follow a god upward; but confounded by the unruly steed, by the mass
stampede of souls seeking to ascend all at once (thus trampling one another
underfoot), by the competition among the souls (jealousy is congenital to
the human choir, it seems), many have difficulty in seeing the Beings.
At best, some souls manage to get the charioteer's head above the surface,
gasping for air as it were, for a few nibbles of the divine feast.[39] Since
they are in motion as they attempt to feast, nongodly souls may see the
little they do see in a blur. Should their wings be broken, they are doomed
to fall into the cycle of birth and death, deprived of the sustenance they
so desperately sought. On the heels of a well-regulated army of gods follows
an anarchic mob striving for self-preservation; this state of nature is, for
nongodly souls, a war of all against all. The origins of human nature are
prepolitical; but these origins are not unambiguously good.

Nongodly souls find it difficult to ascend because the black horse
"weighs down" ("pulls down") the soul, unless it has been well schooled
by the charioteer (247b3–5). Much of the last part of the palinode recounts
how the horse is to be schooled in this life. The black horse seems to have
a natural aversion to reason and a natural inclination for the earth; its

nature is chthonic. Socrates also says that the soul's fall came about because of some "mischance" (248c6), which I take to refer to the destruction of a soul's wings by another soul during the mad rush to the divine banquet. It seems probable that a very disciplined soul could avoid such mischances altogether; hence the fall to earth seems attributable to the charioteer's inability to master the black horse (another example of self-motion!). The process by which a disembodied soul is supposed to discipline itself is left in the dark, however.

Socrates states that some souls are "willing and able" to follow a god (247a6–7) and that to ascend, a soul must "make itself like" the god it selects (248a2). Unlike the gods, the imperfect souls must make a decision as to who they want to be (they do this not by creating a new character type but by deciding which god they want to resemble). The decision cannot be made on the basis of a vision of the Beings, for this occurs *before* an ascent to the divine banquet. In this respect the situation changes for fallen souls; for them, recollective vision of the Beings allows them to master the bad horse. In choosing a specific god, a soul takes on a certain character, that is, it individuates itself and becomes aware of who it is. Since such a choice would seem to require that the soul already be individuated and self-aware, the process in question seems inexplicable. How the choice to follow a certain god is connected to the ability to discipline the horse is also unclear. The soul's inability to follow may be due to lack of self-discipline, and this to ignorance. But if the ignorance cannot be overcome *until* the soul has followed the god to the banquet, how can a soul be held responsible for it? It seems to be a matter of brute ability—hence, perhaps, the "willing and able" phrase. At this level, nevertheless, the whole matter of responsibility, of the relationship between choice and fate, is very murky.[40] The history of the soul prior to the fall seems unknowable. Hence a fallen soul that recollects its character type could not recollect why it chose to be this character type. That is, you cannot know *why* you are, say, an Apollo type, and as just suggested, you cannot know why you saw only such and such Beings. To that extent you cannot know why you are in a certain category of vocation (see below). The most you can do in this area is to understand *that* you are such and such a person, one who knows just so much, belongs in such and such a category, has certain potentialities, and last but not least, knows that it is good (or bad) to be of a certain sort.

The choice as to the subsequent incarnation is different, since the soul doing the choosing is already individuated (there are other differences too between the first choice and the subsequent ones).[41] How the choices and conduct of one's previous lives accumulate to individuate a soul is not explained. Nor is it clear how a soul, when choosing for the second, third, or nth time a cycle of incarnations (when it is not in the presence of the army of gods), can know what character type to choose. I draw three further conclusions from the portrayal of the choosing of lives and the chronology involved.

First, incarnated (fallen) souls have no choice (during the time of their incarnation) about who they will be, at least in the first cycle of a thousand years, or what sort of vocation they will perform. Indeed in none of the cycles does a soul create its character type, since this is pregiven. Yet as we shall see, an incarnated soul is not in every respect unable to make itself. All in all, though, it is Necessity, not Freedom (in the sense of creativity, spontaneity, autonomy, possibility) that rules the cosmos of the *Phaedrus*.

Second, the crucial distinction within Socrates' account of the soul's destiny lies between the category of philosophers and that of all the other soul types; this is clearly the palinode's main diairesis of the human race.

Third, although the soul by nature has an ousia (self-motion) and a corresponding look (symbolized by the winged horses and charioteer), its character is a third stratum of determination, but one that is only ambiguously natural since it is in some sense chosen. Only with this choice can a nonincarnated soul determine not just what but also who it can be (more below on the question of "potentiality"). The task of self-knowledge must therefore be dual, since it must consist of understanding both what and who one is. Since a soul chooses "who" it can be before seeing the Beings, there is no characterless vision of the Beings, no nonindividuated, faceless soul who participates in the divine banquet. Moreover, even if self-knowledge is an activity undertaken by earthly souls only, the myth suggests that the origins of self-consciousness are outside the polis and that the genesis of these origins is inexplicable.

In sum, the myth suggests that human nature cannot be understood historically as a process of social-political development. Man is to be understood primarily in terms of his ends. How an individual understands this is heavily influenced by his natural endowment (the amount of Being he saw, how much of it he forgot, his character type); why he came to have this endowment cannot be analyzed. Further, the chronology of the myth suggests that, so far as human nature is concerned, there is very little possibility of progress. Not only is there a permanent shape to the soul, and a finite number of possible character-god types, the lengthy cycle (a thousand years minimum) during which each soul is trapped in the same character and vocation categories ensures that the turnover rate, so to speak, of types of souls will be slow. The most that can be hoped

for is that eventually all souls will gravitate upward in the hierarchy of
lives, and that everyone will become a philosopher. The myth does not
exclude this happening, but it makes it very improbable. In any event,
it excludes the possibility that political or social reforms can bring it
about.[42] Socrates does allow, however, that an individual soul's actions
in this world can make the soul better or worse by making it forget what
it saw of the Beings (250a; according to 248c7, forgetfulness also precedes
incarnation).

In its first thousand-year cycle of incarnation, a soul is fated to fall
into one of nine hierarchically ranked categories of vocation (248c–e; cf.
256d7). Thus another stratum of individuation occurs at this stage. Evidently the principle regulating which category one falls into concerns the
amount of Being one has seen (248d2) and consequently how much "forgetfulness and vice" one possesses (248c7). It seems impossible, however,
to produce an even moderately satisfying explanation of how a soul's
knowledge of Being is linked with this list (recall that a soul might have
seen different amounts of different Beings); or of the selection of the categories (the mathematician is missing from them, for example); or of the
ranking (granted, the philosopher should be at the top; why is the athlete
higher than the poet?); or of the groupings of vocations within categories
(some categories contain several entries, and it is not always clear how
and when these are meant to be synonymous). The following observations,
though, may be of some help. The first category may be concerned with
care of the soul and with eros, the second and third with care of the city,
the fourth with care of the body, the fifth with care of the gods. I offer
the speculation that the sixth category is concerned with the degenerate
disposition toward the gods, the seventh with the degenerate disposition
toward the body, the eighth with a similar disposition to the city, and
the last with the degenerate disposition toward soul and eros (cf. *Rep.*
573d and context). The lower half of the list is thus like a mirror image
of the upper, though the number of entries under each type varies (for
example, the tyrant alone is in a class of his own).[43]

It is unclear how the twelve character types mesh with the nine vocations. One wonders whether persons of bad character are following their
gods or failing to do so (certainly none is godless), that is, whether there
are gods who symbolize a bad way of life—the description of the behavior
of the followers of Ares must be noted in this respect. The philosophers
(the top category in the list of vocations) are followers of Zeus (252e1–
3) and know the most of Being. Possibly Ares types populate the second
category (law-abiding kings, and so on). Beyond this the issue is murky;
presumably a businessman could be Hera-like or Ares-like; presumably

the philosophers and those who are Zeus-like are the same, in which case
no kings could be Zeus-like—that is, philosophers. Yet there are vocations
linked here for which there are no corresponding gods (or is the tyrant,
say, a stupendously ignorant follower of Ares?).

The many difficulties that surround the hierarchy of nine vocations
illustrate, I think, how difficult it is to find a basis for sorting human
beings into already established categories on the basis of the degree to
which they are possessed by divine erotic madness. That criterion supplies
us with a diairesis, presumably at the "natural joints," of humanity into
philosophers and everyone else. But how that division is linked up to
conventional divisions between occupations as well as divisions into twelve
character types is not clear at all. It is as though we know what the
philosopher is, and that he is superior to everyone else, without knowing
who he is or where in the spectrum of human vocations he is to be found.
We know there is a hierarchy of human beings based on the degree to
which they succeed in fulfilling the soul's highest aims; but we cannot
decide a priori that the usual categories according to which people sort
themselves out correspond to a natural hierarchy.

The description of the lover of wisdom as one who also loves beauty,
as "musical" (perhaps this means a "follower of the Muses"; cf. 243a6)
and "amorous" (erotikos), seems to suggest that the philosopher is an edifier,
a poet, a somewhat romantic devotee of culture. This cannot be accurate,
and indeed the triple identification of the first category in the list of nine
does seem to suppress the role of episteme in philosophy (and with it the
art of division and collection). Since the poet is sixth on the same list,
the philosopher cannot be identical with him. Given that the beauty the
philosopher loves may be found in wise speeches, Socrates' description of
the philosopher suggests that he somehow combines reason with music.
The Phaedrus as a whole will supply us with a clearer view of the sense
in which the lover of knowledge also loves beauty (and so a certain form
of rhetoric) and the Muses (see 259d).

Finally, it is very important to note that the thesis that there exists a
hierarchy of souls points to the problem of rhetoric (and so of communication and disagreement), for a soul in one category will not see things
in the same light as a soul in a different category. Since the central division
in the hierarchy is between the philosophers and nonphilosophers, the
problem of rhetoric is especially exhibited by the problem of the ability
of the former to communicate with—and teach—the latter. And this is
precisely the form the problem will take in the second half of the Phaedrus.

I turn now to the description of the divine banquet (247c–e). Socrates
claims that he is speaking the truth here, though no human poet has ever

composed a hymn worthy of the hyperuranian place or ever shall (247c2–6). One wonders whether a human dialectician ever has or will sing a worthy ode. Since Socrates now speaks as a superhuman poet, he can no longer hide behind Stesichorus' name. This is a concession to what is entailed by the myth itself, since if the myth is true, no mortal could recount what Socrates is about to recount (more on this in chapter 4). Moreover, Socrates must articulate what lies at the very limits of language; he uses spatial metaphors, for example, to describe nonspatial beings. The gods and the gods alone can stand on the outer surface of the universe (the other souls can at best poke their heads above the surface). As the gods (with the exception of Hera) rest on this rotating platform, their charioteer feasts by contemplating what is "outside" the heavens. Since the Beings, the gods, and the limits of the universe are all incorporeal and intangible, it is obvious that the spatial terminology cannot be taken literally. Besides, how could anything exist "outside" the universe?[44] The Beings are everywhere around us, but are *separate* in that (1) they are completely free from the motions of genesis, soul, and life, and (2) they are not *directly* visible to nongodly souls, or to godly souls when they are busied with caring for the universe. The imagery clearly indicates that the work of caring is put aside when theorizing (in the Greek sense of the term; 247c1, d4) occurs. Theorizing requires leisure and, in a sense, passivity; the gods do not *do* anything when they feast except *look*. No labor or techne is required either to cultivate the food they eat or to get themselves to their food. They are carried around by the universe and so do not have to move anything in order to feast. The godly souls do not make their way around *on* a circle, as one would run a lap on a track. Rather, they stand on a circle that carries them around by virtue of itself moving around.[45] When theorizing, each god is "internally" at rest as it is moved in a circle. The ease of their frequent journeys helps account for the absence from this passage of the language of revelation and of the mystery cults.

The net result is that the gods obtain an undistorted vision of Being. Being *appears* to them as it *is*. Unlike the nongodly souls, moreover, the gods are not here preoccupied by themselves; that is, pure theorizing is not an effort to be self-conscious but rather to receive (see the *dexasthai* at 247d3) the Truth. Moreover, the mind's perfection is not to master, shape, make, or alter what *is* but rather to be formed *by* it. The suppression of the subject (if I may use contemporary terms) is its perfection. In this sense eros is the yearning for death. The banquet of the gods represents the state of perfect objectivity. The perfection of the soul is the aperspectival and impersonal activity of thought thinking the purely intelligible (and not, of course, of thought thinking itself).[46]

This is the meaning of my earlier point that one sense in which the Beings are "separate" is that they are not directly visible. To the gods they appear in an unmediated form and so as they are. Socrates contrasts divine Episteme with the episteme "that is neighbor to *genesis* and varies with the various objects to which we commonly ascribe being" (247d7–e1). The appearance of Episteme in this world places it in a context in which it is attached to things that possess both it and many other properties (possibly even opposite properties), and does so in a variety of ways. This, along with the influence in embodied souls of both character and forgetfulness, means that nongodly souls cannot see the Beings directly. Hence they cannot see them in an aperspectival way. Socrates does not say that the colorless, shapeless, untouchable Beings are less real qua embodied in their colored, shaped, even touchable images, even if the things in which they are embodied are less real. He does not say that the beauty of the beloved's shape, for example, only approximates true Beauty. The hyperuranian beings are not literally outside our universe. But Socrates will say that many of them are difficult for us to discern.

The indirectness of the access the fallen souls have to the truth is captured by the nautical terminology used in this passage (247c7, e3, 248a5). This terminology suggests that the universe is like an ocean and the hyperuranian place like the air above the surface. From beneath the moving waters the Beings can appear only in a distorted and refracted way. According to the myth, the motion beneath the surface of the heavens is all caused by the soul; this motion is, in effect, a primary cause for the distortion of the truth. That is, the distortion of the appearance of Being (or the separation of Being and the way it appears) is due not to Being (the Beings do not *do* anything to misrepresent themselves, and they are perfectly intelligible in themselves and are perfectly known by the gods). Nor is it due to the orderly movements of the gods (and these gods do not do anything to man to make knowledge difficult for him). While the inanimate nature for which the gods care might refract the light, the water might be clear if it were perfectly still. It thus appears that man is his own greatest obstacle in his efforts to know the truth, a point also suggested by the account of the prelife and the fall. This is a fundamental teaching of the palinode, which helps explain why self-knowledge is so central for Socrates. I shall return to it below.

The gods, by contrast, have no need for self-knowledge. The entire problematic of self-knowledge is thus deeply revealing of what it means

to be human. To ignore the problematic is to become either sub- or
superhuman. Socrates will mention that no incarnate soul can hope to be
superhuman in this life; hence the price of failing to know oneself is that
one approaches the bestial (for example, see 250e). In sum: the myth
suggests both that the active preservation of the problem of self-knowledge
is indispensable to our humanity and that the preservation of our humanity
is not wholly desirable. If we found what our nature desires, we would
cease to be ourselves. And if we fail to find what we desire, we fall to a
state beneath ourselves. It is as though we must simultaneously try to
find what we "really" desire and be conscious that we cannot find it, and
to be satisfied with (or in) this state of perpetual dissatisfaction. Differently
put, it is the simultaneous awareness of our incompleteness (knowledge
of ignorance), desire to overcome this incompleteness, and awareness that
in this life such overcoming is impossible that defines the "best" *human*
life.

The imagery Socrates uses makes clear that even the gods do not leave
the universe when attending the divine banquet (they stand on the surface
of the rotating heaven). Absolute transcendence of time (247d3) is impossible for an ensouled being. We are given to understand that the outer
edge of the universe rotates in a circle (247d4). The Beings are arranged
around and outside this circle, and thus cannot be said to be ordered
hierarchically. Hence the gods do not choose which Being they will see
or in what sequence; the menu is, so to speak, already decided for them.
Since the divine banquet does not take place outside the stream of tem-
porality, the gods do not obtain a synoptic vision of the Beings. This
point is inseparable from the fact that the Good is nowhere mentioned
in the *Phaedrus*.[47] The absence from the cosmos of the *Phaedrus* of a unifying
and synoptic principle has a bearing (as will become evident when we
examine the second half of the *Phaedrus*) on the endlessness of dialectic.
Dialectic cannot in principle arrive, according to this account, at a comprehensive understanding of reality, a fact that raises the question as to
the fruitfulness of the sequence of partial perspectives which dialectic does
provide (more on this in chapter 6 and the Epilogue). In spite of its
edifying rhetoric, that is, the teaching of the palinode and indeed of the
Phaedrus is disquieting. One begins to see the point of Socrates' prayer
to Pan, at the end of the dialogue, for a harmony between what is "inside"
and "outside" himself.

Socrates tells us that true Being is "visible to nous alone, the pilot of
the soul" (247c7–8). That is to say, the highest form of Episteme is
noetic.[48] There is no mention of logos anywhere in this passage; ocular
metaphors (accompanied by metaphors of eating) dominate. Nous is in-

tellectual vision. Since nous is, in this context, not discursive, I shall occasionally refer to it as "intellectual intuition." Outside of this passage, "nous" does not occur (except in compounds) in the apodeixis; its role is specifically limited to the context of the divine banquet. The palinode is very clear that human beings cannot see the Beings directly; they can only recollect them, and anamnesis is closely associated with both dianoia and discourse (249b5–c6). There is no pure intellectual intuition for fallen souls. Without the accurate guidance of the soul's pilot, of course, a fallen soul will have difficulty in guiding itself rightly.

This difficulty is closely connected, as we shall see, to the problem of rhetoric. Socrates goes on to speak of the dianoia as "seeing" the Beings, and this would seem to contradict his statement that "nous alone" sees the Beings (unless nous and dianoia are identical). But since dianoia is said to be nourished *by* nous, I infer that dianoia "sees" Being indirectly. Here the other metaphor in the passage comes into play. Nous sees the Beings, and dianoia digests the results; nous functions as the mouth, dianoia as the stomach. In the case of the gods, the difference between the two may not matter much.[49] But in the case of the other souls, the difference becomes important once the fall has taken place, as important as the difference between insight and discourse. There is, after all, a tension between the two metaphors in this passage. While the seeing of intellectual intuition is passive and receptive, the digestion process transforms what is seen. The soul is nourished once it has seen and digested; but does it have in mind the Beings as they are in themselves, or as transformed by the living intelligence? Certainly the myth expresses the view that for the gods theorizing is purely objective; but as one contemplates the metaphors Socrates is using in the passage, particularly with reference to nongodly souls, a problem begins to appear concerning the objectivity of a soul's contact with Being. In this passage, the distinction between nous and dianoia is submerged; but for the reasons I have given, the fall disrupts the harmony between the two.

Socrates said that the charioteer is winged, and in a moment he specifies that it is the dianoia that is winged (249c4–5). This is appropriate, for we have been told that the wings in particular are nourished by divine qualities. Socrates never says that nous is winged, and for a good reason; if it were, it would be directly subject to the turbulent movement of eros, and this would make the objectivity of nous suspect. Nous itself must be formless and indeterminate—like a bit of soft wax (though of course even wax possesses a shape)—if it is to receive the imprint of Being. Still, there is no way to check directly on the accuracy of nous by means of, say, a kind of metaintuition. The mind cannot check on its intellectual

intuition by slipping away from itself for another look at Being through
some other faculty in order to compare its first intuition of Being with
its new look at Being. We cannot run that sort of verification test on the
soul's insights. And since nous is not a Being or a form, it cannot be
known Epistemically (if it were a Being, nous itself would be required
to see it, since "nous alone" knows the Beings). If the task of nous is to
assimilate the Beings and if nous is not a Being, then there is no noesis
of nous (there is no self-consciousness with respect to the activity of intuition). Nous is comparable to a mirror of nature; or better yet, it is
like a glass windowpane, the soul's opening to Being. One cannot polish
up this mirror or pane from both sides in order to ensure that the light
enters undistorted. At this level of intellection, then, there is no self-
knowledge if by that we mean "analysis of the self's power of insight into
the Truth." Hence there is no such thing, from this standpoint, as an
epistemology based on the analysis of the structure of the mind (no epistemology in either a Humean or a Kantian sense).

I dwell on this matter because I believe that in the *Phaedrus* the problem
of knowing whether and when one knows something truly is critical. Even
as he suggests that for the gods noetic knowledge is trustworthy (but
uncheckable directly), Socrates is suggesting that for human souls uncritical
acceptance of one's insights is dangerous. Undistorted nous is the realm
of the gods; but men are not gods. Men are endowed with a partial and
possibly blurred noetic vision of Truth that has been digested and reshaped
by dianoia into linguistic form. Noetic insight survives at the fringes of
one's memory. As Socrates paints the glorious picture of the blessed life
of the gods, he also paints a seemingly desperate portrait of the *condition
humaine*. The problems of skepticism and solipsism are thus ingrained
in the *Phaedrus'* account of the knowledge available to human souls. That
rhetoric—the problem of true and false persuasion—subsequently becomes
an issue in the *Phaedrus* should not be surprising once this point is understood. *The problem of rhetoric, which underlies the second half of the* Phaedrus,
is thus generated by the palinode's account of the human condition.

The palinode, however, does not yet suggest that human souls are
entirely condemned to feed on "the food of semblance" (248b5). Might
there not be a kind of rhetoric that, by challenging what we think we
see, reminds us of our deeper insights? A rhetoric that lets us compare
our insights with those of others such that we can clarify or deepen them,
imperfect as they may be? The second part of the *Phaedrus* supplies an
affirmative answer in the form of dialogue. Nous is like the eye of the
soul, and there may be no way for the soul to directly watch itself seeing,
no internal metaintuition. But it can look at itself through the eyes of
others, and an individual can also compare the way in which the eye saw

at one time with the way it sees now. In the course of a conversation, for example, he can experience the gradual clarification of his insights. This experience of learning—or rather, of recollecting—is also crucial to the functioning of philosophical rhetoric as it is outlined later in the *Phaedrus*. If such dialogue is to be more than just a pleasant exchange, it must have the potential of getting the interlocutors closer to the truth. The palinode does not exclude this happening even though it does present a picture of things in which it is difficult for it to happen. When we discuss the notion of anamnesis, we will see in greater detail the sense in which the truth is available, according to the palinode, to fallen souls.

Further reflection on the metaphor of nourishment is helpful in formulating the problem discussed in the previous paragraphs. Socrates is clearly saying both that there is a natural harmony between the soul and reality (see the *prosekon,* 247d2, 248b7) and that knowledge of reality is the natural good toward which the soul is oriented. (Socrates thus retracts the thesis of his first speech to the effect that the soul's orientation to the good, as distinct from physiological pleasure, is acquired rather than natural.) This is the basis for the establishment of a hierarchy within the soul. It is the charioteer alone who sees the Beings; hence he is in principle higher than the other elements of the soul. The nourishment the gods receive makes their dianoia "well contented"; although nothing is said about nous experiencing such feelings, it is clear that dianoia is not unconnected with the emotions. Neither here nor elsewhere in the palinode, indeed, are we offered a conception of the soul in which reason, emotion, and desire are simply indifferent to one another. If one asks *why* knowledge is good, the palinode's answer can only be: because it is valued by reason, and it is valued by reason because it allows the soul to prosper. And that is good because it is, simply, fulfilling. It is the possession of what naturally belongs to oneself and so, in a sense, the possession of oneself. This wholeness is what erotic soul lacks and what contents it; it is what is good. The teaching of the *Phaedrus* is "eudaemonistic" on this point.

The standard modern criticism (such as that of Kant) of eudaemonism is that it supplies only an empirical and subjective criterion for the good and the true. That is, the danger is that various feelings become criterial for judgments about what is being experienced. The pertinent case in the context here concerns the truth of the soul's understanding of the Beings. As I have already noted, at least with respect to the *Phaedrus'* gods, there is no difference between the subjective experience of happiness and the objective truth. The experience of truth *is* the experience of spiritual well-being. To be a god is to live beyond the split between the subjective and objective. What is nourishing to the soul makes it well contented in its freedom from perspectivity. Although the model of rotating nous is not just to be interpreted psychologically, that is, as an empirical model of thinking, it is *also* a model about a psyche and its pathe.[50] But—and this too is a critical part of the palinode's teaching—for nongodly souls, the matter is more complicated, for they might ask themselves whether they are nourished because they know the truth or whether they *think* they know the truth because they *feel* nourished. The doubt here concerns an opposition not between reason and emotion but between one kind of complex of reason/emotion and another (true reason and genuine satisfaction versus opinion and false satisfaction).

To restate the point in the form of a question: what does Socrates mean by "aletheia" in this passage? He describes the hyperuranian realm as the "plain of truth" (248b6; cf. 247c8, d4), but also speaks of truth as both a property of the Beings (247d4; it is something "seen") and a property of the one Being (Episteme) that has as its object the rest of Being (247c8). Thus Socrates speaks of truth both as the object of thought (the mind of god "contemplates truth"; 247d4) and as the place into which mind enters when it contemplates. Since knowledge of Being is (in the best case) noetic and immediate, it seems safe to say that Truth is just the manifestation or presence of Being to the mind. It is, so to speak, the opening up to the mind of what a proposition would be about, and so that on the basis of which correspondences could be set up between discourse and entities. The Truth/Being is what we see in order to talk intelligently; the aletheia of propositions might better be spoken of as a question of "correctness" (*orthotes*) that arises subsequent to the mind's ingestion of truth. The truth is our food for thought, that which sustains genuine thinking, that to which reason is naturally drawn. The *Phaedrus'* formulations are, admittedly, metaphorical here, but how else to articulate the sort of fundamental point at issue?

Given the natural connection between the soul and its nourishment, the mind and Truth/Being, what sense can we give to the thesis that the soul's ousia is self-motion? Is it not also accurate to say (as I just did) that the soul is drawn, that is, moved by, Being? The difficulty lies in the fact that Being seems to be the final cause of the soul's motion, so depriving the soul of self-motion in that sense. It could be responded that Being draws the soul only because the soul confers value on it by desiring it. Yet neither of these views does justice to the fact that, at this highest level, the value of the goal desired by the soul derives both from the goal *and* from the soul. The soul desires Being because Being nourishes it, and Being is desirable because it is intrinsically nourishing. There is just a natural fit between them. But why then still speak of the soul's *self*-motion? The description has, first of all, the advantage of indicating that the locus of activity and life is in the soul (the Beings are, by contrast, lifeless). Second, even though there is a natural fit between soul and Truth, a soul can still fail or succeed in nourishing itself; to some extent it has control over this matter even before embodiment. The notion of self-motion points to the soul's capacity, indeed its freedom, to recover what it naturally desires or to move away from it. The palinode links these movements to the soul's understanding of itself (only a soul that failed to know its own happiness could want to move away from the Beings). Not even the feast of the gods continues ceaselessly; they too must know when and how to move to and from the Beings. This limited freedom gives a role to dialogical rhetoric as the means by which a fallen soul can move itself to what it "really" wants. The change from horizontal to vertical movement comes about through self-knowledge. *Self-knowledge is, in other words, intelligent self-motion.*

Recollection (Anamnesis). I would like to turn now to the description of anamnesis at 249b5–d3. As mentioned above, two kinds of recollection are discussed in the palinode, the one directed to the Beings, the other to the gods. This passage concerns the former sort. Socrates has just described the nine categories of vocations, the chronology of incarnation, and the difference between men and beasts. He is about to portray in detail, from inside the lover's soul, the spiritual páthos involved in the experience of recollection. The transition from the one passage to the other is the abstract-sounding description of the recollection of the Beings. The passage runs as follows:

> For a soul who has never seen the truth [the hyperuranian beings] shall not enter into this human form. For it is necessary for a man [*anthropos*] to understand according to form [eidos] that which is spoken, [the man] going from many sense perceptions to a one gathered together by reasoning; and this [understanding] is the recollection [anamnesis] of those things which our souls then saw when journeying with their god, looking down to that which we now say to be, and lifting their heads up toward real being. Therefore it is just that the intellect [dianoia] of the philosopher alone is winged; for he is always according to his power near in memory [*mneme*] to those things nearness whereunto makes a god godlike. So a man [*aner*], making right use of such memoranda [*hypomnemasin*], always being made perfect by [being initiated into] the ultimate mysteries, alone becomes truly complete. (249b5–c8)[51]

The difficulty of the passage lies precisely in the fact that it attempts to join discourse and eros, thought and desire, the language of reason with that of mystery cults, theory and satisfaction, knowledge and completeness. In recollection, the lover and nonlover are combined. That is, by the very way in which it places logismos and mania side by side, the passage suggests that anamnesis is the language of love. The description of anamnesis is a description of rationality; we are being told that reason and a certain form of madness are the same. Hence Socrates says here that in the philosopher "dianoia" is "winged." The wings, we know, have a natural affinity for the divine, which is beautiful, wise, good, and the like (246d6–e1). To be rational is to know how to be nourished by the divine, and this amounts to knowing how to be whole or complete. Although the talk about recollection is introduced as a way of explaining how men ("anthropos" indicating the generic sense) and beasts differ, rationality is a potentiality in men, not something they possess by nature in the way they possess arms and legs. Human souls must have seen some of the Beings (a point repeated at 249e4–5); but they have forgotten much of it. Their humanity is something they may fail to realize. Thus "it is necessary" for a man, if he is to realize fully this capacity (the necessity to do so being moral since this is something one ought to do), to understand in a particular manner ("according to form") whatever is spoken or expressed. In order to do this, he must want to perform the intellectual process of going from many sense perceptions to a unity. And this process is, in some sense, synthetic, that is, it is a movement of reason toward wholeness.

The reference to the real beings "above" and the less real ones "below" suggests that the wholeness is a bringing together not just of sense perceptions but of the hyper- and hypouranian places, that is, images with their originals, opinions with their grounds. Recollection is both a rational and an ontological unification. Since language and discursivity are strongly present in this passage (and are clearly associated with dianoia),[52] the implication is that logos is somehow intermediate between the hyperuranian beings and the sensible things. Moreover, the contrast between real and less real beings indicates that the relationship between them is hierarchical. The movement of recollective reason is ascending.

The passage also points to a third sense of wholeness, which results from these two sorts of unification. Socrates is quite clear that "recollection" is a way in which a man regains "completeness" or "perfection" (there seems to be little difference here between the two terms), such a man being an "aner" (as distinguished from an "anthropos"). Socrates' remarkable encomium at 250c of our earlier unblemished state points to the wholeness of self which needs to be recaptured: "whole [holokleros] and unblemished were we that did celebrate the mystery [of gazing upon Beauty]. . . . pure was the light that shone around us, and pure [katharoi] were we." The fantastic power of Beauty to attract us is due to the wholeness with which knowledge of Beauty fills the soul. Love of Beauty is, in this sense, self-love, and love of the forms (eide) is self-fulfillment. This point is key to understanding why recollection of the Beings, existential completeness or satisfaction, and self-knowledge are tied to one another. That existential wholeness is one of the benefits of living a life of reasonable desire is also made clear by 256a–b (see too the last words of the palinode)—in radical opposition to the conceptions of reason and desire upheld by the first two speeches of the *Phaedrus*. It is precisely by rejecting their reduction of reason to an instrument and of eros to epithumia (sexual desire) that the palinode preserves a sense of philosophy distinct from the mastery of certain intellectual operations (such as the method of division and collection, or the sterile seduction rhetoric of the nonlover), however sophisticated they may be.

So, in the first place, Socrates is saying that thought is recollective when it is motivated to understand the divine (as opposed to the sorts of things persons in the other categories of the list of nine vocations concern themselves with). Erotic thought is distinguished by the direction of its intentionality. That is one sense in which it is "mad." Furthermore, although the direction of the lover of wisdom's eros detaches him from the world in one sense, it attaches him to it in another: for the "images" of the truths he remembers are "here," reflected in discourses, actions, bodies (see below). These images are sensible things that possess properties corresponding to the Forms. Socrates is clear that no one in this life can circumvent the images altogether and look directly at the Beings. This point is key, I think, to understanding why the philosopher is not a hermit or dweller of the countryside. We must again bring our earlier discussion of the lover and nonlover to bear here. As I indicated in the previous chapter, one of the lessons of the first two speeches of the dialogue is that reason and desire are not separable in the way that the Lysian nonlover pretends. In the present passage, we are being told that the philosopher's detachment from this world, and so from all the desires that bind him to it, actually stems from an attachment to the Being that is "really" desired by everyone else. The philosopher is not the antierotic, intellectualistic nonlover, but the person whose eros is drawn to understand what is really the case in the subheavenly world. This requires the control of some desires, especially that symbolized by the black horse. What is mad about recollection is not that it is in possession of some secret, mysterious method (whether analytical or intuitive) but that it is oriented to understanding what is—"what is" being something other than "what is thought to be." It is not difficult to see how the power of the *question* will be crucial to recollective madness in uncovering the difference between "what is" and "what is thought to be."

The burden of the myth is, in part, to show that the core of recollection is equally existential and theoretical. *In anamnesis we are both recalled to a sense of our primordial status, our place in the cosmos as a whole, and brought by means of lengthy questioning to rational insight into the forms of things. These forms, we're told, nourish the wings and the soul; and in remembering the forms we become again what we were. In this sense insight into the Beings is the same as one's becoming oneself, one's true or whole self.* But the insight is always partial, as the myth also makes clear. Recognition of that fact is knowledge of ignorance, and it is based both on our awareness of our distance from Being and on the experience of aporia engendered through discussion. The aporia and partiality result from our place in the cosmos, a place brought about in large part by the soul's own nature. *Recognition of this is self-knowledge in that it amounts to an understanding of what one desires, of how one is "placed" in a larger context, and so of the self one has all along been, as it were, without realizing it.* It is also self-knowledge in that it is an awareness of one's limits. The relationship between the positive insights into what one really wants and is and the negative insight into the limits of one's understanding is illustrated by the course of a Socratic conversation, indeed by that of the *Phaedrus* itself. Although some of these points must await confirmation from our discussion of later sections of the dialogue, I would like to comment further on the evidence the present passage supplies for them.

What are the "sense perceptions" adverted to at 249b7–c1? At 250a–b we are told that the beings have images in this world that are difficult to perceive *(diaisthanesthai)*. At 250d we learn that Beauty alone is fated to be manifest through sight, the sharpest of the bodily senses *(aisthesis, a word used twice here)*; visually sensed images are the clearest available to us. Phronesis, by contrast, is hard to desire because it is so difficult to perceive, and this because its images, like those of Justice, Sophrosyne, and "other prized possessions of the soul" (every being does have some sort of image in this world), are primarily manifested nonvisually and hence are perceived through less sharp senses.[53] I suggest that the images of the hard-to-know beings are verbal, and that in their case the sense perceptions are primarily auditory.[54] Thought (Phronesis) is hard to see, but winged words can manifest it. This interpretation makes sense of 250a–d as well as our passage at 249b5 and on. To understand what is said (the *legomenon*), one must gather into a unity many auditory perceptions (among other kinds of perceptions). Since recollection seems inseparable from sense perception of one sort or another, it seems that anamnesis cannot take place independently of the body. The body is not simply an obstacle to contemplation. It is worth recalling that the wings, so closely associated with anamnesis, are also associated with the body (246d8).

Socrates is clearly *not* saying, in this passage, that everyone does recollect just by virtue of being human, even though it is true that almost everyone speaks, and understands at a certain level, "what is said." That is, insofar as recollection involves logos, it is (among other things) a way of reflecting on what people think they already understand. This level is generally unreflective and may be very far from the truth; but it is rarely completely devoid of some truth (recall the opening words of our passage: "for a soul who has never seen the truth shall not enter into this human form"). Even what is expressed in logos by a nonphilosophical person (such as Lysias or Phaedrus), and so not with the intention that it be *kat'eidos,* can supply a starting point for the philosopher's recollection. The philosopher must be able to lead opinions to rational unity through insight into eidos. He does this through attempting to "give a logos" of opinions. Thus the standard Socratic claim that one knows something when one can give a satisfactory logos of it is preserved in the present passage. To possess that discursive knowledge is, he is now claiming, to recollect. Although a quick reading of the example of recollection which Socrates proceeds to describe might suggest otherwise, it is fairly clear that anamnesis is not anything like a once-in-a-lifetime religious revelation and conversion (though there may be moments of insight). Recollection is a process that takes place through time. It is an activity, not a state, of the soul.

Anamnesis, then, is not a description of how one understands language simpliciter or of how the ear and eye operate. Anamnesis is in part a description of how someone who already understands language in the ordinary way can understand the truth of things, that is, see them in their context as a whole. Likewise, Socrates' description of the perception of Beauty clearly shows that organized wholes of visual sense perceptions are seen from the start (for example, 251a1–3: "when one who is fresh from the mysteries, and saw much then of the [Beings], sees a godlike [*theoeides*] face or a bodily *idea* that represents Beauty well"). The sense perceptions are not the sense data of the logical positivists. In the case of the auditory sense perceptions, they may be words, sentences, or groupings of these, already unified at various syntactical and semantical levels. Ordinary language, in all its heterogeneity, furnishes the images the philosopher must apprehend by listening (an activity that already involves thought) and thinking things through (via logismos, and kat'eidos). We can now specify more precisely how language is intermediate between the hyperuranian beings and sensible things. Logos *is* a thing perceptible through the senses, but one that has the potential for imaging, reminding, or leading the soul to insights about the topic under consideration. *Socrates' "erotic art" (257a7–8) is the dialectical rhetoric that uses the power of questioning to accomplish this end.*

Perception of the eidos guides the process of recollection, and the ἕν is the result of the process. Presumably the former serves, in the best case, as the standard for the latter; the eidos is that toward which we want to move. If we do so successfully, then the eidos and ἕν would, presumably, end up being the same. In normal situations, however, the relationship between the two would be reciprocal; for surely one's initial understanding of what one wants to say (of the eidos) will develop as one talks and arrives at various levels of unity (the ἕν). It might help give some content to my suggestion that recollection can be exhibited by philosophical speech if we now consider the *Phaedrus* as an example of it.

I shall argue in subsequent chapters that the dialectical progress of the *Phaedrus* cannot be analyzed accurately in terms of the techne of division and collection. The "anamnesis" spoken of at 249b5 ff. and the "collection" of 265d are not identical. Commentators have frequently been too quick to identify "recollection" with the techne of collection. They then have difficulty explaining why division is not mentioned at 249b–c even though it is intrinsically connected with collection at 265c8–266c1 ff. They also have difficulty explaining the sense in which the use of the method of division and collection could constitute divine erotic madness as it is described here. There are, so far as I can tell, no rules for anamnesis as it is described in the *Phaedrus,* whereas the method of division and collection elaborated in the *Phaedrus* does exhibit a rule-governed sequence of steps. There is no indication in the second half of the *Phaedrus* that the method of division and collection can be brought to bear on the Beings; Socrates never associates it with recollection; indeed, the language of eros is absent from the various descriptions of the method. And although definition is central to the method of division and collection, in the present passage nothing at all is said about it.

In what sense is there a movement in the *Phaedrus* toward unity? Socrates gives us a clue later on in the *Phaedrus* when he indicates that the first two speeches of the dialogue articulate only a part of the nature of eros, not the whole. Lysias' speech was thought by Phaedrus to represent the whole truth. As it turns out, the speech was *partially* true, qua representative of one kind of eros (symbolized by the black horse). The palinode gets us closer to the whole of eros of which the earlier speeches captured a part. Is not the dialectical ascent to the palinode, then, an example of reasoning that moves from a plurality of (auditory) sense perceptions (the earlier speeches, theses, and statements in the *Phaedrus*) to a unity (the palinode)? The unity is constituted by the insight that binds the earlier statements about eros together into a larger context. Of course, this unity is itself stated through a plurality of statements. Thus the movement from many sense perceptions to a one is not a movement to something that is known in the absence of all sense perception (nor is it somehow a movement to one sense perception). It is a movement from partially true (partially insightful) statements about something to a coherent discourse based on a unifying insight of eidos. The extreme brevity of Socrates' description here of the process masks its complexity. As we shall see, the palinode itself must be retracted; it is not the final whole of the *Phaedrus*. It is necessary to see it from a still broader standpoint and so to recollect that standpoint, too. The insight that we still have not settled on the whole truth is knowledge of ignorance. The progress from less to more (though not perfectly) satisfactory insights amounts to the progressively deeper understanding of one's aporia.[55]

The "dialectical" use of words is, then, the "right use" of "memoranda." In the last pages of the *Phaedrus* the word "hypomnemata" is used to refer to the written word, and when we get to that part of the dialogue the wrong use of "reminders" will be discussed. The right use is closely connected with the distinction between what is within the soul (the traces of the Beings) and what is not.[56] In the context of the beauty manifested visually in the love affair that Socrates now describes, their misuse would presumably consist of a response to representations of beauty that remained at the level of sexual desire.

I think that it is possible to connect the eidos of Beauty (which is so pivotal in the palinode) with the one exhibited by the palinode, as well as by the *Phaedrus* itself. In spite of the emphasis on the visual manifestation of Beauty, we should not be misled into thinking that Beauty cannot in any way show itself in speeches or deeds. The Greek *kalon* can also mean "admirable," "fair," "noble," "suitable," "appropriate," "measured." In the palinode the eidos that guides the dialectical movement from the earlier speeches to the palinode (and then to the remainder of the *Phaedrus*) would seem to be Beauty understood in the senses just discussed. Knowledgeable unity in a speech seems, at least in the *Phaedrus*, to be a manifestation of Beauty in that the speech says what is appropriate, suitable, right, true. Correspondingly, beauty is not an aesthetic quality here. In the *Phaedrus*, "beautiful" is not said of speeches that are *simply* "pleasing" in the ordinary sense; indeed, a major thesis of the second half of the dialogue is that a *rhetorically* good speech is *not* just pleasing at the expense of also being true. Thus Socrates refers to his palinode—the contents of which he has claimed are true—as "most beautiful" (257a3–4). The lover of wisdom, we recall, is a lover of beauty (248d3), and at 250b5–c6 Socrates indicates that he, along with the followers of Zeus—the philosophers—saw Beauty in all its splendor. Beauty does not seem to be so much an object of discourse as that which illuminates it. Hence the association, at 250b–d, with light, manifestness, visibility. It makes a body shine, gives splendor to images "here," and bestows clarity and illumination on intelligence.

In what sense, then, are the Beings present in their "images" (*homoioma*, 250a6; *eikones*, 250b4; *eidola*, 250d5)? Is it the blurred images of the eide that serve as the guides for recollection, or is it the eide that are present in blurred images? Are the Beings difficult to see in the images because the images necessarily distort them (regardless of how wise the man is who grasps the images) or because of the defective "organs" of the souls that apprehend the images? These questions bear directly on how successful anamnesis could be in principle. The *Phaedrus* does not provide altogether unambiguous answers.

Socrates indicates that some people cannot see the eide in their images because in the previous life they saw little or because they have forgotten much through misdeeds in this life or some other cause (hence it is helpful to be *neoteles*; 250e1). The reference to misdeeds recalls the roles of character and vocation I discussed above. Even in the case of the philosopher, character will shape the manner in which the truth is discerned. Character even seemed to influence the extent to which a nongodly soul originally saw the truth, since much depended on how well the black horse had been schooled. These shortcomings help explain why our organs for apprehending these images are said to be dim (250b3–4). Further, immediately after Socrates says that in the likenesses of our soul's prized possessions (such as justice and sophrosyne) there is no "luster" (*pheggos;* 250b3), he seems to suggest that the locus of the difficulty lies in this dimness. Thus far, the obscurity of the eide would seem to be the soul's fault, as it were—a point that fits in nicely with the notion that through self-knowledge progress toward recollection of the Beings is possible.

On the other hand, the facts that the soul is embodied and must therefore recollect with the help of sense perception and that the eide show themselves in images (such as logos) that are part of the sensible world seem to constitute constraints on the side of the object, constraints about which the soul can do nothing. So too with the fact that the eide have different sorts of images (Beauty alone being visible to sight) and some therefore are easier to know than others. The thesis that soul cannot in this life see the Truth directly, but only recall the imprints left over from an earlier time, signifies that the fallen soul necessarily knows the Beings (to the extent that it does) in the context of a world in which things such as body and soul, and sense perception and thought, are mixed together.

Yet these facts do not entail the view that the sensible world conceals the eide, such that the guides for recollection are only blurred images approximating the eide. Were that the case, it would be difficult to explain how anyone could ever be reminded of what *is*. The *Phaedrus* does not in fact advance that view. In the palinode Socrates provides an example of recollection in which the beloved's beauty does show itself, and with shocking force. The lover suddenly remembers that quality isolated from the beloved in which it is embodied (Beauty on its "holy pedestal"; 254b7). The beauty in the beloved really is beautiful, but the beloved himself is not essentially beautiful; he may thus be ugly in comparison with a god.[57] When the lover comes to understand that, he realizes that what he really wants is not so much the beloved but the beauty he exhibits, the Beauty that is in all ways and all times beautiful. If he fails to understand that, then (as Socrates will soon recount) he attempts to possess the beloved sexually. Differently put, the lover must come to see the beloved as an *image*, and so as lacking some of the characteristics of the original. The Beings, for example, are essentially, forever, and in every respect whatever they are; the beloved lacks these critical characteristics. That is to say that a divine quality 'is neighbor to *genesis* and varies with the various objects to which we commonly ascribe being' (247d7–e1).

That the eide are mingled in sensible things may make them extremely difficult to see. This is especially true when it is a question of discourse and so when the sense perceptions are primarily auditory rather than visual. Logos is fantastically complex. Eide are present in it in such a way that they are always obscured by the countless and often contradictory opinions, beliefs, predispositions, and prejudices expressed by a language. Words have multiple and even shifting meanings depending on the time, context, and the speaker. This fact provides fertile ground for rhetoric, which, as Socrates points out at length later in the *Phaedrus,* can (mis)lead his auditors from a position to its opposite, gliding through the small similarities that connect the intermediary steps (262a–b).

Moreover, the wholes expressed by the contexts of discourses seem always to fail to capture all the characteristics of the topic and so fail to exhibit Beauty in the sense of the measured, appropriate, suitable. As no act is just in every conceivable context, so no logos (whether it is a word or a discourse) articulates what justice is from every possible perspective and with respect to every conceivable state of affairs. Yet the complexity and ambiguity of language reflects the level of the persons who speak and write it. If logos is like water (to use the simile discussed above), that water is stirred up and set in motion by soul. As Socrates will say later in the *Phaedrus*, logos is brought to life by the soul. Once again, the soul is the key to generating the difficulties in which it finds itself. As we saw several times above, the dimness of our powers of understanding (owing to a soul's forgetfulness, limited vision of the Truth earlier on, and character) prevents a soul from coming to a perfectly aperspectival insight into what is the case. Self-knowledge nevertheless provides a means for partial progress toward that end.

The *Phaedrus* does not suggest that logos is bent on deceiving us, or that the truth it images only approximates what *is*. Nor does it suggest that all articulations of, say, the nature of justice are equally good. On the contrary, the *Phaedrus* itself shows how progress can be made from partially true logoi about something (such as eros) to more adequate logoi that call upon a larger context closer to the whole truth of the matter. Hence the connection between the emphasis in the description of recollection on movement toward wholeness and the movement of the *Phaedrus* itself. This movement develops, as we saw, between the insights into the eidos contained in what begins by saying and the "one" (ἕν) which is gradually articulated. The *Phaedrus* does allow, that is, that our knowledge of what *is* is approximate and even that in principle it must remain limited. This is quite different from the view that the universe is itself in some way unintelligible, absurd, or fundamentally lacking form.

In sum, the eide orient us all along; the true shapes of things are present as informing or illumining the things that, in doxa, we mistakenly trust to be the primarily real. Recollection and dialectic can begin with doxa because that "everyday" world of experience is not devoid of truth. Yet that same truth is not self-evident. From what I have said in the previous paragraph, it is evident that division and collection will serve a useful function in sorting out the various meanings of terms, even though the method of division and collection cannot be identified with anamnesis. Socrates' distinction later on in the *Phaedrus* (263a–c) between words whose meanings are "disputed" (such as "justice," "good") and those that are not ("iron," "silver") provides a clue as to which kinds of terms are hard to understand deeply (they especially are without light; 250b3). Concerning these problematic words we do not agree, he says, either with ourselves or with others. The phenomenon of internal disagreement shows that it is difficult to arrive at an insight into the whole truth. The phenomenon of unfounded agreement shows how easy it is to persuade oneself that one possesses the requisite insight. Socrates' praise at the end of the *Phaedrus* of "living" dialogue is, as we will see, a response to the dimness of our understanding and the complexity of the sensory images we must rely on. *Thus Socrates' commitment to dialogue is ultimately based on the teaching of the palinode.*

Section Two: Beauty, Gods, and Eros, 250c7–253c6

Having ended his encomium to the "memory" (250c7) of things past, Socrates turns to the function of Beauty and the gods in the context of love and desire. This middle section of the apodeixis and the last section (253c7–257a2) are sequential in the order of presentation but not in the order of things they describe. The last section is a detailed description of the pathos of eros already adumbrated in the middle section (especially 251a–252a). Thus the one must be superimposed on the latter in order to convey the complete picture. Moreover, the two halves of the middle section of the apodeixis (the quotation from the Homerids divides the section into two) must also be read simultaneously, as it were. The second half must be folded back over the first half; the lover's divinization of the beloved is amplified by the account of the way in which lovers select beloveds possessing the same character type as they. The diairesis of this speech about love is not a division of eros itself.

The picture of eros contained in the middle and last sections of the apodeixis is extremely complex. The complexity is a result of the central thesis of the apodeixis of the nature of eros, namely, that the experience of eros is, whether the lover is aware of it or not, actually a yearning for a return to the origins (the Beings and gods). The telos of eros—and of course the picture of eros here is, so to speak, intensely teleological—is a return to the arche. When this yearning is successful, that is, when the lover comes to understand his eros, the experience is called anamnesis. When it is not self-conscious, eros is the blind and comic groping for the divine. Socrates' myth understands the present and future tenses of love in terms of the past. While this will remind contemporary readers of Freud, Socrates' principle of explanation is in fact the inverse of Freud's. Stated very crudely, instead of explaining the desire for philosophy as a modification of sexual desire, Socrates explains sexual desire as a low manifestation of the desire for wisdom.[58] As this section of the myth teaches us, even physiological desire holds the promise of spiritual perfection *if* this desire is rightly understood (this is part of what is meant by saying that even the black horse of the soul is winged). In the palinode (unlike the first two speeches) eros is not reducible to a desire for pleasure.

The second and third sections of the apodeixis describe the reascent of the soul to the divine. This process itself becomes part of the soul's history, that is, part of the soul in question. In spite of all the talk about the soul already being its true nature, once the soul has fallen away from its original state it is unfinished and incomplete until it finds itself again. To do this it must come to understand the body it now inhabits. Self-control, and indeed the entire experience of eros and attraction to a beloved, is an experience foreign to the heavenly topos and so to the soul's original nature. The point of all this is that self-knowledge possesses a "practical" dimension; it is a matter of a person's *acting* in a certain manner, of *living* his life in a certain way. As we shall see, the soul's original character type (represented by a god) is really a potentiality for being a certain character; a soul does not become its character type until it lives out the character and *acts* accordingly. Correspondingly, the emphasis in this middle section of the myth is not so much on the structure of the soul (with which the third section begins) as on the soul's incompleteness and potentiality for change and even growth. The experience of eros is that of lacking something, whether Beauty or godlike character.

Self-knowledge includes, then, the ability to affirm a certain way of life and to live it. That the affirmation must be repeated over and over is part of what is meant symbolically by the portrayal of the philosophical soul as having to choose three one-thousand-year periods of a philosophical life before it is truly a philosopher (truly winged). The need to renew the affirmation recurs, if not endlessly, at least continuously for a long time. The analogy between recollection and remembering may be misleading in this respect, since the latter, unlike the former, need not involve anything more than a momentary intellectual operation. Of course, at this point it does become extraordinarily difficult to analyze precisely the relationship between choice and fate, a problem I have already touched on above.

Self-knowledge is not then something one pursues *in order* to live a philosophical life at some future date, as, say, an athlete limbers up in preparation for an Olympic wrestling match (cf. 256b5). Rather, self-knowledge is this living out of a philosophical life. Hence it is something that cannot be "finished" until that life is over (though obviously the converse does not hold). This is implied in the crucial metaphor of "following the god" used in the palinode; no fallen soul was able in the earlier life to follow the god perfectly and so no fallen soul perfectly has the character he desires. Nor could an earthly soul in this life perfectly follow a god, for the god is, after all, divine (hence the qualifications at 253a4–5, b7). That is, even character remains a telos that is never quite fulfilled. Character is not present in this world in the way that, say, Beauty is (more on this below). Is this not why an elderly Socrates can claim, at the start of the *Phaedrus,* that he does not yet know himself? Is this not why Socrates can claim to lack self-knowledge and yet also claim, at the conclusion of the palinode, to possess an "erotike techne" (257a7–8), that is, the art of continually striving (or yearning) for something he cannot ever fully possess while a man? As Socrates interprets it, the Oracle's command also means "Become thyself!" But this becoming is based on an understanding of the "good for man," a good captured by Socrates' image of the soul's idea: the soul is a being that functions well when it is hierarchically organized.

Let me turn now to the middle section of the apodeixis. As already noted, this section is divided in half by an apocryphal quotation from the Homerids, the main point being the identification of Eros with the wings.[59] The first half of the section deals mainly with Beauty and eros, the second with the gods and eros. Nowhere in the whole section are the elements of the soul referred to; that is reserved for the third section of the palinode. In the present section there is a remarkable emphasis on the soul's being bound into a whole by the pathos of love (for example, 251b6–7, 253e5–6); eros has a totalizing effect on the soul. When inner conflict and self-control become an issue, the elements of the soul are distinguished and then reintegrated at a higher level. We wonder immediately how recollection of Beauty and that of the gods are connected. A prior question must be raised first, however: what importance should be attached to the fact that Beauty is chosen to illustrate the process of recollection? We know that Beauty is unique among the Beings in showing itself to sight (250d). The choice of Beauty is fortunate in that it anchors a connection between the literal and metaphorical senses of eidos/idea ("look" and "essence" being the two senses), and between these senses and the faculty of sight (eidos and idea being derived from the verb meaning "to see"). There are good contextual reasons for the selection of Beauty. Socrates is trying to retract speeches that dealt with eros in a sexual context, and so he must offer an alternative account of that same context. But it does not follow that Beauty is the only paradigm to illustrate anamnesis. The account of recollection would surely have been somewhat different if, say, Phronesis (250d4) were selected. Indeed, Socrates narrows even the scope of his treatment of Beauty by implying that Beauty is manifest *only* to sight (250d1–3). He thereby excludes the beauty of the soul as well as that of speeches (the latter is a topic of the second half of the *Phaedrus*). Still further, he deals only with the beauty of the human form.[60] I infer that the description of recollection in the palinode is not exhaustive.

Socrates begins his brilliant phenomenology of love—or, perhaps it would be more accurate to say, of the experience of falling in love—by distinguishing between someone whose memory of Beauty is still fresh and someone whose memory is dim. Socrates' account is about the former, Zeus-like, types. That is, his account cannot be a description of "the human response to physical beauty" as such. Such an account would be considerably less edifying than the one Socrates actually produces. Nevertheless, even the true lover's response seems, by the time we get to the quotation from the Homerids, to be indistinguishable from the conventional response (252a and context). By this point the lover thinks sex and only sex is the solution to his aggravating aporia (251d7–9 and context). The last section of the apodeixis picks up at this point and describes how a vision of Beauty and Sophrosyne rescue the lover's madness from decaying into merely human insanity.

When the true lover sees "a godlike face or the look of a body that represents Beauty well" (251a2–3), he undergoes a violent reaction, since his mind recollects Beauty Itself (also 254b). Socrates uses a startling mix of metaphors and images in describing the experience; as the roots of the wings are warmed and watered, they melt and the wings grow, the pain being like that felt by a teething child. This impossible mix of natural forms nevertheless seems to produce a good description of a state of the soul. Sense perceptions and intellection are inseparable here. Hence in the case of the lover, body and soul begin by cooperating with each other. Thanks to the force of his recollection of beauty, as we learn in the third section of the myth, the lover's attraction for the beloved's beautiful bodily shape can be transformed into a concern for his spiritual well-being. This impressive feat is accomplished through the uplifting growth of the wings, which itself depends on both reason and the beauty perceived by the senses. When the soul in question is Zeus-like, reason can have motivational force and the ability to control sexual desire. The growth of the wings is initially stimulated by physical icons of Beauty; but presumably if memory of Beauty is lacking, the wings wither and the sexual desire dominates (cf. the *apteroi* at 256d4 and context).

The lover treats the beloved as though he were an image (or statue; *agalma*) of a god (cf. *Symp.* 215b and 216e–217a, where Alcibiades claims that Socrates, like a Silenus, contains agalmata of the gods inside). The lover idolizes the beloved's bodily shape ("idea") and would prepare sacrifices to him were he not afraid of being thought "mad" (251a). At this point convention still has some hold on the lover (others see the beloved's body but not the divine beauty in it; hence in their eyes it is madness to worship that beloved). Presumably it is in these ways that the true lover differs from the forgetful lover. The latter immediately objectifies the beautiful beloved by responding in simply sexual terms; devoid of a sense of "shame," he wants to "mount" the beloved like a four-footed beast so as to get pleasure (250e1–251a1).[61] For him, the beloved is not godlike. The lover thinks that he can grasp physically the quality that the eyes alone among the senses can communicate. This degenerate lover, in short, no longer understands the difference between Beauty and that in which it is present. Socrates allows that people will see beauty in different ways, but he does not infer that beauty is in the eye of the beholder (or at least, not just there); some eyes are keener than others.

The lover is struck by beauty and *then* he divinizes the beloved (*hotan, proton, eita;* 251a2–7). It is the beloved's beauty and not his character that attracts the lover. Presumably if the beloved's soul were the object of the lover's attentions, it would be because it was beautiful.[62] In contrast with the approach of the nonlover, the lover does not calculate his potential profits and losses in selecting a beloved. Indeed, he does not really stop and choose the beloved at all, though as we learn later, a principle of selection (sharing the same god) does govern this process. Nor will the beloved respond to the lover with a computation of gain and losses. Nevertheless, there is a significant difference in the present description between the ways in which Beauty and the gods are present in the beloved. Unlike the god-type (= character), beauty is visible to the senses. Most of the visual metaphors in these passages are used with reference to the perception of beauty; different metaphors (having connotations of "production," "grasping," "participating") dominate the account of character. There seems to be no necessity to track down Beauty, as there is in the case of the god (this is partly due to the restricted scope of this discussion of Beauty). While Beauty strikes the lover with great force, character does not. Character does not stream into the lover as Beauty does. Although not a word is said about the lover's being beautiful (except so far as he reflects the beloved's beauty), it seems that he is the source of character for the beloved (see below). There is no indication that the beloved is beautiful because he *knows,* in a discursive sense, *what* beauty is (this fact seems connected to the fact that the beauty of the soul, which would presumably arise from the soul's possession of knowledge and the like, is not mentioned here). The beloved just *is* beautiful; he does not have to *do* anything to be beautiful in the way that one might have to do something to be just or wise. Character, unlike physical beauty, is not something "there" in a finished form. Perhaps we are meant to think of the perfection of character as itself being beautiful. Although Socrates speaks of both knowledge of character and knowledge of Beauty as being sorts of "memories" (253a3, 254b5), the differences I have outlined remain.

Why does the lover divinize the beloved? The lover's actions here seem to repeat the events connected with the divine banquet. Just as then a

soul followed a god in an effort to see the Beings, so now the lover makes
the beloved into his god and thinks that his enthusiasm is caused by the
beloved (253a5–6). But because of the separation now between soul and
Beings, the path of the soul back to Beauty is torturously complex. Now
the lover does not just follow a god, he re-creates him in the beloved.
The beloved is not, in fact, a god any more than the lover is. The god
is within (as the etymology of "enthusiasm" suggests). In his initial response to the beloved, the lover in effect allows himself to be possessed
by the beloved's beauty to the extent of forgetting himself. The lover
loses himself in order to find himself at a deeper level. The lover uncon-
sciously transfers his own character-ideal to the beloved to whom he has
taken a fancy, and then sees himself in the beloved. The role of the imagination is crucial here; the lover in effect fantasizes about the beloved and
imposes the fantasy on the beloved, so externalizing his own self and
thereby creating for himself a route to self-knowledge. *This illustrates how
the soul can move itself through the excitation of eros.*

The beloved eventually identifies with the lover by, in effect, accepting
as true the lover's fantasy about him. When the lover is overfull with the
beloved's beauty, some of it streams back into the beloved through his
eyes ("as a breath of wind or an echo, rebounding from a smooth hard
surface, goes back to its place of origin"; 255c4–6). The wings of the
beloved's soul then become moderately excited. It seems clear that the
beloved is here enjoying his own beauty, not the lover's beauty; in particular, the beloved's desire is aroused because the beloved is desired by
the lover. The lover manages to change the beloved's self-image. Hence
the beloved's soul too moves itself. Eros is the synthesizing force uniting
these star-crossed souls. Not surprisingly, the beloved "loves, but is in
aporia as to what he loves; and what he has experienced he does not know
and is not able to articulate it, but like one who has caught a disease of
the eye from another, he cannot account for it, not realizing that his lover
is as it were a mirror in which he beholds himself" (255d3–6).[63] The
lover reproduces in the beloved the experience the lover is undergoing,
thanks to the beloved's presence. The lover does not know what he is
looking for since he does not understand his own eros; he thus creates
what he is looking for and then finds it. The beloved's "counterlove"
(*anterota;* 255e1) is an eidolon of the lover's eros. Just as the lover pours
into the beloved draughts drawn from Zeus and thinks that the beloved
is pouring them into him (253a), so the beloved pours a stream of beauty
into the lover and then perceives reflected beauty pouring back into him
(255c–d). We seem to have here a case of continual transference and coun-
tertransference, as it is called today. The beloved, however, is not said
to recollect anything or to become enthusiastic. Nor does he try to shape

the lover as the lover has him. The beloved is remarkably passive; thus the relationship between lover and beloved is asymmetrical.[64] While the counterimage is not a copy of the lover's love, it does share in common with it an initial stage in which the soul is mistaken or ignorant about what it loves and a second stage in which love of another becomes self-recognition. Friendship is eros undistracted by the black horse and focused on simultaneously benefiting both of the friends and recollecting the Beings.[65]

Socrates shows himself wonderfully sensitive here to the role imagination plays in desire—and what is closer to the pathos of love than the power of fantasy? Now, this process can easily go awry if the dialectic of love degenerates into sexual desire alone (more on this later) or if the lover's intuition about his own and the beloved's nature is mistaken. The danger of such a mistake is clear from the extraordinary terms with which Socrates characterizes the lover's efforts to divinize the beloved. Socrates says that a lover selects a beloved for himself in keeping with his own character and that he "fashions for himself [*tecktainetai*] an image [= the beloved] even as if the beloved himself were a god, and adorns it [*katakosmei;* 'arranges'] it" (252d6–7). The lover "makes" (252e4, 253a7) that beloved to be a certain way (the Zeus-like in particular impose their "hegemony"; cf. 252e3) once he has "acquired" (253b5) the beloved. The lovers "persuade and discipline" the beloved (253b6). Yet at 252e4 and 253b2 Socrates speaks of the lover's "discovering" the beloved's "nature." Is the beloved's nature created or not? One could answer that his potentialities are discovered and then developed; but while 252e4–5 might suggest this, the other descriptions conflict with it.[66]

The problem also holds for the lover's understanding of which of the gods he should follow. Socrates says:

> If they [the lovers] have not aforetime set upon this pursuit [philosophy], then they endeavor to learn [the way] from wherever they can or they find it for themselves, and tracking it down within themselves they find a way to discover the nature of their god insofar as they are intensely constrained to look toward the god, and reaching out to him in memory they are enthusiastic, and they take from him their ways and pursuits, insofar as a man can partake of a god. But all this, mind you, they attribute to the beloved, and they love him all the more; and the draughts which they draw from Zeus they pour out, like Bacchants, into the soul of the beloved, thus creating in him the closest possible likeness to their god. (252e5–253b1)

The Zeus-like, to repeat, are the philosophers; thus what is being described here is the effort of a person to be a philosopher. The difficulty in being a philosopher seems here to be inseparable from knowing what a philosopher is. An "intense necessity" compels a potential philosopher to search for an understanding of what a philosopher is, and in doing so, he is in fact acting like a philosopher. This is the self-motion of soul, how the intentionality of eros works out its fulfillment. Just as the lover discovered himself surreptitiously, as it were, so now the philosopher (who in this account is just a particular kind of lover) ends up "remembering" that he is Zeus-like even though he did not know exactly what he was doing when trying to track down his character. Perhaps philosophical self-knowledge, then, is retrospective in that its logos of itself is dependent on its prior ergon (more on this in chapter 6 and the Epilogue). But since being Zeus-like remains an ideal, this self-knowledge includes awareness of the extent to which one falls short of the ideal (and so the extent to which one is *imperfectly* a philosopher). Hence it would seem to include knowledge of ignorance: knowledge of what, in general, one lacks and should go looking for, as well as of the difficulty of attaining it (this is the sort of knowledge Socrates claims to have; *Phr.* 257a7–8, *Symp.* 177d6–8, *Lysis* 204b8–c2, *Theages* 128b).

As the passage quoted indicates, the lover's search for himself must take place through his divinization of the beloved. The search for one's own god, and the effort to pattern the beloved after a god, go hand in hand, guided by eros and worked out with the help of imagination, insight, and projection. *When all is said and done, what the lover really wants is himself as he would like to be: himself fulfilled, whole, perfected, godlike.* From Socrates' standpoint, it is equivalent to saying that the lover is "intensely necessitated" to become what he *ought* to be, to be what he *truly is.* Clearly the soul's nature is being conceived of here teleologically. The lover's love is self-love, but not selfish love; he loves the beautiful in himself understood as the type of character he potentially is. By a kind of invisible hand, the lover's effort to try to do this for himself leads him to do the same for the beloved.

It has been maintained that this picture of love turns it into a selfish process, neither the lover nor beloved being appreciated without qualification as an "individual."[67] These criticisms of the palinode's description of love have already been ably responded to by others,[68] and I limit myself to the following. The lover and beloved described in the palinode are distinguished from the nonlover and nonbeloved of the earlier speeches precisely in that they do not treat each other simply as means to the satisfaction of their physiological desires. Hence, in the palinode's account of love, individuals are loved for the true selves they can become again, and not just for what they are (potentially Zeus-like, beautiful in physical appearance). The lover makes the beloved resemble him qua follower of a god, that is, as striving for the perfection of godlike character. The lover's actions are not motivated by vanity, by a bloated estimation of what he has achieved or is endowed with at present.[69] Moreover, the palinode in no way recommends that either lover or beloved be left in the dust in favor of a transcendent Being. The mirrorlike nature of the other's soul is indispensable if one is to see oneself, a point that will become clearer when we consider the importance of dialogue for self-knowledge.

Socrates' account here of love differs from two familiar positions. The one, popularly (and so loosely) known as Christian agape, is the love of a person as a human being and as a creature of God, regardless of that person's individual qualities. In this sense it is possible to love someone who is far from admirable. This does not exclude the individual as an object of love, but does not require it either. The other position is the love of a unique individual, and so of her good *and* bad qualities alike. Phenomenologically, it seems true to say that individuals can love a person who seems physically beautiful to them but spiritually mediocre, and yet not love them just "for" their physical beauty. In this case we have a love of a person that stems neither from a love of mankind nor from a love of noble qualities, but that is somehow a love of one individual. I suppose that if there were an Idea of the Soul, that Idea might function as the Platonic correlate of the creature of God in the Christian view; in any event, Socrates is clearly not talking about love in that sense, especially if (as I have argued) he is not assuming that there is such an Idea. He is also not talking about love in the second sense; or at least, his description of the Zeus-like love differs from it, though conceivably the love between the followers of other gods might come close to it. Let us grant that the love Socrates is describing is not selfish and not limited to sexual gratification. I think that one must admit that Socrates' goal is to describe a rare and noble form of love rather than to produce a phenomenology of every sort, or even of the very common sorts, of love. Socrates' lover and beloved love each other so as to love themselves, not in a selfish way, but in a way that helps the other to love himself qua whole and fulfilling his nature. Socrates' lover and beloved love each other not as unique individuals but as exemplifying certain qualities. Yet they do seem attached to each other as individuals, perhaps because they have had the experience, which they have not shared with others, of helping each other learn over a lifetime (256b). Such a friendship is not unknown, surely, between a philosopher and a former student. Though love may ultimately be of certain divine qualities, lovers and beloveds are still residents of a world in which those qualities are present in images preserved in embodied souls.

As already noted, the philosopher tries to "persuade" (253b6) the beloved to follow along. This persuasion will be discursive. It is a matter

of discursively "leading" (253b7) the beloved's soul down the path of
philosophy. And this observation points to the topic of rhetoric, defined
later in the *Phaedrus* as the ability to "lead souls" by means of discourses.
Indeed, in the passage quoted above, Socrates alludes to a phrase ("following in the tracks of a god") that crops up twice more in the *Phaedrus*,
once in connection with the art of division and collection (266b)—itself
discussed in the context of rhetoric—and once in connection with the
writings a dialectician will leave behind for benefit of those who follow
(276d4–5).[70] The description at the end of the *Phaedrus* of the relationship
between dialectician and student (a relationship explained in the context
of a discussion about rhetoric) is grounded in the present description of
Zeus-like lover and beloved.[71] In this manner the teaching of the palinode
continues to frame the subsequent discussion of rhetoric and dialectic.

That the description of the love between the Zeus-like is meant to tell
us something about the relationship between the dialectician and his student is confirmed by Socrates' sudden return at 252b2 to the dramatic
framework of the palinode. The beautiful boy is being played by Phaedrus,
and the lover, by Socrates. Certainly, Socrates is trying to educate Phaedrus
and has been moved by Phaedrus to deliver these discourses. Yet it would
be absurd to think of Phaedrus as capable of becoming truly Zeus-like,
though it is plausible to think of Socrates in this way. In the pretense
that Socrates and Phaedrus are equal and, by the end of the dialogue,
interchangeable (having "everything in common" like true friends, as
Phaedrus—not Socrates—will say) lies the comedy of the *Phaedrus*. Socrates
and Phaedrus belong to different types; or at least, Phaedrus is a laughable
imitation of the Zeus-like. When the palinode's edifying portrait of lover
and beloved is compared to reality, we come across a large discrepancy
between the two. We are led by our perception of the comedy to reflection
about the palinode's teaching, and this amounts to a kind of metalevel
reflection, which leads (as we shall see) not to outright rejection but to
partial qualification of the palinode.

When we reflect on the issue of the mutual pursuit of self-knowledge
in the context of the drama of the *Phaedrus* or of our own experience, we
begin to realize how precarious that pursuit is. How can the lover be so
sure that in "persuading" and "making" the beloved he is not just compelling the beloved against his nature to fit the lover's own mold? Just
as the perception of Beauty could degenerate into the desire for sex, so
the perception of godlike character might degenerate into the desire for
mastery (indeed, in Socrates' first speech there occurred terms similar to
those used here for the lover's "preparation" of the beloved: 239a2, a6,
b6). Might the lover, indeed, *not* succeed in laying hold of his own character

type, whether because of the sheer complexity of the task, the dimness
of his memory, or the allure of another type (he might pursue Apollo
instead of Zeus)?[72] To put the point in terms of the tracking metaphor:
where will the potential philosopher find the imprints of the footsteps he
is to follow? And if, as will certainly be the case, he is presented with a
number of footsteps—a multitude of imprints leading in all directions—
how will he identify those he is to follow?

One could reply that every lover has, after all, been educated at an
earlier time to understand these matters by another lover. Lover and beloved
will be of the same soul type. But the very parochialism entailed by this
account—each character type will be interested only in others of the same
type (252c3 ff.)—brings us to the problem of perspectivism. That this
problem is a real one for intellectuals as well as for other types of human
beings is obvious from the prevalence of schools of thought on every conceivable topic as well as the unending and far-reaching disagreements
among them. Each group firmly believes that *it* is composed of the *truly*
Zeus-like and continually uses all its powers to initiate new disciples into
its ranks. It is a banal fact that people (including those who call themselves
philosophers) see different things and see them differently. The truth
cannot be seen by those not able by nature to be persuaded of it. But
men often create conventions in the light of which they persuade themselves
that they are by nature wise. The palinode, as I have tried to show, gives
a detailed explanation of this phenomenon in terms of the prelife of the
soul. It thus sets the stage for the problem of rhetoric and for dialogue
(along with its theoretical discourse). A great deal hinges on one's appraisal
of the banal fact just mentioned. The palinode tells us, in effect, that
there is no neutral self-understanding or understanding of the Beings;
every human soul is biased in its pregiven nature. Even the Zeus-like
philosophers exist because they *failed* to see all the Beings. Of course, we
might say that the Zeus-like are truth seekers and so are precisely the
ones able to escape from the parochialism and bias of character; their
character is the one that possesses objective knowledge. Even if this is
true as an ideal, though, no philosopher is perfectly Zeus-like. A philosopher will know this, that is, know his ignorance; he thus continues
to be Zeus-like, but in a way that reflects his imperfect nature. This is
the stance taken by Socrates and Plato in the *Phaedrus*. It is at the root
of the importance of dialegesthai. But dialogue is not a solution to the
problem in a sense that gets rid of the problem.

That is, distinguishing between the truth about oneself and what one
has been persuaded of always remains a grave difficulty. There is no objective check by which a fallen soul can, as it were, escape from itself

momentarily in order to see what is *really* the case. *And precisely this is the crux of the problem of rhetoric in the* Phaedrus. The problem consists of distinguishing between true discourses and those that are persuasive but untrue—between true and false persuasion. I am arguing that the palinode's account of the soul and of recollection (whether recollection of Ideas or of gods) makes the problem unavoidable. Indeed, it actually *establishes* the problem. The problem is signaled by the astonishing parochialism of the erotic relationship, by the characterization of these relationships in terms of leaders and followers, and by the very heavy emphasis placed on the leader's formation of the follower (a political version of all this is not difficult to imagine). The heart of the matter lies in the account of the soul's separation from the plain of truth and the consequent alienation from divine Episteme.

To put all this in one last, but still preliminary, way: the palinode teaches that in thinking we cannot safely distinguish theory (in the sense of theoria; 247c1, d4) and production (as *poiesis;* 252e4, 253a7, c2), that is, between what we *see* to be the case and what we (falsely) *make* to be the case. As I shall argue at length in chapter 5, the creation of a methodological episteme, such as that outlined in the second half of the *Phaedrus,* by no means solves the problem, for it itself is a form of rhetoric (this does not mean that it is an illusion).

One cannot solve the problem by depriving oneself of intercourse with other philosophers, by removing oneself—perhaps along with a book or two—to the banks of a charming stream in the countryside. This move only increases the danger of self-deception, of the soul's keeping from itself (by forgetting it) the truth it has in itself. Self-knowledge, far from being sharpened by the absence of a mirror in which one can see oneself, is dulled thereby. This is why Socrates declares, at the start of the *Phaedrus,* that he never leaves the city: the trees and open country have nothing to teach him (230d3–5). This is also why both Socrates and Plato take the extreme position that only dialectic is an appropriate medium for philosophizing (more on this in subsequent chapters).

Before commenting on the last section of the palinode, I would like to point out that Socrates' description at 252a of the public behavior of the true lover is indistinguishable from the negative description in the first two speeches of the lover's behavior. In both cases, the lover abandons all family, friends, and concern with reputation, wealth, mores, in order to slavishly serve the beloved. What power the world of society held over the lover has disappeared; the lover does not now mind being thought mad (cf. 251a5–6). Perhaps even Socrates' attitude toward wealth, family, and reputation could serve as an example of such behavior. The difference between the divinely mad and humanly mad lovers resides in the causes of their love, and these causes are not visible to the external, sane, observer. Hence the judgment of the detached observer ought not to be criterial for anyone's deciding whether or not the lover is divinely mad. Similarly, once the true lover has restrained himself (thanks to renewed recollection of the Beings), he looks very much like the nonlover with respect to their mutual sophrosyne. The differences between the latter's mortal sophrosyne (256e5) and the former's divine sophrosyne resides in the *reasons* for which they restrain themselves. The meaning of the philosopher's eros, as well as the relationships in which it works itself out, are fundamentally private, as the dramatic setting of the *Phaedrus* emphasizes (though of course in some other dialogues many people listen to Socrates' conversations). This is also clear from the description of lover and beloved in the palinode, that of the dialectician and student at the end of the *Phaedrus,* and that of the philosopher's "art of rhetoric" later in the *Phaedrus* (that art being effective with individual souls rather than masses of people). The message of the *Phaedrus* is clear: philosophy is a form of private eros, and it is essentially nobler and higher than the political concerns and the public rhetoric of the polis. Philosophical madness cannot double as political doctrine without losing its divinity.

Section Three: Self-Control and Eros, 253c7–257a2

As is evident from the description in the *Phaedrus* of the lover's infatuation with the beloved, even a lover whose memory of Beauty is sharp tends to degenerate into an ordinary lover, one who thinks that only sex with the beloved will cure his "madness" (252b1, 251e). Consequently Socrates turns now to the issue of self-control, and he paints an extraordinarily vivid picture of the horses and their struggle with the charioteer. This section is demarcated from the rest of the myth by the return to the division of the soul into forms. At this point we come to the most consistently introspective section of the myth; the inner world of the soul comes fully alive in the context of moral conflict (in contrast with the lack of subjectivity in the souls of theorizing gods). The thesis embedded in this section is that virtue is knowledge, as is the view that no man does evil knowingly. That men have a natural desire for the good is, as I have argued, also a fundamental thesis of the palinode. Without recollection of noetically presented truth, eros degenerates into sexual desire; with it, true sophrosyne (= divine erotic madness) results. Socrates rather surprisingly refers to this process as the "capture" of the beloved (253c6); what is really at stake is the genesis of self-possession and of true philia. We are also shown that the knowledge associated with genuine virtue is not merely intellectual. It is not reducible to the capacity to utter a moral truth, to produce an argument about or analysis of the ethics at issue here. It is not an episteme or *methodos* in the sense in which these terms are used in the second half of the *Phaedrus*. The kind of "knowledge" (perhaps it would be better to speak of "understanding") described here is, if I may put it this way, able to persuade the entire soul; indeed, it alone allows the charioteer to master the immensely powerful black horse. The white horse's sense of shame (253d6, 254a2, c4, 256a6) and the application of the whip to the black horse are insufficient restraints. The good horse obeys the "word of command" (253d7–e1, 256a6); this logos, if not animated by anamnesis, is not enough to ensure sophrosyne.[73] The sources of true self-restraint are suprapolitical. That the horses and charioteer can be swayed in one direction or another (by means of the charioteer's actions with respect to them) foreshadows again the importance of rhetoric in the effort to control the soul.

It is important to note that self-control through time depends on continually renewed recollection (254e6). Socrates is not, as I have already mentioned, suggesting that recollection is a once-in-a-lifetime revelation that permanently alters one's life. Indeed, when seeing the beautiful beloved for the first time, the lover recollects Beauty and then proceeds to absorb himself in idolizing the beloved's body—unless he recollects further. When the charioteer recalls Beauty and Sophrosyne, he falls backwards in amazement, thus inflicting excruciating pain on the black horse. The charioteer has thereby been reminded of a crucial fact about the soul, namely, that it lacks the true nourishment provided by the hyperuranian beings. This self-knowledge leads to repetition of self-restraint, which in turn produces a conditioned reflex in the black horse, who becomes habituated to reacting with "fear" (254e8) every time the beloved comes into sight. Note that according to Socrates the lover's mind recollects, at this stage, both Beauty *and* Sophrosyne (254b5–7). Does the sight of Beauty alone not generate self-control? To this tantalizing question the myth offers no answer.

In this last section of the myth, then, Socrates depicts reason's ability to motivate the soul toward a goal not shared by another part of the soul. We have thus gone from the view that reason is an instrument of desire (in Lysias' speech) to the view that reason is desirable as a means of fulfilling epithumetic desires (Socrates' first speech), then to the view that reason has desires (earlier on in the palinode), and finally to the view that the desire of reason can control the other desires. The crux of the matter is couched in the depiction of the charioteer falling backward as he is struck with the vision of what is truly beautiful and sophron. Why does the vision have any force to motivate the soul in a new, higher direction? The charioteer is not portrayed as presenting the black horse with an ethical argument in favor of self-restraint. Nor does he restrain the soul on the basis of perception of its self-interest understood in the manner of the nonlover. Just the force of the recognition of what one has been lacking, and so what one really desires in the beloved, is enough to compel the black horse to behave modestly. This depiction of self-restraint depends crucially on the assumption that the vision is a return to the origins, in the sense of return to what naturally and truly is nourishing for the soul.

That is, the notion that reason can restrain the passions in the way described here follows from the notion of the soul and of its place in the whole offered earlier in the myth. The virtue-is-knowledge thesis depends on a comprehensive view of the soul and cosmos. This is one reason the description of the soul's self-restraint must occupy the last section of the myth, after the other topics have been discussed. Since self-knowledge includes knowledge of the soul and so knowledge of the Ideas the soul desires, it will also be a necessary condition for true sophrosyne. Unlike the self-restraint of the nonlover, that of the philosopher is based on an understanding of what is good for the soul as a whole. Anamnesis, and its repetition or development, is the path to this good. According to the myth, to understand that is to possess the beginnings of self-knowledge.

Socrates praised "pederasty in conjunction with philosophy" (249a2), and he now suggests that lover and beloved will be philosophers when they abstain from sex (250e, 256a–b). These philosophical pederasts will bear children of the psyche, not of the body. Pederasty without sex is friendship between unequals (between teacher and student); it is this sort of uranism, and not pederasty as such (let alone any other form of what we call homosexuality), that the palinode praises. The suggestion that the lover must abstain from all sexual relations seems to result in asceticism. This final part of the palinode does seem to endorse complete abstention from sex, even when this abstention is arrived at in the proper way. Taken literally, this view would entail the eventual termination of the human species. This scarcely seems in line with the whole of the palinode, however. Quite possibly the point is that only pederastic sexual relations (which are "unnatural"; 251a1, 254b1) and sex indulged in for pleasure alone are to be rejected completely.

Indeed, the palinode as a whole suggests that a successful lover *integrates* the various elements of his soul into a hierarchically organized whole, and that this cannot be accomplished without an understanding of these elements, which in turn is dependent on the capacity to experience the powers (cf. 246a7) of these elements. The true philosopher is not, according to this account, the unemotional intellectual or the ascetic bent on obliterating all thought of his body and the desires centered around it. Self-knowledge includes an understanding of the black horse too; and the black horse is a desire for the particular person, not for a universal. The palinode does not indicate (as I commented above) that the body per se is evil, but that the wrong understanding of the body makes it the instrument of wrongdoing. The lover cannot escape becoming a slave to his desire for the beloved by pretending there is no beloved.[74]

Concluding Words (257a3–b6)

Having just addressed the boy, Socrates concludes by addressing Eros directly. Socrates alludes indirectly to Phaedrus (256e3, 257b4–5), thus making Phaedrus too pray for his own deliverance from Lysias and holding a mirror up to him. Socrates expresses his hope both that his discourse has been faithful to Eros and that it will persuade Phaedrus to turn to philosophy. That is, Socrates hopes that his discourse fulfills the two main conditions for noble rhetoric outlined later in the *Phaedrus*, namely, that one should both speak the truth and suit one's words to the soul of one's auditor. In delivering this speech with this purpose in mind, Socrates has cast himself in the role of Phaedrus' lover, but only with the purpose of yoking Phaedrus into a joint pursuit of philosophy. Socrates has attempted to induce Phaedrus' soul to move itself toward philosophy. Thus the workings of Socrates' pedagogy and rhetoric confirm the abstract definition of the soul as self-motion. Even though Socrates seems to acknowledge that Phaedrus will turn to philosophy only if his beloved Lysias is so turned, the ultimate goal is to persuade Phaedrus to "live his life for Eros in singleness of purpose with the aid of philosophical discourses" (257b5–7) rather than to be the disciple of either Socrates or Lysias. Further, Socrates prays on behalf not just of Phaedrus but of himself. His own "erotic art" is at issue. Underneath the various guises Socrates has assumed, Stesichorean and otherwise, he is the discursive erotician par excellence.

Why should the fact that he delivered a speech praising the nonlover and implicitly criticizing Eros make Socrates fear that he will lose his erotic art? His knowledge of eros is self-knowledge in the ways I have discussed in this chapter: knowledge of what he and others lack, knowledge of himself as self-moved soul and as a certain character type, knowledge of himself in terms of a larger Whole, and knowledge of the limitations of his knowledge. That is, knowledge of eros is finally knowledge of being intermediate or, in the *Symposium's* language, "in between" wisdom and ignorance, Beauty and ugliness. The palinode has provided a psychology, set out against the vast canvas of the cosmos, in terms of which knowledge of ignorance or knowledge of eros makes sense. As it turns out, Socrates exhibits this knowledge through the "art" of dialogue. His ability to ask and answer questions depends on his ability to move from partial under-standing of the Truth to a greater understanding of it. If he says things that are untrue *of* himself and so of his whole project of dialogical erotics, he is untrue *to* himself and risks becoming untrue *as* a self. He risks debasing his eros, for there is a close connection between the way one is, and the way one talks about oneself as being. This is why Socrates fears that, having debased Eros, his erotic art will be taken from him.

By reminding us that the palinode is a logos directed to a certain end, and by emphasizing the whole issue of discourse, Socrates invites not just reflection on the problem of rhetoric (which of course is precisely what he and Phaedrus turn to next) but also a self-conscious appraisal of the palinode in terms of its own teaching. The palinode is presumably not just a discussion about self-knowledge and its conditions but an example of self-knowledge. Several questions naturally arise from this observation, among which are the following. Is the myth an example of a *philosophical* logos? What is the logos appropriate to self-knowledge? The second ques-tion in particular leads to the topic of rhetoric, which therefore occupies the remainder of the *Phaedrus*. As I have indicated repeatedly, the palinode's descriptions of character and of the soul's forgetfulness also lead to the topic of rhetoric. The unity of the *Phaedrus* will become still clearer, how-ever, if we pause to reflect on the first question just mentioned, that is, on the rhetoric of the palinode itself.

4

Excursus: Myth in the *Phaedrus* and the Unity of the Dialogue

*The Myth belongs to the pedagogic stage of the human race
. . . . When the Notion attains its full development, it has
no more need of the myth.*
HEGEL[1]

*Thus the myth-lover is in a sense the philosopher, since
myths are composed of wonders.*
ARISTOTLE[2]

The first half of the *Phaedrus* is normally thought of as being mythic and playful in tone, whereas the second half seems considerably more technical and sober. Indeed, it is this fact that has helped make the unity of the *Phaedrus* so problematic and the significance of the first half of the dialogue so difficult to gauge. After all, how "serious," from a philosophical standpoint, *is* myth? To properly understand the unity of the *Phaedrus,* we must evaluate the role of myth in the palinode. For the limitations as well as benefits of myth emerge when we reflect on the palinode's use of it, and this reflection will shed further light on the sudden turn to the topic of rhetoric.

Of course, the *Phaedrus* gives us a warrant for reflecting on myth as a form of rhetoric. In the discussion in the second half of the *Phaedrus* about the art of rhetoric, the speeches of the first half of the dialogue are used as examples of artful and artless rhetoric. One might thus argue that the unity of the *Phaedrus* is that of an example and the rules it exemplifies. For reasons I will discuss in chapter 5, this argument (which most interpreters reject anyhow, since it does not explain the length and complexity of the palinode) is not a sound one. At the present juncture, I will consider the myth not in terms of the putative artfulness of the speech it graces (techne is later said to constitute one criterion of the new rhetoric) but in terms of its claim to truth (which is also said to constitute a criterion). In sum, before proceeding to the next section of the *Phaedrus*, it is important to move from reflection on the details presented *within* the myth to reflection on the speech *as* a myth.

The scope of my discussion will be extremely limited. I do not intend to discuss myth as such or the interpretation thereof. Nor will I be discussing the issue of myth as it arises in the Platonic corpus. My discussion will draw upon and is intended to illuminate the *Phaedrus* alone (though it might also clarify other dialogues). The topic of myth, like the literature on the topic, is vast, and I will make little effort to take much of it into account in my own discussion. Anyone who has tried to deal with the topic of Platonic myth knows how difficult it is not to skate over some very thin ice. The severe restrictions I am imposing on my own discussion are meant to help me stay as near to terra firma as possible, while casting some new light on the *Phaedrus*.[3]

Some preliminary remarks are in order. In general, a Platonic mythos is a fictional story whose symbolically expressed meaning requires interpretation in order to be understood. As a rule, it cannot be understood literally.[4] A logos, by contrast, may be among other things a factual account or an argument. But as the *Phaedrus* shows, the distinction in question is not absolute either substantively or terminologically. Socrates refers to his first speech as a "myth" at 237a9, 241e8, and 243a4 ("mythologia" adverts, in the context, to Socrates' first speech). However, at 241d3, 242e3, 243c2, 244a1, 264e7, 265c6, d7, e3, and 266a3, Socrates refers to the same speech as a "logos." Likewise, at 253c7 and 265c1 Socrates refers to the palinode as a "mythos," and it is clear from 253c7 in particular that he is referring to the part of the apodeixis that begins with the image of the soul and ends with the prayer to Eros. At 265b8 he refers to the identical section as a "logos," and at 252b2, 265b8, c6, d7, e3, 264e7, and 266a3, he refers to the whole palinode as a "logos." Lysias' speech, by contrast, is referred to by both Phaedrus (234c6, 264e3, inter alia) and Socrates (227c4, 234d3, inter alia) as a "logos," but never as a "mythos." At 229c5 Phaedrus refers to the "mythologema" concerning Boreas and Oreithuia; at 229d2 Socrates refers to it, or possibly to an interpretation of it, as a "logos." The Theuth/Thamus myth is called a "logos" (275b4), but not a "mythos" (though it bears all the traditional markings of being a myth). Some of the "logoi" are myths, though they are not denominated as such. The cicadas myth is introduced by the traditional *legetai* (259b6); while it too seems clearly mythic, it is not explicitly called a "logos" or "mythos." Mythos and logos, then, seem not to be mutually exclusive.

It seems odd that Socrates' first speech is referred to as a "myth," though the reference is in keeping with the ironic references to the Muses and to Socrates' enthusiasm. Simply put, there does not seem to be much that is mythic about this speech except for the bare pretense that it is a seduction speech delivered by a fictional concealed lover to a beloved. Indeed, when we recall that the first part of this myth advocates the rudiments of a dianoetic method as a solution to conceptual confusion, the term "myth" seems to take on a sense familiar to us today (as in "the myth of science," a phrase referring to the rhetorical advocacy of the powers of science).

THE PHILOSOPHICAL INTERPRETATION
OF MYTH

Two questions arise immediately with respect to the philosophical interpretation of Platonic myth. Are we to understand that these myths are integral to articulating the truth about self-knowledge? How far can they be so interpreted? (Is there always a residue, as it were, that resists further interpretation?) That the answer to the first question is affirmative should be evident from the following considerations.

Whereas Socrates' first speech was "neither healthy nor true" (242e5–243a1), he claims to speak the truth in his second speech (247c4–6). We are also given to understand that the Theuth/Thamus story is true (274c1–2, 275c1). Thus a logos that is called a "myth" can be true or not true without ceasing to be a myth; the same situation holds for logos. Socrates suggests both that one cannot piously accept myths to be true without interpretation and that one cannot dismiss a myth as false in every sense merely because it is a myth. Granted, he later refers to the palinode's myth as a "not altogether implausible logos" in which "we perhaps attained some degree of truth, though we may well have sometimes gone astray" (265b6–8). These statements cast a shadow on the claim that the palinode speaks the truth but in themselves do not undo this claim.

Toward the start of the *Phaedrus* the issue as to the truth of the my-thologema concerning Boreas and Oreithuia is explicitly raised by Phaedrus. Socrates obliges Phaedrus with an instant translation of the mythic tale into materialist terms as an example of the sort of logos Phaedrus thinks underlies the myth (that is, a report of what "really" happened).

Phaedrus seems to treat myths as imaginary stories or fables, as his comment at the end of the dialogue also indicates (276e1–3).[5]

When Socrates connects Pharmakeia with Oreithuia and Boreas, he shows that he is perfectly willing to amend the traditional stories. In general, Socrates appropriates myths for his own, philosophical, project and thereby takes up a quite radical stance toward them. As he tells us explicitly, he cares only about knowing himself; his use of the Typhon myth is regulated by this predetermined project. However much he bows in the direction of the ancients who know things through myths, Socrates in fact makes his own use of them, rewriting them to suit his needs.[6] Indeed, he does not hesitate to just make up stories and pass them off as the wisdom of the ancients; if Frutiger is correct, the *Phaedrus* contains the two myths (that of the cicadas and that about Theuth and Thamus) that are entirely invented by Plato.[7] When Phaedrus points out that the latter is an invention, Socrates snaps back that what counts is the "truth" of such stories (275b3–c2). He thus implicitly grants Phaedrus' point that the story is a fiction but once again insists that such a story is acceptable as a way of discovering the truth about the sort of subjects at issue here, namely, those concerned with the right conduct of one's life. Implicit in Socrates' response is a distinction between literal and nonliteral truth. Socrates' demand that myths serve his effort to know himself means that the myths must be subjected to *interpretation,* as is evident in his use at the start of the *Phaedrus* of the figure of Typhon. We are meant to interpret the myths nonliterally in a way that assists self-knowledge rather than, say, in ways confined to the study of the historical traditions of myth-making or the antecedents of any particular myth.

The key to Socrates' general approach to myth is his dedication to self-knowledge. His *Phaedrus* myths seem designed, in part because of their intentional ambiguity, to lead the reader to engage in a complex hermeneutic task whose result is philosophical reflection. As is true for the Platonic dialogues in general, the partially buried meaning of Plato's myths is accessible only to the reader willing to engage in a dialogue with them. This in turn requires that he be willing to reflect on his own experience in terms of the myth, for the myth (as is especially clear in the *Phaedrus*) is a complex mirror of human experience (see below). Surely this reflection is intended to help the reader better understand his own experience and so to know himself. The mirrorlike nature of a myth such as that of the palinode allows the reader to identify with the events narrated in the story in a way that is difficult to do with the logical syntax of an argument. Thus Socrates' myths in the *Phaedrus* (or at least that of the palinode) are excellent examples of the philosophical rhetoric recommended in the second half of the dialogue. A similar function is served by many of the myths in dialogues such as the *Phaedo, Gorgias, Symposium,* and *Republic,* in which the core motif is the soul in its cosmic situation. I shall return to this issue later when I discuss in greater detail *how* myths may be important to Socrates' articulation of self-knowledge.

Neither in the *Phaedrus* nor, so far as I am aware, in any other Platonic dialogue is an explicit answer proffered to the second question mentioned earlier—how completely can Plato's myths be interpreted? We are never presented with a theory of interpretation (analogous, say, to a structuralist theory) that informs us how to interpret mythic symbolism. To be sure, in the second half of the *Phaedrus* Socrates looks at his two discourses as paradigms of the art of rhetoric, and he sets out (with the help of numerous distortions and omissions) their formal structure. This scarcely qualifies as an interpretation of the myth. However, we need not rely *only* on the interpreter's *esprit de finesse* in this matter. Given my remarks in the Introduction to this book and Socrates' remarks about "logographic necessity" at 264b7 and context, we can at least say that the interpreter must assume that a Platonic myth is perfectly composed, and so that every detail has *some* point to it relative to the whole of the myth. The palinode's myth contains several inconsistencies (see below); we must begin by assuming that these are not the result of carelessness. Nor can they be ignored on the basis that this is, after all, just a *myth*.

The answer to our second question can be pursued further as follows. It is sometimes suggested that the reason for Plato's use of myth is that what he wants to communicate transcends all "rational" (that is, from this standpoint, nonmythic) explication. The initial difficulty with this suggestion is that it is open to the following reply: if a myth's meaning can be completely translated into nonmythic terms (there being no symbols or explicit interrelations among symbols left unanalyzed), then there is no surplus of meaning expressible just through mythic discourse. Is it not the goal of every interpreter, the reply might continue, to exhaust a myth in precisely this sense? Is this not precisely what I have attempted to do in the previous chapter? Indeed, is it not the case that material that is presented mythically in one dialogue is presented nonmythically in another (the discussions concerning self-motion in the *Phaedrus* and *Laws* X could be offered as an example)? Let us suppose that someone offers a comprehensive interpretation of a myth. Every symbol, relation between symbols, every image and relation between images, the allegorical content of the symbols, in short, every detail seems to have been accounted for in nonmythical language. How could anyone defend the claim that the meaning of the myth "transcends" all interpretive efforts unless he says what this transcendent meaning is—so contradicting the premise that it is transcendent (that is, untranslatable)? Of course, an interpreter might find it difficult to show that further fruitful interpretation is impossible; someone might be able to point out that a detail of the myth has not yet been accounted for satisfactorily. This is different, however, from arguing that some dimensions of the myth *cannot* in principle be accounted for. (This is also different, incidentally, from claiming that some aspect of a myth—such as the fanciful chronology of the palinode—does not have *any* meaning.) In sum, the suggestion that Plato's myths convey something transcending nonmythic rational communication seems contradicted by our practice of interpretation. Even the effort to say what it is in myth that is so irrational (or at least nonrational) seems to contradict itself. Most interpreters seem to assume that Plato's myths are like cryptograms; once one has the key, the meaning of an enciphered message is no more mysterious than the meaning of the same message once deciphered.

Nevertheless there does seem to be a difference between mythic and nonmythic logoi, regardless of how much one translates the one into the other, in a way that is similar to the situation in the interpretation of poetry. One might take, say, a Shakespeare sonnet and interpret it using nonpoetic language. But once this is done, the beauty, charm, and force of the original are lost. Yet our rationalist might again reply: even if this is so (and it would be difficult to deny that, say, an analysis of the palinode's description of the pathos of the soul in love is a lot less impressive than the description itself), are not these rhetorical qualities extrinsic to the poem's (or myth's) meaning? They might be good (so he might continue) for pedagogic purposes, but rational thought, whose purpose is to say without embellishment what the meaning of something is, can dispense with it. This sort of reply is widespread among philosophers; one finds a good statement of it in Hegel.[8]

Let us take a closer look at the palinode's myth in order to get a better grasp of the problem of interpretation. The mythic section of the palinode begins, as already mentioned, at 246a3 with the famous eikon of the soul. Socrates does not say that the soul *is* a winged charioteer and horses, of course, only that it is *like* them. A very large part of the ensuing myth concerns the experiences and deeds (*pathe kai erga;* 245c3–4) of this strange apparatus. Thus the soul's experiences are meant to be *like* those Socrates describes. The myth is an allegorical history of the soul's nature constructed around the image of the soul's idea. The places the soul goes to and from can be, moreover, only likenesses of the place in which we now find ourselves. As I argued in the previous chapter, to speak of hyperuranian beings, that is, to give spatial location to what is nonspatial, is to simultaneously make Being visible to the mind's eye and to distort it (until the mind corrects the misleading impression, that is).

Likewise, it would be absurd to suppose that the chronology of·the myth is to be taken literally; it too is part of the allegory about a winged charioteer and horses. Some souls in this tale are "gods" whose own journeys are an intrinsic part of the allegory. One might say that the gods too are *like* the description of them in the myth. The gods of the palinode are like those of Homer in little more than name. Indeed, one might say that the palinode's gods are likenesses of the souls of human beings as they would look if perfect and unembodied. The gods of this myth do seem to be (among other things) idealized human types who serve the crucial purpose in the story of helping articulate the notion that we are imperfect in specific ways. If the soul does not literally have wings, then it cannot gain or lose them. Is not the talk about "falling" to earth (the wings being "broken") also a likeness, along with the talk about like-winged souls flying heavenward after three one-thousand-year cycles? It is the soul that "falls," but what does "falling" mean? To "fall from heaven" means, in the *Phaedrus,* to be separated from a condition of wholeness and knowledge. If in a literal sense there is no fall from heaven, then the notion of a prelife, like that of the afterlife, constitutes not a declaration of literal truth but an extension (or extrapolation) in symbolic language of the idea that the human soul is by nature deficient (fallen, cut off from immediate access to truth) but able to discover ("remember") it "from within" (by dialectical reflection). Thus while an image (such as the icon of the cave in the *Republic*) is not a myth, the myth of the palinode is fundamentally built around an image and is constituted by images, none of which can be interpreted literally.

This point seems at odds, though, with the fact that the section of the palinode in which immortality is (ostensibly) established precedes the myth and does not seem to be a "likeness." Yet that section does not establish personal immortality. I argued that "cosmic soul" was not the meaning of "psyche pasa." At best, then, the passage could be taken as arguing in favor of the immortality of nonpersonal bits of soul. Only in the myth do we get a description of what "immortality" means for souls, and we hear only of souls that are individuated (capable of making choices, at any rate), never about nonpersonal bits of soul (whatever that may mean). Moreover, no one maintains that the palinode's argument for immortality (whether the immortality is of the personal sort or not) is sound. I suggested in the previous chapter that Socrates understood this fact. Is there a nonliteral sense of "immortality" that is compatible with the rest of the myth once the myth has been interpreted in the manner sketched in the preceding paragraphs and the previous chapter?

Immortality in the usual sense of "survival through time" is a presupposition of the myth read literally. Once interpreted as an allegory, however, the myth does not necessarily require this. "Immortality" expresses the view that the human, earthbound soul by nature knows (though it may have forgotten) the Truth and that it can, in principle, know it again. "Immortality" expresses, at this level, the thesis that a person can in principle transcend the obstacles posed by the dimensions of time and space to which a soul is, to borrow a phrase from the palinode, bound as an oyster is to its shell. The transcendence, again, occurs not by a soul's literally *leaving* this life via the gates of death but by means of *knowledge*. "Immortality" is a way of expressing the primordial connection between the soul and Being. It expresses, if you like, the capacity of a mind that exists in time to think what is eternal. Socrates says at one point that it is the gods' nearness to Being that makes them godlike (249c5–6). It is man's nearness to Being (but, again a "fallen" nearness contaminated by "forgetfulness") that makes him human; and both of these points can be expressed by saying that the soul is "immortal." In this interpretation, immortality does not seem to be very different from that referred to at *Symposium* 212a7 and context, at the very end of Diotima's description of the "major ascent."[9] Correspondingly, the "punishment" a person undergoes for having lived a nonphilosophic life is simply the quality of that one life—a life devoid of true happiness, satisfaction, love (cf. *Theae.* 177a).

One could argue that the notion of "immortality" in the sense of "perdurance through time" is required in order to explain how an embodied soul "already knows" and so can re-cognize the Forms. The answer begs the question, however; for how did the soul in the prelife recognize the Forms when seeing them for the first time? One might reply that the soul has *always* known the Forms, every vision of them in this life or at the divine banquet being a re-cognition. But this just amounts to saying that the soul by nature knows the Forms, no further analysis of *how* it came to know them being possible. The mind *just is* suited to knowing them. For this thesis, however, "immortality" in the sense expressed by the myth when it is read literally is not required, though the notion when interpreted along the lines I have just sketched is still helpful in expressing (among other things) the ability of the timebound mind to apprehend the atemporal. Immortality *is* required to explain anamnesis, but not "immortality" in the literal and obvious sense of "existing forever through time."

The mythical notion of immortality also allows Socrates to express the view that one cannot explain the soul's nature historically, that is, anthropologically; one cannot explain the genesis of one part of the soul as arising out of another part. For example, reason cannot be understood as a faculty created through time by the interaction of desire and the environment (or as created out of the body). And this allows Socrates to maintain the thesis, crucial to the whole palinode, that philosophical reason is as natural as the passions and, still more strongly, that it *is* passionate. In Socrates' first speech, by contrast, it was argued that desire is natural and reason acquired.

The interpretation of immortality sketched in the preceding paragraphs—one I believe correctly represents the palinode's teaching on this score—in effect denies that soul and body are separate in the sense that the former can live without the latter. It points to a very close relationship between the two, even as it tells against a reduction of the one to the other. In the previous chapter I argued that at several junctures in the myth precisely such a relationship is implied (for example, in the reference at 246d8 to the proximity of the wings to the body; in the obvious connection of the horses to physiological desire, the horses being "naturally grown together" with the charioteer; in the description of recollection at 249b–c; in the physiological terms used to describe the pathos of love). Indeed, the very use of mythic language to describe the soul, such language being closely bound with sense perception (see below), suggests a similar point. The unease interpreters feel with the idea that the black horse is immortal along with the rest of the soul disappears once immortality is understood along the lines I have suggested.

By providing for a prelife and afterlife, the notion of immortality allows Socrates to say something about the origins of self-consciousness, the soul's natural suitableness for understanding the Truth and its alienation from this nature, and to do so in a way that suggests that the soul is not an acquisition of the body. Talk about the soul as immortal in its self-motion also lets Socrates indicate that soul is to be understood neither as an Idea nor as an instance of one. It would be an "altogether divine and long narrative" (as Socrates says) to put all this nonmythically. In short, the mythic formulations of this issue allow Socrates to make very complex points simply, elegantly, and economically. And this is why the translation of the myth's picture of immortality provided above—and the interpreter of a Platonic myth cannot avoid offering one translation or another—need not reduce myth to the status of extrinsic, dispensable rhetoric.

A reader generous enough to go along with this line of reasoning would nevertheless be justified in pushing some questions. If this is what Socrates meant by immortality, why did he not say so? Why did he not state at least a couple of the main points about immortality in nonmythic terms? Why did he rely wholly on mythic formulations? So far I seem to have gone along with the usual view that a Platonic myth is, in principle, *completely* translatable, the remainder of the myth being a matter of form, albeit elegant and economical form. This view, to repeat, is different from Phaedrus' reductionistic approach to myth. Yet it seems to provide only a weak rationale for myth.

WHY DOES SOCRATES USE MYTHS IN THE *PHAEDRUS?*

On the assumption that the palinode's myth is, of the *Phaedrus* myths, the discourse that is a "myth" in the paradigmatic and exemplary sense, I am going to confine my discussion to it. As argued in the previous chapter, the palinode is above all else a psycho-logy. *The* topic is the soul; the rest is brought in to the extent necessary to explain what the soul is (this is one reason very little is said about the nature of the hyperuranian beings; these are not even called Forms or Ideas). Self-knowledge and the use of myth here seem closely connected. But how?

To the extent that a discussion about soul must include a discussion about eros, particularly about the sort of eros directed toward another person, an answer seems available. Is not mythic language appropriate to desire and love? More specifically, is it not appropriate to articulating our *experience* of desire and love? As I noted in chapter 1, Socrates orients himself from the start toward human experience, refusing to rationalize myths about human beings in terms of subhuman principles or events (for example, materialistic ones). Our ordinary self-understanding serves as the basis and touchstones of our explanation of experience. An analysis of *what* we are cannot but proceed on the basis of our understanding of *who* we are. A myth, unlike a syllogism, has the capacity to act as a complex mirror in which people can recognize not just who they are but who they might become at their best. Platonic myth is a mirror that can not only reflect one's hopes but also seek to realize them. While it preserves contact with our ordinary self-understanding, it also deepens it. As already suggested, myth serves in this way a valuable function. In part, myth retains its tie to our ordinary self-understanding by constantly transposing the language that describes objects experienced through the senses to objects not accessible to the senses (such as the hyperuranian beings and the soul). This rootedness of the abstract in the concrete assumes, it seems, the interdependence of mind and body, of discourse and the senses, an interdependence implied in the myth itself (see above).

We understand ourselves at least in part as embodied, particular persons, possessing a world of inner experience. While the palinode's myth has a good deal to say about the soul as such, it also discourses in a way that depicts our individual experiences as embodied selves. In part this is accomplished by the heavy use of imagery, metaphor, and symbols in which the world revealed by the senses is transposed to the inner world of the soul. This poetic dimension of Platonic myth is lost when its contents are translated into the medium of abstract propositions and arguments. In holding up a mirror, the myth is *personal* in a distinctive way. Although the *Phaedrus* tries to show that self-knowledge must include discourse about the soul, it also insists that self-knowledge always return to the level of the individual.

The myth of the palinode provides us with a whole that both initiates and guides the commentary. It is like an eidos in the sense of shape or visible form, the "one" that inquiry both begins with and ends with. Even as it calls for philosophical reflection, a Platonic myth keeps the phenomenon of human experience in front of us. It preserves the shape or look of man as it attempts to explain what human nature is. It tells us what we are by telling us what we are like rather than by dissolving or reducing us into sub- or suprahuman principles.

Given the assumption that the sense of eros is to be uncovered and displayed with constant reference to the *Lebenswelt,* does not Socrates' mythic language in fact tell us what eros is? From the standpoint of the experience of love, in fact, the talk about the gods may be taken descriptively. Phenomenologically speaking, the lover may indeed feel that the beloved is godlike and that he himself ought to develop the seed of godlike perfection he feels is already present in him. Moreover, the language of myth (including the metaphoric mystery-cult idioms) is appropriate to articulating the experience of insight, as noted in the previous chapter. Socrates said that his eikon of the soul supplied a human form of discourse (246a5), and this is so not just in that the mythic form of discourse falls within the capacity of a man to utter but also in that it proceeds from within a human standpoint. The second half of the *Phaedrus* tells us that good rhetoric conveys the truth, that it both expresses the truth and expresses it *to* persons of suitable disposition so that they are led to think it to be true. In the present case, we are also trying to express what is true *of* these persons (or at least, potentially true of some of them). Although I do not know how one would *prove* to a skeptic that the palinode's myth does all this, it does seem to me (and I am scarcely alone in this) that the myth very nicely gives form to the dimension of eros that is at issue in the palinode. If this is a pedagogic justification of the use of myth, it is so in the sense of the term specified in the second half of the *Phaedrus*.

Another result achieved by the poetic imagery of the palinode's myth is the portrayal of the soul both *as a whole* and as a part of the larger Whole. No one who has read the myth can fail to retain a coherent picture of the soul, the cosmos, and the soul's place in it. The capacity of Socrates' well-composed imagery to convey a synoptic understanding of these issues would seem impossible to realize in the medium of bare analyses, arguments, propositions. Moreover, the picture of the winged charioteer and horses is both very simple and very complicated. The simplicity of the image allows the mind to see at once the soul as a whole; its complexity becomes apparent when one tries to interpret it, to draw out all its implications. This is a capacity of Socrates' mythic speech that does not seem translatable into a conceptual idiom. Given the objection sketched in the first part of this chapter to the possibility of stating coherently that a certain dimension of myth cannot in principle be accounted for, one may wonder how we are to demonstrate the view that the palinode's myth possesses an ability to convey a meaning as a whole that is lost when it is translated. The answer to the objection is, I think, just a comparison of what we understand when we read the myth and what we understand when we read an interpretation of it.

Moreover, Socrates said, in introducing the image of the soul's ἰδέα, that it is the "shorter" sort of speech (246a6). The image is meant to compress into a few words a long, perhaps endlessly long, commentary or psychology. As I suggested above, mythic speech can be an extraordinarily economical form of speech. The economy of myth is especially important because (as I have shown in previous chapters) Socrates wants to argue that the soul cannot be understood independently of its place in *the* Whole. Since refutation of the standpoint of the earlier two speeches requires a comprehensive description of the soul, Socrates must produce a speech that also describes the Whole. The vast expanses of time and space, of matter and form, must somehow be woven together with the account of the endlessly variegated and tangled experience of soul into a coherent picture.

If it is the case, as argued above, that there is no Idea of the soul, then myth seems all the more appropriate as a logos of the soul. This is so because myth, while capturing in words the whole of the soul, does not necessarily assume that the soul has an Idea-like essence. Indeed, the wholeness of the soul, as pictured in the myth, is perfectly compatible with the view that not all parts of the soul are forms (as is the case with the wings that represent eros), that the soul gains and loses its unity, that there is no form connecting the various parts or aspects of the soul. It is compatible with the fact that there is no logos of the soul's ousia independent of the multitude of pathe and erga the soul undergoes through its mythical history. With respect to expressing the soul's fluctuating wholeness (the fluctuations are due especially to the omnipresence and nature of eros in the soul), myth is superior to the method of division and collection Socrates goes on to formulate.

In the palinode, Socrates wants to explain the nature of the soul in terms that do not reify it, terms that articulate its nature in the context of the genesis of the soul's pathe and erga but that are not about historical development. Socrates does not want an anthropological story of the genesis of the soul out of the subhuman. Yet he wants to preserve the notion that soul has a nature. Myth is an ideal way to accomplish all this simultaneously. If the soul must be described as a process of motion, there being no Idea of this process, and if myth (allegory, simile, metaphor, and imagery being part of myth) is able simultaneously to convey the motion as a whole without committing itself to the view that the soul possesses a formal metaphysical nature of a certain sort, then myth is well suited to the psychology in question. I am suggesting, in sum, that given the particular notion of soul Socrates wishes to propose, myth is a reasonably good idiom.

I do not claim that any one of the points sketched thus far about the utility of myth, that is, discourse about the soul, is in and of itself enough to explain Socrates' use of myth, or that when taken together they justify it in some conclusive way.[10] Taken together they do, however, supply a plausible rationale for Socrates' use of myth. This rationale is inseparable from the self-knowledge problematic as it has been developed in the *Phaedrus*. A consequence of this argument is that the commentator cannot ever claim to have produced an interpretation of a myth (such as that in the *Phaedrus'* palinode) that exhausts the meaning of the myth and so allows us to dispense with it. The shape of things described in the myth needs to be seen; that shape is a primary phenomenon. At the same time, as I have said above, we are required to reflect on what we see and indeed on the difficult problem of articulating what we see (the latter has been a focus of this chapter). Pious observance of the literal meaning of the palinode's myth is unwarranted, as is an indifferent disregard of the rhetoric of myth.

Is not Socrates' mythic palinode, however, superhuman in its very comprehensiveness? Is this not at odds with the recognition of the limits of a man's knowledge which initiates the myth?

THE SELF-QUALIFICATION OF THE MYTH
AND THE TURN TO *TECHNE*

Socrates' palinodic myth is meant to produce a conception of the soul and the Whole within which it makes sense to be a philosopher. The earlier speeches rendered the love of wisdom unintelligible. Likewise, the discussion of techne does not provide a picture of things which legitimizes the love of wisdom. That discussion is remarkable, indeed, for the extraordinary *contraction* of the vast horizon of the palinode. Socrates' discussion becomes neutral with respect to the palinode precisely by ignoring, at least on the surface, its substantive teachings. The discussion of techne does not explicitly challenge the authority of the palinode (techne is not explicitly substituted for mythos), let alone submit the palinode to dialectical examination (cf. Socrates' treatment of Protagoras' myth in the *Prot.*). These are reasons the unity of the *Phaedrus* is puzzling. In the previous chapter I have already indicated, however, senses in which the problem of rhetoric is anticipated, and indeed established, by the palinode. The transition to the discussion of the techne of rhetoric must also be understood in terms of the self-qualification of the myth. As we shall see, this transition is philosophically revealing.

Socrates introduces the myth with the image of the soul, citing as a reason for doing so the necessity of speaking in a way that is human rather than divine. He thus begins the myth with a statement about the limitations of human cognition. This sophron start seems soon forgotten, since Socrates madly claims to say what no earthly poet ever has or ever will say (247c3–6). Although commentators like to think of Socrates' recitation of the palinode as inspired, with one rather ambiguous exception (265a5) Socrates never characterizes himself as such.[11] The sense in which the speech is both self-controlled and mad, both aware of its limits and forgetful of them, is more complex than is usually thought. To grasp fully the complexity of the problem we must keep in mind the sense in which the notion of limit can be a dialectical one. That is, every philosophical statement of the limitations of knowledge seems to presuppose knowledge of what one (ostensibly) does not know (this is at the root of the knowledge-of-ignorance paradox). The relevance of this point to the present discussion will become clear momentarily. Let me begin by specifying the sense in which the myth is inspired.

There is a gap between what the myth says and the telling of the myth, between its logos and its ergon. This fact is intrinsically connected to the fact that Socrates attempts to give a comprehensive account of the soul and that he does so monologically, all this being part and parcel of the fact that he is narrating a *myth*. According to the myth, the sort of knowledge accessible to fallen souls is anamnesis. We are told that to a limited extent people can recollect some of the hyperuranian beings and their god, though presently they are not able to see either of them directly. Now, everything that Socrates recounts in the myth cannot, according to the standards presented within the myth itself, be a product of anamnesis (even though at 250c Socrates does seem to suggest that his account of the divine was a memory). Socrates produces an account of things that, *according to the myth's own standard* (anamnesis), no human soul could possibly know. Socrates' comprehensive account far exceeds the scope of anamnesis (as the latter is described at 249b–c). Some of the things he speaks of, such as the nine categories of lives and the chronology of the soul's journeys, are not possible objects of recollection since they are not Ideas. In narrating the myth, Socrates goes beyond the grave and returns knowing all—an impossibility according to the myth itself.[12] A sure sign of this problem is Socrates' hubristic self-promotion to the rank of divine poet (247c). Still further, the myth suggests that recollection arises in the context of a passionate love affair between lover and beloved. Although Phaedrus plays the boy (243e, 252b2) of whom Socrates, as narrator of the palinode, is the courting lover, it is obvious that their relationship is not much like that described in the myth.[13]

The palinode is thus mad in the sense that if it is true the person narrating it could not know it is true (given the criteria for knowledge presented within the myth itself). The madness consists at least in part in the myth's lack of reflexivity and self-consciousness—a defect that characterizes the creations of ordinary poetic inspiration, too, as Socrates' criticisms of poetry in *Republic* X show.[14] The apodéixis in its totality is not self-grounding; in lacking philosophical self-possession, it lacks sophrosyne. It seems that the madness of the speech about erotic madness is not just erotic but also an amalgam of the other three kinds of mania. The speech about love is not mad in the same sense love is; yet it does seem to share with the madness of love (at least love in its initial stages) the lack of self-possession.

Because the palinode recommends a synthesis of madness and sophrosyne, it calls upon the reader to reflect on whether the palinode itself exhibits this synthesis. Initially, it does not seem to exhibit it. Ironically, the palinode thereby signals its own limitations as well as the necessity of progressing to a self-conscious discussion about logos—and this is precisely what occurs next in the *Phaedrus*. Differently put, the palinode itself calls for the broader reflection initiated by Socrates' prayer at the end of the speech for Phaedrus' conversion to philosophy. The prayer is in a sense external to the palinode; the prayer looks back on it *as* a speech directed to Phaedrus. The palinode is thereby considered as an example of rhetoric that is part of a dialogical context. By returning to the dramatic or dialectical level of the *Phaedrus,* in other words, we are compelled to think about the myth self-consciously and so to understand its limitations. This dialogical level thus functions here as a sort of metalevel that regulates the object-level speeches presented within it. By compelling this reflection, the palinode provides us with a lesson about the nature of philosophical sophrosyne and so about self-knowledge, thus combining, in a way, madness with sophrosyne.

The palinode, then, recants itself when we compare its ergon with its logos. As is the case with respect to the palinode's relation to the earlier two speeches, this recantation is not an outright cancelation or negation. Elements are preserved but also placed within a larger, more complete, more self-possessed context. In the following chapter I will spell out the sense in which the palinode continues to mold the discussion (I have already mentioned some ways in which it does so with respect to the theme of rhetoric).

This self-induced movement is what I have in mind in referring to the self-qualification of the myth (this qualification points to another sense in which the myth is a human, that is, limited, mode of speech). The movement expresses the dialectical nature of limit mentioned above. The myth's teaching marks off the limits of human knowledge and in so doing presupposes a standpoint beyond them. That standpoint in turn shows itself in the need for limitation, a limit realized by the turn from myth to techne. The dialectic fluctuates between madness and sobriety, and this suggests that in the final analysis the two cannot in practice be combined to the extent of making them identical. Yet this fluctuation is not a vicious circle, since there is a complex sense in which the palinode's teaching is preserved even as it is transcended. There *is* progress in the *Phaedrus*. It is not as though the palinode is just a wild, irrational, unprovable inspiration that can be left behind with a few compliments about its charming diction. The significance of dialogue as a striving to know the Ideas again, of the soul as self-motion, of reason as motivating the soul, and of the mirrorlike nature of self-knowledge becomes intelligible in terms of the palinode. But it seems that Socrates cannot, in a single monologue, simultaneously present all this *and* the grounds for it. In my interpretation of the *Phaedrus,* Socrates and, of course, Plato understand this, the result being that the putative incoherence of the *Phaedrus* is an intentionally generated step in the development of the self-knowledge theme.

This interpretation suggests that Plato does not think that it is possible fully to justify a comprehensive insight in the same logos in which that insight is articulated. This is equivalent to saying that Plato does not think that the insight can be separated from noetic madness. Since Plato is aware of this point, the use of monologic myth to articulate such an insight thus looks like a self-conscious decision on his part. That self-consciousness would itself be an example of philosophical sophrosyne, or self-conscious madness. On this level it is difficult to tell madness and sophrosyne apart. At the same time, however, the self-consciousness includes an awareness of the limitations of madness and so of the need to go on to talk about one's talk—which is what occurs next in the *Phaedrus*. Had the *Phaedrus* come to a close with the palinode, our evaluation of the relationship between madness and reason as they are exhibited by the myth would have been quite different.

The dialectic of the myth's self-limitation is the dialectic of self-knowledge. We are told by the myth that self-knowledge is both erotic madness and sophrosyne (though not of the merely "mortal" variety; 256e5); we are told indirectly by the myth's self-qualification that self-knowledge cannot simply be a sustained identification of madness with sophrosyne. Throughout, we are given to understand that self-knowledge is (among other things) the effort of knowledge to ground itself, take hold of itself, be self-conscious; self-knowledge is *reflection*. But as a search for grounds that knows its own ignorance it simultaneously exhibits a synthesis of madness and sophrosyne (for example, in the form of a monologue, mythic or not, or a series of comprehensive images, or prophecies and guesses— all of which are common in the Platonic dialogues) and a dissolution of the synthesis (and so the need for further search for a more comprehensive and reflexive logos). The two "moments" here, namely, mania and sophrosyne, were present in debased form in Lysias' speech in the personae of the lover and nonlover. The doctrine of the concealed lover in Socrates' first speech showed the impossibility of separating reason and desire. Now, on a much higher level, their problematic relationship has become clearer. The prophetic insight of the enthusiastic narrator (of the lover of recollected truth) that produced the myth cannot express itself to the satisfaction of the self-possessed speaker (the nonlover), *but the lover and the nonlover are functions of the same soul:* on the one hand, the silent but elevating, indeed soaring, desire for a comprehensive and beautiful mythos about the soul; on the other, a desire for detached analysis, for logos, feet firmly on the ground. Both desires animate the philosopher's soul. The drastic turn midway through the *Phaedrus* illustrates the problem of the relationship between madness and sophrosyne in a particularly shocking, but also illuminating, way. The disunity of the *Phaedrus* thus has, among its philosophical purposes, that of stating a genuine philosophical difficulty.[15]

As we shall see, the *Phaedrus* does offer a medium within which the seemingly antithetical elements of madness and sophrosyne can be combined to some extent. This medium is dialectic (dialegesthai). The myth threatened to charm us by means of its beauty; the discussion about techne, to which I will turn momentarily, embodies the equally powerful charm of technical competence. These potential poisons are transformed into remedies when they are regulated by dialectic. That myth is meant to be supplemented by dialectic is suggested by the remark that precedes the Theuth/Thamus story (274c1–3); indeed, Socrates and Phaedrus do go on to examine dialectically the content of that myth. After the conclusion of the palinode, we are treated to a call for dialogue (258d7 ff., though the call is immediately cast in the form of another myth!), and after Socrates' first speech we hear a similar appeal (242a6). Dialogue is something Socrates and Phaedrus produce out of themselves and through their own efforts. The monologue (Lysias' speech) and all the myths in the *Phaedrus* (including Socrates' first speech), by contrast, are said to have a source external to Socrates and Phaedrus.

The palinode's final teaching about philosophical madness is a teaching not just about the madness of true (erotic) moderation but about the moderation of madness. The indirectness with which this point is made is a form of irony. We have here several levels of meaning among which there exists a tension. A difficulty with the first level, that of the myth itself (what the myth says, as it were) manifests itself when this level is seen as part of a larger context (in terms of *who* is doing the speaking, for example). The disparity between the two (between the logos and ergon) suggests the deeper meaning intended all along. The notion that Socrates' philosophical myths and his irony are akin has already been suggested by Friedländer.[16] The quasi-structural use of irony exhibited by the self-qualification of the myth and the surface disunity of the *Phaedrus* has the advantage of suggesting that the necessity for movement forward from the palinode is immanent in the palinode itself. Indeed, two components of irony—the presence of a meaning "beyond" the obvious one and the tension between these two levels of meaning—seem, as H. Gundert has pointed out, to be very much like enthusiasm or madness itself.[17] As ironic, Socrates' enthusiastic speech contains a third element, namely, the requirement that the speaker (and auditor) become self-conscious about his own presuppositions. The "beyond" turns out to be near at hand, though still elusive.

Finally, by means of the complex construction of the dialogue Plato is able to communicate to the reader an equally complicated thesis about the nature of philosophical self-knowledge. The interpretation of the unity of the *Phaedrus* that I am outlining (I will say more about it in chapter 5) is warranted in principle by the interpretive maxim outlined in the Introduction to this book, and specifically by the fact that it leads us to a coherent and fruitful understanding of the dialogue's unity that is consistent with the details of the text. The alternatives are either to hold that the dialogue is just massively incoherent and the palinode simply self-contradictory, and to leave it at that, or to produce some other explanation that assumes that the apparent disunity and incoherencies are intentional.

In sum: reflection on the question of myth in the *Phaedrus* brings us back to the question of self-knowledge with respect to Socrates' interpretive approach to myth (myth is valuable as a means to self-knowledge and can be translated accordingly), the reasons for *using* myth (the wholeness issue, among others), and the reasons for progressing beyond it (the self-qualification issue). The self-qualification of the myth also establishes the limitations of our self-knowledge. Reflection on the question of myth and on the development of the *Phaedrus* generates *knowledge of ignorance*. And this knowledge, we are given to see, is part and parcel of self-knowledge.[18]

5

Rhetoric

No man knows, or ever will know, the truth about the gods
and about everything I speak of: for even if one chanced to
say the complete truth, yet oneself knows it not; but fancy is
wrought in the case of all men.
XENOPHANES [1]

THE UNITY OF THE *PHAEDRUS:*
FURTHER REFLECTIONS

With the termination of Socrates' great palinode, the *Phaedrus* is only half finished. Since the palinode is itself only a step in a larger dialogue, we would expect that it would now become a subject of discussion. Yet beyond being used at one point as a paradigm of formally correct speech, this does not occur. This is part of what is meant by the famous "problem of the unity of the *Phaedrus*." The problem is also caused by the sudden shift in the style and tone of the dialogue; roughly speaking, the enthusiastic and erotic idiom of the first half seems replaced by a detached and analytic idiom. Thus at least on the surface the two halves of the dialogue seem to stand to each other as the lover did to the nonlover in the prepalinodic speeches of the *Phaedrus*. Furthermore, there seems to be a change in topic: we hear virtually nothing more about eros and instead hear a lot about rhetoric, a theme that was barely even explicit in the first half of the dialogue. The palinode over, we come tumbling down from the heights to the more familiar earth—to the level of Phaedrus, in effect.

The stark contrast between the two levels is also evident when we compare the "immortality" a successful "rhetorician or king" achieves (258c1–2) with the "immortality" spoken of in the palinode (so closely linked to knowledge of the hyperuranian beings). So too with the "equal to god" epithet (258c2), which was used in the palinode to describe the way in which the beloved is treated by a self-controlled lover. Moreover, the beauty of speeches is initially thought of by Phaedrus in a way that shows that Beauty Itself has been forgotten. Finally, the first half of the *Phaedrus* is dominated by speeches or monologues, whereas the second half is dominated by dialogue, and this change also contributes to the problem of unity. In chapter 4 I have already given some reasons for my view that the problem of the unity of the *Phaedrus* is intelligible in terms of the self-knowledge issue. I would like to spell this thesis out further.

The immediate blame for the discontinuity of the *Phaedrus* may be put on Phaedrus, who, as Socrates' respondent, certainly had the option of raising some questions about the palinode. Phaedrus' response is, instead, quite pitiful. He says only that he finds the speech more beautiful than the previous one and that he is afraid Lysias will not be able to match it. This is a weaker response than that which Phaedrus originally felt toward Lysias' speech. Yet Phaedrus seems to have progressed a bit: Socrates' incredible rhetorical powers have made Phaedrus wonder whether Lysias really is the ablest writer of the day after all (cf. 228a1–2). Hence Phaedrus refers here (for the second and last time) to Socrates as "thaumasie" (257c5; cf. 230c6).

Yet because Phaedrus is responsible for the turn the dialogue named after him now takes, he may also be said to supply the solution at the dramatic level to the problem of its unity. As just indicated, Phaedrus views the palinode simply as a piece of rhetoric in a very narrow, formal sense of the term (Phaedrus ignores *what* is said in the speech). This is in character for Phaedrus. Since Socrates still wishes to talk with him, the discussion shifts to the topic of rhetoric. Phaedrus fathers yet another logos. As we saw in chapter 1, Phaedrus is extremely interested in beautiful speeches (especially when they are about eros understood from a certain standpoint), of which he considers Lysias' speech an example. Socrates used this passion to seduce Phaedrus into listening to some more philosophical, and so more beautiful, speeches. Socrates thereby engaged in a contest of rhetoric with Lysias. The combination of Phaedrus' character and Socrates' desire to converse with Phaedrus (a desire I discussed at length in chapter 1) ensured that rhetoric was an implicit theme from the start of the dialogue; and together with Phaedrus' poor reaction to the palinode, all this ensures that rhetoric will become an explicit theme. In chapter 1 I tried to explain Socrates' desire to talk to Phaedrus on the basis of Socrates' desire for self-knowledge. In that sense (as well as others

I will specify in a moment) the self-knowledge theme continues to underlie the twists and turns of the *Phaedrus*.

Still further, there is an obvious connection between rhetoric and eros. The connection is exhibited not just by Socrates' relationship to Phaedrus but by that of the nonlover and beloved of Lysias' speech, of the concealed lover and beloved of Socrates' first speech, and of the erotic madman and boy of the palinode. The connection is, simply, that the desire to seduce requires rhetoric, whether one's purpose is to lead one's beloved into philosophy or into a sexual relationship. In the second part of the *Phaedrus*, rhetoric is defined as the art of leading the soul through words. This definition makes explicit the connection between eros and logos exhibited throughout the first part. The rhetorician, that is, is a lover in that he attempts to lead the soul of his beloved (his audience) to a mutually desired goal.[2] Indeed, Socrates now argues that to lead effectively the rhetorician must possess a techne of speech, and in this respect the effective lover-rhetorician must be a nonlover (more on this below).

Having said all this, however, there is still a problem in understanding the unity of the *Phaedrus*. It remains a fact that there is a sudden shift in style and tone here, as well a turn to questions of method and techne from questions about eros, hyperuranian beings, and so on. More needs to be said about the connection between the explicit themes of the first half of the dialogue and those of the second. Let us do so by starting with the conversation that immediately follows the palinode.

Phaedrus gives initial direction to the discussion by remarking that a politician recently attacked Lysias for being a speech writer (logographos), and that Lysias, desiring to preserve his reputation, might cease writing as a result (and so might not compete with Socrates' palinode). For great writers are "ashamed," Phaedrus says, to leave behind their compositions lest at a later time they be called sophists (257c–d). As Socrates' reply soon makes clear, politicians are themselves speech writers (Socrates expands the meaning of "logographos" by taking the word literally); they shame others into not writing though they do the same thing and for the same reasons (desire for reputation and power). The notion of shame thus continues to play an important role in the dialogue. In an almost prophetic manner, Phaedrus connects rhetoric, politics, sophists, writing, honor, and popular appeal. All these are ingredients, as it turns out, of non-philosophical or shameful rhetoric.

Socrates seizes this opportunity to try, once again, to make Phaedrus understand the defects of his conception of beautiful discourse. Socrates does this by phrasing the main question here in terms Phaedrus can understand immediately: when is a discourse composed shamefully and when beautifully (258d)? This question, the answer to which is withheld until the end of the *Phaedrus* (274b6 ff.), will be preceded by another one that is closely related to Phaedrus' interest in both the form of speeches and the power of their beauty. When is rhetoric artful and when does it lack art? This latter question occupies, roughly speaking, the first section of this half of the *Phaedrus* (257c–274b), and the former question the second ection (from 274b–end). They are related as is techne to telos. By "techne" Socrates means here an intellectual procedure (which he compares to the art of medicine) that involves a determinate sequence of steps (first do this, then that, and so on), that operates on complexes of elements via division and collection, that is a means to a goal, and that is teachable. Techne is value free in the sense that qua techne it is not knowledge of how its objects (or possibly products) should be used. The art of casting bronze does not include the knowledge of whether it is better to cast tripods or spear tips, or of what those objects should be used for. Similarly the art of rhetoric, as Socrates will soon say explicitly, can be used to lead to the truth or away from it; nothing in the knowledge of the art informs the technician as to which of these ends ought to be pursued. Arts have a delimited material they work on or with (in the case of the art of rhetoric, this material is the soul and discourse, respectively). The art of division and collection (of which the art of rhetoric turns out to be only a subdivision), however, is extraordinarily comprehensive. It is presented in the *Phaedrus* as capable of being applied to anything, including other arts (see below). Socrates thus uses the word "techne" interchangeably with "methodos."[3] Although the internal structure of the second half of the *Phaedrus* is much less clear than that of the first, this diairesis between techne and telos does help make explicit the organization of the second half. The joint connecting them is the Theuth/Thamus myth. Speaking and writing are not distinguished until the telos of discourse is considered (in the section on techne, they are sometimes referred to together, sometimes not, as though it were a matter of indifference). Philosophical dialogue is not equivalent to technical discourse—a point crucial, as we shall see, to understanding the status of the art of division and collection (265d–266b) and of the epistemic method of thinking which is based on division and collection (270c ff.).

Socrates' strategy at this stage is to try to get Phaedrus to see that the problem of rhetoric is an extremely broad one. As already mentioned, Socrates first convinces Phaedrus that politicians in composing laws and submitting resolutions are also acting like speech writers. Socrates concludes from this ad hominem argument that writing per se is not shameful

(258d1–2). Should the politician be persuasive, he gains great power and prestige and even a sort of immortality among men, since he is thought to be "equal to god." Should he fail to persuade, then he and his friends leave the stage of the "theater" of politics (258b–c). In other words, the discourse of politics is rhetoric.

Having placed the nature of rhetoric on this broad political level, Socrates goes still further. The question "when is writing shameful and when beautiful?" is to be raised with respect to all those "who have written or shall write, whether in the field of public affairs or private, whether in the verse of the poet or in the plain speech of prose" (258d7–11). After recounting the cicada story, Socrates proceeds to get Phaedrus to agree that rhetoric is present wherever and whenever men speak (261d10–e4 and context), and not just in a political context. As Socrates also puts this extraordinarily comprehensive definition of rhetoric: rhetoric is the "art of leading souls through words, not only in law courts and other public gatherings, but also in private ones too, the same art being concerned with both small and great issues, its correct employment commanding no more respect when dealing with important matters than with unimportant ones" (261a7–b2). This is an indication that logos itself is to be understood as being fundamentally rhetorical (hence at 271c10 we hear that "the dynamis of logos is psychagogia"). Phaedrus emphatically declares that this is not what he has heard about rhetoric, and he obviously believes what he has been told (261b3–5)—though if he were right in limiting rhetoric to the law courts and assemblies, the first three speeches of the *Phaedrus* could not be counted as examples of rhetoric. Rhetoric is eventually shown to include dialectic, and once the ends of rhetoric are considered (in the Theuth/Thamus story and subsequent passages), it becomes clear that philosophical dialogue is the perfection of rhetoric.

That is, the second half of the *Phaedrus* is a voyage from a narrowly and politically defined conception of rhetoric to a much more comprehensive, and for Socrates paradigmatic, conception. It is a voyage from the cave of the polis up to the pure realm of dialectic, and in this respect it is analogous to the first half of the *Phaedrus* in which we went from a narrowly defined conception of eros to a comprehensive and paradigmatic view of the matter. The second half of the dialogue thus seems to parallel the first half. This thesis is confirmed by a number of other observations. The passage from the end of the palinode through the story of the cicadas reminds us of the start of the *Phaedrus* in several respects (in chapter 6 I will add to my comments of chapter 3 about the relationship between the end of the *Phaedrus* and the palinode). The cicadas were mentioned in Socrates' encomium to nature (230c2); Socrates now adverts again to the spring Ilissus (259a6); further, the heat of the day and the comfort of the body are issues both now and at the start of the *Phaedrus*. Thus we have here a kind of return to nature. Just as the theme of leisure was brought up at 227b9–11, so it is now at 258e6. As much of the discussion then centered around Lysias and his speech making, so too now. Phaedrus' mad passion for discourses is once again emphasized (258e1–5). Then the issue of Socrates' attitude toward myths arose, and he claimed that he did not care about their literal truth or origins, although, as we saw, he did want to use them for self-knowledge. Now Socrates makes up a myth to encourage Phaedrus to philosophize about the objects of his desires (beautiful speeches), and so to know himself.

Moreover, the return to the first half of the *Phaedrus* is emphasized by the reference to the Muses (259b–d), for they figured prominently in the genesis of Socrates' first speech. Indeed at 262d2–6 Socrates suggests that the local gods, or the prophets of the Muses (the cicadas), are responsible for his first speech and Lysias' speech. This clue to the structure of the *Phaedrus* is important. The reference to the Muses heralds a discussion that is strikingly similar to Socrates' first speech. There are crucial parallels between the emphasis in that speech on "agreement," "definition," and generally the whole "methodological" nature of "clear" thinking, and the similar emphasis in the first section of the second half of the *Phaedrus* on the same issues (on techne, in short). Indeed, the tone of this section resembles that of Socrates' first speech, and the general orientation here cannot but recall that of the nonlover of Lysias' and Socrates' first speeches. The astonishing disappearance, in the first section of the second half of the *Phaedrus* (the section on techne), of the vocabulary and propositions of the palinode (virtually all of which are omitted even in Socrates' formal analysis of the palinode) confirm that we have, in a sense, regressed to the ontological level of Socrates' first speech. And just as a palinode was needed then (as Socrates warned at the start of his palinode, the servant of the Muses who pours out song [*ode*] on the basis of techne alone is bound to fail; 245a), so now a retraction of the dominance of techne will be required. The retraction occurs in the form of another myth (the Theuth/Thamus myth), in which the matter of the *ends* of life (and so the issue of anamnesis) is again discussed. Socrates' first speech played the role of intermediary between the other two. Correspondingly, its emphasis on orderly, rule-governed thinking occupied an intermediate position between the self-interested calculations of Lysias' speech and the reasonable madness of the palinode. So too now, the techne of thinking is pedagogically useful because it is inferior to philosophic rhetoric but superior to merely popular rhetoric. The Theuth/Thamus myth and ensuing discussion stand to the discussion of techne as the palinode stands to Socrates' first speech.

Thus, in addition to this parallelism between the two halves of the dialogue, or rather because of it, the transition from the first half of the dialogue to the second looks like a regression, a step backward to an ontological level that preceded that of the palinode. This is true only up to a point, however, for we are now in a position to grasp technical thinking *as* less elevated than the anamnesis described in the palinode. Moreover, the present discussion of techne builds upon the palinode and leads us to a new discussion of dialectic. Thus the parallelism of structure and the consequent regression do not entail repetition; the sun is passing overhead, and much has transpired since its rising. Moreover, there is another sense in which the turn to rhetoric and techne represents progress beyond the level of the palinode. I have already discussed this sense in the "Excursus" on myth. The main point can be restated as follows.

In my interpretation of the palinode I argued that recollection would certainly include the understanding of wholes of discou.se and that the palinode's answer to the question "when is a discourse composed beautifully?" would be: when it is recollective of Beauty. Yet discourse was barely mentioned in the palinode, and both beauty and anamnesis were conceived of primarily in visual terms. We were thus left without a clear understanding of what sort of philosophical discourse would qualify as recollective. We were left wondering just how an erotically mad philosopher would go about philosophizing. Indeed, the palinode itself cannot be an example of recollection; reflection on its status as a logos, and so (as we now learn) as an example of rhetoric, is therefore required. This is the "self-qualification" discussed in the "Excursus." The fall from the end of the palinode to the start of the second half of the *Phaedrus* is dialectical in the sense that the palinode *on its own grounds* requires us to go beyond it. We need, then, to talk about talking, and this is precisely what occurs next. This turn gives the discussion a certain metalevel abstractness, an air of detachment, distance, reflection, and self-consciousness. The use of the method of analysis Socrates goes on to delineate demands the self-conscious awareness that in order to reach a given goal one must take a determinate series of steps. Like nonlovers who discuss eros objectively and critically, Socrates and Phaedrus now talk about the speeches about eros (as well as about discoursing in general) in a relatively sober and uninspired manner. We are treated to speech (dialogue) about speaking (the method of division and collection) about speeches (the discourses earlier in the *Phaedrus*). To understand the sense in which the palinode retracts itself, in sum, it is necessary to perform what amounts to a metaphilosophical reflection, and this sort of reflection is naturally focused on matters of procedure and method, and therefore on our language. This kind of reflection is one dimension of *self-knowledge* in that it is an effort to understand how the soul understands things.

I have spoken about the sense in which the second half of the dialogue parallels the first, as well as the sense in which it both regresses and progresses from it. It is also necessary to say more about the sense in which the two halves are continuous. I have already pointed out how Phaedrus himself, along with Socrates' desire to converse with him, provides a sort of continuity. I also argued in my treatment of the palinode that the *problem* of rhetoric was defined in the myth. Indeed, the demand, repeatedly stressed in the present section of the *Phaedrus,* that good rhetoric be ad hominem and a leading of the soul, seems to presuppose the palinode's thesis that the soul's nature is self-motion. In order to induce a soul to do or think this or that, one must appeal to that soul in terms of the values that move it. The palinode's view of the soul, the cosmos, and Being supplies a framework, not available when Socrates delivered his first speech, in terms of which techne (as well as rhetoric) can be placed at its proper level. In this way the palinode is not so much superseded as worked out further. Its formulation of the terms of the problem of self-knowledge is preserved by the direction the discussion now takes as it attempts a solution of the problem. The palinode seems to determine not just that a further retraction must be undertaken but also what kind of retraction must occur. The parallelism and regression spoken of above are called for by the palinode and so are dialectical consequences of it. This is key to the *Phaedrus'* unity. The chronology of the *Phaedrus* nicely captures the various dimensions of this unity as I have just adumbrated them: the sun now begins its long *descent,* yet a descent that *completes* the visible portion of its *periodos.* At the end of the day it is lower, and yet farther along, than it is at midday (which is where we are at the conclusion of the palinode).

As I have indicated, the self-knowledge theme is the key to understanding the *Phaedrus'* typhonic unity. On the dramatic level, Socrates' desire to converse with Phaedrus stems from his desire for self-knowledge. The self-qualification of the palinode arises out of the demand for self-knowledge in a metaphilosophical sense. The importance of the theme of rhetoric is established in the palinode, that is, in a myth about the soul, and in close connection (as I argued in chapter 3) with the whole problem of a fallen soul's self-knowledge. And the praise of dialectic (particularly of dialogical rhetoric) will make sense, as we will see, in terms of Socrates' desire for self-knowledge as well as of the difficulties, set out by the palinode, of attaining it. Thus the various dramatic, structural, and thematic threads of the dialogue's unity harmonize with one another perfectly. Their complex interaction creates the *Phaedrus'* difficult, but beautiful, dialectic of self-knowledge.

I would like to turn now to the cicada story, the discussion of which will confirm the remarks I have made thus far about the unity of the *Phaedrus*. The remainder of this chapter deals with the cicada story (258e6–259d9); the problem of rhetoric (259e1–262c4); division, collection, and the paradigms of rhetoric (262c5–266c5); and the manuals, the masters of the techne, and the five descriptions of the method of knowing and of psychagogia (266c6–274b5). A recapitulation closes my discussion.

THE CICADA STORY (258e6–259d9)

Robin justly refers to this story as the "pivot du *Phèdre*."[4] The story takes place at high noon (259a2, a6, d8), the halfway mark; this is a time of the most intense light and clarity, and yet also of the greatest danger of "darkness at noon." Correspondingly, the story is ambiguous in its meaning. It is occasioned by Phaedrus' enthusiastic exclamation that life would not be worth living without the pleasures of discourse, for unlike those of the body, they contain no pain and hence are not "slavish." Transcendence of and freedom from the body was an important theme in the palinode. But Phaedrus replaces the noetic contemplation of the hyperuranian beings with the painless activity of listening to beautiful discourses. It is true, as I remarked above, that for fallen souls discourse is necessary for recollection of the Beings. The problem is to determine *how* we are to talk in order to fulfill the palinode's aims. For Phaedrus pure pleasure is freedom; he does not understand that painful philosophical labor is required to answer the question at stake. That is, as I remarked in chapter 1, Phaedrus does not particularly care for the exigencies of Socratic dialogue.

The cicada story is in part a warning to Phaedrus about the dangers of a drugged mind, and in part it turns our attention from the political goal of the cultivation of honor among men to that of pleasing the Muses. But whereas earlier the cicada choir was innocently sweet (230c2–3), now its charm is Siren-like and menacing, an invitation to deadly sedation. Our innocent pleasure lost, for safety we must now secure ourselves with laborious "dialogue" (a term Socrates mentions several times at 259a). We must be able to imitate the "dialogue" of the cicadas (259a1), but in such a way as to resist being lulled by their humming. The cicadas, who in the story are the representatives of the Muses, report back to them (including those of philosophy—Calliope and Urania—according to Socrates) about who among men has honored them. Presumably those who pass the cicadas' test are those who at the very least are not lulled into sleep, that is, those who can resist the cicadas' charms. On the one hand, there is slavelike sleep, thoughtlessness, poisonous beauty of song, the oppressiveness of the sun's heat, nature that is no longer simply good in its beauty, a test for leisured souls, and on the other, wakefulness, awareness of a danger, a question about the true beauty of artful discourse that leads to self-conscious talk about techne and method.

The cicadas used to be men in an age preceding the advent of the Muses. When the Muses came to be, some of these men were so struck by the pleasure of song *(ode)* that they went on singing and utterly forgot to nourish themselves, to the point that they died without realizing it (259b6 ff.). As in the Boreas/Oreithuia story, a tale about love turns into a tale about death. Presumably the human race has survived because some men resisted the charm of the Muses; perhaps they felt the need to analyze, or at least talk about, the magic worked on them by the Muses. As we already learned in the first half of the *Phaedrus,* eros requires the dianoia and sophrosyne of the nonlover if it is to escape self-destruction. Phaedrus is referred to here as a "lover of the Muses" (259b5), and as we have just seen, he is dedicated to the pleasure of discourse unmixed with the pains and pleasure of the body. The "prize" awarded the precicadic men was not just to become cicadas but to have no need of food or drink (259c2–6), that is, to be free from bodily pains and pleasures (cf. *Symp.* 191c1–2; the cicadas generate by spilling their seed onto the earth). We thus cannot avoid comparing Phaedrus to the men who were enthralled by the Muses, entranced by the pleasure of song, forgetting themselves to the extent of ignoring nourishment. Undoubtedly Phaedrus expects that the question of rhetoric will itself be discussed through long speeches. Surely Socrates is suggesting that Phaedrus is altogether too apt to lose himself in the pleasure of listening to odes he finds charming (such as Lysias' speech and perhaps Socrates' speeches as well). The sleep Socrates warns against corresponds to the death of those precicadic men; both are easy to fall into without noticing it. The mind dies or falls asleep when it fails to remember or take hold of itself; and this self-consciousness is to be achieved, Socrates suggests, through dialogue. Otherwise Phaedrus and Socrates risk degenerating into cicada-like creatures whose "dialogue" or "singing" (258e6–259a1) is no longer rational discourse or recollective thinking.[5]

If this interpretation is correct, then the song that preceded the death of the precicadic men corresponds to the speeches that precede the sleep now threatening Socrates and Phaedrus. Since we have just heard a "mythical hymn" (as Socrates calls the palinode at 265c1; cf. 247c4) that was compared to Stesichorus' "palin-ode" (Stesichorus, the "musical" poet; 243a6), an ode that was beautiful and pleasurable to hear, we can hardly avoid thinking that Socrates is indirectly telling us here something about his second speech. Indeed, at the start of his first speech Socrates called on the sweet-sounding Muses' song (*ode*) to assist him in his tale,[6] and at 262d1–6 he suggests that the cicadas singing overhead were the cause of his first speech (as well as that of Lysias). If we were to take both of Socrates' speeches as one (Socrates himself will soon do so), the implication is that both of Socrates' speeches are the song of a Muse-inspired, precicadic man. And after having heard so much in the palinode about a divine banquet and the food that truly nourishes the soul, we must wonder: did Socrates' songs, however beautiful, somehow fall short of nourishing the soul? Are they, in other words, somehow lacking in knowledge and truth (recall the nourishing "plain of truth" at 248b5–c2), causing us to "die" without noticing it?

In my discussion of the nature of myth, I argued that the palinode could not have been spoken by Socrates with the knowledge that it is true (given the standards of the palinode itself for knowledge). The self-qualification of Socrates' monologic palinode is an effort, in effect, to avoid the fate of the precicadic men. Correspondingly, not just dialogue but dialogue about how to speak and think follows the story. The moral of the cicada story applies not just to Phaedrus but also at a deeper level to Socrates. The deficiency in question is remedied by dialogue and the turn to method and techne formulated within its course. Thus the cicada story provides us with a confirmation of my earlier remarks about the unity of the *Phaedrus*.

Socrates brings the cicada story to a close by remarking that they should attempt to honor Calliope, the eldest of the Muses, as well as Urania, for these are the patronesses of philosophy, and theirs is the most beautiful music whose "theme is the heavens and all the story of the divine and human" (259d3–7). That music sounds very much like the palinode, in which the heavens and the doings of gods and men were discussed. The palinode also discussed erotic matters, of course, and came to a close with a prayer to Eros. Thus it is odd that Socrates now says that those who "worshiped in the rites of love" honor Erato and that he does not try to associate that Muse with philosophy (259d1–2 and context). Are we to honor philosophy in a way that excludes eros (for example, by defining philosophy simply as the method of division and collection)? Given what I have said above, it would seem strange that Socrates would recommend that he and Phaedrus continue to try to please the Muses at all.[7] As just noted, however, the Muses are explicitly associated by him with his first speech, a speech that exhibited the techne of speaking but not truth (262d1–6). The Muses were capable of inspiring deceitful as well as true speech, forgetfulness as well as rememb rance.[8] The techne of rhetoric that Socrates is about to articulate can be used for deceit as well as for conveying the truth.

In sum, the reference in the cicada passage to the Muses seems to me to suggest the following: the section of the *Phaedrus* that unrolls between the cicada and Theuth/Thamus stories is meant to avoid the un-self-consciousness of Phaedrus and of the precicadic men (who died without noticing it and then found themselves reduced to a lower species), as well as of the beautiful monologic palinode. At the same time, this section will not proceed at the highest possible level. Its results, and in particular the implicit equation of philosophical dialectic with techne, resemble Socrates' Muse-inspired first speech in important ways. In that respect Socrates and Phaedrus continue to honor the Muses. The doctrine of techne will itself need to be qualified by the consideration of telos, a consideration introduced in the Theuth/Thamus story. Correspondingly, just before narrating that story, and just after summarizing once again the techne of rhetoric, Socrates remarks that one should speak in a way that is pleasing to the gods rather than to men (273e7, 274b9). He does not mention the Muses; unlike them, the gods are (as the palinode suggests) "the best and from the best" (274a2; cf. 246a8).

THE PROBLEM OF RHETORIC (259e1–262c4)

In the cicada story we heard a good deal about sound, about singing both in the usual sense and in the metaphoric sense relevant to logos. The turn to logos from the primarily visual metaphors of the palinode is part of the turn to the problem of rhetoric. The question with which Socrates begins the investigation of rhetoric is a surprising one: does not a beautiful *(kalos)* discourse presuppose a knowledge in the speaker's mind (dianoia) of the truth of the matters discoursed about? Needless to say, this is not the ordinary view: the only thing that matters to one who wishes to persuade the crowd is what they opine to be just and good and noble and the like, not what is so in truth. Socrates immediately casts doubt on this popular view by pointing to a situation in which deeds speak louder than words. Regardless of what the crowd is persuaded of, someone who rides a donkey instead of a horse into battle is going to pay a heavy price (260b). Socrates aptly quotes (260a5) part of a line from *Iliad* II. 361, which illustrates the relationship between rhetoric and the truth in the context of war.[9] There is a hint here of a pragmatic argument for the connection between rhetoric and truth; if you want to stay alive, you had better be able to tell the difference between true and deceptive rhetoric.

Socrates draws an analogy: just as an orator and his audience who ignorantly talked themselves into believing that a donkey is a horse would be "laughable" (and in a war, dead as well), so too if they became persuaded that what is really evil is good (and vice versa). In their actions, they would make asses of themselves; they would harvest a poor crop from the seeds of ignorance (260c). The claim being made here is a complex one. Certainly Socrates is not making the contrary-to-fact claims that the speaker of just rhetoric will not be laughable to the many, that the actions taken as the result of such rhetoric will necessarily be profitable or will save lives (consider the circumstances of Socrates' own demise), or that rhetoric based on truth is per se persuasive. When we consider the matter in the context of the *Phaedrus* as a whole, it becomes clear that Socrates is claiming that actions undertaken in the mistaken belief that what is evil is good will at the very least cause the actors to destroy what capacity for virtue and happiness their souls possess. The seeding/harvesting metaphor comes up again at the end of the dialogue, with reference to the dialectician and his follower (276b ff.), a private relationship analogous to that of the lover and beloved in the palinode. The *Phaedrus* as a whole also suggests that true virtue is not available to the "masses" (260c9). And this points to the political dimension of the art of rhetoric. Although one who knows the truth may not be able to persuade the masses unless he possesses the art of rhetoric (260d3–9), he may not be able to persuade them of the *truth* even if he *does* possess the art. Still further: the truth-knowing rhetorician, especially if he *writes,* will address a mélange of people, some of whom can and many of whom cannot understand the truth. Thus his rhetoric must be ad hominem and, in this case, capable of moving on several levels at once. He must also dissuade the nonphilosopher from doing wrong, including wrong to him.

The art of rhetoric is meant to supply rules for accomplishing *part* of this complex task. It is important to see, however, that one could possess this art but *not* the truth about the facts (*ta onta;* 260d8). It is hardly the case that the artful rhetorician cannot be persuasive unless he knows the truth of the matters about which he discourses. Moreover, Socrates cannot seriously hold that the rhetoricians cannot be persuasive unless they possess the art (though he implies that the leading rhetoricians do not possess the art). This assertion is disproven by the fact that the nontechnical rhetoricians *do* persuade. As Socrates later acknowledges, they "know all about the soul but keep their knowledge hidden" (271c2–3). Socrates does not even say that to be artful the rhetorician must speak the truth. Indeed, the man who possesses the art of speech can make the same thing appear *either* just or unjust as he wishes (261c10–d1). He can make anything seem like anything else, within the limits of possible comparison (261e2–3; the limits are, presumably, determined by the gullibility of the audience). Socrates alludes to Zeno's dialectical displays, which, despite their logical sophistication (and *so* their persuasiveness to a certain audience), exemplify the power of artful rhetoric to proceed without bothering with the question of truth (261d). The possessor of the art can even expose the attempts of others to do the same thing (261e3–4). This point introduces an elenchic element into the art, but at the price of expanding it so much that Socrates adds the qualifying "if it is an art" (261e2).

Socrates goes on to explain that people are misled when they are led step by small step from X to ~X (262a; at *Rep.* 487b–c Socrates is accused of doing something similar). It is at this point that Socrates connects the art of rhetoric with the need for the rhetoricians' knowledge of the truth, and the connection is made thanks to a proviso that confirms my remarks so far. In order to *deceive* one's audience, one might tell them that X is Y, though one actually believes that X is Z (and it is important that Socrates speaks here of deception, not just error). Unfortunately, it is possible to deceive others while also being deceived oneself—hence the crucial proviso (repeated twice) that the artful rhetorician must know the truth *if he is himself to avoid being deceived* (262a5–7, b7). One ought to avoid persuading oneself of what seems to be true, not in order that one might possess the art of rhetoric but that one might avoid being deceived. Socrates concludes that an "art of words" possessed by someone ignorant of the truth would be laughable and not really an art (262c1–3). But this conclusion makes sense only with the addition of the just mentioned proviso. It is the spectacle of someone who does not know his own ignorance that can be laughable (cf. *Phil.* 48c–49c). Though Socrates tries to persuade Phaedrus otherwise, it is possible for someone to possess the art of rhetoric (as defined further on in the *Phaedrus*) while being deceived about the truth.

But if one can possess the art of rhetoric and not the truth, might one not pursue the truth and simply dispense with the whole issue of art, rhetoric, and persuasion? The *Phaedrus* provides a negative answer to this question. And here we come to the crux of the *problem* of rhetoric, a problem that was already visible in the palinode (see chapter 3). Stated very broadly, the *Phaedrus* suggests the following line of reasoning.

The philosopher can either express his views in discourse or forgo discourse in order to contemplate in silence. Unfortunately, the philosopher is not one of those blessed gods whose minds are nourished by unmediated vision of the truth (247c–e). For an embodied soul, logos is unavoidable in its effort to remember what *is*. This accounts for the important place of discourse in the description of anamnesis at 249b–c; discourse functions as a reminder and image of Being. The issue of images and likenesses of entities is explicit, in fact, in the present passage (262a–b). The self-qualification of the palinode also brought our attention to the status of logos. Now, if the philosopher cannot express in discourse, even to himself, what he contemplates, then he cannot distinguish himself from the zealot or the dogmatist and so ceases to be a philosopher. In terms of the palinode, this means that he cannot be sure whether he is at the top of the list of nine vocations or somewhere else on it (248d2–e3), whether he is a follower of Zeus rather than another god. The philosopher is then merely certain of himself in his contemplation; he simply *believes* that contemplation reveals something true to him. But he cannot know on this basis that the revelation of which he is so confident *is* true. The palinode described the situation in terms of which a soul's access to the truth is so questionable and problematic. Some of the ingredients of this situation were these: the soul's limited vision of the hyperuranian beings originally; the forgetting of even that limited insight; the problem of remembering the truth by means of verbal and visual images when direct vision of the Beings is impossible and when the images are themselves only partially representative of their originals; the influence of character on one's understanding of things, as well as one's inability fully to embody one's character type (this holds true for the philosopher as well); and the necessity of coming to know oneself through the mediation of another soul and the parochialism of this leader/follower relationship. I summarized these difficulties by remarking that according to the palinode there is no way for a fallen soul to distinguish with certainty theory (vision of what is) from production (the transformation of what is into what one makes of what is). We saw too that the divinely erotic madman appeared to behave very much like the humanly erotic madman; public opinion, that is, cannot serve as a basis for distinguishing a sophist from a philosopher.

The genuine philosopher will understand this situation and will respond to it with an effort *not* to be persuaded that what reveals itself to him is true just because he sees it as true. He must create a context of disagreement for himself. He will be persuaded only if he hears himself giving reasons for what he sees. He will therefore break his silence and express himself in discourse, at least to himself. *But in this case rhetoric is already present.* The philosopher is his own audience as he speaks to himself. The one side in him will claim that such and such is the case in order to persuade the other side of its truth. The other side will respond with a question in order to check that this is an adequate truth (this is an internal "antilogike techne").[10] The philosopher's thinking will perfect the soul's ability to carry on a dialogue with itself (cf. *Theae.* 189e and *Soph.* 263e). But this dialogue is an instance of rhetoric, as Socrates' comprehensive definition of rhetoric suggests (261a7–b2, d10–e4). Speaking (and writing) is always a matter of a soul's leading or following, even if it is only leading or following itself. Logos and persuasion are inseparable.

However, the *Phaedrus* indicates that the philosopher who discourses to himself alone cannot ultimately be sure that he has secured the difference between unwarranted self-certainty and discursively warranted self-confidence, between mistaking a false image for a true one and correctly identifying the true, or (in an equivalent formulation) between sophistry and philosophy. The isolated philosopher cannot be sure that his conviction stems from the truth of his answer (the right correspondence between his words and the subject matter) rather than from the persuasiveness of the words he has used in formulating his answer. The palinode's description of character and its relationship to the soul's effort to know, along with the theses mentioned above concerning forgetfulness, the partiality of our vision of Being, our separation from Being and the omnipresence of images (discursive and otherwise), all make solipsism a formidable threat. This danger seems closely connected, in the *Phaedrus,* to the difficulty of coming to know oneself and so to the difficulty of avoiding self-deception (falsely allowing oneself to think that one knows something when one has not "remembered" what is really the case). Socrates makes a similar point at *Cratylus* 428d.[11]

That is, in the present context the issues of truth and persuasion are tied together through the proviso that the rhetorician who does not want to be deceived himself must know the truth. But, we might ask, deceived by whom? The palinode suggests that the answer is "by the rhetorician himself." The likenesses to truth deceive only if one allows them to deceive; strictly speaking they do not deceive at all, but are (mis)understood in a way that leads to the soul's being deceived. Such deception would be, in the palinode's terms, an example of soul moving itself defectively, but nevertheless moving itself. Every soul knows something of the truth; if it fails to remember it and bring it to the level of reflection, and allows itself to mistake a distorted likeness for the original, it has itself to blame. In this sense the rhetorician's being deceived is an example of self-deception. In sum, just as the rhetorician may use the art of rhetoric to mislead others, he may use it in such a way that he ends up misleading himself.

The problems of self-knowledge and self-deception lie at the heart of the problem of rhetoric. Rhetoric is inseparable from discourse and therefore from philosophizing. This brings us to a question critical to the remainder of the *Phaedrus:* given that rhetoric and logos are inseparable, and that the philosopher must articulate his insights in discourse, and that it is dangerous for a philosopher to talk to himself only, what kind of rhetoric best avoids the dangers of solipsism and self-deception? What kind of rhetoric, that is, best furthers self-knowledge? The *Phaedrus'* response to the problem, namely, dialegesthai, is not made explicit until the retraction of techne is introduced by the Theuth/Thamus story. But it is implicit throughout in the way that Socrates and Plato practice philosophy. Now, the standard antidote for the dangers at issue is to acquire knowledge in the company of others: crudely put, "objectively certifiable" is often taken to mean "publicly certifiable," the public being the relevant community of experts. Socrates endorses the notion that he must come to know himself through the mediation of others, that is, through dialogue. But he rejects the most obvious means of communicating with a relevant public when he rejects the written word as a rhetoric suitable for philosophizing. Socrates endorses the spoken word, which is interpersonal and fundamentally dialogical ("fundamentally," because long speeches, such as the palinode in the *Phaedrus,* can also be spoken). The interlocutors he actually chooses (such as Phaedrus) do not, moreover, initially look like experts in the area of self-knowledge. I have already said something in chapter 1 about Socrates' choice of Phaedrus as interlocutor; but more needs to be said about the peculiarities of Socratic dialogue, and I will do so in chapter 6 and the Epilogue. At this juncture I am only trying to establish in a general way a connection between the themes of self-knowledge (and so self-deception), rhetoric, and dialogue.

DIVISION, COLLECTION, AND THE PARADIGMS OF RHETORIC (262c5–266c5)

Let me begin with some general observations about division and collection. Putting aside 265b–266b, the *Phaedrus* as a whole emphasizes division instead of collection. There are six explicit references to a division type of process *(temnein, diairein).*[12] A survey of them shows two things.

First, the meaning of "division" is very loose, ranging from "distinguish" to a technical sounding "diairesis according to [or into] forms."[13] Second, it is clear that division is not limited to operations on Ideas or even to "forms" in any one sense of the term.[14] Nevertheless, five of the six references to division occur in connection with Socrates' effort to formulate an art (techne) or method of thinking. The attempt to give division a formal appearance as a technique of analysis (or more literally, of dialysis) is explicit at 265d–266a (see below).

Outside of 265d–266b, there is one explicit reference to collection in the palinode (249b7–c1), which I have discussed already (and the *sunagagonte* of 256c3 does not refer to a discursive process). A second more ambiguous reference may occur at 273e2–3 in the context of one of the formulations of the method of thinking. We are told to "bring together each one thing under a single idea." However, Socrates does not refer to a "many," and the process involved does not seem to amount to more than identifying something as an instance of a form (a capacity called for earlier at 272a).

The fact that at 265d–266b collection seems to be assigned a preliminary and subordinate role (even the description of collection here is shorter than that of division) supports the suggestion that the method of technical thinking is primarily analytical. Yet it would seem that the limits of analysis are its boundaries with nontechnical synthesis, since every analysis (literally, "unloosing") or diairesis would seem to presuppose a collected field of objects or activities as its starting point. Synthesis is the context of division. In a sense, the discussion about rhetoric in the second half of the *Phaedrus* is—quietly, as it were—about collection rather than division. The emphasis is on composing wholes of discourse in the proper manner. Lysias' speech (like Midas' epitaph) lacks *taxis* and "logographic necessity," the result being a sum rather than whole of words. Socrates uses an image here (264c2–5) in order to articulate the notion of organic unity. He implies that his two speeches possess such unity; the method of division therefore operates, in this case, on pregiven wholes. Given the paradigmatic status of this example, we might infer that all divisions assume previously collected wholes. There must already be something to be divided. Natural or artificial wholes seem naturally to be prior to divisions. Analysis presupposes synthesis.

That this is, again, too simple a picture is obvious when we recall that the wholes are articulated unities; whether division is used in the service of producing a speech or for understanding an already given whole (whether natural or artificial), division is implicitly coeval with collection. In choosing out a whole, we must *distinguish* it from other wholes; every collection seems to presuppose prior division. If collection is a collection of parts or elements, then what is collected has already been articulated by division. Thus division and collection seem to interpenetrate. Differently put, one cannot establish the similarities between things without also understanding their dissimilarities (the "same" and "different" are inseparable). For example, when dividing complexes into other complexes and finally into simples (cf. 270d–271b), at each stage the subordinate complexes and simples must be grasped as wholes before further division is attempted, and concurrently each whole must be divided from the others (whether the "whole" is simple or not). Or again at 263a–c, Socrates (silently) takes the class of words as a collected field and so as distinguished from, for example, letters, syllables, and the rest. In order to know how to divide it he looks at how we speak and notices that some (particular) words are disputable and that others are not (cf. *Alc. I,* 111b–c, *Euthyphro* 7b–e). Then he collects the disputables and indisputables into two "forms" and finally suggests that they are divisions of the previously collected class of words. The procedure is itself complex.[15] But when he turns all this into a techne, the procedure is artificially simplified according to the following rule: first collect and then divide (see also 277b5–6; the steps to be taken receive more elaborate formulation at 270d ff.). Unfortunately, this rule-governed procedure distorts the underlying complexity of the situation.

Thus the formal or consciously rule-governed use of collection and division seems to presuppose implicitly both collection and division in their various senses. That is, before Socrates creates an official classification of "words," he must already be acquainted with words; he learns from consulting his experience that some are disputed and some are not. This context already involves divisions and collections, as pointed out in the previous paragraph. The comprehensive context within which we formulate our analytical procedures is that of ordinary experience or, to use a Platonic word, opinion.[16] As Plato's dialogues themselves suggest, opinion is the starting point which we have already made.

The genesis of an explicit techne of thinking, the refinement of procedures already implicit in opinion, has clear pedagogical advantages in the *Phaedrus* and in other dialogues. Such an art requires one to stop and think, and so to put a hold on automatically espoused opinions. This is exactly what Phaedrus still requires.[17] But as we shall see, the art of thinking is subordinated, in the *Phaedrus,* to the artless path of dialogue and so to the explicit process of bringing opinion into question. Dialogue must, as it were, declassify the structures built up by techne, without simply imitating the forgetfulness of opinion. Differently put, the dialect of techne must be reabsorbed into the dialectic of philosophizing. We will see that this questioning of opinion is superior to the reconstitution of opinion into a techne and that the former but not the latter is associated with anamnesis. Opinion unravels its intuitions unreflectively; techne grapples with them and imposes an order; and dialegesthai forces reflection on them by means of questions.

The mutually disruptive qualities of opinion, techne, and dialegesthai must not be allowed to conceal the fact that they all depend on the capacity to *see* what it is we wish to say or analyze, to see how to analyze it, and to see when the analysis is finished and completed. This capacity is one form of noesis (not necessarily the same as the sort described at 247c–e, however), and it may be connected with division and collection in the following way. In order to analyze an articulated whole or to combine it with other wholes, we must first divide this whole from others and also collect it into a single whole. If apprehension of a whole—whether in the course of ordinary discourse, a philosophical dialogue, or at the start of an analysis—requires that divisions and collections be reciprocally carried out, there would be no such apprehensions for the divisions and collections would be endless. Still further, divisions and collections could not be carried out at all: for upon what would they be carried out? Intuitions must accompany our discursive specifications of ones and manys, and there is a corresponding emphasis in the passages on division and collection on verbs related to "seeing." These intuitions might be characterized as acts of simultaneous divisions and collections.[18] By the time that thinking has been codified into a method of division and collection, the heuristic work (which includes intuitions, as well as division and collection in a variety of informal senses) has already been accomplished. However, intuition or insight may be molded by opinion (the *trophe doxaste* of 248b5) or by anamnesis. That is, these insights may or may not be grounded in an understanding of the hyperuranian beings. The techne alone does not, unfortunately, resolve the critical problem of distinguishing between intuition of the Beings and intuition governed by opinion, even if the techne is helpful in training the mind to make some steps in solving the problem. That is, the techne does not resolve the problem of rhetoric as I have defined that problem in the present chapter. I will argue below (as I have here) that Socrates and Plato offer dialogue as their response to this problem.

Let me turn now to the passages that immediately precede the section in which the earlier speeches are divided and collected. The discussion is explicitly about techne and the lack of it in speeches. It seems that "by chance" the previous "two speeches" (262d1)[19] offer helpful "paradigms" of how someone "knowing the truth" can lead his audience astray. Lysias' speech is one of these paradigms; Socrates is ironically crediting Lysias with knowing the truth, albeit speaking it artlessly and misleadingly (cf. 242e5–243a1; the first two speeches of the *Phaedrus* were "neither healthy nor true"). This point further substantiates the argument that truth and techne are not indissolubly connected. Moreover, Socrates goes on to abstract completely from the differences in content and narrative frame that exist between Lysias' speech and Socrates' first speech— a preliminary indication of the distorting powers of the techne in question.

In order to specify what he means by artful writing, Socrates performs the division, already discussed above, between two kinds of words (those whose meanings are agreed upon and those about which there is disagreement) and then suggests that a discussion that concerns a disputed topic (such as eros) should begin with a definition. Lysias' speech failed to do this and so is artless, whereas Socrates' first speech not only did so, but made a point of saying how important it is to do so if one is to eliminate disagreement. Now in itself this is a trivial criticism of a speech. The presence or absence of a definition at the start of a speech is unrelated to whether the speech is disorganized and repetitious. Further, the presence of a definition might actually be out of place in the context, as was certainly the case with a seduction speech, which, in however absurd a fashion, Lysias' speech was intended to be.[20] On the other hand, Socrates does have a point with respect to Lysias' speech: for the speech was thoughtless, as was Phaedrus' response to it. Both Lysias and Phaedrus could have benefited from the demand that they stop and think about their overly clever pronouncements about eros, and this is what the demand for definition can accomplish. But it is scarcely a demand that is defensible without qualification.

Still further, the presence of a definition at the start of a speech guarantees neither agreement nor truth, or agreement based on truth, for that matter. (I have already discussed this point at some length in chapter 2.) I suggest that the demand for definition, a demand inseparable from the whole method of division and collection, is better suited to generating clarity and possibly internal consistency (the very qualities Socrates cites in its behalf at 265d6–7) than it is to generating a logos that lays hold of the truth. These qualities of clarity and consistency are undoubtedly helpful pedagogically; as Socrates puts it here, they are useful "in order that defining each thing one might make clear whatever one might ever wish to teach" (265d4–5). In this respect the techne's virtues and defects parallel those of the written word, against whose false certainty and clarity Socrates warns at the end of the *Phaedrus* (275c6, 278a).

The paradigm of writing composed according to techne is expressed by Socrates in the famous image of the body (he does not refer to the soul) of an animal (264c2–5). It is not difficult to see how this image might easily be taken to illustrate both the systematic procedure of division and collection and the ideal organization of a written treatise. In explaining the process of diairesis, Socrates uses the very same image of an animal (265e–266a), and in explaining the nature of the written word, he compares writing to *zōgraphia* (275d5), whose products stand there as though "living" (*zōnta,* 275d6; cf. the *graphein* at 264c5, which can mean "write" or "paint"). Paintings depict the visible form or body of the animal. The written word, Socrates will argue, is somehow "dead," whereas the spoken word is "living and ensouled" (276a8). The body of the animal is lifeless (soul is the principle of life; 245c7). As the reference to the "butcher" at 265e3 also makes clear, the animal is dead when it is operated upon by the art of definition, division, and collection. The metaphor of life and death is present too in the reference here to the epitaph written on Midas' tombstone (264d).

The written treatise (however well organized) and the art of division and collection thus look like "phantoms" (see 276a9) of the "live" activity of dialegesthai. Correspondingly the *Phaedrus* itself does not fit the treatise form or meet the standards of the art of division and collection, as is amply confirmed by Socrates' own attempt to divide the first half of the *Phaedrus* (see below).[21] Socrates tries to overcome this difficulty by pretending, through a series of confusing references in the singular and dual to the three speeches of the *Phaedrus,* that his two speeches are one. Socrates seems to treat his two spoken logoi as though they had been *written* artfully in treatise form. An attempt to subject the second half of the *Phaedrus* to the art of division and collection would suffer a similarly unfortunate fate. The dialogue does not begin with a definition and defies the rules of techne. Yet it does exhibit perfect "logographic necessity" (I shall return to this point in chapter 6). Thus the formal art of methodological dialectic is rhetorically advocated in the *Phaedrus,* while the dialogical rhetoric of the *Phaedrus* is informal, artless dialectic.[22]

At 265a–c Socrates suggests that he madly began his speech with the following definition: "eros is a sort of madness." He says that he then performed the following diaireses:

Socrates does not explain where he obtained the notion of madness or its divisions, but as I have already intimated, it seems that it all derives from current knowledge of the culture and times. The description of the fourth part was, we are told, a "not altogether unbelievable" myth, that is, it is not fully believable. Ostensibly rigorous divisions seem to terminate in explicitly unrigorous knowledge of parts.[23] The schema attributes artfulness to Socrates' first, base speech, as well as to the second, noble speech. But their baseness and nobility is invisible structurally; the analysis of the molecular composition of the speeches detaches form from content in such a way as to conceal a major point of the speeches.[24] Hence the passage "from censure to encomium" (265c5–6) is not explained by the formal art of rhetoric. The schema altogether omits the pivotal interlude that joins the two speeches, though it was precisely there that the questionability of the thesis of the first speech was raised. The method is directed only to the monologues of the *Phaedrus,* and even these it distorts. The schema does not explain the shamefulness of the first speech. Questions do not figure in this schema; the schema is, so to speak, a declarative statement. The reasons for which the palinode was necessary, then, are omitted here; the sense in which it is a retraction is no longer visible; hence the true unity of the speeches cannot be understood on the basis of the diairetical summary. Still further, Socrates' speeches did not proceed in the way here characterized.[25] The theory of method and the practice of dialogue in the *Phaedrus* do not mesh, as I have already noted. This observation is crucial. I want to argue that the fault is intentional and that it serves as a way of pointing out the limitations of techne.

According to Socrates, two "forms" whose function it would be "not unpleasant" to grasp were alluded to earlier (it is not clear where!). The first of these consists of "leading a plurality dispersed in many ways into one idea, seeing it all together, in order that defining each thing one might make clear whatever one might ever wish to teach" (265d3–5). The description is general: whether the dispersed things are particular objects, forms, sense perceptions is not specified. In its very generality, this procedure differs from that of recollection (249b5–c4). The meaning of the adverb *pollachē* is also unclear here: it seems to be a concession that the dispersed things are not just numerically separate but also distinct in some qualitative sense—perhaps like the different kinds of eros. The ontological status of the "idea" is utterly undefined here. There is no suggestion that the word refers to a hyperuranian being, and no suggestion that there is an ascent or separation involved. There is no reason, then, that this procedure could not be used on, say, fictional objects (mythological monsters, and so on). "Seeing together" appears to be a prerequisite for "leading." But this does not mean that the seeing is an insight into an eternal order of Ideas.

Socrates goes on to give a further specification of the rule: "for example, take the things that were said just now about eros; once eros has been defined, whether well or badly, as to what it is, at least [*goun*] the logos was by that means able to speak with clarity and internal consistency."[26] I take the *ta nunde* to refer to the earlier speeches about eros and madness; these contain the "plurality dispersed in many ways." The definition has just been offered at 265a6–7: "eros is a sort of madness." We have already seen how this definition is not quite an accurate report of what was said earlier. Lucidity and truth are not identical. Eros and madness are seen as one here, presumably on the basis of the generally available opinion that eros and loss of sophrosyne are, in human beings, closely related phenomena. That is, the rule-governed procedure Socrates points to here is insensitive to the difference between knowledge and opinion, or original and image, whereas anamnesis heavily depends on seeing the world as saturated by images of the divine.

This definition precedes the divisions in that it supplies the teacher with a way of focusing and giving preliminary direction to the divisions. One wonders how, if this starting point is a synthesis of fairly conventional views, the analysis or divisions of the definition could possibly yield "natural" articulations. Further, what is being defined here is "eros." But it appears that eros is not the "one idea"; that title belongs to "madness," which is the "one" of which eros is *a* "part." It would seem that "eros" is an example of the "each thing" (*hekaston:* 265d4) that is being defined. Yet the many instances and kinds of eros must themselves be seen together in the one-form "eros" before "eros" can be said to be a kind of madness. The instances and kinds of madness too must be gathered into one form in order for the definition "eros is a sort of madness" to be uttered.

I turn now to the description of division. This description is lengthier and more detailed than that given of collection. Socrates had previously used the image of a natural body of an animal to illustrate the need for literary wholeness: now the same image is used to illustrate division. Artful writing was said to be constructed like the body (not the soul) of a living animal; now we see that artful division is like carving up the body of a dead animal (perhaps having taken the animal's life).[27]

The procedure of division is "the reverse, to be able to cut through into forms, following the joints in the manner that is natural, and not to try to break off any part by proceeding in the manner of a bad butcher" (265e1–3).[28] Socrates then goes on to illustrate the correct execution of this rule with his two speeches. The result is the following:

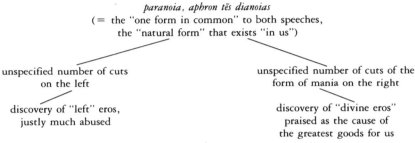

paranoia, aphron tēs dianoias
(= the "one form in common" to both speeches,
the "natural form" that exists "in us")

unspecified number of cuts
on the left

unspecified number of cuts of the
form of mania on the right

discovery of "left" eros,
justly much abused

discovery of "divine eros"
praised as the cause of
the greatest goods for us

Although the language here strongly suggests that the divisions are dichotomous, the two speeches as well as the diaireses given at 265a–c (see above) show that this is not so at every stage of the division (the subsequent descriptions in the *Phaedrus* of the method drop the suggestion that the divisions are dichotomous). Not everything about the animal's body is twofold. Once again, the schema does not accurately summarize what actually happened earlier. The first speech, the second, and their connection are not faithfully represented here, as is noted by Hackforth.[29] Without repeating my earlier observations about these divisions, I add that in Socrates' first speech hubris is said to have "many names, many branches, many parts" (238a2–3), of which eros is just one. Hubris should thus be a part of paranoia. Since the parts of hubris, like those of mania, are not contraries, some divisions cannot be guided by contrariety.

Moreover, among the important themes of Socrates' two speeches that are omitted here is that of the soul! Looking at these divisions one would never know that the introduction of *psyche* was crucial to the transition from the first to the second speech.[30] Soul, the principle of life, is now omitted. Is this not in keeping with the fact that the whole image here is that of a dead body of thought?

I have been arguing that much of the content and significance of the speeches is lost when they are dissected by the butcher's art. What is being mapped out is a pale shadow of those speeches, no longer animated by the dialectic of discovery and philosophizing. I have pointed to the connection between this method and written word.[31] Thus Phaedrus is not mistaken in dividing, at 266c, the dialecticians (understood as the practitioners of divisions and collections) from the rhetoricians (the specialists in live discourse).

None of this means that the method is useless. On the contrary, it can be a helpful check on thoughtlessness, and it supplies a rule-governed discipline that can help put a stop to one's absorption in speeches (such as Phaedrus' comic infatuation with Lysias' speech). The method directs the mind's attention away from sensible particulars to concepts and their interrelations. Moreover, it is undeniably the case that any investigation must make distinctions, stake out a field of inquiry, and so on. It is not as though Socrates' earlier speeches were seamless. It is true that the various informal and intermingled senses of division and collection are indispensable. But the method (whether in the form already examined or that which Socrates goes on to deploy) is not in itself a means by which one may rejoin the gods at the divine banquet. It is perfectly suited to tilling the soil of opinion and as a sort of catharsis aimed at preparing the soul for true dialectic (dialegesthai). This is precisely the pharmakon Socrates is administering to Phaedrus. As is clear when we consider the techne in relation to the telos presented at the end of the *Phaedrus,* the techne is *a* means to the goal of anamnesis. But it is a mistake to identify the two. One must not follow uncritically in the steps of the technician. Hence the appropriateness of Socrates' quotation at 266b6 from Homer,[32] a quotation also alluded to at 252e7 ff. (in the palinode) and at 276d4 (in the discussion of the true dialectician). Surely we are meant to see the three passages together and to grasp the subservient position of techne relative to dialectical anamnesis (more on the connection between dialogue and recollection in chapter 6). In short: when viewed relative to its context—the whole of which it is a part—the method comes alive.

At the conclusion of the present section (266b3–c1), Socrates exclaims: "Of these divisions and collections, Phaedrus, I am myself a lover, in order that I may be such as to speak and think; and whenever I think someone else is able by nature to look to a one and upon a many, I follow him 'from behind in his track [which is] as though of a god.' Furthermore, those able to do this I for the present call—whether I address them rightly or not, god knows—dialecticians."[33] This passage contains the first use of "synagoge" in the *Phaedrus,* and the first use of the word "diairesis" in the present description of the two procedures (265d–266a). Possibly these words are introduced to shift our attention away from the techne at issue here and to a broader horizon (Socrates does not say he is a lover of techne or method); for Socrates' declaration here is extremely general.

By "these divisions and collections" he obviously does not mean only the particular ones just performed. I do not think he means to limit himself to the particular *kind* of divisions and collections just performed (those that Socrates describes further on in the *Phaedrus* should also be included, presumably). Rather, it seems that "divisions and collections" in any of the senses I have discussed above are the objects of Socrates' praise. Hence Socrates here refers to the "one" and "many" in a *very* broad sense; the operation he is adverting to could take any number of forms. Even so, the love of wisdom entails something more than the love of divisions and collections; it entails dialogue. Hence Socrates hesitates to identify the dialectician with the man who can collect and divide (thus the "for the present" qualifier). Indeed, by the end of the *Phaedrus* the dialectical art is explicitly shown to be something grander than the capacity to divide and collect.[34] As Socrates puts it here: he loves divisions and collections *so that* he may "speak and think"; that is, they are means to this general goal. As we learn further on, the true rhetorician must possess natural ability, episteme, and practice (269c6–d1).[35] Episteme seems to include "garrulity and high-flown speculation" about nature (see 269c6–d8).[35] This does not sound much like rigorous method, but it does sound like Socratic dialogue (see the "dialegesthai" at 269b6).

I would like to bring my discussion of this section of the *Phaedrus* to a close with several observations about the references to "nature" in the present passage. We hear of "carving in the manner that is natural," of a "single natural body" (Hackforth's translation), and of a "natural form of madness existing in us." Talk about method and the naturalness of its objects also comes up in subsequent descriptions of the method (for example, 270b–c, d1, d4, d7, e4, 271a6–7, a11, 272a1, 273e1, 277b8, c1, c4). Taken at face value, these references suggest that the skillfull butcher operates on natural entities and in a way that reveals their nature, that is, what they really are (cf. especially 270e2–5). After all the laborious dialogue so far in search of the meaning of eros and soul, after all the palinode's teaching about the difficulty of distinguishing between originals and images, after all the puzzles surrounding self-knowledge, it turns out that one need only divide and collect artfully to find the nature of something. Not only would this be a surprising result; my remarks above have suggested that the method of division and collection operates, in the present context, on opinions. Opinions may, or may not, reflect the natures of things. Further comment on the talk about nature and its connection to division and collection is thus called for.

We are not actually told here that the joints are natural, but rather that one must cut according to them in the manner that is natural (nor does Socrates actually say here that the forms produced by division are natural). Presumably the criterion for what is and what is not a natural way for cutting resides in what is being cut. At least, "nature" and "natural" are used, in the passages of the *Phaedrus* adverted to in the previous paragraph, with reference to what is being cut. What is meant by "nature" or "natural" here? In the *Phaedrus* Socrates gives us no answer to this question. But I think that it is clear that the "forms" and "natures" he is referring to are *not* hyperuranian beings, that is, Ideas. The examples he calls upon are eros and soul; I know of no one who maintains that for Plato there is an Idea of eros, and I have argued that there is no Idea of the soul. Furthermore, Socrates soon makes clear that the method of division and collection can be extended to any object whatever (see below), and it would be difficult to maintain that there are Ideas for everything to which one might apply the method of division and collection (such as all the arts divided in the *Sophist* and *Statesman*). There is no reason why there cannot, in a Platonic universe, exist things that have a determinate nature but no Idea.

The animal/body image appeals to our everyday knowledge of an articulated nature. It is a rhetorically effective image because the body and its joints (the body being the main form to be cut) seem obvious and natural. Perhaps, though, the image is somewhat deceptive. Are there not joints that would come to light from the perspective of, say, a veterinarian but not that of a butcher, and vice versa? The veterinarian might see that while there is a joining of two bones at the elbow, there are arteries and nerves that do not divide there. If his purpose in cutting is to heal the patient rather than to contribute to the preparation of a banquet, he might cut halfway between elbow and shoulder, this being *for his purposes* the natural place. Or the layers of skin and muscle might be seen as the relevant parts; or perhaps internal organs might be divided off, even though here (as in the skin and muscle) the location of the joint is not at all obvious. There would seem to be many natural joints; on the basis of our desires and goals we select some as the place for cutting. Indeed, one might take an axe and butcher that pitiable animal; why can we not say that where the axe falls is a natural joint, given that we wish to deform or kill the beast?

To be sure, the fact that a plurality of different divisions can be performed on a single object does not constitute a reason for rejecting division. In fact, both the opening divisions of the *Sophist* (which yield several different descriptions of one object) and divisions in the *Statesman* (265a and context) acknowledge the manifoldness of divisions in this sense. But the plurality in question suggests that no one set of divisions performed in the service of some given purpose yields the *whole* nature of the object divided. For example, in a moment Socrates will outline the method of division further and will argue that the rhetorician must apply it to the soul if rhetoric is to be technical. But the use of the method *for the purposes of rhetoric* yields only *a* perspective on the soul, one in terms of which the soul is divided into a variety of character types. An unmistakable and critical indication of the limitation of the use of the method for the purposes of rhetoric is the complete absence, in Socrates' descriptions (from 270c on) of the art of rhetoric, of any mention of eros. Correspondingly, he says nothing there about the soul as self-motion, about the soul's transcendence of this world, about the hyperuranian beings, about the necessity for understanding the soul in the context of the Whole, about souls as mirrors of each other, or about madness. It seems to me that while no account of an entity can dispense with divisions and collections in the informal sense discussed earlier in this chapter, any effort to understand what a philosophical logos is in terms of a techne of division and collection is bound to fail for the reason just discussed (among others). To repeat: logos in the sense of techne does not grasp the whole of the nature to which it is directed. That the issue of wholeness is not absent from the discussion about techne is clear from 270c1–2 and elsewhere (see below).

Further, the techne's retrospective organization of its materials partially distorts them (hence the inaccuracies in Socrates' formal analysis of the speeches), for it elicits one aspect of the subject matter at the cost of capturing the whole of it (hence the absence in the descriptions of the method of references to eros, madness, and anamnesis). As I said above, the technician can proceed technically while being deceived about the truth. The natures would best be understood in the light of anamnesis, and anamnesis must be articulated dialogically. I have specified above why the techne of division and collection is a helpful step in this process.

Socrates uses the previous speeches of the *Phaedrus* as paradigms of the art of division and collection. The material or natures Socrates analyzes are thus pregiven; his divisions and collections are retrospective in that they are dependent on a prior understanding and articulation of the natures (eros, madness, soul) in question. This aspect of the structure of the *Phaedrus* (the fact that the techne is illustrated by speeches provided earlier in the dialogue) confirms an important point about the status of the techne of division and collection. The techne is not a way of discovering new knowledge; it is a way of organizing something one already knows or thinks one knows. That is to say the techne is retrospective, but not recollective in the palinode's sense. I made essentially the same point above in my discussion of intuition.

How then *do* we grasp the whole of a nature? In my discussion of myth I argued that Socrates' eikastic myth has the unique ability to let us see the whole of a nature, and in particular of the soul. But I also argued that the myth qualified itself; in the final analysis, when subjected to metaphilosophical reflection, the myth could not claim to represent the whole picture. What is required, I suggested, is reflection on logos and so (as it turns out) on rhetoric. This we are presently doing, and the shortcomings of the interpretation of logos in terms of techne will lead us to an understanding of the importance of dialogue. If there is a way of grasping the whole of a nature, and of preventing a confusion between a false opinion and a true opinion about something (whether that thing has an Idea or not), it ultimately resides in dialogue (of which myth and techne may be elements). We are not yet ready, however, for a consideration of dialogue. That theme is introduced in the Theuth/Thamus myth, along with the reintroduction of the theme of anamnesis. But Socrates has only just started the discussion about the method of division and collection and has more to say about how the rhetorician is to use it.

THE MANUALS, THE MASTERS OF *TECHNE,* AND THE FIVE DESCRIPTIONS OF THE METHOD OF KNOWING AND OF *PSYCHAGOGIA* (266c6–274b5)

Phaedrus rightly insists that the eidos of the dialectician as it has just been described does not include that of the rhetoricians (266c6–9), for the ordinary, *but nevertheless effective,* rhetoricians lack the knowledge of the dialectical art. Socrates' initial response is to suggest that what has been omitted consists in "the antecedents of the art," that is, all the tricks and technicalities described in the manuals. What is remarkable about the ensuing discussion is that Socrates shows himself to be thoroughly acquainted with these manuals and with the vast and amorphous field of rhetoric. Not all the niceties are frivolous; Prodicus' principle that one's speeches should be neither too long nor too short, but of fitting length, is echoed by Socrates at 272a. Indeed, the contrast between short and long speeches, one on which Socrates elsewhere insists, reminds one of the contrast between Socratic dialegesthai and the long epideictic monologues of the sophists.[36] Tisias' and Gorgias' principle that probabilities (*ta eikota*) deserve more attention than truth (267a) since probabilities are so much more persuasive is precisely the principle that entrances Phaedrus (260a, 272d–273a; cf. 268a3–4), and on which much of the second half of the *Phaedrus* is focused (hence Tisias is addressed directly at 273d2). Tisias' and Gorgias' skeptical objections to the techne pop up several times in this section of the *Phaedrus;* they correspond to the denial, implicit in

Lysias' speech, of the importance of knowing what is really true about eros and soul. Unfortunately the techne does not, as I have argued above, present an adequate response to the problem of rhetoric, namely, the problem of self-deception and of coming to know oneself.

In a rhetorical effort to display more clearly the power of the art of words, Socrates constructs three dialogues within a dialogue between a claimant to knowledge and, in sequence, (1) Eryximachus or Acumenus, (2) Sophocles or Euripides, (3) an unnamed musician, and (4) the true rhetoricians Adrastus and Pericles. In each case, the master of the art distinguishes between the antecedents and a substantive knowledge of what is appropriate, suitable, or kalon. "Episteme" and derivates are used frequently in this passage, synonomously with "techne." Socrates wants to imply, of course, that the art of rhetoric is an episteme comparable to the arts of medicine, music, and the composition of tragedy. Since the art of rhetoric needs supplementing by the knowledge of the soul and of the things one is discoursing about (see below), Socrates is trying to suggest that there is an episteme of the soul and of "the beings" (see also 273d6, 277b8), but in a sense that cannot be identical with that of the palinode (247c ff.).

Medicine is an episteme because, in addition to being the (teachable) knowledge of how to change the body's temperature and the like, it is the diagnostic knowledge of which patients should be given which treatments and when, for how long, and in what dosage (268a–b). To lack knowledge of the right occasion for the application of rules is, as Phaedrus says, just to have a book knowledge of the art (268c2–4), and so only knowledge of the antecedents. Thus true episteme seems to include sound judgment, and this can be perfected only through experience. Although Socrates wants to distinguish techne from *empeiria* (270b), there is certainly an empirical dimension to episteme. It seems doubtful whether this aspect of the episteme is teachable in the sense in which the antecedents are teachable.

Similarly, the episteme of composing tragedies requires not just the ability to write long or short passages about small or great topics in various ways (with pathos or a menacing tone, and so on) and the ability to teach others to do so, too—these are the antecedents—but also the ability to arrange the passages suitably so as to produce a whole (268c–d). How does an accomplished writer learn to put together a whole discourse? Like the "sound judgment" of the physician, this capacity of the tragedian is his "genius" or "madness" and is very hard to formulate in terms of rules (cf. the remark about techne at 245a6). It would also seem to be very difficult to teach. Once again episteme includes an element that transcends

book knowledge. We begin to see why Socrates will say that the true
rhetorician must have the right nature in addition to acquiring episteme
and practice (269d), and why he says that the great arts "need supplementing" (Hackforth's translation) by garrulity and high-flown speculation
about nature (this is what Pericles is supposed to have learned from Anaxagoras; 270a).

The musician's episteme consists of more than the ability to produce
high and low notes. Since the musician is *mousikos,* he is pictured as re-
proving in a most gentle, indeed rhetorical, way the person who thinks
that such an ability constitutes knowledge of music (268d–e). But we do
not learn what the true knowledge of harmony would require. Presumably
it would consist of both a knowledge of the ratios between notes and a
knowledge of how to produce a beautiful combination of notes. Again,
it seems doubtful whether the ability to make beauty palpable in sound
is teachable or intelligible solely in terms of rules.

Finally Socrates draws the analogy between these arts and rhetoric. The
true rhetorician must know not just the devices explained in the books
about rhetoric—these are the teachable antecedents—but also (a) how to
speak persuasively and (b) how to put together a "whole" of discourse
(269a–c). The demand in (b) echoes the description at 264c of "organic
unity." Once again, it is hard to say how (b) is a teachable, rule-directed
sort of knowledge. It certainly seems to be the case that the art of rhetoric
as Socrates outlines it does not provide one with a handy way of either
composing wholes, or recognizing a whole. The art of division and collection as it is outlined in the *Phaedrus* does not explain the wholeness of
the *Phaedrus* itself, for example.

The *Phaedrus* indicates that there are two criteria for wholeness of discourses, namely, what is "persuasive" (or "probable"; *pithanos, eikos*), and
what is in accordance with the structure of "the beings." That is, a perfected (a truly well-balanced and whole) speech is one that can successfully
communicate what is true. Wholeness is thus a function of both the "logic
of the subject matter" and the "logic of persuasion." I have suggested
that the Platonic dialogue form and Socratic dialogue possess a kind of
wholeness or logic of development that does not characterize the standard
treatise or the art of division and collection. The discussion of the art of
division and collection is itself an effort to reach a definition, and Socrates
has Adrastus and Pericles explain that the claimants to the art of rhetoric
confuse the art and its antecedents precisely because they do not know
(*mē epistamenoi*) dialectic (dialegesthai; 269b). But this knowledge of dialectic is not reducible to the clean-cut and methodical exercise of the art

of division and collection. As if to underline this point, Socrates produces no less than four definitions of this art between 270c and 274b, and a fifth recapitulative one at 277b–c (see below). Although great emphasis is placed on the exactitude of the method, the method itself does not receive an exact formulation. The descriptions vary from one another in nontrivial ways, and no one of them mentions all the important points.

Indeed, will not the true rhetorician (the dialectician) have to combine qualities of the doctor, tragedian, and musician?[37] He must be able to administer the pharmakon of rhetoric in just the right dose, at and for the right time; he must compose wholes of discourse; and by means of beautiful discourses he must remind the soul of the Ideas. But in saying this, one is demanding something that goes beyond the limits of techne. Correspondingly, Socrates' sketch in the passage under discussion as to what a true episteme would ideally consist of in fact suggests that true episteme, including the episteme of rhetoric, goes beyond the techne he actually outlines. There is an underlying tension between the tremendous demands placed on the art of rhetoric in the present passage (268a–270b) and the character of rhetoric as an *art* (as art is defined in the five descriptions below). Perhaps the distinctions at 269d among the rhetorician's episteme, his nature, and his practice of (or care for) his art is meant to acknowledge that much is needed in addition to the techne. The qualifying phrase at 269d6 (Thompson translates it as "for as much of it as is technical") suggests the same (cf. 261e2). So too with the reference here to the rhetorician's need for "garrulity and high-flown speculation about nature and reason" (that is, nature as a whole). The reference reminds us of the palinode and so suggests requirements for the art of rhetoric that surpass the limits of art. That the tension between the nature of techne and the demands placed here on techne is evident to Socrates is clear from the eventual subordination of techne to dialogue, anamnesis, and erotic mania (see below). I thus infer that the *Phaedrus'* discussion about techne is intended to point out the limits of techne even as it praises techne.

As I have already noted, at 270b Socrates suggests a connection between rhetoric and nature by means of a comparison between medicine and rhetoric. If the analogy here holds for all the terms as they are stated, medicine stands to the nature of the body as rhetoric does to that of the soul; the body's health and strength correspond to the convictions and virtue of the soul, respectively; and the doctor's *pharmaka* and regimen correspond to the rhetorician's logoi and prescribed practices, respectively (270b). The analogy is suggestive, particularly with respect to the pharmakon/logos comparison, one that will come up again in the *Phaedrus*. Virtue was mentioned in the first half of the dialogue, but it is not mentioned in the descriptions of the art of division and collection or of the art of rhetoric.

The analogy also prompts the following question: is knowledge of the soul's nature inseparable from knowledge of the truth about virtue and rules of conduct, that is, in the language of the palinode, about the "hyperuranian beings"? As if in anticipation of this question, Socrates asks, "Do you think it possible to understand the nature of the soul in a way worthy of being mentioned without taking the soul as a whole?" (270c1–2). The phrase may also be translated "Do you think it possible to understand the nature of the soul in a way worthy of being mentioned by taking the soul independently of the nature of the Whole?" Scholarly opinion is split as to which reading is correct.[38] I would suggest that the ambiguity is intentional. It accurately reflects at least one aspect of the unity-of-the-*Phaedrus* problem. In the palinode "soul" is understood in terms of its place in the Whole—hence the emphasis on eros. In the second half (up to the Theuth/Thamus story) the soul is understood simply in terms of its internal articulation in abstraction from its place in the Whole—hence the absence there of references to eros (as well as to madness and anamnesis). And this means that the conception of the human person assumed by the method is far more limited than that developed hitherto in the *Phaedrus*. From the standpoint of the palinode, the techne does not yield knowledge of the soul as a whole. Thus this grammatical ambiguity keeps before the reader's eyes an issue about self-knowledge of the greatest importance.

Correspondingly, in the techne section of the second half of the *Phaedrus*, there is no reference to the hyperuranian beings. The issue as to how 270c1–2 is to be translated is, then, closely connected to that concerning the relationship between knowledge of the soul and knowledge of the cosmos, and finally between self-knowledge and knowledge of the Whole. In the *Phaedrus'* descriptions of the method applicable to the soul, knowledge of the soul and knowledge of the Whole are detached from each other. Thus while Socrates does say that the rhetorician must know the facts about which he is discoursing (*unless* he is to be deceived himself) as well as the souls of his interlocutors, he does not say that the rhetorician must know the soul *as* a knower or lover of the Ideas. Moreover, the "facts" (*ta onta*) cannot be equated with the hyperuranian beings. The cosmos required for the art of rhetoric is considerably narrower than that depicted in the palinode. Presumably the artful rhetorician could apply his art to himself and so discover precisely what forms his own soul has, how it could be persuaded to do this or that, and so on (see below). The sort of self-knowledge provided for by the five descriptions of the art of division and collection will dispense with all the "mysteries" (recall 250b8, c4, and context) described in the palinode. Thus from the palinode's standpoint, the techne does not yield knowledge of the soul as a part of the Whole.

Not without reason, Phaedrus is a bit hesitant about the suggestion that the true rhetoric is like medicine (270b10); surely it is not a self-evident one. Phaedrus does have a certain respect for doctors, however (see chapter 1); Socrates thus seizes upon Phaedrus' reference to Hippocrates and asks what both Hippocrates and the true logos have to say about how one must think about *(dianoeisthai)* the nature of anything. He then launches into the descriptions of the art of division.

The first of these occurs at 270c9–271a2. To reflect (dianoeisthai) on the nature of anything, one must (1) see whether it is simple or polyeidetic; (2) if simple, investigate its dynamis, and determine both its natural capacity for acting on something else and its way of doing so, or determine its natural capacity for being acted on and by what; and (3) if complex, enumerate its forms, and follow step (2) for each of them. All this will tell us precisely what the ousia is of the nature about which we wish to speak, which in this case happens to be the soul. Socrates makes clear here (as he does in all five descriptions) that the steps of this rule-governed procedure are to be followed in a set sequence, that one must do this if one wants to make others scientific *(technikoi),* and that the art is teachable.

The method is introduced here in an extraordinarily comprehensive manner. This is not just a techne of rhetoric; psychology is only one of its subdivisions. The method is indifferent to ontological differences among its objects; it treats body and soul as though they occupied the same ontological plane. Soul will be, to repeat, one among many objects of dianoeisthai. It is to be understood just as one would understand anything else; it has no logos peculiar to itself. For the method, the disputable topics can be brought into the eidos of the nondisputables (263a–c) by means of clearheaded analysis. Certainly nothing could be further from the teaching of the palinode. The method is formulated in advance of its application to this or that being—hence the essentially preparatory tone here. Phaedrus and Socrates do not actually apply the method; they lay down in advance of any effort to know something *how* it will be known. As a result, they also determine a priori what the nature of a knowable thing shall be. To the extent that nature is knowable, it is so as an extension of the method. Entities are assumed to be the sum of eidetically distinguishable parts acting upon and being acted upon by each other. Nature is the orderly and intelligible sequence of actions and reactions of single and clustered monads. This method is intended to deliver us from intellectual blindness and deafness (270d9–e5); it is the key to enlightenment. The technician is sober, clearheaded, methodical; like the concealed lover of Socrates' first speech, he knows precisely what will satisfy his demands. So far, nothing has been said about the proper and improper uses of this techne, and in this sense the techne is value free, as I remarked above. For us the method has a remarkably modern ring to it. As though the techne also struck Socrates and Phaedrus as innovative and nontraditional, Socrates will regulate its use by introducing an (ostensibly) ancient, rustic, and conservative Egyptian story, the Theuth/Thamus myth.

So far Socrates has outlined the method in a general way. Now he wants to show its use for rhetoric. The art of rhetoric, to repeat, is only a special application of the art of thinking applied to souls, speeches, and beings in a particular way. Hence he begins this second description with a reference to Thrasymachus, thereby focusing attention on the question of rhetoric in particular. The turn to soul is dictated by the turn to rhetoric: the ousia of the nature of the soul is, as Socrates says, what they must describe exactly (270e3–5) if they are to possess the art of rhetoric. The implication that the soul's ousia can be exhaustively analyzed is breathtaking. All of a sudden Socrates seems to be promising us that divine narrative about the soul that he claimed in his palinode to be beyond the reach of mankind (246a3–6). Or is this comprehensiveness achieved, as just suggested, by limiting the depth of our analysis? The palinode's myth was an inspired, deep, but finally self-forgetful monologue; the techne of division and collection is an uninspired effort at accountability, which seems purchased at the price of superficiality. I have said above that the discussion of techne regresses to the level of Socrates' first speech in its emphasis on definition and method and, in general, in its indifference to the hyperuranian beings and to soul understood as erotic self-motion. Most of the vocabulary of the palinode is absent in the discussion of techne. The reintroduction of soul at the start of the second description of division and collection is the exception that proves the rule, so to speak. For soul is now understood in a rather different way than it was in the palinode.

The second description of the method (271a4–b5) contains three steps, which are to be followed in sequence. They are (1) very precisely make the soul visible, specifying whether it is one and by nature homogeneous (*homoion*) or rather polyeidetic like the body; for to do this is to show a thing's nature; (2) describe how it by nature acts and how it suffers and through what; and (3) having classified forms of discourse and soul and the passions (*pathemata*) of the latter, explain the causes (*aitiai*) in each case, suggesting what type of speech is suitable for what type of soul and showing what kind of speech will necessarily cause a soul to be persuaded. Socrates thus indicates that discourses too are classifiable into types. Their actions would presumably be their capacity to affect people, and perhaps their passions (neither a specific action nor a passion being mentioned here by Socrates) would consist in their being molded or suited to the disposition of an audience. Indeed, logoi can themselves be viewed as actions of the soul; hence the rhetorician's study of the soul would seem to lead to study of logos. However, while we might want to speak about the soul's actions and passions as natural, it is not clear that we would want to do the same thing with respect to the soul's discourses.

The first step here draws our attention to three important points that were implicit in the first description of the techne. To begin with, the method does not provide a way for explaining how a *complex* whole acts or is acted upon. Now, embodied souls are certainly complex or polyeidetic; but the method provides us with no way of understanding a soul's erga and pathe (cf. 245c3–4) *as a whole.* This is related, I think, to the fact that the method does not call for a teleological understanding of soul, whereas the palinode did do so (in the palinode the notion of the soul's telos was crucial to explaining how the soul could be a whole). In the palinode the ergon and pathos of the whole soul was understood in terms of erotic self-motion. But self-motion and eros are not mentioned in the descriptions of division and collection we are examining. Second, the present description of the method makes no allowance for parts of the soul that are not forms. But the palinode suggests that eros (represented by the wings) might be such a part. This point is obviously related to my first point. Finally, the method excludes the possibility that something might be both simple and complex. An Idea might be such an entity.

All the descriptions proceed without the slightest suggestion that the ousia of things might be unavailable to us. Perfect objectivity is assumed to be attainable. The psyche is assumed to be completely visible to the trained observer and fully accessible within (broadly speaking) a political context. This view stands in obvious contrast with the palinode's teaching in which, as I have already remarked, the soul is understood as erotic and so as capable of transcending the political. Moreover, there is no overt suggestion here that the user of the art of rhetoric is himself subject to the power of rhetoric. That the rhetorician must himself be persuaded that his analysis is correct before he persuades others is altogether over-looked; hence the whole problematic of self-deception and self-knowledge discussed above is silently passed over. There is, in other words, a kind of self-forgetfulness attached to the use of this method. This point is also evident in that the rhetorician seems to proceed in his analysis in a wholly nondialogical fashion. From the perspective of the palinode, for example, we might want to ask: will not the soul of the rhetorician have a certain character that will influence his perception of other souls as well as of reality? Might it not be that ousiai reveal themselves only through images, and if so, how are we to say which image is the correct one? Will not self-knowledge, then, be important for accurate use of the method?

Socrates does not answer these questions, but instead makes a rather odd comment. The popular rhetoricians about whom Phaedrus has heard are cunning people who "know all about the soul but keep their knowledge hidden" (271c1–3). Yet if they know all about the soul and do succeed in persuading, why should they object to Socrates' techne? Indeed, do they not in fact possess the techne, even though they do not make this knowledge explicit? So far, the popular rhetoricians would not find much to object to in Socrates' sketches of the techne of rhetoric, for nothing has yet been said about the necessity for knowing the truth about the subjects discoursed about. Socrates will return to that issue in a moment. Now, the rhetorical powers of the orators depend on a factor not yet mentioned by Socrates, namely, the ability to size up an audience on the spot and produce the appropriate speech. Thus Socrates goes on to produce another description of the art in which this point is made prominently. Besides, Phaedrus is still puzzled about what art the rhetoricians are supposed to be lacking (271c5), and so another statement of the matter is called for.

The third description (271c10–272b4) of the art begins by reminding us that the power of discourse is its capacity for psychagogia (at 261a7–8 we were told that the "art of rhetoric is a sort of psychagogia through words"; the reference to "art" is absent this time). According to this third description, (1) one must know the forms of the soul; these are of a certain number and sort (the variety of individuals being determined by them); (2) having divided the souls, one must recognize that there corresponds to them a determinate number of forms of discourse (a certain type of hearer will be easy to persuade by a certain type of speech to take such and such an action for such and such reason, whereas another will be hard to persuade); (3) one must observe all this happening in men's actions, being able to sharply perceive it all and apply in practice what he has learned, knowing which speeches will persuade this or that soul; and (4) one must know when to speak and when to be silent, and when to use the different forms of speech detailed in the manuals (such as brachylogy). This description makes especially clear that the purpose of the analysis of soul is to persuade this or that soul. The purpose is not theoretical, but practical. What counts as a kind of soul and a kind of discourse is de-

termined within the horizon of rhetoric, presumably by diaireses yielding
a working knowledge of the soul, a knowledge that is key to successful
practice. It is assumed, of course, that the soul does have a finite number
of stable and determinate forms which do not change. One detects in this
assumption a faint echo of the palinode's description of the twelve soul
types.

Yet there is a deceptive simplicity to the method's recommendations
for the classification of souls. What type of soul does Socrates, for example,
possess? To answer "philosophical" is not terribly helpful, unless one goes
on to explain in detail what the term means. And is this not what the
palinode—indeed, the whole of the *Phaedrus*—does? Still further, what
sort of speech *is* suitable to the soul of the Socratic philosopher? In the
fifth description of the method, we are told that one must be able to
address a variegated soul in a variegated manner (277c2–3). If Socrates
himself could find the variegated speech that is based on knowledge of
the truth and that is suitable to his own typhonic soul, would he not be
closer to knowing himself? In order to find such a speech the budding
student of the techne of rhetoric must surely push beyond the limits of
techne to philosophy as such.

The third description of the method confirms that the empirical element
cannot be removed from the art of rhetoric. Moreover, it is difficult to
see how this method could be useful for the rhetorician who addresses
large audiences. Yet there is no hint at all in the descriptions that the
rhetorician will proceed dialogically with an individual soul. The method
is unilateral rather than bilateral. The technician seems strangely detached
from the individuals he is addressing, as though he did not require a
continuous response to his words in order to determine whether his perception of his audience's nature is correct. Indeed, it is initially difficult
to see how it could be useful for a writer (mentioned here; 272b1), since
the text may fall into the hands of persons not known by the author. But
the stipulation (which anticipates the last section of the *Phaedrus*) that
the rhetorician know when to speak and when to be silent (272a4; cf.
275e3) is suggestive. Might not Socratic and Platonic irony be ways of
doing both simultaneously? We shall have occasion to consider this issue
further in chapter 6.

Socrates' third description of the art stipulates a project of considerable
magnitude. When Phaedrus observes this fact, Socrates replies, for the
first and last time in the *Phaedrus*, "you speak truly" (272b7).[39] But, as
a matter of fact, the description of the art does not yet provide a convincing
reply to the popular conception of rhetoric, whose claims are once again
summarized. Phaedrus recalls that these claims had been mentioned at

the start of the discussion (259e–260a). Yet another description of the art will thus be necessary. Socrates starts by speaking "on behalf of the wolf." He does this by repeating Phaedrus' favorite observation, which Socrates now associates with Tisias, to the effect that in matters concerning the good and the just what counts is the probable (eikos, pithanos), not what is true. Socrates then describes the method for the fourth time, addressing himself directly to Tisias (273d2–274a5). In this description, we are told that since the likenesses of truth by which the many are persuaded are best discovered by one who knows the truth,[40] one must (1) count up the natures of the auditors, (2) be able to divide into forms the beings (ta onta) and to bring together each one thing under a single idea, and (3) speak and act in a way that is pleasing to the gods. Socrates is again implying that one must know the truth in order to successfully manipulate one's audience by means of half-truths. As I have already argued, this implausible point is refuted by the fact that the popular rhetoricians do not know the truth but are quite successful in persuading their audience. One might wish to know the truth in order to avoid being deceived about oneself (262a–b) or to benefit truly one's auditor. Neither reason is mentioned in the five descriptions of the method, but both become important once the telos of speaking and writing is considered.

Socrates brings this section of the *Phaedrus* to a close with the demand that we speak in order to please the gods, not our "fellow slaves." He thus suddenly tears rhetoric out of its technical and political context. We have heard little about the gods since the palinode. Evidently the transformation of merely artful rhetoric into noble, philosophical rhetoric depends on the distinction between man and god, and so on the dual recognition of human limitations and of the divinity of the goals men should aim for in their discourses. Is it possible to combine the teachings of the palinode with the teachings about psychagogia? Socrates attempts to do so in the final section of the dialogue.

The fifth and last description of the method (277b5–c6) is intended to summarize the results of the discussion of the art of rhetoric (as distinguished from the goals of rhetoric). This final description occurs in the course of the critique of the written word. The steps there are (1) one must know the truth about each of the things one speaks or writes about and must be able to define the whole of it, (2) having defined it one must know how to cut into forms until one reaches the uncuttable, and (3) having followed this method with respect to the soul, one must discover the form corresponding to each nature and then establish and arrange the logos in an appropriate manner—a variegated speech for a like soul and a simple one for a simple soul. Until one has done this, Socrates adds, one will not be able to teach or persuade successfully. Step (1) would seem to correspond to collection (cf. 265d, where definition is associated with collection and precedes the divisions). The reference to the "un-cuttable" appears here for the first and last time in the *Phaedrus*, although the idea of a limit to division may be implied by the description at 266a of the method of division and collection. It is not clear whether the un-cuttable is what cannot be divided in any way or what cannot be divided according to the method of division. Given the emphasis in the techne section of the *Phaedrus* on the comprehensiveness of the art and on the idea that nature consists of denumerable forms which are entirely intel-ligible, it would seem that the "uncuttable" is what the method cannot cut further.

RECAPITULATION

In the last chapter I discussed the self-qualification of the palinode's mythos. I began this chapter with an explanation of the reasons for the turn to logos and rhetoric. I described the sense in which the discussion of techne progresses beyond the palinode, even as it represents a descent from the palinode's exalted vision and so a regression to the methodo-logically oriented procedure of Socrates' first speech. The cicada story and reference to the Muses illustrated this complex unity of the *Phaedrus*. I also analyzed the sense in which the turn reflected Phaedrus' interests and the nature of his reaction to the palinode, as well as Socrates' continuing desire to converse with him. That desire stems from Socrates' own preoc-cupation with self-knowledge.

The seeds of the turn to rhetoric were sown in the palinode itself, and reflection on the palinode as a logos brought them to maturity. This reflection is metaphilosophical in character; it amounts to reflection on procedure, method, and language, and on the ways in which we persuade ourselves of something. The problem of rhetoric is rooted in the problem of attaining *self-knowledge*. The ingredients of the problem are set out in the palinode's description of the influence of character on thought, and of the limitations imposed on thought by the soul's separation from what *is* as well as by the partialness, indeed the partiality of its original un-derstanding of what is. Discourse is an image of the hyperuranian beings, but one that cannot be dispensed with. Furthermore, discourse and per-suasion are inseparable. Even the soul's inner discourse with itself is an effort of the soul to persuade itself of something, to lead itself from one thought or opinion to another. The effort to know oneself cannot be severed from discourse and rhetoric; but at the same time they pose a series of dangers and traps for self-knowledge. The most obvious of these is the danger of self-deception or of lapsing into mere popular rhetoric. Our wisdom is as disputable as a dream (cf. *Symp.* 175e2–4) and is always shadowed by a sort of internal sophist (cf. *Crat.* 428d). Socrates' response to the danger is dialegesthai, that is, the effort to create a context of disagreement between himself and others that will demand genuine attention to the question and that will check, so far as is possible, unwarranted persuasion. Discourse of any sort is an influencing of the soul, and this illustrates the soul's nature as self-motion. The question then concerns what sort of discourse directs this self-motion correctly.

The notion of dialogical rhetoric is not made explicit, however, until after the Theuth/Thamus story. Socrates first develops the techne of rhetoric, a techne that is one instance of the techne of division and collection, that is, of dianoetic episteme. In the *Phaedrus,* techne is a rule-governed, precise, comprehensive, and rigorous method of analysis that is teachable and that allows one to know whatever one wishes. It requires that one follow a series of determinate steps in a set sequence, and it operates on determinate forms. It is not concerned with the uses to which its results are put, and in that sense it is value free; techne is a means to a goal, not a science of the ends. Epistemic techne is meant, in part, to yield definitive results and so to dissolve disagreements. That is, it is meant to transform the disputed class of words into the undisputed class (263a–c). "Eros," along with "soul," "knowledge," "justice," and the like, should be as uncontroversial as "iron" and "silver."[41]

There is no question of dispensing with divisions and collections in the variety of nontechnical senses of these terms. Moreover, the techne of division and collection introduces a certain self-consciousness and accountability into speaking and thinking, and in this lies much of its value. By arresting opinion and compelling reflection on *how* we are to proceed, it enables persuasion to rise above the level of "mere" rhetoric. In the final analysis, however, the techne suffers from a number of critical shortcomings as well. I discussed and illustrated the sense in which it relies on opinions. The method is a classificatory and so a retrospective, rather than a heuristic, procedure. The body of thought on which it operates and so the forms it brings to light are supplied by pretechnical understanding of things—hence the appropriateness of Socrates' taking his previously generated speeches as material with which to illustrate the method. The method also suffers from inability to specify the whole of its object (and in particular the whole of the soul) and from its indifference to the place of its object (especially the soul) in the Whole. From this is derived the inaccuracy of Socrates' schematization of the first half of the *Phaedrus*, the uninspired and sober tone of the discussion about techne, and the absence in the descriptions of the techne of references to eros, self-motion, and divine madness. Correspondingly, in the hands of the technician the soul comes to be understood in what we would call a psychological way. That is, the technician is to understand a soul's various character traits, how these traits interact with various kinds of talk, and how they represent instances of a determinate number of types of traits. The metaphysical, mythic, and religious considerations suggested by the palinode are not invoked in that context.

Socrates argues that the techne of rhetoric includes not just knowledge of the soul but also knowledge of the truth of the subjects the rhetorician discourses about. But the only real basis for the argument lies in the proviso that if the rhetorician does not wish to deceive *himself* he must know the truth. He can possess the art perfectly and still deceive himself. He can certainly be the most persuasive of men and be sadly deluded himself. The discussion of techne does not explain why it is better to avoid self-deception, and this because it does not explain the ends to which rhetoric should be put. Moreover, the art of division and collection goes only so far in helping us avoid self-deception and find the truth. As I have mentioned above, the method does impose an invaluable discipline on thinking; but one can speak half-truths artfully, as Socrates did in his first speech (262d1–6 and context). Indeed, the self-consciousness generated by the method goes hand in hand with self-forgetfulness. In the face of the techne, questions about the nature of the soul understood as erotic self-motion, that is, of the soul as a lover of *ta onta* and so of one's own soul understood in the same way, retreat to a pretechnical, forgotten past. Yet the question of the ends of the soul ought to arise not only with respect to the soul understood as the object of analysis but with respect to the soul of the analyst: to what end ought the rhetorician bother persuading others? Such questions, recalled at the end of the discussion of techne, necessitate another myth (the Theuth/Thamus story) and then a discussion of dialogue.

The importance of the issue of ends or purposes can also be put as follows. It initially seems odd that a technique of analysis should be presented in the context of a discussion about rhetoric. The art of rhetoric is, we recall, just one use to which the technique of analysis can be put. But that fact itself helps explain the connection between knowledge and rhetoric, for in the service of rhetoric, techne brings things to light from the perspective of the goals of the rhetorician who is trying to get his auditors from one position to another. Given that purpose, a number of aspects of the soul are not even mentioned, whereas others take on great importance. This is an illustration of the general point that analysis is itself a form of rhetoric: not "mere" rhetoric necessarily, but still governed by the phenomenon of persuasion and leading and following, and so (to use the palinode's terms) of "self-motion" and "eros." The practicing philosophical rhetorician will ask certain questions and not others of his auditor, depending on what aspect of the auditor's soul needs to be articulated next and on where he thinks his auditor needs to be led. In practice, analysis and (literally) education are inseparable. The artful rhetorician will ask certain questions about the subject matter depending on what he is persuaded needs illumination. He is always in the position of having educated himself and of trying to improve his education. The issue is then how to educate oneself best and to what goals. None of this can be adequately accomplished, according to the *Phaedrus*, without self-knowledge.

The palinode offers us a conception of self-knowledge fundamentally dependent on an everyday and doxic understanding of ourselves. The dependence is a complex one; the palinode is a mirror not just of how we think of ourselves but of how we ought to think of ourselves. It is on the basis of such understanding, as we saw in chapter 1, that Socrates avails himself of various myths and images. The techne, by contrast, objectifies the soul as well as logos. The tension between a mythically articulated self-knowledge and an epistemically articulated self-knowledge (a tension that is part of the problem of the unity of the *Phaedrus*) must strike us as an intimation of the by now familiar split between humanistic and scientific self-knowledge. Representatives of the view that epistemic or technical knowledge reifies and distorts accounts of human nature, and that a pretechnical understanding of ourselves as residents of the "life world" is the key to understanding man, would certainly include thinkers such as Kierkegaard, Sartre, and Heidegger. The modern advocates of the scientistic program for self-knowledge are numerous; Descartes, Leibniz, Spinoza, and Kant immediately come to mind as central figures of the earlier phases of the movement.

Obviously I cannot pause to sketch in any detail the extremely complex debate between the philosophers just mentioned. I refer to it only so as to indicate that the issue of the unity of the *Phaedrus* signals not so much a literary as a deeply philosophical problem. If I were to take the sketch in question further, I would suggest that Hegel represents the modern counterpart of the mediating position the *Phaedrus* is about to make explicit. I have indicated in several ways how the *Phaedrus* unifies mythic and technical self-understanding. Yet we still seem to lack a middle term, as it were. As it happens, the *Phaedrus* does not close with the discussion of methodological episteme. We are treated instead to a short myth and then to a discussion about dialogue. The transition from myth to techne itself has (in the *Phaedrus*) a dialectical character, as does the transition from techne to the Theuth/Thamus myth. We have seen that the analysis of techne qualifies itself and how it does so; it now turns out that techne must be subordinated to telos. This subordination is a kind of palinode. The hymn to methodological episteme (the antistrophe of myth) was only one phase in a complex ode whose truth can be grasped only when it is seen as part of a larger whole. That ode is the dialogue itself, the whole of which myth, techne, and their relationship are parts. The discussion of dialogue to which we now turn will permit us to grasp, once again through metaphilosophical reflection, what we have been engaged in all along, namely, dialegesthai. "We" includes the readers of the written dialogue as well as the interlocutors speaking in the dialogue. Now the difference between the written and spoken word will also become an issue. Reflection on that difference is an exercise in self-knowledge and so an antidote for the self-forgetfulness entailed by myth as well as techne.

6

Dialogue and Writing

THEUTH, THAMUS, THE CRITICISM OF WRITING, AND THE PRAISE OF DIALECTIC

Having said enough about the techne of words, Socrates turns to the matter of its "seemliness" (*euprepeia*). As noted in the previous chapter, the second half of the *Phaedrus* is divided in accordance with this distinction between techne and telos. That the former should be subservient to the latter is explicitly asserted in the story Socrates proceeds to invent. Theuth (whom Thamus addresses as "technikotate") stands for the autonomy of the arts, and Thamus, for the conservative telos to which they must be subjected. It is the hierarchical distinction between Theuth and Thamus that is the principle on the basis of which Socrates discriminates between spoken and written discourse. The remainder of the *Phaedrus* cannot be understood adequately unless this point is kept in mind. This distinction constitutes a retraction of the discussion of techne to the extent that the discussion left techne unregulated and to the extent that it did not distinguish between the written and spoken word. In the previous chapter I discussed the question of the unity of the *Phaedrus*. I pointed out that the Theuth/Thamus myth both parallels, in its palinodic function, Socrates' great second speech and at the same time progresses beyond that self-qualifying speech. A major task of this chapter is to show what this progress is and so how dialogue (in its spoken and written forms) is intended as the whole of which myth and techne are parts.

Socrates begins by making up an "Egyptian" myth, a myth of the ancients who "knew the truth." As was the case with the other myths in the *Phaedrus*, this story is not intended to be literally true (see chapter 4), and it once again allows Socrates to articulate his views on several levels at once. To begin with, the myth not only is handed down by the wise men of old but also refers to that ancient and pious society, Egypt. Indeed, Socrates reports fragments of a dialogue between two divine beings, Theuth and Thamus,[2] which took place before the introduction of various arts among men. Socrates goes back to the beginning, the fundamentals, the first principles. The myth thus contrasts sharply with the emphasis earlier on in the dialogue on the formulation of a new and autonomous techne of thinking.

Socrates' ostensible piety and respect for tradition contrasts sharply with, and is no doubt meant to influence, Phaedrus' affection for the avant-garde and the modern. Socrates' antiquarianism suggests the superiority of a turn to origins over the blind acceptance of progress. Our knowledge of the fundamentals, like our knowledge of the hyperuranian beings, is described as being in the remote past; that is, it is not our invention. The idea of returning to the origins, the mention of the gods and the soul (275a2), the references to memory and recollection, and the whole mythic character of this story take us back to the substantive teachings of the palinode. But the debate now is also about writing, an art not mentioned in the earlier palinode. The Theuth/Thamus story thus unites elements of that palinode with elements of the discussion of techne that succeeded it.

Socrates clearly sides with Thamus' view, which is extremely conservative and old-fashioned. Thamus is prepared to restrict the dissemination of knowledge (for example, the knowledge about writing), whereas Theuth favors universal enlightenment. Theuth is willing to proceed democratically, allowing the consumer of the arts to decide whether to use them.[3] Thamus proceeds monarchically, deciding for all potential users what "harm and benefit" (274e9) will arise as a result of the art. The relationship between inventor and user cannot simply be that of seller and buyer; a competent judge must decide what may suitably be put up for sale (cf. *Rep.* 601d–e, *Crat.* 390b–c). Though Socrates and Phaedrus have just tried to invent the true art of rhetoric, the more philosophical task seems to be that of Thamus—of evaluating the claims inventors of arts make about their creations. Moreover, by conjuring up a mythical moment in which the introduction of several arts into society is being debated, Socrates allows the question as to the worth of these arts to be formulated bluntly in abstraction from the actual role these arts have played in human history.

Socrates does not explicitly say that Thamus prohibited the gift of writing to men, but this is strongly implied. Since all the arts Theuth invented actually do exist among men, Thamus' implied prohibition of the dissemination of writing was violated. The myth offers, in a tremendously compact form, a standard according to which we may evaluate this violation. The mere fact that Theuth and Thamus debate in the medium of the spoken word the virtues and vices of the written word anticipates Socrates' evaluation of the relative merits of oral dialogue and writing: dialogue ought to be the ruling medium of all forms of philosophical rhetoric.

That the story requires interpretation is evident from, among other things, the fact that Egypt was scarcely a stronghold of philosophy. Egypt would have been a far less hospitable home for Socrates than was Athens. Thamus does not say, in this story, whether he approves of the spoken word when it becomes infused by Socratic dialectic—a dialectic that, after all, made Socrates seem impious. Socrates has more in common with the "moderns" than his use of this story lets on. It is difficult to believe that Thamus is really a philosopher king, though he is more philosophical than Theuth. Was it not, indeed, the pharmakon of Lysias' written text that drew both Phaedrus and Socrates out of the city and into a discussion with each other? Is it not ironic, indeed, that a god of tradition-bound Egypt refuses the Egyptians access to an art so important in codifying their traditions (cf. *Tim.* 23a–b)? With respect to the meaning of certain key words (such as "mneme," "graphe," "paidia," and "pharmakon"), as well as with respect to the criticisms of writing themselves, this last section of the *Phaedrus* is full of double entendres. Indeed, the fact that Socrates has obviously made up the Theuth/Thamus story (as Phaedrus immediately objects)—a modern fiction posturing as a time-honored account provided by the ancients who knew the truth—adds to the playfulness of the story. In his unconcern for the historical truth of myths and in his care for the truth about memory and soul, Socrates manifests the same view we discovered in his treatment of the Typhon story: myths are to be used for the purpose of self-knowledge.

Theuth invented, first, number, calculation, geometry, astronomy; still further, draughts and dice; and above all writing (274c8–d2).[4] Thamus had praise and criticism for each of them, but Socrates reports only the criticisms of the art of writing, along with Theuth's claim on behalf of the art. Perhaps the absence of a dialectical explanation (such as the one Socrates and Phaedrus now produce) by Thamus of his judgment is one reason Socrates calls it a "prophecy" (275c8; note the use of the future tense at 275b1). Writing seems especially important because of the magnitude of its effects on human beings. The principle Thamus and Theuth use for judging the worth of writing is nothing other than its benefit for the human soul (*psyche;* 275a2). Both Theuth and Thamus connect the art of writing with the soul's capacity to remember. The metaphysical sense of "remembering from within" is not mentioned in the criticisms of writing formulated after the conclusion of this myth (275c–e; though there are references to "reminders"). As was the case in the palinode, *mneme* and anamnesis are discussed in a myth when their metaphysical significance is at stake. I shall thus distinguish between two sets of criticisms, the one formulated in the Theuth/Thamus story, the other immediately after it. I begin with the former.

Theuth claims that his art will "make the Egyptians wiser and improve their memories; for I have discovered a remedy [pharmakon] for memory [mneme] and wisdom." The medicine analogy is by now familiar to readers of the *Phaedrus* (268b–c, 270c), as is the association of "pharmakon" with the written word (230d6, 268c3). "Pharmakon" can also mean "drug," and clearly Thamus thinks that Theuth's invention will drug memory, not remedy it. Thamus' response depends on a distinction between mneme and *hypomnesis.* Thamus agrees that Theuth has found a "remedy" ("pharmakon," 275a5) for the latter, but he suggests that students will take an overdose of it, thus turning it into a poison destructive of mneme. The written word is an "aid to memory"; to use such a *hypomnema* would be to "remember" in the ordinary sense of the term. If Phaedrus forgets exactly what the first lines of Lysias' speech are, he can (in an act of hypomnesis) recall them by glancing at the text, which thus remedies his faulty memory. Its fixity and unchangeableness allows for precise repetition, and this is particularly useful in subjects of great technical complexity.[5] Needless to say, this virtue of the written word is exactly the source of its greatest danger. I have argued in the previous chapter that writing and techne are related earlier in the *Phaedrus.* The criticism of writing constitutes an implicit criticism of techne, as the remarks made in the Theuth/Thamus story indicate. At 275c5–d2, moreover, Socrates claims that anyone who thinks that a techne transmitted by means of writing can escape the inherent defects of the written word is simpleminded.

What then is the sense of the "mneme" of whose destruction Thamus is so fearful? The distinctions between *sophia* and *doxosophia,* and between "truly understanding" and "having heard much" (or "seeming to be much knowing," 275a6–b2) parallel that between mneme and hypomnesis. The

most obvious interpretation of Thamus' point is this: people who rely on
books do not exercise their capacity to remember ideas and so lose this
capacity. They thus become thoughtless. But Thamus is getting at something deeper than this. The persons characterized by the second member
of each of the pairs have memorized a lot of information. They thus acquire
the ability to talk about virtually every subject and so become, as Thamus
wisely says, "difficult to be with." These literati think themselves wiser
than they are, thus exhibiting a lack of self-knowledge (cf. the use of
"doxosophia" at *Phil.* 49a2). They do not know their own ignorance and
have forgotten to philosophize about all the information they have stored
in their memoriès. The distinction at issue is not between someone who
remembers everything he sees and hears (having a photographic memory,
as we say) and someone whose memory is so bad that he has to keep
looking everything up to refresh it. Thamus is worried about people whose
memories are full, not empty—but full of "book knowledge." This is
"dead" as opposed to "living" knowledge, as Socrates will shortly put it.
Thamus' fear is well founded; consider the familiar spectacle of the fantastically erudite scholar who has forgotten to search for answers to the
fundamental questions. Thamus' argument, in short, gives support to the
intuition many people have that there is a difference between a learned
professor and a man who really understands things. Socrates later draws
a complementary picture of a poet, a speech writer, and a writer of laws
who spends all his time twisting his phrases this way and that, collating
and taking them apart (278d8–e2).

At the same time, the portrait of the doxosophos who *appears* to be a
know-it-all fits the sophist. The seeming and comprehensive "wisdom"
the sophist exhibits in a monologue is very much like that which the
written text exhibits, at least according to Socrates (cf. *Prot.* 329a). In
neither case is genuine dialectic present. Thus it is not inaccurate to say
that, for Socrates, books are in an important sense sophistical, dwelling
in the realm of what *seems* to be rather than of truth. Yet the phenomenon
of sophistry also suggests that "living" speech can drug the soul as much
as "dead" speech can. But Socrates thinks that a certain form of living
speech offers an antidote to spiritual narcosis, whereas the written word
lacks this redeeming feature (see below).

Thamus uses another parallel set of distinctions that help clarify what
he is driving at. The written word will introduce forgetfulness into the
souls of men since they will no longer practice their memory and "since
they trust in writing, recollecting [*anamimnēskomenous*] by means of external
marks, not from within themselves by means of themselves." The inner/
outer and anamnesis/hypomnesis distinctions clearly indicate that the sort

of "memory" Thamus wishes to safeguard is precisely the "anamnesis" of Socrates' palinode.[6] The *Phaedrus'* critique of writing calls upon a set of parallel distinctions, namely, those between mneme (or anamnesis) and hypomnesis, real wisdom/apparent wisdom, truly understanding/seeming to be much knowing, inner/outer, alive/dead, responsive/rigid, remedy/ poison, legitimate/bastard, reality/appearance, original/image, long-term growth/short-term growth, and seriousness/playfulness. These distinctions parallel the palinode's distinction between the hyperuranian and hypouranian places. Thus the criticism of writing and praise of speaking rely on the notion of anamnesis, a notion that, as we know from the palinode, is inseparable from a conception of the true ends of human life, all of which Socrates now wants to connect with the dialogical process of question and answer (see below). Far from having been left behind, the palinode is now integrated into a larger whole. The question put at the start of the second half of the dialogue (258d), namely, "when is discourse beautiful and not shameful?" only now receives an answer: when it is recollective and dialectical. This answer incorporates elements from the previous sections of the *Phaedrus*.

Even if there is a difference between apparent and real knowledge, and the latter is somehow connected with anamnesis, how is this difference to be connected with the written/spoken distinction? Socrates attempts to answer this question in the second set of criticisms of writing, a set he articulates nonmythically. These criticisms fall into two groups.

First, Socrates states several times that the written word cannot convey knowledge that is "clear" (*saphes*), "certain" (*bebaios*; "permanent" is a possible meaning here as well), "complete," and "worthy of seriousness," though it *seems* to possess just these characteristics (275c5–7; 277d8–9, 278a4–5). The written word can easily take on an authority, inviolability, and finality it does not possess, and its weighty pronouncements a specious lucidity that seems to answer all questions. Socrates seems to fear the canonization of a *biblos*. That is, the written word lets us *persuade* ourselves too easily that we are in irrefutable possession of the truth, while in fact we are not. It facilitates our tendency to become dogmatists or zealots rather than philosophers. It does not provide a reliable means of distinguishing between a waking and a dreaming vision of things (277d10). We desire knowledge and believe that the written word will help procure it for us. Socrates fears that we will become dominated by the instruments of our desire.

The second group of criticisms specifies how the written word accomplishes this. Socrates compares writing to a painting of a living animal that looks alive but is not. Like a painting, the written word remains

silent when questioned, saying the same thing over and over. The original
of which the painting is an imitation is *alive,* and the principle of life,
as we know from the palinode's apodeixis, is soul. Moreover, once something is written it floats about, getting into the hands of those who understand it as well as those who do not. It does not know when to speak
and when not. Finally, when it is unjustly criticized, it cannot defend
itself (cf. *Prot.* 329a, *Theae.* 164e; *Stm.* 294 ff. contains a critique of
written law, in which the medicine analogy is again used).

In what sense can a book, for example, harm those who misunderstand
it? Is it not the case, after all, that those who do not understand a complicated philosophical text will simply ignore it? In the wrong hands,
Socrates argues, the remedy will become the poison (hence the aptness of
the use of "pharmakon" with respect to the written word); the written
word cannot be medicinal, varying treatment in accordance with the spiritual state of the reader. Historical examples of this problem are not difficult to find, I think; consider the misuses to which some of Nietzsche's
writings were put not long ago. Perhaps the Good Book itself has on
occasion served as an excuse for some cruel piety. The deleterious effects
of the written word that Socrates has in mind seem analogous to the
damage that infatuation with philosophical dialectic can do to someone
too young to use dialectic properly (cf. *Rep.* 539b–c, *Phil.* 15d–16a, *Soph.*
251b–c). Under these conditions philosophy can have the same corrupting
influence that sophistry does or worse. An immature philosopher easily
becomes overly ironic and finally cynical (cf. *Pho.* 89d–e).

This second group of criticisms might nevertheless look like a trivial
catalog of complaints about some empirical characteristics of the written
word. One might as well complain, say, that the written word is not as
useful as the spoken to a man who is lost in a forest and must call for
help. When the criticisms are connected with the problem of rhetoric as
I have outlined it, however, they become much more interesting.[7] It does
seem impossible to engage in a live dialogue with a book. And since a
book cannot easily adjust its words to suit the soul of each reader, it may
fail to challenge him. Hence it is simple enough for the well-intentioned
reader to either reject or accept the book's "teaching" without adequate
grounds and so, again, to *persuade* himself that he knows what he does
not know. Correspondingly, writing seems to be an inappropriate medium
for the pursuit of self-knowledge. The problem Socrates is worried about
is grounded in the difficulty, established in the palinode as a condition
endemic to the soul, of separating truth and persuasion. This is the problem, as I argued in previous chapters, of self-deception—an issue at the
heart of the problem of self-knowledge and of the corresponding problem

of rhetoric. The *Phaedrus'* criticisms of writing make sense when understood in the light of the self-knowledge problematic. It is the nature of the soul that makes the spoken word preferable to the written.

Yet the criticisms of writing and praise of speaking may still seem wildly overstated. Surely writing can be dialectical and nonmonologic. The writer can anticipate objections, mention possible misunderstandings by others, and cite other authors for support. Moreover, it seems that writing never occurs in as anonymous a context as Socrates implies. One always assumes an audience, and this audience is always a reflection of a tradition in which certain sorts of questions are asked and certain sorts of answers anticipated. Still further, there would seem to be varieties (such as epideictic monologues) of the spoken word that are as destructive to self-knowledge as the written word, as my reference above to the damage caused by the improper use of dialectic suggests.

Socrates does not in fact endorse the spoken word without qualification. At 277e8–9, moreover, he criticizes the declamatory recitations of the rhapsode that aim to "persuade," not genuinely teach, others. Clearly Socrates would not approve of the sophistic speeches (alluded to earlier in the *Phaedrus*) just because they are spoken and not written. At 257b2 Socrates refers to Lysias as the "father of the logos" given earlier on, and this "logos" must include Socrates' first speech, which thus is a sort of "illegitimate son," though it is spoken. Socrates is well aware that the spoken word can have enormous power in the assemblies and therefore enormous capacity for harm.[8] Hence, in the palinode, Socrates said in the course of his description of anamnesis that a man must "use the reminders [hypomnemasin] correctly" (249c6–7). The phrase suggests that the (spoken) reminders can be used incorrectly, in a way that does not stimulate anamnesis.

Likewise, Socrates does not banish the written word altogether. He has already argued at 258d1–2 that writing per se is not shameful. As I have noted, he does allow that the serious dialectician might *playfully* provide himself with a written "thesaurus" of his thoughts so as to have good "reminders" in the "forgetfulness" (*lethe*) of old age (276d3–4). "Reminder" should be taken, in this instance, in its ordinary sense. Socrates is making a concession to the frailty of our mnemonic powers.[9] Socrates does not say precisely how far one could use this rationale to legitimize the written word. Clearly he does not think it a very significant exception to the rule. More important, he also allows that the dialectician may write for the sake of those who "follow in the same track" (276d4–5). This phrase derives from Homer and is also alluded to at 252e7–8 and 266b6–7; I have already commented on it in the previous chapter. The use of it here links the recollection and eros of the palinode's "follower of Zeus," the expert in division and collection, and the farmerlike lover of dialogue. Socrates may mean by all this that the dialectician might also write playfully so that his followers, in *their* old age, will have reminders. But this weak concession to writing could be taken to suggest much more. If the reminders are to help the young follow, indeed find, the dialectician's tracks, they must also be useful to the young before they reach frail old age. The young must philosophize and know themselves if they are to follow successfully in the dialectician's steps. And this can mean only that the "reminders" the dialectician leaves the young must help them "remember" in the sense of "recollect," and so that the "lethe" the young must overcome is that mentioned in the palinode (248c7). If so, then this redemption of the written word must be connected with Socrates' twice-stated view that the written word can at best "remind [hypomnesai] one who [already] knows the things the writing is concerned with" (275d1–2; 278a1), for the dialectical follower (the potential philosopher) might be taken to "know" these things in the sense specified in the palinode. His knowing is covered over with "forgetfulness"—not that of old age but that coeval with being human.

Yet Socrates immediately goes on at 276e4 to contrast very unfavorably the value of such writing with that of the spoken dialogue the *serious* dialectician will use in educating the young. The serious dialectician's lessons will be "written in the soul of the learner" (276a5–6, 278a3). Evidently the written text as Socrates conceives it is not even worth playing with. To anticipate somewhat: Socrates seems not to have conceived of the Platonic dialogue—a form of the written word that can remind (hypomnesai) in the sense of "kindle anamnesis" and so a form of rhetoric that can function fruitfully in the service of self-knowledge. Socrates says that if a dialectician or philosopher does write at all, he will do so not only in play but will also be able to "demonstrate the inferiority of his writing out of his own mouth" (278c5–6). As we shall see, in a certain sense Plato's dialogues do indeed point playfully to their own inferiority.

What does Socrates mean when he says that the logos that is "written *met'epistemes* in the soul of the learner" (276a5–6, 278a3) is superior to the written word since it can defend the dialectician who sowed it and knows when to speak and when not, and again that the dialectician sows words "met'epistemes" ("together with knowledge") which can defend him and also generate new growth in other souls (276e7)? As I have already noted in the previous chapter, episteme is associated in the second half of the *Phaedrus* with the techne of rhetoric, and so with the art of speaking and writing (cf. 272a4 where the issue of knowing when to speak and when not is mentioned). This is what is alluded to here. In his dialogue with his beloved potential philosopher, the lover of wisdom avails himself, to the extent appropriate, of the techne of rhetoric. Knowing how to carry on a dialogue and to seek the self-knowledge that may result from it are not, however, reducible to techne or episteme, as I have argued at length.

The language about the growth of the soul, the externality of the written word, and the view that philosophy is a search for wisdom involving all one's being indicate that Socrates is praising a way of life as opposed to a *merely* intellectual occupation. That is very much in keeping with the palinode (for example, see 257b5–6). He is also arguing that the written word will encourage the reduction of philosophy to a merely intellectual business, devoid of the recollective insight into Truth and so of the madness of eros. He fears that information will be engraved on the outer surface of one's memory, taking the place of knowledge "written in the soul." What should be written in the soul is the permanence of the erotic *search* for wisdom.

It is not difficult to see, in sum, that Socrates is endorsing dialectical discourse of the sort to which his name came to be attached. This "alive and ensouled" discourse *can* defend itself, and knows when to speak and when not, and to whom (276a). Indeed, spoken words can defend not only themselves but also the one who sowed them in the soul of the student. This spoken dialogue is not characterized by "persuasion without questioning and teaching" (277e8–9; "without teaching" repeats Thamus' words at 275a7). Legitimate discourse is discovered by its speaker; it has as its primary goal self-instruction, and its secondary goal the generation of similar discourses in the souls of others (278a). The serious man who can discourse in this way, and with an understanding of the reasons for which spoken dialogue is superior to written text, is not so much wise as a lover of wisdom (278d3–6). The distinction between wisdom and the love of wisdom here is important. For it is precisely the condition of loving wisdom rather than possessing it—the condition of a man rather than a god, as Socrates says here—that is bedeviled by the problem of self-knowledge. This insight is key to the praise of the spoken word and the criticism of the written. Socrates is emphasizing the connection between his conception of dialectic and the notion that there are limitations inherent in being human (a notion cast in terms of a distinction between man and god, a distinction that initiates this last section of the *Phr.*; 274b). That he should do so is in keeping with the *Phaedrus* as I have interpreted it. Even the statement here that the chain of dialectician-students is "im-

mortal" (277a2—note the "dunaton" at A4) very strongly suggests that
dialectic will always be a *search* for wisdom and not the possession thereof,
and so that in the essential respects a certain form of spoken discourse
will always remain superior to written discourse.

The main reason Socrates rejects writing concerns the danger that writing will not adequately induce self-questioning in its readers or author.
He clearly has in mind a certain conception of the written word. At 264a–
e he argued that the written work should be constructed like the body
of a living animal: not lacking head or feet and having "a middle and
extremities, so composed so as to suit each other and the whole." Such
a work, in other words, should have an introduction in which key terms
are defined (the "head" of the work), then should continue with an analysis
of its theme (the "body" of the argument) and perhaps with a few secondary
developments of the analysis (the "limbs"), and finally conclude with an
apt summary. The paradigm of a written work that does not meet Socrates'
strictures for good composition is Lysias' treatise, but not simply because
it is a treatise. The epitaph on Midas' tombstone (264d), which is an
example illustrating a certain defect of Lysias' text, incidentally points to
the connection between the written word and the absence of life. The
butcherlike method of division and collection outlined at 265d–266b seems
to articulate the structure of such a work (the image of the body of an
animal is also used to illustrate the method). In short, Socrates' model
fits the *artfully* written treatise perfectly. At the end of the *Phaedrus* he
once again uses the image of the body of an animal when comparing the
written work to a painting (a painting of a living animal is a picture of
its body, not its soul). However tightly knit its unity, a text of that sort
is dead. It cannot really guard the readers and author against false certainty
in the area of the disputable topics. If Socrates is taking the artful treatise
as paradigmatic of the written word, then his criticisms of writing are
not implausible. Yet they may not hold, or not hold with the same degree
of force, against a different form of writing, such as that exhibited by the
Platonic dialogue (see below).

The decisive advantage of the spoken word, in Socrates' view, might
also be put this way: it can embody the priority of the dialectic of question
and answer to assertion and statement. It suggests that thoughts are answers
to previous questions as well as preparations for further questions. It constitutes a denial of the self-sufficiency of thoughts and an affirmation of
the view that thoughts expressed in logos are interdependent (though not
in a way that yields a self-sufficient "system"; more on this below).[10] It
suggests that no philosophical position about the disputable topics is so

strong that only arguments in favor of it are sound. It also indicates that the *persuasiveness* of an argument depends on many considerations.

The written monologue, on the other hand, possesses the dangerous tendency to drug living thought. The *Phaedrus* is named after a man who perfectly exhibits this danger. At the start of the dialogue we find that Phaedrus is intent on memorizing, in the solitary splendor of the countryside and without critical reflection or effort to question the author or himself, the text with which he has fallen in love. Lysias' text was compared by Socrates to a pharmakon (230d6), and in spite of the playful suggestion that Socrates is the one who is drugged by it (see also 242e1), it is obviously Phaedrus who has succumbed. The critique of writing is therefore a critique of Phaedrus as well. The title of the dialogue thus refers indirectly to the problem of writing. But the problem of writing is ultimately grounded in the problematic of self-knowledge.[11] As I argued in chapter 1, Phaedrus is markedly lacking in self-knowledge. The dramatic and the thematic dimensions of the *Phaedrus* are perfectly harmonized.

The topics about which the philosopher will discourse are, Socrates says here, "the just and unjust and evil and good things" (277d10–e1), the "just and noble and good" (278a3–4; cf. 276e2–3). These are some of the disputable topics mentioned at 263a–c, the ones about which we disagree "both with others and with ourselves." As I argued in chapter 5, it is the truth about these issues that is haunted by the problem of distinguishing between persuasion and truth. Of course, *the* disputable topic for Socrates concerns the nature of the soul; this has been the battleground between Socrates and Lysias all along in the *Phaedrus.* Socrates is now arguing that spoken dialectical discourse is the best available means for avoiding self-deception in these areas.

Socrates characterizes the relationship between dialogue partners by means of two metaphors, the one agricultural and the other erotic. Along with a third metaphor, namely, that of play (adverted to explicitly, as well as in the reference to the festival of Adonis), they frame the closing pages of the *Phaedrus.* The partnership is between unequals and seems modeled in this and other ways on that of the lover-beloved relationship as portrayed in the palinode. Dialecticians do not "plant" discourses in each other; a dialectical relationship between dialecticians is not envisioned here or elsewhere in the *Phaedrus.*[12] As in the palinode, Socrates also avails himself of the language of sexuality in order to articulate the self-motion of the soul. The eroticism now attaches itself from the start to the beauty of a soul and logos rather than that of the body. Rhetoric, not physical beauty, is now the medium of seduction.[13] Although the notion of education is important both in the present passage and in the palinode, we have learned in the second half of the Phaedrus that the soul can never free itself entirely from the danger of seduction by the charms of this or that teaching. The activity of philosophizing cannot free itself from rhetoric; it can only minimize the dangers by relying on dialectical rhetoric.

The soul of the beloved or learner is now compared to the earth, not to a winged charioteer and horses; the metaphor for the soul is now agricultural rather than aeronautical. The metaphors of nonhuman and human or nonsexual and sexual generation blend in Socrates' description of the farmer-dialectician planting seeds in the soil/soul of the student, who in turn produces plants/sons containing new seed. It is true that agricultural metaphors were not absent from the palinode (talk about "watering" the soul occurred at 251b3, c8, and about the "roots" of the wings at 250b). The metaphor of nourishment was also prevalent in the palinode. Still, the eroticism at the end of the Phaedrus is permeated by talk about the *generation* of discourses, whereas that of the palinode barely referred to either discourses or the generation thereof, emphasizing instead the nonproductive vision that takes the soul out of the realm of genesis. Socrates indicates that "happiness" (*eudaimonein:* 277a3)—a term not used since the palinode (256d8)—will be the successful lover's reward in this life. Nothing is said now about the blessedness of souls in the next life. Correspondingly, Socrates' notion of "immortality" here (277a2; cf. 258c1–2), unlike that in the palinode, remains earthbound. The vision of the soul presented at the end of the Phaedrus is not as exalted as that of the palinode, and for good reason, given the palinode's self-qualification, the subsequent emphasis on self-conscious logos, and the development of the problem of rhetoric. It does not follow from this that the teachings of the palinode are thereby abandoned. We are instead called upon to understand anamnesis from the standpoint of dialegesthai. The "winged words" in a philosophical dialogue are to embody the erotic madness of recollection.

An intelligent farmer will not sow the land as one sows the gardens of Adonis. The true teacher will aim for long-term growth in the soul of the beloved (276b–c)—a point that has obvious parallels in the palinode.[14] No doubt the pedagogy of the sophists is to be compared to the cultivation of the Adonis gardens (it is such sophistical speeches Phaedrus seems to be thinking of at 276e1–3). The philosophical "farmer," by contrast, possesses a "dialektike techne" (276e5–6). This is the last reference in the Phaedrus to dialectic. The context makes it clear that by "dialectic" Socrates has in mind the "art" of conversation (of dialegesthai). The dialectician, according to this description, knows what soul to pick and how to make it dialectical. That is, the dialectician possesses Socrates' "erotike techne" (257a7–8).[15] The dialectician is an expert psychologist, a practitioner of psychagogia. *Dialectic is inseparable from rhetoric.* Socrates speaks repeatedly here of teaching (277e9) and learning (275a6–7, d9, 276a5, 277c5, e9, 278a2). Since dialectic is supposed to engender recollection, the terms "teaching" and "learning" cannot be taken in their normal senses (cf. *Meno* 81e–82a). Socrates claims not to be a teacher (for example, *Apol.* 33a); dialectic is not fathered in the way that other species of knowledge are.

Yet why must Thamus and Socrates mention the student/teacher relationship at all? Socrates seems to be suggesting that the spoken word is superior to the written word *and* that it is superior to the inner dialogue of a solitary mind with itself. As I have argued already in chapter 5, Socrates' decisions to engage in discourse and to do so in the company of others are inseparable. We saw that where there is discourse there is rhetoric. Even the soul's inner dialogue with itself is a matter of persuasion, of leading and following. The problem is then to distinguish misleading rhetoric from the sort that leads one to what is really the case. That is, the problem is to determine how a soul is to move itself recollectively. As was evident from the palinode, recollection is a precarious business. The soul and the hyperuranian beings are connected by the finest of threads, and the limitations of vision, the parochialism of desire, the inseparability of persuasion and truth, of images and originals, of character and intellect, the uplifting but potentially destabilizing energy of eros, the partiality of single discourses and the seeming impossibility of a final and whole discourse, the difficulty of distinguishing between intellectual *theoria* and *poiesis*—all these factors combine to generate what I have called "the problem of self-knowledge" and *therefore* Socrates' rather extreme views on the defects of the written word and the virtues of the spoken. The danger of substituting an opinion for knowledge is so ubiquitous and unavoidable (as the palinode demonstrated) that a special form of discourse is required if the danger is to be checked. By questioning others and defending itself (as well as the reverse), the movement of thought does not settle artificially on a single system, concept, theory, method, proposition—on a single dogma, in short. Recollection that is not sustained dialogically soon degenerates into the moribund rhetoric that Socrates associates with the written word.

Socrates practices his dialectic for his own benefit primarily. He teaches others insofar as he prepares the ground for them to recollect, and this consists in disabusing them of their firmly held opinions, showing that things are not as they seem to them to be, and in sparking their eros for wisdom. This teaching is, though, a by-product of Sócrates' main concern, namely, his own self-knowledge. In chapter 1 we saw that Socrates' desire to converse with Phaedrus is to be explained along these lines. As Socrates puts it in the *Charmides,* where he defends himself against the charge that he talks to others just in order to refute them for the sake of refuting them: he discusses with others "the meaning of my own words—from a fear of carelessly supposing, at any moment, that I knew something while I knew it not. . . . I am examining the argument mainly for my own sake, but also, perhaps, for that of my other intimates" (166c7–d4; cf. *Prot.* 348c5–d5, *Meno* 80c8–d4, *Gorg.* 453c1–4, *Pho.* 91a, *Crat.* 428d).[16] As Socrates says here, the discourses a man gives birth to in himself are "legitimate" in the highest sense of the term, and the sons or brothers of these, which arise in other souls, are such in a secondary sense (278a5–b2).

The concern for self-knowledge underpins the contrast, pervasive in this last section of the *Phaedrus,* between playfulness and seriousness. The former is consistently used (with an exception I will discuss below) to characterize the diàlectician's attitude to the written word and the latter his attitude toward the spoken. The reasons dialogical discourse is more serious have been discussed above. Though Socrates envisions a playful use of the written word, he himself declined to put his philosophical thoughts into writing, and so is interested exclusively in the serious use of dialectic. This suggests that in his opinion the assistance the written word might offer in the matter of self-knowledge is so slight, and the dangers so great, that the risk was not worth taking. It would seem that in the calculation leading to this conclusion, the other factor Socrates mentions—the utility of written memoranda in old age—receives very little weight. By refusing to write, Socrates also indicates that teaching others is not his highest priority; as already indicated, it is for him more a by-product of his quest for self-knowledge. The chain of dialecticians and students he envisions depends on the spoken word. Though Socrates promises "immortality" for the words sown in this manner (277a2), such a chain would be extraordinarily fragile, a fact of which Socrates was surely not unaware. Indeed, the survival of even his reputation as a teacher seems of little importance to him, and for the same reasons. Writings by Socrates would have virtually ensured immortality for their author. That pedagogy is of secondary importance for him, however, does not mean that dialogue is of secondary importance. It is indispensable precisely because it alone fulfills his desire to educate himself. Finally, it does not seem that Socrates could have been terribly concerned with leaving behind logoi (of the serious, spoken sort) that would defend him before the tribunal of future

generations. It is the written works of Plato and others that have presented
(at least for posterity) Socrates' *apologia,* a complex defense that could not
have been handed down verbally through the centuries.

Socrates prays that he and Phaedrus might become dialecticians (278b3–
4 and context),[17] and with this he sends Phaedrus off to deliver to Lysias
and all composers of discourses, to Homer and all the poets, to Solon and
all the law writers, a report of their dialogue. Phaedrus' role as intermediary
between Socrates and the city is thus affirmed. The private discussion
between Phaedrus and Socrates has results relevant to the "public opinion
makers." Judging from the specifics Socrates mentions, however, only
the results of the immediately preceding discussion are to be conveyed to
them. The talk about eros, soul as self-motion, hyperuranian beings, division and collection is to remain private. Perhaps it could not be com-
municated effectively to the persons in question, and certainly not by
Phaedrus, who probably has understood little of it.

Yet does not Plato's written text also serve as an intermediary between
Socrates and the groups mentioned? Phaedrus is sent by Plato out into
the world under cover of a text named after him. The *Phaedrus'* message
is far more complex than that which Phaedrus is charged by Socrates with
delivering, since the *Phaedrus* includes all the "private" talk just mentioned.[18] That is, a simple act of reflection reveals a puzzling dimension
to this last section of the *Phaedrus.* Socrates' criticisms of writing are
themselves written. Is not the *Phaedrus, according to its own standards,* an
"illegitimate brother" of true living discourse, a dead painting or imitation
of Socrates himself? But why then did Plato write? Must not Plato either
reject the criticisms or weigh them differently than Socrates does? Just
as in considering the status of the palinode and the art of division and
collection, so too now is it not necessary to reflect on the difference between
the theories being propounded and the context within which they are
propounded?

Socrates himself sets this process in motion when he refers to the preceding discussion (*ta peri logōn* at 278b7 refers, strictly speaking, to the
entire second half of the dialogue) as play. This is the exception mentioned
above to Socrates' use of the play/seriousness contrast. Just as Socrates
detracted from the significance of his first speech by ironically referring
to it as the product of inspiration; just as he qualified the solemnity of
the palinode by referring to it as a "not altogether unbelievable logos"
and as a "mythical hymn" (265b8, 265c1), and to both his speeches as
"play" (265c9); just as he restricted the importance of his new "method"
of thought by means of a playfully concocted Egyptian tale; so now Socrates, having just spoken of the inferiority of play to seriousness, undercuts

the seriousness of the whole second half of the *Phaedrus* (including the distinction between play and seriousness itself!). The serious dialectic of Socrates now appears playful, but in a different sense of "playful" than that which held for the literary Adonis gardens of nonphilosophical writers, as well as that which held for the memoranda of dialecticians. Socratic playfulness has a serious intent, namely, self-knowledge and recollection. At this level, *paidia* is genuine *paideia*. The sense in which it is seriously playful (for the apparent oxymoron one should blame Socrates) is inseparable from the qualifications with which all the phases of the *Phaedrus'* discussion are framed.

That is, the playfulness of the dialectic in the *Phaedrus* is inseparable from Socratic irony.[19] The development of the *Phaedrus* is thoroughly permeated by irony, not just with respect to the drama but with respect to the development of the themes.[20] In typically Socratic fashion, various points of view are presented as though they were final and are then purposely undercut to reveal a further, unanticipated, meaning. The original meaning is not simply rejected. As I have argued repeatedly in this and previous chapters, the movement from one level to the next resembles the way in which Socrates' first speech is recanted by his second speech (up to a point, one might also speak of Socrates' first speech as recanting Lysias' speech). An act of reflection brings us to see that a given view cannot be complete; it is not wholly true nor wholly false either. For this reason, I offered the suggestion that the development of the *Phaedrus* is palinodic. I now suggest that this amounts to saying that the development is playful and ironic. But since reflection on partial views is meant to lead us back to the discursive whole of which they are parts, and since this whole is marked by the orderliness, harmony, and symmetry of the parts—that is, by perfection or Beauty—it may also be called "recollective" in the sense described in the palinode and mentioned in the Theuth/Thamus story. The repeated movement from an "ode" to "palinode" (the latter serving as an "ode" for a further "palinode") is the *recovery* of a larger context that is "already there." I shall say more about this below and in the Epilogue.

For now, I return to the irony of which Socrates cannot, qua persona in the dialogue, be aware—namely, that his criticism of writing is itself written and so itself recanted—by Plato. This deed suggests that Socrates' critique of writing may be true in part, but not wholly or without qualification. Plato's recantation of Socrates' critique thus puts that critique in a larger, more complex perspective in a manner analogous to the other palinodes just mentioned. To restate the matter: the *Phaedrus* offers us a palinode recanting the first two speeches of the *Phaedrus;* then a recantation (in the form of a discussion of the techne of words) of this palinode; then a recantation (introduced by the Theuth/Thamus story) of this recantation; followed by Plato's recantation (visible in his *deed* of writing) of the critique of writing expressed by the personae in his text. But a self-qualification of Plato's irony will also appear, for the deed of writing can be seen to acknowledge its inferiority to living dialogue between philosophers (see below). This fifth palinode of the *Phaedrus* returns us to something like Socratic dialegesthai as the proper medium for philosophizing (more on this below).[21] For Plato, too, dialogue is the living self-motion of thought.

PLATO'S WRITTEN DIALOGUES

Plato's decision to write, and to write dialogues, can be understood on the basis of the *Phaedrus* itself if the reader is prepared to compare what Plato has his characters *in* the *Phaedrus* say with the fact that they are "saying" it in a *written* text whose form is that of a dialogue. In this sense, Plato's *Phaedrus* contains within itself the possibility of reflection on its own status qua written work. This is in keeping with the view that the written word is an "image" of the spoken (276a8–9) and the assumption that the image is to be understood relative to its original. The *Phaedrus* not only *shows* dialectic at work; it indirectly supplies (by virtue of being a written work that comments about written works) a commentary *about* the dialectic. An immanent understanding of Plato's decision to write dialogues, then, is possible.

As already mentioned, Plato's decision to write shows that he does not agree with Socrates' position (as presented in the *Phaedrus*) on the matter; else he would have followed in the latter's steps in this regard. Plato must think that the criticisms of writing are answerable at least to some extent, that some benefit Socrates did not acknowledge follows from the use of the written word, that the criticisms of writing are just not that powerful, or, finally, that some combination of these alternatives is the case. Plato's position in this matter cannot be assessed without reference to the *kind* of writing he uses.[22] If it is the case, as I have argued above, that the sort of writing Socrates is thinking of in his critique is the treatise form, then Plato's divergence from Socrates here is connected with his having discovered an extraordinary species of the written philosophical dialogue— a form of writing not adequately assessed by Socrates.[23]

It is obvious at a glance that Plato's dialogues are not modeled along the lines touted by Socrates as definitive of a well-composed text. This is a fortiori so with the *Phaedrus*. By writing a dialogue that seems shock-

ingly disunified and in which unified writing is defined and praised by
someone who refused to write, Plato thrusts the point at the reader. Unless
one believes that Plato could not follow the advice about good writing
he puts into Socrates' mouth, one must infer that Plato did not accept
the assumption about the form of writing that underlies the advice. It is
this latter inference I wish to argue in favor of. Moreover, I shall argue
that the dialogue form of writing, as it is used by Plato, blunts the force
of Socrates' and Thamus' criticisms of writing. That is, by *writing,* Plato
signals a disagreement with Socrates' criticisms, and by writing *dialogues,*
he signals an agreement with them. A number of peculiarities of the
Platonic dialogues, peculiarities that can be understood as part of Plato's
response to Socrates' criticism of writing, mark out the Platonic dialogues
as a distinct literary-philosophical genre. Among these peculiarities are
their unsystematic and noncatechistic character; Platonic anonymity and
irony; the presence of several layers of meaning contained within one another, the more difficult lying underneath the simpler; the interplay between drama and argument and so between showing and saying; the mimetic and mirroring nature of the dialogues; and the absence of a dialogue
between mature philosophers. I shall comment on these points below.

A Platonic dialogue does not present a clear and certain (permanent),
or complete teaching. In general, Plato's dialogues look like a buzzing
confusion of ideas, arguments, images, myths, digressions, and interjec-
tions by characters meeting at a variety of places and times. To find a
system of thought in the dialogues would require a massive effort of interpretation, for such a system (if it exists at all) can only lie buried deep
in the dialogues (hence the connection between the old view that Plato
is an esotericist and the view that he has a system). Spinoza's *Ethics,* by
contrast, trumpets its systematic nature from start to finish. The Platonic
corpus does not present the aspect of a system either. This fact is visible
if one asks whether the coherence of "Plato's philosophy" would be upset
if a new Platonic dialogue were discovered, or if one of the dialogues in
our possession had never been written, or if some of the dialogues (say,
the *Statesman*) turned out to be inauthentic and others (for example, *Erastai*
and *Alcibiades I*) indubitably authentic. There is no preface or conclusion
to Plato's thought within the corpus—no head, middle, or extremities.

Moreover, since Plato does not speak in propria persona in his dialogues,
they cannot be canonized without further ado as "the teachings of Plato"
unless one makes the arbitrary assumption that character X is Plato in
disguise. Plato's anonymity or silence, that is, is an indispensable element
of his use of the dialogue form and so his response to Socrates' criticisms
of the written word. In these ways the Platonic dialogue form goes some

way toward countering Socrates' fear that writings will serve as pretexts for dogmatism. The dialogue form has been used in a catechistic manner, but not by Plato. The author is also prevented thereby from expounding a doctrine in a dogmatic way as The Truth, armed with impressive declarations and polemics. A Platonic dialogue could, presumably, be memorized, just as Thamus feared. But for the reasons just stated, such memorization seems altogether pointless if the expected effect is to acquire the capacity to lecture on Plato's philosophy.

Socrates objected that the written word cannot ask or answer questions, does not know when to speak and when not, and cannot defend itself. Plato's dialogues do, however, overcome these objections at least in part. If it is the case that a Platonic dialogue contains several layers of meaning (such as the difference between words and deeds, as well as levels within them), then it is the case that in a sense they do know when to speak and when not.[24] For they announce their deeper message only to those readers able enough to find it. To those unsuited to philosophizing, the Platonic dialogues are closed books. Again, I infer from the nature of the dialogue form and from the study of particular Platonic dialogues, as well as from the assumption that Plato knew what he was doing when he wrote them (see the Introduction), that the stratification of meanings in the dialogues is purposely designed by Plato to achieve this goal. By contrast, the ideal of modern academic writing in philosophy is clarity of argument, univocacy of meaning, and overt statement of the author's intentions and theses, however difficult the subject matter may in fact be.[25]

Plato's dialogues are medicinal in that they vary the treatment with the patient. The medicine is conservatively applied by Plato; philosophy is not beneficial for each and every person. However radical the deeper meaning of the dialogues, on the surface they generally present a fairly edifying teaching: be virtuous, be pious, do not break the law, stay away from sophistry, cultivate the desires of the soul rather than those of the body, and do all this lest you be unhappy or punished in the next life. My point is *not* that Socrates and Plato secretly held views contrary to each of these beliefs but rather that they may not have held exactly these views and certainly did not hold their views for the same reasons non-philosophical people might. Plato and Socrates did not, however, think it is possible or desirable to try to transform everyone into a philosopher. For this and other reasons, neither of them was a revolutionary, let alone an advocate of "universal enlightenment."

At the same time, the levels of meaning in Plato's text are not disconnected from one another, such that the "real" message is indecipherable without clues supplied from the sources external to the dialogues. Indeed, a good deal of the message concerns the relationship between these levels and their inseparability. The nature of Socratic-Platonic philosophizing is, in fact, written all over Plato's dialogues in the practice of the dialectic which always, in one form or another, shapes each of Plato's texts.

Correspondingly, it also seems that Plato's dialogues do ask and answer questions in that they pose riddles and aporiai (some of which are obvious, like that of the unity of the *Phaedrus,* and some of which are not) to the reader and then supply, in the form of deeper strata of significance, partial answers to the questions. The riddles and questions posed by the text are always near enough to the surface, but always phrased in conservative enough ways to enable Plato's dialogues to approximate one of the characteristics that Socrates attributes to the spoken word, namely, the ability to select and fertilize the soul of the potential philosopher, as well as to further cultivate that of the accomplished philosopher—an astounding feat of rhetoric on Plato's part.[26] As was the case in the palinode, so now the crucial diairesis of mankind is between the philosophers and the nonphilosophers. Platonic rhetoric is intended to speak on these two levels and, equally important, to locate potential philosophers and transform them into philosophers. Moreover, the ability of a Platonic dialogue to defend its author is provided for, to some extent, by its ability to answer questions. If one takes Platonic anonymity or silence seriously, as one must, then the problem receives a radical solution: since *Plato* does not say anything in his own name in the dialogues, there are no statements *by Plato* to be attacked or defended.[27]

That is, Plato's dialogues seem designed to function as mirrors of a peculiar sort, for they allow the reader who is unsuited to philosophy to see himself in the text (that is, to "find" in the text only what he expects or wants to find), and the reader who is suited to philosophy to glimpse something that he has not yet achieved and that he desires (for example, self-knowledge). Even the failures and the mistakes of so many of the characters in Plato's dialogues may confront the philosophical reader with an occasion for reflection on himself, that is, on a probable (and defective) way of understanding a part of the soul or of responding to some question. By functioning in this manner, the dialogues satisfy the requirements of the *Phaedrus'* art of rhetoric, which stipulate that one's words be suited to the soul of one's auditor and not just to the subject matter, that one introduce into the mysteries of philosophy only those able to undergo them successfully, and that philosophical rhetoric lead to self-knowledge. Hence they also succeed, to a considerable degree, in avoiding the danger of turning those who are unsuited to philosophical dialectic into sophists or eristical debaters. Plato's anonymity reflects his pedagogical awareness of the danger his authority poses to his student's growth.

Socrates agrees with Thamus that a chief objection to the written word is that it stymies the activity of recollection. This activity is, as I interpreted it, that of living dialogue. The written word fails, Socrates suggests, to seduce the reader into undertaking the lifelong search that is the love of wisdom. Insofar as the Platonic dialogues do not present a dogma, system, or teaching (in the usual sense of the term), they are not liable to this criticism. *Platonic anonymity also attests to the core meaning of philosophy as questioning directed to self-knowledge.* The dialogues not only *encourage* the search, and even *defend* the view that philosophy *is* a search (more on this in the Epilogue), they also *portray* this very activity. By being imitations of a peculiar sort, they *show* rather than *tell* us that philosophy has this character. Plato shares with Socrates the view that dialectic, as the knowledge of asking and answering questions, cannot be taught verbally in the way, say, that someone might be taught to count from one to ten. Dialectic can be learned only by the practice of it; it depends on something like phronesis rather than rule-governed methods. The activity of coming to an insight, and the insight itself, must be experienced in order to be understood. To do otherwise is to fall prey to the danger prophesied by Thamus—that of memorizing information obtained from without, instead of remembering knowledge from within.

Hence it makes sense for Plato to *show* us what dialectic is.[28] Moreover, writing *dialogues* also allows Plato to emphasize the view that philosophy cannot remove itself totally from the level of particularity. The goal of the whole pursuit is self-knowledge, and this must ultimately focus on knowledge of oneself as *this* individual in this time and place and in these circumstances. The beginning point of philosophizing, namely, ordinary experience, is never left behind. It is not just the banal fact that one is always a resident of the everyday world but that this world supplies and gives significance to the basic issues (the disputable topics) which shape our philosophizing, that makes Plato's imitation of the everyday philosophically important. Recall Socrates' refusal, at the start of the *Phaedrus,* to substitute a reductive, materialistic explanation of myths (including myths useful for self-knowledge) for one that takes its bearings by doxa. By writing dialogues that imitate the activity of philosophical dialogue, Plato prevents the logos from becoming completely autonomous; even the most abstract monologues (the premier example being the second half of the *Parmenides*) are bound to a dramatic, rhetorical, human, and empirical context. In the Platonic dialogues, the soul's pathe and erga are always before us. I have argued throughout this study that this context is not dispensable.

The Platonic dialogue actually seems to surpass the spoken word in two areas Socrates professed to be concerned with, namely, the creation of an "immortal" chain of discourses stretching from teacher to student, and the capacity of a dialectician's "plants" to "defend" he who planted them. Plato's writings are far more effective means of defending Socrates and his way of life than Plato's oral teachings would have been (at least this is true before the tribunal of history, if not before the Athenian court that tried Socrates). For the written word does possess a permanence and repeatability denied to the spoken word. Thus Plato's written dialogues are also better suited to creating that "immortal" chain of philosophers than is Socrates' spoken dialectic. Since the written dialogues can reach a far wider audience than Socrates can, they can cultivate, across the expanses of time and space, larger numbers of philosophers than is possible for the spoken word.

In sum, Plato's dialogues do answer, in part, Socrates' criticisms of writing. Plato's decision to *write* is inseparable from his discovery of a marvelous kind of written dialogue. But his decision to write *dialogues* is inseparable from his acceptance of the very same aporiai that led Socrates to criticize all forms of writing, as well as of the very same telos (self-knowledge) that Socrates thinks is achievable through philosophizing. That is, Plato does not simply reject Socrates' criticisms of writing; he thinks he can meet them adequately enough to balance the dangers associated with the written word. Plato thus accepts the basis of these criticisms, namely, the whole problematic of self-knowledge.[29] Thus Socrates and Plato share, in their mutual and extreme devotion to dialectic and nothing but dialectic, the same premises about the difficulties and value of self-knowledge. Plato also accepts the critique of writing as applied to treatises; up to a point, he accepts the critique as applied to other forms of writing, but thinks he has found in the dialogue form a way to blunt some of its force. Like the gramma of the Delphic Oracle, Plato's texts command "Know thyself!" To ask why Plato wrote dialogues is to ask a philosophical question about the foundations of Platonic philosophizing.

If this interpretation is correct, then Plato does not mean to substitute the study of his texts for the live activity of philosophizing. The texts are still dead and external compared to the living and internal self-motion of the soul. Plato's writings demote themselves in rank relative to the truly serious activity of "writing in the soul," even as they defend themselves as useful memoranda for the lover of wisdom. In this sense, Plato has fulfilled Socrates' demand that an author be able to demonstrate out of

his own mouth the inferiority of his own writings (278c6–7). Though he
was a consummate writer, Plato would never agree to the deification of
The Text popular among contemporary poststructuralists, for example.
As I put it above, Plato's dialogues themselves recant their authority as
written in order to return the reader to the life of ensouled discourse.[30]

A qualification is necessary here, however. For Plato's dialogues do not
necessarily recommend dialegesthai in precisely the form it is pictured
within the dialogues. Missing from these dialogues is, as noted above, a
conversation between mature philosophers. Yet philosophers such as Socrates and Plato must have had conversations with each other in which
they questioned and answered each other. The phenomenon is not unknown
to each of us, though fruitful dialogue between mature philosophers is
difficult and rare. Such a dialogue cannot escape being a paradigm for
the Socratic who believes that dialectic and philosophy are inseparable.
If Socrates converses with others in order to prevent himself from thinking
he knows something when he knows it not, would he not do everything
within his power to seek out other philosophers? The reasons Plato did
not write such a dialogue are complex;[31] I do not think, however, that
we are meant to infer from the absence of such a dialogue in Plato's corpus
that Plato thought it either undesirable or impossible for philosophers to
talk to each other. Possibly he thought that such a dialogue could not be
written, at least not in a way that would have preserved his anonymity
(this being an essential factor in the success of the dialogues in blunting
Socrates' criticisms of writing). By virtue of being written, in any event,
Plato's dialogues succeed in narrowing the gap between a conversation
between philosophers and a conversation of a philosopher with someone
like Phaedrus. Thanks to the absolute control the author of a text can
exert over the conversation presented in it, such a conversation is far more
perfect than one taking place in real life. To that extent the dialogues are
distortions of the reality (such as that of philosophical conversation) they
ostensibly represent.

That is, in a written Platonic dialogue, there are no accidents. Every
seeming accident and chance occurrence is planned in accordance with
"logographic necessity" (264b7; see also the Introduction to this book).
Consequently the actions and pronouncements of a character such as Phaedrus are far more interesting in the context of Plato's text than they would
be if they occurred in the course of life. In the context of this written
work, Phaedrus' mediocrity becomes very illuminating, whereas in the
course of life we would be tempted to dismiss a Phaedrus without further
ado. Correspondingly, the perspectives of the reader of a dialogue and of
the participant in a dialogue are bound to be different. In a philosophical

dialogue such as the *Phaedrus,* for example, Phaedrus' mistakes and ignorance about the nature of eros are for the reader an occasion for learning
about, among other things, the reasons and effects of the ignorance of
people such as Phaedrus.[32] Phaedrus "means" a lot more than he is conscious of, and in this way his words and deeds become genuinely interesting
for the philosophical reader. All this is made possible by the fact that we
are dealing with a written text.

When we combine this observation with the point made earlier about
the conservative and mirrorlike character of the dialogues, another observation suggests itself. The Platonic dialogues are "imitations" in the
sense of being "phantasms" rather than "eikons" (*Soph.* 235d–236c). That
is, the proportion of the parts of the written dialogue do not precisely
reproduce those of the original, but instead are suited to the multiple
perspectives of types of readers, with the aim of interesting them in bringing the original to life in themselves. The original represented in a variety
of ways and with varying degrees of explicitness and comprehensiveness
by Plato's texts is the soul's pursuit of self-knowledge. Socrates in effect
rejects the possibility of a phantasm that could successfully lead a reader
to engage in that pursuit. Plato's brilliant use of the dialogue form shows
that Socrates was mistaken on this point.

THE PRAYER TO PAN AND CONCLUDING
WORDS

The prayer to Pan is Socrates' next to last pronouncement in the *Phaedrus.* The prayer summarizes, in an extraordinarily compact form, the
major themes of the dialogue. The distinction between the inner and the
outer, the talk about beauty, the references to Pan and the other local
gods, the mention of the outer possessions being disposed in a manner
that is friendly to those within, the desire for sophrosyne and wisdom—
all these have come up repeatedly before. Moreover, the prayer needs to
be read on both literal and metaphorical levels, and in this it resembles
many other passages in the dialogue. Possibly the "wealth" and "gold"
Socrates refers to, for example, may be taken literally; but surely they
also refer to spiritual riches.[33] Although the prayer does not explicitly
mention self-knowledge, I do not know what sense to make of it except
by understanding it in connection with Socrates' passion for self-knowledge, as that theme has been developed in the *Phaedrus.*

The prayer has a precedent in Socrates' prayer to Eros at the conclusion
of the palinode. In both cases, the prayer is an expression of hope. The

prayer to Pan is explicitly oriented toward the future and thus seems to express with special clarity Socrates' sense of incompleteness and imperfection. Socrates prays for wisdom, but has acknowledged that only a god can possess it (278d3–4). He knows his limits; the prayer is indeed *metrios* (279c4). Both of these prayers have something in common with his formulation, at the start of the *Phaedrus,* of the self-knowledge issue. In all three cases, Socrates is focusing primarily on himself as a particular person (in none of these cases is the "soul" mentioned). He wonders whether he is typhonic or not; he prays that he will not lose his erotic art; he prays that he will reconcile what is inside him with what is outside him. As at the start of the *Phaedrus,* so now at the end self-knowledge is conceived of on the level of the individual's particular self and way of life rather than on the soul or general philosophical issues concerning self-knowledge. Thus the vocabulary we have become used to (including "soul," "episteme," and so forth) is no more present here than it was at the start of the dialogue. We begin and end with an interpretation of the Delphic imperative that is guided by the individual's concern for himself, that is, by the question "how should *I* live my life?" The underlying ethical imperative that explains *why* Socrates cares about self-knowledge also explains why self-knowledge begins and ends with an individual's effort to know himself in particular, however complex and necessary the intervening discussions about soul and related topics may be. The point of engaging in such discussions is, finally, to help the discussants live the life that is best. Moreover, in all three prayers the initial threat that confronts the desire for self-knowledge remains the same. The problem of a psyche's disharmony that was so vivid in Socrates' comparison of himself with Typhon is still present. A similar problem suggested itself in terms of Socrates' prayer for possession of the erotic art, that is, for the art that focuses the soul's desire on the unifying pursuit of truth. The threat may also consist in the loss of sophrosyne that was exhibited by Typhon, characteristic of unphilosophic eros, and earlier associated with Pan (at 263d Socrates connects Pan with his first, "enthusiastic" speech). Thus the madness/self-control issue, so prevalent in the *Phaedrus,* is also embedded in the final lines of the dialogue.

In Socrates' two prayers as well as in his comparison of himself with Typhon, Phaedrus takes a backseat. It is amusing that Socrates turns to Phaedrus after reciting the prayer to Pan and asks whether "we" still lack something further. The "truly golden" Phaedrus (235e2) seems to think that what is good for Socrates is good for him: he joins Socrates in the prayer, for "friends have all things in common." It is Phaedrus, not Socrates, who recalls this maxim; Socrates could not think that he and Phaedrus have all things in common (indeed, Phaedrus was intent on leaving without any prayers). Phaedrus misunderstands their relationship. A solemn prayer is immediately followed by a bit of subtle humor. The comedy of the *Phaedrus* is thus sustained to the end, as is the question "why does Socrates talk to Phaedrus?" Surely one of the things Socrates is praying for is a harmony between himself and persons such as Phaedrus. He seems to have achieved it, but only on the basis of his companion's deficient knowledge of both himself and Socrates. Socrates does not try any longer to disabuse Phaedrus of his illusion. Nevertheless, Phaedrus is not altogether wrong that inner wisdom can be shared and can serve as a basis for friendship, unlike material gold whose power tends to be divisive. As 228a3–4 indicates, Phaedrus prefers discourses to gold, and this preference helped join Socrates and Phaedrus together in dialogue (as I argued in chapter 1). Thus once again Phaedrus does, *malgré lui*, have an inkling of the truth.

Socrates does not pray for an episteme or techne; the prayer has a strongly existential slant. He wishes to "become" a certain kind of person (cf. 278b3–4 and context). Heavy emphasis is put on the value of unity, harmony, and integrity in the face of the natural differentiation of life. The "inner" and "outer," for example, were mentioned explicitly at 245e; they referred to the soul and body, respectively. The terms were also mentioned at 275a in the context of the discussion about anamnesis; there they served to help characterize the "reminders" that are within the soul and are accessible through live, spoken dialogue, as distinct from those that are external to it in that they are embodied in the written word. Hence the whole problem of rhetoric is also alluded to here. On the basis of the palinode, we would have to add that things that are outside oneself can also be the hyperuranian beings (consider *ta exo*, 247c2). Each of these associations articulates a dimension of the self-knowledge issue. The prayer to Pan, and Phaedrus' response to it, must be understood in the light of the whole of the *Phaedrus*.

At the start of the *Phaedrus* Socrates wonders whether he is tame and a participant in some divine destiny or whether he is tremendously complex and hubristic. That issue too still seems present here. According to the *Cratylus* (408b–d), Pan is the "double-natured" son of Hermes (the inventor of logos). Pan and logos are twofold; their upper part is true, smooth, and godlike. The lower part is false and goatlike; it shares in myths and tragedy, dwells among men, and is dangerous to sophrosyne. Pan can inspire, but sometimes in the wrong way; as already noted, Socrates suggests that Pan and the other local gods animated his first speech. Has not the *Phaedrus* suggested that the soul is, in fact, this unnatural and monstrous synthesis of species, being partly godlike and part beastlike?[34] and that logos too can ennoble a man or (especially in the form of the written word) drug him into forgetfulness? The *Phaedrus'* own discourse is dual throughout. The duality in question seems appropriate to a man who is "in between" the merely mortal and the divine. Socrates, who is eros incarnate and an avid lover of dialectics, is paradigmatically *metaxu* and knows himself to be such.[35]

Just as the prayer for unity between inner and outer reminds us of the difficulty of harmonizing them, so the very distinction between inner and outer reminds us that self-knowledge is, as Socrates has shown in the *Phaedrus,* inseparable from knowledge of oneself as part of a greater Whole. We can scarcely avoid thinking here of "pan" in the sense of the "All" or "Whole" (cf. Crat. 408c10–d1); and in this way also the prayer alludes to yet another major theme of the dialogue.

Socrates' last word in the dialogue is "let us go." The *Phaedrus* closes as it began, with an indication of movement. We now understand this to be a matter of spiritual self-motion. Their physically sedentary "feast of words" over, Socrates and Phaedrus return home, as do the gods at the conclusion of their banquet (247e4 and context). The feast took place outside the walls of the Athenian universe, but could not have taken place in the absence of the polis. Like the gods who must stand on the back of the heavens in order to ponder what lies beyond and outside them, Socrates too is supported by his cosmopolitan city (especially by its so-phisticated discourse) and is thus enabled to look beyond the polis's limits to what lies inside himself. The nourishment the "atopotatos" (230c6) lover of wisdom seeks both is and is not within the city's confines. Thus the return to Athens is both good and bad. The potential disharmony to which Socrates' prayer addresses itself is reflected in the ambivalent de-sirability of the deed which the last word of the *Phaedrus* prefaces.

Epilogue: The Defense of Dialogue

The Soul has its own Logos, *which increases itself.*
HERACLITUS[1]

The "dialogue" discussed in the previous chapter would seem to be an endless enterprise. One of the questions outlined in the Introduction thus returns with added force: is not dialogue a Sisyphean exercise? It might well seem that if the goal of wisdom or Episteme (in the sense of 247d7, e2) is not achievable, then it ought to be forgotten. For perpetual dissatisfaction scarcely seems desirable, and in any event we seem hopelessly muddled about what we are supposed to "really" want. Given the endlessness of philosophical conversation, it would seem impossible to distinguish between progress and regress except by reference to the conventional rhetorical standards of the day. We might thus conclude that it is preferable to carry on conversations simply in order to satisfy our individual interests and without any thought of reaching a mythic "Platonic Truth"—whatever that may be.

In this Epilogue I show in greater detail how this conclusion, so damaging to the *Phaedrus'* explicit teachings, would seem to grow out of the *Phaedrus* itself as I have interpreted it. I shall then show, in a way that sheds further light on the self-knowledge theme, how the *Phaedrus* counters this apparent conclusion with a defense of its claims concerning the desirability of philosophical dialogue. In my formulation of the criticisms of Platonic dialogue I will call upon a well-known essay by Jacques Derrida

on the *Phaedrus*,[2] as well as the equally well-known notion of "conversation"
recently proposed (in explicit opposition to Plato) by Richard Rorty.[3] For
my purposes, Derrida and Rorty form natural allies.[4] This strategy offers
the additional advantage of bringing the themes I have been discussing
into a contemporary context.

I have argued that the main and unifying theme of the *Phaedrus* is that
of self-knowledge. The theme is deftly presented by Plato through the
dramatic context of the dialogue and is developed gradually by means of
a series of statements and retractions (or palinodes) of various positions.
What emerges is not just a commentary about the philosophic life but a
number of specific theses about the objects and preconditions of such a
life. First among these is, obviously, the view that self-knowledge is the
goal of the philosophic life. There is, correspondingly, an irremediably
existential dimension to philosophy, namely, the living of a certain kind
of life, a purpose that can be realized only by each individual. The *Phaedrus*
also attempts to show that living philosophically requires us to conceive
of ourselves as souls having a certain nature oriented toward the Whole,
or cosmos. To understand how best to live we must know what we desire,
which in turn requires us to recognize the unchanging principles that
sustain the well-ordered person. Being well ordered requires that the reasonable desires restrain the unreasonable ones.

The defense of these propositions becomes difficult on grounds provided
by the *Phaedrus* itself. The main point can be stated as follows: while
human beings are (we are told) souls participating in a natural order, it
is also their fate to understand that order only dimly. Differently put, it
is not our lot to see the unchanging principles (the Forms or Ideas) without
interference. Instead, we see them in the extremely complex and confusing
context of actions, things, and discourses, and from the perspective of
our character and intelligence. Desire alone is not enough to clear the
way to the Forms; as even the nonlover of Lysias' speech understands,
desire unrestrained by logos destroys itself. This lesson is further developed
in Socrates' speech on behalf of the concealed lover, in which it is shown
that logos unanimated by desire remains a form of unelevating and hence
unsatisfying calculation. Logos becomes the tool for the prudent satisfaction
of bodily desire. Yet even winged words seem at best to be undependable
substitutes for the nondiscursive banquet of the gods described in Socrates'
great myth.

The radical separation of human nature from what nourishes it leads
to the unavoidability of discursive reminders (as is shown in the second
half of the dialogue) and therefore to rhetoric. The problem of distinguishing between warranted and unwarranted persuasion then becomes

pressing indeed if truth is to remain our goal. The art of thinking and speaking epitomized by the method of division and collection is no doubt useful in this regard, but far from sufficient. Socrates finally proposes spoken dialogue, that is, his unmethodical erotic art, as the best available response to the problem posed by rhetoric. But the very conditions that generated the problem in the first place—not just the thesis that there is soul and that it is a part of a Whole but the suggestion that the soul no longer remembers and no longer has unmediated access to the principles that enlighten the Whole—seem to guarantee that the problem is insoluble. And this in turn seems to guarantee that philosophizing will be an endless process in pursuit of a mostly imagined goal. This unfortunate conclusion seems further supported by yet another of the *Phaedrus'* theses, namely, that there is no Idea, Form, or essence of the soul. This thesis seems to guarantee that there does not exist a definitive logos of the soul's nature.

We might reply that the *Phaedrus* nevertheless gives us grounds for holding that an account of the soul's nature can be pursued, an account guided or measured by a potential answer about "what it is to be human" that is a fixed, unchanging answer. It is not the case, the *Phaedrus* tells us, that only opinions about the soul are possible, or that the soul is mere material for techne, to be molded and transformed through history by rhetoricians. In the course of the *Phaedrus* itself, several kinds of talk about the soul occur, particularly "mythic" and "technical" discourse. An intelligible progress from one to the next is presented to us. The reasons for the steps in this development make sense, and each step permits us to recognize the advantages as well as shortcomings of the preceding kind of discourse. A tremendous virtue of the *Phaedrus*—we might continue in reply—is that it leads us to see how self-knowledge is tied not just to what we desire but to our talk about ourselves. The progress of the *Phaedrus* itself shows that our talk about ourselves must extend to talk about our talk about ourselves. This peculiarly metaphilosophical aspect of the *Phaedrus* explains, together with the various strands of the self-knowledge theme, Socrates' devotion to the living dialectic portrayed in Plato's composition. The unique knowledge of the soul that neither reduces it to a special type of abstract object nor confines it to images of edifying poetry is exhibited in dialectical discourse. The heterogeneous vocabulary of this gnostic rather than epistemic (since a form of gignoskein rather than epistasthai) knowledge retains critical elements of the language in which people ordinarily articulate their self-understanding. And even as the self-knowledge thematic explains the unity of the *Phaedrus,* it also explains the dialogue's existence as a literary artifact of a certain type. More gen-

erally, it explains why Plato wrote dialogues, indeed dialogues possessing
a number of specifiable characteristics (such as the distance of the author
from the text, the text's mimetic capacity, and the role of irony).

It is precisely in saying all this, however, that we seem to undermine
the intended result. For the peculiar self-commentary of the *Phaedrus* might
be taken to suggest that, in the final analysis, there are only discourses
and discourses about discourses, and no Truth by which they can be measured. Each discourse seems to undermine itself in a way that generates
yet another discourse. Even the theses that make sense of the *Phaedrus'*
progressive self-commentaries are presented in the course of the same text.
As I indicated in chapter 6, the distinction between spoken and written
dialectic might seem to correct the view that the text is an all-enveloping
world unto itself. But this is so only if the spoken word is—as Socrates
claims explicitly and as Plato claims (if my interpretation holds) implicitly—not just other than but superior to the written. And this claim can
be maintained only if the related theses concerning recollection, the Ideas,
eros, and the soul are also upheld. But are not all these theses themselves
just phases in the self-enclosed cosmos conjured up by Plato's literary
artifact? Indeed, are they not presented in, and as, *myths*?

Is Plato's artifact even a result of the dialogic process praised by Socrates
in that very artifact? Phaedrus' self-absorption in a text, whose novel thesis
he intended to recite aloud to himself outside the boundaries of the polis,
is checked by Socrates' passion for self-knowledge. Although Socrates prefers to stay within the city where he can question and be questioned, this
one time he follows Phaedrus out into unquestioning nature in order to
examine Phaedrus and so himself, filled with premonitions and warnings
about the danger of their situation. This scene, as I showed in chapter
1, certainly prepares us for the self-knowledge theme as it is developed
in the *Phaedrus*. Yet at the very end of the dialogue we are led to reflect
on the *Phaedrus* as a literary artifact. As the written text of one author,
it is in effect a monologue. Might not then the *Phaedrus* be the playful
daydream of a solitary *promeneur* rather than the result of Socratic dialogue?
Differently stated, one might question whether the Platonic dialogue form
is (as I argued in chapter 6) meant to lead the reader back to living dialogue.
Perhaps the fact that Plato chose to write signals the rejection (however
reluctant Plato may have been to accept this rejection) of the view that
spoken dialectic is superior to the written. If so, the *Phaedrus* is ultimately
a defense of Phaedrus.

Let us go still further. Plato's text has generated an "immortal" (cf.
277a2) series of discursive artifacts (of which my own text is an example)
devoted to commenting on its meaning. Like devoted children of father

Plato, we converse with ourselves in the antiquated vocabulary of "souls" and "hyperuranian beings" and "palinodes" about fictional speeches put in the mouths of fictionalized characters who play in a dialogue that never took place. The critic of Platonism might add that whether the endless interpretations are spoken or written matters little. The central point is that these interpretations seem, like the Platonic corpus, to be in principle open-ended, and in a way that is far removed from the notion that philosophy approaches Platonic Truth—that notion being itself a myth recounted somewhere along the way. Differently put, the statement that "the soul has its own logos, which increases itself" is congenial to the *Phaedrus* as I interpreted it. But for the critic who holds that philosophy is a never-ending exercise in self-commentary, this statement ironically recants itself, since the soul now seems to be the invention of a logos, a moment in the immortal self-motion of discourse. The statement (logos) thus becomes: "the logos increases itself."

The conclusion I have sketched in the previous paragraph is worked out by Derrida and Rorty in the texts cited above. Derrida deconstructs the *Phaedrus* by concentrating on the ambiguity of the pivotal word "pharmakon," a word that can mean "cure" or "poison." He grants that Plato intends to keep the two meanings of this word apart, but argues that Plato has led himself to the brink of a *topos* in which the required metaphysical distinctions cannot be sustained. Plato reveals his difficulty even as he attempts to distinguish between spoken and written discourse, for he uses the language of the latter in order to articulate the former: true spoken dialectic will, Socrates says, be "written" in the soul of the learner (276a5–6). Similarly, the distinction between two senses of the word "play"—one referring to the activity of philosophizing and the other to the nonphilosophical activity of writing—also blend. Consequently, all of Theuth's inventions—among which are writing and the games of draughts and dice—turn out to be on a par. The very list of his inventions hints at the problem. Plato is not, Derrida suggests, unaware of the duplicity in which he has become ensnared. Plato glimpses a richly textured plain, not of Truth, but of fluctuating and multihued images for which there are no stable originals, a kaleidoscopic play of opinions, interpretations, all bereft of "serious" intent. Plato divines that the world is, so to speak, a sophist. At which point, "Platon se bouche les oreilles, pour mieux s'entendre-parler, pour mieux voir, pour mieux analyser."[5] Plato responds by divinizing the method of division that seems to give rigor to distinctions such as that between original and image, soul and body, the inner and the outer, and repeats them to himself as though they were a charm, an antidote to the poison into which his very own pharmakon (namely, the dialogue form of writing) against sophistry has metabolized.

Although Derrida's interpretation of the *Phaedrus* does focus on a genuine difficulty, it is nevertheless extraordinarily arbitrary when judged by the principles that have guided my interpretation of the dialogue. Derrida pays virtually no attention to sections of the *Phaedrus* other than the last one in which the speaking/writing issue is raised. The notions of logographic necessity and of the text as a whole, so crucial to my reading of the *Phaedrus* and praised in that dialogue itself (264b7, c2–5), carry no weight in his reading of texts.[6] Since for Derrida the "author" of a text is merely the interpreter's construction out of the text, he has no way of distinguishing between a mistake and an intentional irony in the text, and no way to distinguish between the text's meaning and its significance to the interpreter. Derrida also fails to consider in detail all of Socrates' criticisms of the written word, including the criticism to the effect that the written word does not know when to speak and when to be silent. Correspondingly, Derrida does not ask why Plato wrote *dialogues,* and most important of all, he takes no account of the fundamental role attributed in the final section of the dialogue to the *question.* Yet, as I have shown in chapter 6, Socrates' and Plato's evaluation of the power of questioning to arouse the mind to look beyond what it is persuaded to be true is the key to the one's praise of spoken dialogue and the other's decision to write dialogues.[7]

Thus, even while my interpretation of the *Phaedrus* points to a problem that is the focus of Derrida's interpretation, our approaches to the dialogue are radically different. Roughly put, his is in principle anti-Platonic and mine Platonic. Here we may seem to have a basis for refusing to accept Derrida's deconstruction of the *Phaedrus,* however much the *Phaedrus* itself tempts us in that direction. Given his anti-Platonic assumptions, he reaches anti-Platonic conclusions about Plato. Hence his approach seems circular. This observation would not in the least disturb Derrida, for he has tried to show precisely that no philosophical activity, even when focused on the interpretation of texts, can claim to measure itself by some objective standard. He might then proceed to argue that my interpretation is circular in a way analogous to his. Efforts to defend the surface thesis of the *Phaedrus* to the effect that dialogue is a means by which the soul can recollect the Truth then begin to look like confirmations of Derrida's own suggestions concerning the self-enclosed and hence self-vitiating character of objectivist hermeneutics. What is left is agreement or disagreement regulated by our foundationless assumptions or purposes. Given that this point is anticipated in the *Phaedrus*, it would seem that the dialogue does after all establish that dialectic is a Sisyphean enterprise.

The challenge to my interpretation of the *Phaedrus*—a challenge which, ironically, that interpretation itself summons—is still more formidable that this. The *Phaedrus* is explicit that there exists strong disagreement about disputable topics such as eros, justice, and the good (263a–d). If the dialogue Socrates lauds at the end of the *Phaedrus* is to have any significance, it must have the potential to mediate these disagreements by showing that either one or both sides fails to measure up to the truth of the matter. Since one of the disputable topics might be said to concern the meaning of "dialogue" itself, the disagreement between interpretations of the *Phaedrus* that I have discussed ought in principle to be soluble by means of dialogue. Yet it may be doubted whether this is the case, precisely because the standpoint taken by Derrida is not a philosophical one but a nonphilosophical one. While he attempts to deconstruct philosophical positions, deconstructivism is not itself a position. As Rorty puts it with reference to his own efforts, "Edifying philosophers have to decry the very notion of having a view, while avoiding having a view about having views. This is an awkward, but not impossible, position."[8] Consequently it seems that every effort to criticize Derrida or Rorty necessarily assumes a framework repudiated by them (but not repudiated in the name of an alternative framework), and so is question begging. Every construal of a common ground or (in Rorty's vocabulary) "commensurating principles" will seem to be merely an expression of assumptions made by the philosopher. The Derridean may seem to agree to the assumptions of his opponent, but he does so only in order to show that they undermine themselves. The Derridean's participation in a discussion with the philosopher thus contains an element of ruse and dissembling.[9]

The result is that the "recollective dialogue" praised in the *Phaedrus* seems impossible, even when the topic of the dialogue concerns the correct evaluation of the *Phaedrus* itself. And this result is once again satisfactory from a Derridean standpoint. Moreover, Derrida might maintain that— regardless of Plato's intentions—the absence of a dialogue in the Platonic corpus between two mature philosophers concedes the same result. In sum, philosophizing would seem to be the imaginative play of the mind whose fruit is an endless interplay of discourses. The game can be played in a variety of vocabularies and according to a variety of rules once claims to objectivity are deconstructed, that is, shown on their own grounds to fall apart. The deconstructed dialogue that is then the intellectual's playground is what Rorty means by "conversation." Rorty's notion of conversation may well look like a plausible embodiment of the seemingly unsustainable notion of dialogue praised in the *Phaedrus*. As I have indicated, "conversation" may even look like the natural outgrowth of the way in which dialogue is *practiced* in the *Phaedrus*.

The Platonic response to this line of reasoning might take an intensely reflexive metalevel course analogous to Aristotle's response in *Metaphysics* Gamma to the person who denies the principle of noncontradiction. Plato might argue that at some metalevel Rorty and Derrida must make some claim to truth, even if only in the form of the claim that he has truly understood and deconstructed his opponents. Rorty's book is, as a matter of fact, filled with a number of positive assertions, as the closing reference to the philosopher's "moral concern" indicates.[10] Plato's powerful strategy would seek to establish that *there is intelligibility* in a sense that is assumed by every deconstructive effort.

The *Phaedrus* suggests such a strategy indirectly, as a result of what I take to be another equally compelling sort of response. If the *Phaedrus'* notion of dialogue is to hold, then a connection between conversation and self-knowledge must be established, as must a connection between conversation and anamnesis. The first of these requires us to hold that the point of conversation is to know ourselves, and the second to hold that the "hyperuranian beings" or Forms are *present* in the world. Plato does not begin the *Phaedrus* by proposing either of these views as theses to be defended. Instead, through the drama of the dialogue he presents us with a phenomenon that is strikingly apposite to the present discussion, as though in anticipation of the difficulties the reader will encounter in defending the reflections prompted by the conclusion of the *Phaedrus*. The phenomenon in question is the passion exhibited by Phaedrus and mimicked by Socrates for novel and possibly absurd discourses. As is clear in Plato's portrayal of Phaedrus, this passion is brother to the view that rhetoric has no connection with truth. Phaedrus has completely forgotten himself in the World of the Text. Not only are the consequences amusing; the *Phaedrus* shows that there is a dialectic between desire and speech, or between attraction and detachment, which generates self-conscious awareness of desires as well as speeches. This can lead to a desire for a true speech as well as speech about the difference between noble and base desires. The dialectic is not automatic or autonomous; Phaedrus is led to reflect about himself by Socrates' complicated rhetoric. Unlike Phaedrus, Socrates already possesses a passion for self-knowledge.

In the way the *Phaedrus* goes on to demonstrate, this exercise in self-knowledge leads the interlocutors in the conversation to a number of specific theses not just about their own nature but about the nature of what they desire. They come to see, for example, that they cannot and do not wholly lack what they desire. Just as desire requires speech to articulate itself—if only to solve the "paradox of desire," namely, that we cannot know that something is desirable if we do not and never have possessed it—so there would be no speeches without the lack that is desire. Still further, there would be no speeches unless we already knew in some sense, and so already possessed, what we were speaking about. The objects of desire and speech must be detached and separate, precisely "for the sake of" these same phenomena. These objects are, ultimately, the Forms. This line of reasoning is first developed in terms of the nonlover's speech and then on successively more complicated levels. In short, the defense of recollective dialogue I am outlining begins with the phenomenon common both to Phaedrus and to Derridean textual interpretation, namely, the passion for beautiful speeches which ignores the Delphic "Know thyself." The *Phaedrus* then describes the dialectical development of this passion.

These considerations suggest that a defense of the *Phaedrus'* notion of dialogue might begin not with metaphysical or epistemological doctrines but with an exercise in the art of rhetoric also described in the *Phaedrus*— the effort to lead one's interlocutor to reflect on himself. And this effort can be initiated with the apparently simple kinds of questions with which the *Phaedrus* (like so many other Platonic dialogues) begins, such as: why do you desire what you desire? Are the speeches you find beautiful really satisfactory? It is above all in addressing questions such as these that the pretense to the effect that your own life is a discourse deconstructs itself. Our sense that the conversation advocated by Rorty and the deconstructivism practiced by Derrida are entertaining but ultimately frivolous ways of occupying one's life derives from the fact that they cannot (given the meaning of the terms "conversation" and "deconstruction") question with a passion for self-knowledge. For that passion is informed by what I have called the ethical dimension of the Delphic imperative, namely the view that an individual's most important task is his living a worthwhile life. The *Phaedrus* shows that reflection on that task—that is, philosophy— necessarily leads to general issues concerning the soul, desire, logos, and the like. But the seriousness such notions, along with our discussion about them, retain derives from the importance they hold for us as individuals who understand ourselves as possessing the ability to fulfill, or to fail to fulfill, the excellence our natures may promise. Philosophical dialogue does require a good deal of self-commentary, but the "self" that is commented upon includes the individual person and not just the commentary about the individual. The everyday, with its prophetic preawareness (cf. 242c6–7) of what philosophers make explicit (including the notions of the soul, and cosmos, and the difference between the inner and outer), is in this respect not just preparatory for philosophy but regulative of it. By contrast, these and other terms (notions such as knowledge, self, and excellence) seem not to carry, for the deconstructivists, the objective referents that are attached to them even in everyday life. One's life becomes a language-game (a sentiment that seems appropriate to Phaedrus as he is described at the start of the *Phaedrus*). The Derridean and Rortean deconstruction of philosophy is also a deconstruction of prephilosophic life, and this is why their playful palinodes finally resemble merely sophisticated poems of the "clever" (229d4, 245c2). Especially as it is exhibited in the *Phaedrus*, Platonic playfulness seems very similar in execution to the Derridean and may well seem to foreshadow the latter, as I have pointed out in the preceding paragraphs. At the same time it is dissimilar to the nontelic conversations of the deconstructivists in (among other things) its "trust" (cf. 245c2) in the seriousness of the ethical imperative that initiates and closes the *Phaedrus*.

Thus Plato's decision to write dialogues whose characteristics include the ability to challenge the reader to know himself (rather than to confine himself to "collating and pulling apart" the phrases of his composition; 278d8–e2) reflects a philosophical understanding of the problem of defending dialogue itself. The literary or dramatic aspect of Plato's artifacts is intended to prevent readers from becoming absorbed in them in the way that Phaedrus does in Lysias' text. By raising the issue of *self*-knowledge on the level of the individual, and by deepening rather than transcending that level, Plato's dialogical pharmakon is the antidote for the sorts of consequences that, as Derrida rightly detects, the *Phaedrus* itself confronts us with. Differently put, Socrates is not only a "philologist" (a lover of discourses; 228c1–2); he is a "philomathist" (a lover of learning; 230d3) and in particular a lover of self-knowledge in the ethically charged sense conveyed by the reference to Typhon (230a). One ought not be satisfied only with loving beautiful discourses.

To read the Platonic dialogues as complex images or mirrors of human reality is ultimately to demand that the interpretation of a Platonic dialogue be guided by the standard of self-knowledge. I argued in the Introduction that to begin by assuming that the text is a whole designed by the author to convey a meaning—that is, to begin by taking seriously the text's claim to articulate the truth—is warranted by the reader's desire to learn whatever the text may be capable of teaching. As should now be evident, this maxim of interpretation is grounded in the importance of the reader's search for self-knowledge. The reader must approach the Platonic dialogues in the way that he approaches a promising discussion. This does not mean that my defense of the *Phaedrus'* notion of dialogue is circular in a self-vitiating sense. The importance of self-knowledge is not an axiom from which a specific interpretation of the *Phaedrus* follows. The result of interpretation is not predetermined by the reader's desire to learn the truth. Even though the reader approaches the *Phaedrus* with the desire to know himself, it may still turn out that the text is incoherent. Different readers may still arrive at differing interpretations.

A successful defense of the *Phaedrus* must awaken and cultivate our sense that the way in which we lead our lives is important. As mentioned above, it must also show how our inquiry is connected with anamnesis, and so to the true shapes and forms of things. These shapes (εἴδη, ἰδέαι) are, as the *Phaedrus* indicates, apprehensible only by means of our experience of and reflection upon ourselves—our desires, speeches, actions, bodies, world. For us, the "beings" (*ta onta ontos*) are not apprehensible in complete isolation from the world; Socrates reserves pure aperspectival "giveness" for the blessed gods. *Nevertheless we cannot infer, as Derrida attempts to do, that the true shapes of things are simply absent.*[11] These shapes are present in the "look" of things. The *Phaedrus* suggests that something of the Truth is visible to nonphilosophical vision, the most obvious example being the universally recognized presence of Beauty (cf. 249b5–6; no soul that has seen none of the Truth can enter into a human form). Of course a person's response to Beauty may be reflective or corrupt. The strange development (and corresponding unity) of the *Phaedrus* exemplifies the reflective response. The unfolding of the *Phaedrus* shows us how dialogue can recover a context that is already present. As I argued in chapter 3, in the palinode's description of recollection Socrates provides some specific clues as to how the beings are connected to discourse. In the realm of discourses, Beauty (τὸ καλόν) includes the fitting, the commensurate, the measured, the appropriate, that is, that which allows us to see what needs thinking about and how to think about it, to know what to say next, to know when to say it and to whom, and to know when a discussion is unfinished or complete. Here the beautiful is that which guides and frames the sense by which we are properly oriented to our subject matter and interlocutor. Anamnesis is a description of the way in which insight, awakened by questioning, comes to recognize the shape a conversation must take if it is to get us nearer to the truth. This process is fundamentally different from that of rote memorization, as Thamus pointed out, as well as from the rhetorical question whose purpose is simply to persuade.

It is true that no Platonic dialogue offers anything like a theoretical "proof" of the proposition that there are Forms. In the *Phaedrus*, the Forms are mentioned in a myth. It may therefore seem that the existence of the

Forms is asserted dogmatically. But as I have shown, the myth is itself
recanted in a way that preserves its teaching and frames it within a more
comprehensive context. This process recurs several more times in the dialogue until we are brought back, by means of the kind of reflections I
have just discussed, to Plato's opening portrait of Phaedrus' passion for
novel and clever speeches. Phaedrus' passion is so laughably self-forgetful
as to impress on us once again the importance of self-knowledge. The
Phaedrus' development thus suggests indirectly an intensely reflexive defense of dialogue. The *Phaedrus'* elaboration of human experience retains
a commitment to the reality of certain elements of that experience, but
in an interrogative way. To call the various speeches and stages of the
Phaedrus (including the myth about the soul and Forms) into question is
to be true to the idea of dialogue. And to question dialogically is in effect
to exhibit τὸ καλόν, since it is to act in a way that is fitting, appropriate,
measured by an awareness of the soul's simultaneous recognition and forgetfulness of the whole truth. Such awareness manifests self-knowledge.
That the search for self-knowledge should begin anew with each of us is
as it should be. The boundaries of the soul will not be reached, and the
logos of the soul will increase itself. Recognizing that the unexamined
life is not worth living, one searches out oneself.

Notes

Introduction

1. F. E. D. Schleiermacher, *Introductions to the Dialogues of Plato*, trans. W. Dobson (New York: Arno Press, 1973), p. 59 ff. Schleiermacher adduces "innumerable proofs of the youthfulness of the work generally." His more persuasive discussion of the significance of the dialogue form occurs in the General Introduction to his *Introductions*.

2. Other references to Socrates' desire for self-knowledge may be found at *Alc. 1*, 128e ff.; *Prot.* 331c, 348a; *Lach.* 187e–188c; *Apol.* 20d ff.; *Charm.* 164d–165b, 166d–e. See also *Theae.* 174b3–6, *Erastai* 138a, *Hipparchus* 228e. The *Phr.*, however, contains the strongest statement of the matter. Unless otherwise indicated, I have relied in this study on J. Burnet's edition of the dialogues (*Platonis Opera* [Oxford: Clarendon Press, 1967–68]). The translations of the *Phr.* cited in the text are, unless otherwise noted, from R. Hackforth's *Plato's Phaedrus* (Cambridge: Cambridge University Press, 1972), though I have frequently amended them. Where my emendations significantly change the sense of the passage or are substantive enough to require defense, I supply further discussion of the matter. Page references in the text advert directly to the *Phr.* unless otherwise noted. I shall distinguish, as is customary, between Plato's "Socrates" and the historical Socrates. In this study I shall be concerned with the former, and all references to "Socrates" advert (unless otherwise indicated) to Plato's "Socrates."

3. To the best of my knowledge, this thesis has never been argued in detail and has been suggested only once before by G. E. Mueller in "The Unity of the *Phaedrus*," 2 pts., *Classical Bulletin* 33 (1957): 1:50–51.

4. S. Shoemaker, *Self-Knowledge and Self-Identity* (Ithaca: Cornell University Press, 1963). Shoemaker himself begins the book by remarking that "The term 'self-knowledge' is used here, not in the Socratic sense, where it refers to something that few are able to attain, but in such a way that a person can be said to have self-knowledge whenever he knows the truth of a statement in which there is reference to himself" (p. vii).

5. For an account of the traditional interpretations of the Delphic command, see E. G. Wilkins, *"Know Thyself" in Greek and Latin Literature* (New York: Garland, 1979).

6. By "Lysias' text" I mean, in this study, the speech that is attributed to him in the *Phr.* I agree with Hackforth (*Plato's Phaedrus*, p. 17) that the speech is probably Plato's invention, though no definitive evidence is available, and that, in any event, Phaedrus and Socrates assume the speech is by Lysias (p. 111). As is noted by Robin, the ancient testimony on the question of the authenticity of the speech is largely inconclusive, with the exception of the remarks by D. Laertius and Hermeias, both of whom state that the text was composed by Lysias (*Phèdre*, in *Platon: Oeuvres complètes*, Tome IV, 3ᵉ Partie [Paris: Collection des Universités de France, 1970], p. lx). P. Shorey's study of the particles of the speech indicates that the speech is a subtle exaggeration ("On the *Erotikos* of Lysias in Plato's *Phaedrus*," *Classical Philology* 28 [1933]: 131–32). Similar results are arrived at by G. E. Dimock, "'ΑΛΛΑ΄ in Lysias and Plato's *Phaedrus*," *American Journal of Philology* 73 (1952): 381–96.

7. See P. Friedländer, *Plato: An Introduction*, vol. I of *Plato*, trans. H. Meyerhoff (Princeton: Princeton University Press, 1973), chap. 7–8; R. Brague, Introduction to *Le restant; Supplément aux commentaires du Ménon de Platon* (Paris: Vrin, 1978); F. E. Sparshott, "Socrates and Thrasymachus," *Monist* 50 (1966): 421–59; P. Shorey, *The Unity of Plato's Thought* (Chicago: University of Chicago Press, 1968); M. H. Miller, Introduction to *The Philosopher in Plato's Statesman* (The Hague: Nijhoff, 1980); H. Gundert, *Dialog und Dialektik; zur Struktur des platonischen Dialogs* (Amsterdam: B. R. Grüner, 1971); R. Schaerer, *La question Platonicienne*, 2d ed. (Paris: Vrin, 1969), and "Le mécanisme de l'ironie dans ses rapports avec la dialectique," *Revue de métaphysique et de morale* 48 (1941): 181–209; J. Klein, Introductory Remarks to *A Commentary on Plato's Meno* (Chapel Hill: University of North Carolina Press, 1965); S. Rosen, Introduction to *Plato's Symposium* (New Haven: Yale University Press, 1968); L. Strauss, chap. 2 of *Persecution and the Art of Writing* (Westport: Greenwood Press, 1973), and *The City and Man* (Chicago: University of Chicago Press, 1964), pp. 50–62; D. Hyland, "Why Plato Wrote Dialogues," *Philosophy and Rhetoric* 1 (1968): 38–50; R. K. Sprague, "Logic and Literary Form in Plato," *Personalist* 48 (1967): 560–72, and *Plato's Use of Fallacy* (New York: Barnes & Noble, 1962); H. G. Gadamer, "*Logos* and *Ergon* in

Plato's *Lysis*," in *Dialogue and Dialectic: Eight Hermeneutical Studies on Plato,* trans. P. C. Smith (New Haven: Yale University Press, 1980), pp. 1–6; J. Dalfen, "Gedanken zur Lektüre platonischer Dialoge," *Zeitschrift für philosophische Forschung* 29 (1975): 169–94; G. Krüger, Einleitung to *Einsicht und Leidenschaft; Das Wesen des platonischen Denkens* (Frankfurt: Klostermann, 1973); W. Wieland, Einleitung to *Platon und die Formen des Wissens* (Göttingen: Vandenhoeck & Ruprecht, 1982); T. Ebert, Einleitung to *Meinung und Wissen in der Philosophie Platons* (Berlin: de Gruyter, 1974); J. J. Mulhern, "Treatises, Dialogues, and Interpretation," *Monist* 53 (1969): 631–41; E. Hoffman, "Die literarischen Voraussetzungen des Platonverständnisses," *Zeitschrift für philosophische Forschung* 2 (1947): 465–80; P. Merlan, "Form and Content in Plato's Philosophy," *Journal of the History of Ideas* 8 (1947): 406–30; and J. Sallis, Introduction to *Being and Logos; The Way of Platonic Dialogue* (Pittsburgh: Duquesne University Press, 1975). While I share with these authors a general approach to interpreting Plato, it would be inaccurate to equate my view with any of theirs. Further, these authors do not agree on every aspect of the theory of interpretation (the disagreements between Gadamer and Strauss are especially important; see the following note). For an overview of the history of Plato interpretations, see E. N. Tigerstedt, *Interpreting Plato* (Uppsala: Almquist & Wiksell, 1977).

8. For criticism of J. Klein's approach to interpretation, see J. Gould's "Klein on Ethological Mimes, for example, the *Meno*," *Journal of Philosophy* 66 (1969): 253–65. A criticism of Strauss (directed more to his theory of interpretation than his practice) occurs in Gadamer's "Hermeneutics and Historicism," supplement to *Truth and Method,* trans. Sheed and Ward Ltd. (New York: Seabury Press, 1975), pp. 482–91. Some of Strauss's exchanges with Gadamer on this issue may be found in "Correspondence concerning *Wahrheit und Methode,*" *Independent Journal of Philosophy* 2 (1978): 5–12. For further criticism of Strauss's approach to interpretation as presented in *Persecution and the Art of Writing,* see G. H. Sabine's review of the book in *Ethics* 63 (1953): 220–22. Strauss's response to the review, "On a Forgotten Kind of Writing," is reprinted in the *Independent Journal of Philosophy* 2 (1978): 27–31. M. Burnyeat's "Review of L. Strauss's *Studies in Platonic Political Philosophy,*" *New York Review of Books,* May 30, 1985, pp. 30–36, provides a rather acrid critique of Strauss, which illustrates how thoroughly assumptions about interpretation divide scholars working on the same texts and how important it is to get clear about one's own assumptions. In a similar vein, see the exchange between H. C. Mansfield and J. G. A. Pocock about L. Strauss's interpretation of Machiavelli in *Political Theory* 3 (1975): 372–405. For a criticism of the interpretative assumptions made by G. Vlastos in his *Platonic Studies,* see D. Clay's "Platonic Studies and the Study of Plato," *Arion,* n.s. 2 (1975): 116–32, and in a similar vein, D. Bolotin's review of T. Irwin's *Plato's Moral Theory,* in *St. John's Review* 32 (1981): 95–97, as well as K. R. Seeskin's "Formalization in Platonic Scholarship," *Metaphilosophy* 9 (1978): 242–51. For a co-

gent critique of R. Robinson's principles of interpretation (presented in *Plato's Earlier Dialectic*), see the article by Mulhern referred to in the previous note. Robinson's principles are also sharply criticized by Tigerstedt, *Interpreting Plato*, pp. 22–23. Tigerstedt cites a number of other reviews critical of Robinson's procedure. For discussion of analytic and nonanalytic approaches to Plato, see Y. Lafrance, "Autour de Platon: Continentaux et analystes," *Dionysius* 3 (1979): 17–37, and D. Lachterman's "Review of Jacob Klein's *Plato's Trilogy*," *Nous* 13 (1979): 106–12.

9. I add here that, as is normally acknowledged, the rules of a language (for example, as embodied in grammar) supply a basis for excluding some interpretations of a text. An interpretation must at least be linguistically possible.

10. *Plato's Phaedrus*, p. 136.

11. Ibid., p. 133*n*1.

12. Ibid., p. 136.

13. Ibid., p. 137.

14. L. Strauss, *The City and Man*, p. 60: "In a word, one cannot take seriously enough the law of logographic necessity. Nothing is accidental in a Platonic dialogue; everything is necessary at the place where it occurs. Everything which would be accidental outside of the dialogue becomes meaningful within the dialogue. In all actual conversations chance plays a considerable role: all Platonic dialogues are radically fictitious. The Platonic dialogue is based on a fundamental falsehood, a beautiful or beautifying falsehood, viz. on the denial of chance."

15. Gadamer, for example, objects that to take the author's intentions as criterial when interpreting the meaning of the text is to reduce interpretation to irrelevant historical research and to assume a "historicist" position (*Truth and Method*, pp. 336, 356–57). Gadamer is objecting to an approach to the issue of the author's intentions other than the one I am endorsing. For further discussion of the matter, see P. Juhl, *Interpretation: An Essay in the Philosophy of Literary Criticism* (Princeton: Princeton University Press, 1980). Juhl distinguishes an author's intention from his motives and from what the author planned to write or to convey (p. 14). He defends the view that a literary work possesses one and only one meaning (as distinguished from significance) and that this meaning corresponds to the author's intention. A similar (but not identical) approach is to be found in E. D. Hirsch's *Validity in Interpretation* (New Haven: Yale University Press, 1967). As I have adumbrated it above, my position is closer to Hirsch's than Juhl's. Gadamer's theory of interpretation is convincingly criticized in Appendix 2 to Hirsch's *Validity*, and in the Appendix to Juhl's *Interpretation*.

16. For a similar point, see Wieland, *Platon*, p. 10. Of course, I am also arguing that Plato "articulates the truth" in an indirect and rhetorical way. The point of view I am sketching (with its emphasis on the speaker's or writer's intentions) permits us to refer to "irony" in a text or verbal speech act.

For an excellent argument in support of this statement, see W. Booth, *A Rhetoric of Irony* (Chicago: University of Chicago Press, 1974), pp. 91 ff., 120 ff. (and notes), et passim.

17. Cf. E. D. Hirsch, *The Aims of Interpretation* (Chicago: University of Chicago Press, 1976), p. 91: "Few critics fail to show moral indignation when their meaning is distorted in reviews and other interpretations of their interpretations." And p. 90: "Unless there is a powerful overriding value in disregarding an author's intention (i.e., original meaning), we who interpret as a vocation should not disregard it" (italicized in the original). Hirsch argues in these pages that the basis of this approach is in the final analysis a moral one.

18. For a statement of this view, see J. Derrida, *Eperons: Les styles de Nietzsche,* French with facing translation by B. Harlow (Chicago: University of Chicago Press, 1979), especially pp. 95 ff.

19. For a discussion of the question of Platonic anonymity, see L. Edelstein, "Platonic Anonymity," *American Journal of Philology* 83 (1962): 1–22. Edelstein is right to insist that Plato cannot be identified with any of his characters, and that Plato "always preserves his anonymity, but conceals himself in various ways, just as he retains the dialogue form in all his works, although he gives it many variations. . . . This use of many masks constitutes a unique feature of Platonic anonymity" (p. 16). My own explanation of Plato's reasons for using the dialogue form is, however, rather different than Edelstein's. I discuss the matter and (briefly) the question of the *Epistles,* in chap. 6. I add that "Plato" is mentioned in the *Apol.* as being present and in the *Pho.* as being absent; in neither case are any specific utterances attributed to "Plato."

20. It might be inferred that those doctrines articulated by the Platonic Socrates that were not espoused by the historical Socrates are attributable to Plato. This inference is a non sequitur. Indeed, many of the characters in Plato's dialogues are a combination of historical and fictional elements; why not infer that, say, the doctrines of Plato's "Protagoras" that were not espoused by the historical Protagoras represent Plato's views?

21. See F. E. Sparshott, "Socrates and Thrasymachus," p. 421: "The normal implication of dialogue form is that the author is disengaged from his characters. Even if he usually uses one of them as his mouthpiece, we cannot assume that he stands by every word he makes him say, or that he dissents from every word the others say. He is, after all, the author of all their words alike. Where there is a genuine interchange between characters, we may look for the author's 'doctrine' not so much in what any one of them says as in *what happens between them.* That is to say, a writer of dialogues is necessarily an ironist." I would offer a small clarification of this statement: since one of the things that happens between the characters is what they say to each other, the author's "doctrine" must be elicited from both what they say and what they do, as well as from the relationship between their "words" and their "deeds." See also Rosen, *Plato's Symposium,* p. xxv: "Platonic irony means that every

statement in a dialogue must be understood in terms of its dramatic context";
and p. xiv: "Only by the recognition of irony as the central problem in the
interpretation of Plato, do we honor the demands of rigorous and sober philosophical analysis" (the sentence is italicized in the original).

22. *Lectures on the History of Philosophy,* trans. Haldane and Simson, 3 vols.
(Atlantic Highlands: Humanities Press, 1974), 2:11–12.

23. Thus a specific statement made by somebody in a dialogue may or
may not be ironic. But the whole of the text always exhibits Platonic irony.
For further discussion of the difference between Socratic and Platonic irony,
see W. Boder, *Die sokratische Ironie in den platonischen Frühdialogen* (Amsterdam:
B. R. Grüner, 1973), and my "Irony and Aesthetic Language in Plato's Dialogues," in *Literature as Art,* ed. D. Bolling (New York: Haven Press, 1986).

24. Schaerer, "Le mécanisme," p. 185: "En quoi se distingue la dissimulation ironique? Par un paradoxe fondamental: elle n'existe que pour être démasquée, bien plus, qu'à l'instant où elle est démasquée, soit par celui qu'elle
vise, soit par un tiers. L'ironiste ne trompe pas pour tromper, mais pour qu'on
devine qu'il trompe. Sa dissimulation ne devient ironique qu'au moment où
elle se dénonce comme telle." See also Klein, *A Commentary on Plato's Meno,*
pp. 5–8.

25. The inference is made by G. Vlastos in his "The Individual as an Object of Love in Plato" (reprinted in *Platonic Studies,* 2d ed. [Princeton: Princeton University Press, 1981], pp. 3–34). The relevant passages are cited in D.
Clay's critical discussion of the book, "Platonic Studies and the Study of Plato," pp. 123 ff.. Another example of a commentary in which the views of
Plato's dramatis personae are regularly attributed to Plato himself is T. Irwin's
Plato's Moral Theory: The Early and Middle Dialogues (Oxford: Clarendon Press,
1977). My own standpoint is compatible with C. Kahn's statement that "as
works of art they [Plato's dialogues] produce an effect of literary 'distancing'
between author and audience which prevents us—even in works as late as the
Parmenides and *Theaetetus*—from simply reading off the author's thoughts in
any straightforward way from what is said by some character in the dialogues"
("Did Plato Write Socratic Dialogues?" *Classical Quarterly* 31 [1981]: 305).

26. A longer discussion of Platonic irony would include an analysis of the
sense in which the titles of the dialogues, the dramatic time, the place, the
sequence (in the fictive chronology) of the dialogues, and finally the division
between narrated and performed dialogues, provide clues to Plato's intentions.
I will comment below on these points as they arise in the context of the *Phr.*

27. For a discussion of types of irony and of the ways in which intended
ironies can be detected and the underlying meaning reconstructed, see Booth's
indispensable *A Rhetoric of Irony.* In the concluding pages of the book (pp. 267
ff.), Booth correctly classifies Platonic irony as an instance of intended, stable,
covert, infinite irony. That is, at each instance of irony in a dialogue a determinate (if complex) covert meaning can be discovered, though the ultimate
Truth underlying the ironies may not be fully knowable. The "absurdist"
irony of some modern writers (such as Camus or Beckett) may, by contrast, be

intended, *un*stable, covert, and infinite, such that any knowledge of the Truth is impossible in principle. For still further discussion of the various sorts of irony and ways in which they may be detected, see D. C. Muecke's *The Compass of Irony* (London: Methuen & Co., 1969), and the works cited in n. 23 above.

28. For further discussion of the fictive chronology of the dialogues and its relationship to interpretations that are based on the chronology of the composition of the dialogues, see Wieland, *Platon,* chap. 1, sec. 5.

Chapter 1: The Dramatic Scene and the Prologue

1. In *The Portable Nietzsche,* trans. W. Kaufmann (1954; reprint. New York: Viking Press, 1974), p. 475.

2. Hence at 257b2 Socrates makes Lysias the "father" of the first two speeches of the *Phr.* At 244a1 he claims that his own first speech was "by Phaedrus." Moreover at 264e3 Phaedrus refers to Lysias' text as "our logos" (Phaedrus' and Lysias'). And of course Phaedrus is absolutely enthralled by Lysias' speech. At 257b4 Phaedrus is referred to as Lysias' *erastes,* at 257d1, 264c7, 278e4 as his "friend," and at 236b5 and 279b3 Lysias is called his "darling." At 257c Phaedrus worries that his hero will have a difficult time matching Socrates' palinode.

3. For further comments on the relationship between the *Symp.* and *Phr.,* see S. Rosen, "Socrates as Concealed Lover," in *Classics and the Classical Tradition* (University Park: Pennsylvania State University Press, 1973), pp. 163–77; and "The Non-Lover in Plato's *Phaedrus,*" *Man and World* 2 (1969): 423–28. Also Z. Diesendruck, *Struktur und Charakter des platonischen Phaidros* (Wien-Leipzig: W. Braumüller, 1927), pp. 33–37.

4. For support of this point and for further discussion of the *Symp.*'s portrait of Phaedrus, see Rosen, *Plato's Symposium,* pp. 39 ff.. Rosen explains here the apparent contradiction between the main thesis of Phaedrus' speech and Phaedrus' interpretation of Achilles' death (*Symp.* 180a).

5. According to Hackforth, the dramatic date of the *Phr.* is about 410. But as M. Nussbaum points out, the historical Phaedrus was forced to go into exile between 415 and 404 (" 'This Story Isn't True': Poetry, Goodness, and Understanding in Plato's *Phaedrus,*" in *Plato on Beauty, Wisdom, and the Arts,* ed. Moravcsik and Temko [Totowa: Rowman & Littlefield, 1982], pp. 96–97 and notes). Nussbaum's suggestion that Phaedrus' presence in the dialogue constitutes Plato's wishful palinode of Phaedrus' misbehavior is a good one. This explanation of the historical impossibility of the *Phr.* certainly helps to remind one of the dialogue's status as a literary artifact, and so as a written work. I shall from time to time refer to the "dramatic date" of the *Phr.,* but always with the just mentioned problem, and suggested solution, in mind.

6. Phaedrus thinks Prodicus "most wise" (267b6) and Lysias the "cleverest of those now writing" (228a1–2), and he refers to Thrasymachus and friends as "kingly" (266c6). He has thumbed Tisias' manuals carefully

(273a6); indeed, it is Phaedrus who reminds Socrates of the rhetoricians' manuals (266d5–6). At 265a4 Phaedrus remarks that in his speeches Socrates "very courageously" opposed the thesis of Lysias' speech; such is the esteem in which Phaedrus holds Lysias' speech.

7. At *Phr.* 268a8–9 Socrates refers to "Eryximachus or his father Acumenus," and to Eryximachus as Phaedrus' "friend." At 227a5 Phaedrus refers to Acumenus as his own and Socrates' companion. In the *Prot.* (315c) Phaedrus and Eryximachus are sitting together.

8. The issue of effeminacy also arises in Phaedrus' remark that the place they will be sitting near is a good spot for girls to play (229b7–9; and according to Socrates the place they are sitting in is consecrated to the nymphs); in Socrates' oath by Hera (230b2, this being a woman's oath); in Socrates' and Phaedrus' shared passivity (Socrates denies that he generates his own speeches, and Phaedrus reads someone else's speeches); in their desire to sit and talk (outside the walls of the city, in fact) instead of participating in the manly activities of politics and war within the city; and in Phaedrus' sensitivity to the well-being of his body. For further discussion of the matter, see A. Philip's excellent "Récurrences thématiques et topologie dans le *Phèdre* de Platon," *Revue de métaphysique et de morale* 86 (1981): 458–59.

9. A quick glance at Phaedrus' oaths further illuminates his character. In all cases except one he swears by Zeus. Phaedrus' oath by the plane tree (236d9–e3) manifests, in a comic way, his love of speeches. The oath by Zeus at 229c4 signals his great interest in reductionistic interpretations of myths. The oath at 234e2 emphasizes his high opinion of Lysias' speech, and the oath at 243d2, that he is receptive to moral criticisms of even Lysias' conception of eros. Phaedrus' oaths by Zeus at 261b3 and c1 show that he endorses the ordinary conception of rhetoric and is shocked by Socrates' effort to redefine it. The oath at 263d4 shows that he was very impressed with the emphasis on techne at the start of Socrates' first speech.

10. 227c11, "gennaios"; 230d3, 269e1, "ariste"; 235c5, 268a5, "daimonie"; 236d4, 241e1, "makarie"; 242b8, 243c1, 260d3, "agathe"; 242a7, "theios . . . peri tous logous." Cf. also 257c8, "neania"; 238d8, "pheriste"; 228e1, "philo se"; 237a10, "beltistos." On the other hand, see the "miare" at 236e4.

11. The quotation is from *Isthm.,* 1:1 ff. The ode begins with "Mother, Theba of the golden shield, / yours is the moment now: / I will set you above / my want of leisure. / May rocky Delos, in whose praises / I have been absorbed, / not reproach me. / What is dearer to the good / than their own beloved parents?" (*Pindar's Victory Songs,* trans. F. J. Nisetich [Baltimore: Johns Hopkins University Press, 1980]). Pindar was in the middle of writing a poem to the Delian Apollo when he was called upon by Thebes, the town of his origin, to compose a poem in praise of Herodotus, who had won the chariot race in the games. By contrast, the chariot and driver that Socrates ends up praising do not belong to any city; Socrates puts the command of the Delphic god (or, in the palinode, of Zeus) above even the concerns of his city.

Socrates has leisure only for self-knowledge (229e4–230a6). Pindar suggests here that the supreme prize is the immortality obtainable when one is praised in speech by citizen and stranger alike. Though this view is not foreign to Phaedrus (cf. *Phr.* 258c1–2), Socrates argues against it in the *Phr.* The whole of the ode contains interesting differences with and parallels to sections of the *Phr.*

12. Herodicus was a physician and a specialist in "physical culture"; he is not Gorgias' brother (*Gorg.* 448b) but a Megarian (*Prot.* 316d; Protagoras refers to him as one of the disguised sophists). In *Rep.* 406a–b it is said that Herodicus combined gymnastics and medicine in his teachings, and was slavishly devoted to prolonging life. The doctor Socrates quotes, at least, prescribes a much tougher regimen than Phaedrus' doctors do.

13. See also Rosen, "Socrates," p. 169, who suggests (with reference to 236d) that Phaedrus is a corrupt "archon" who as partly vulgar and partly refined can mediate between Athens and philosophy. Note also that at 261a1–4 Phaedrus is called upon to respond on behalf of popular rhetoric. Of course, Phaedrus reminds Socrates that he too has a message to deliver to Isocrates.

14. At 266a Lysias' speech is said to have advocated a "left" (*skaios*) eros; the "sinister" connotation is difficult to overlook; 253d implies that the good horse is on the right side, the bad on the left. Lysias' conception of desire is represented by the bad horse.

15. It is Phaedrus who first introduces the crucial term "dianoia" and who distinguishes between words and their meaning—a crucial distinction with respect to the notion of rhetoric, especially the rhetoric of irony. Socrates later says that one must suit the truth to the soul of one's interlocutor (271d–e); that is, the words and their meaning may not be identical.

16. The switching of roles between Phaedrus and Socrates is visible in the prologue itself. Phaedrus is heading for the countryside, and Socrates will therefore follow; at 227c1 Phaedrus tells Socrates to lead; at 227d3–5 Socrates says he will follow Phaedrus to Megara and back; at 228c1 Socrates recounts that Phaedrus bade him to lead the way; at 228e4–229a1 Phaedrus asks where they should sit, and Socrates suggests any spot along the Ilisus Phaedrus wishes to choose; at 229a7 and b3 Socrates tells Phaedrus to lead on, and Phaedrus then points to a comfortable spot; at 230c5 and d5–e1 Socrates characterizes Phaedrus as his guide and himself as the animal dominated by the book Phaedrus carries. The very last word of the dialogue, by contrast, is a first person plural, signifying a mutual and equal decision to leave together.

17. Cf. Rosen's comment that the relationship between lover and nonlover in the first two speeches of the *Phr.* is a "fruitless dialectical circle" ("Socrates," p. 177).

18. Since the correspondences between the *Phr.*'s topology and the palinode are nicely treated by Philip (in his "Récurrences"), I will say little more about them. The two trees named here, the plane ("platanos," sacred to Dionysus) and the agnus (230b3; a tree sacred to Hera) are also symbolic, as is shown by K. Dorter in his "Imagery and Philosophy in Plato's *Phaedrus*,"

Journal of the History of Philosophy 9 (1971): 281–82, 286. See also F. Daumas, "Sous le signe du Gattilier en Fleurs," *Revue des Etudes Grecques* 74 (1961): 61–68.

19. We are not told why Lysias has come to town. He certainly is not staying with distinguished citizens or at a house of illustrious lineage. Morychus achieved a reputation for high living; he was a heavy drinker and a glutton. It is appropriate that his house was the scene of this "feast of speeches" (227b6–7); both Morychus and Lysias supply "food of semblance" (248b5). Plato thereby signals the baseness of Lysias' speech. Obviously Phaedrus was the perfect guest for the occasion. Epicrates was a rhetorician, demagogue, and orator of the democratic party. Lysias himself subsequently proved to be a champion of the democratic cause (and his brother lost his life fighting for it). The thesis of Lysias' speech seems suited to democratic sentiment (227c9–d2; it is "demophelic," "useful to the people"); hence the setting for Lysias' feast is appropriate on this score too. Yet Lysias has come up to a house located near the temple of the Olympian Zeus, a god who, in the *Phaedrus,* is the leader of the philosophers (252e). On Morychus and Epicrates, see W. H. Thompson, *The Phaedrus of Plato, with English Notes and Dissertations* (London: Wittaker & Co., 1868), pp. 2–3.

20. In reference to Socrates' encomium here, E. A. Wyller remarks "Im Text folgt die erste und wohl auch lichtvollste Schilderung der sinnlichen Natur in der klassichen griechischen Prosa (bes. 230BC)" (*Der Späte Platon* [Hamburg: Meiner, 1970], p. 128).

21. As is noted by R. Burger in *Plato's Phaedrus: A Defense of a Philosophic Art of Writing* (University: University of Alabama Press, 1980), p. 14 and notes, Phaedrus is indirectly associated by Socrates with Oreithuia, and Pharmakeia with Lysias' text (the "pharmakon" of 230d6 which Phaedrus "plays" with). Socrates is thus associated with Boreas, who will "carry off" Phaedrus, having been lured to Phaedrus by the seductive drug he is carrying. The Boreas/Socrates and Phaedrus/Oreithuia linkages are also proposed by Hermeias of Alexandria in his intricate interpretation of the passage (*In Platonis Phaedrum Scholia*, ed. P. Couvreur [Hildesheim: G. Olms, 1971], p. 29).

22. We should note that in the conjunction of "truth" and "persuasion" here the ingredients of the problem of rhetoric are already present. And the question as to whether the Boreas/Oreithuia story should be understood "literally" points not just to the problem of rhetoric but also to that of interpreting the rhetoric of myth. The latter problem is closely connected to that of interpreting a Platonic dialogue (see the Introduction and chapter 4 of this study).

23. In his note to this passage, Thompson cites Metrodorus' explanation of Zeus and the other gods as "physical substances or elemental arrangements" (*The Phaedrus*, p. 7). Cf. also C. Ritter's n. 15 to p. 32 of *Platons Dialog Phaidros,* 2d ed. (Leipzig: Meiner, 1922).

24. Of course, Socrates did not invent the connection between love and death, one that is discussed extensively by E. Vermeule in *Aspects of Death in Early Greek Art and Poetry* (Berkeley: University of California Press, 1979),

chap. 5. On p. 159 she comments that "Eros with the wand of Hermes, Eros the killer, Eros and Thanatos: it was a formal principle of Greek myth and literature that love and death were two aspects of the same power, as in the myth of Persephone or Helen of Troy." Vermeule also discusses in this chapter the strange conjunction of love and death represented in stories focused on the rape motif, as in the Boreas/Oreithuia story.

25. *Contra* H. W. Meyer, "Das Verhältnis von Enthusiasmus und Philosophie bei Platon im Hinblick auf seinen *Phaidros*," *Archiv für Philosophie* 6 (1956): 271: "Die Haltung des Sokrates gegenüber dem Mythos ist frei. Er weiss, dass die Kenntnis der Mythen keinen philosophischen Wert enthalt und dass in deren allegorischer Interpretation kein Wissen gewonnen werden kann, wie die Sophistik es beansprucht." Plato thus shows us, according to Meyer, how we are to interpret Socrates' own palinode: "Wir sollen nicht skeptisch sein wie die Sophisten und versuchen, in allegorisierender Interpretation einen Sinn in sie hineinzupressen; wir sollen sie andererseits nicht als Offenbarung höchster philosophischer Wahrheit hinnehmen . . .''; the myths "Poesie sind und keine Philosophie" (p. 277). I agree that we must not try to translate the myths like "sophists," that is, into materialistic terms. But there are other kinds of translation.

26. Apollodorus, *The Library*, trans. J. G. Frazer, 2 vols. (Cambridge, Mass.: Harvard University Press, 1976–79), 1:47–49. See also J. Fontenrose's discussion in chap. 4 of *Python: A Study of Delphic Myth and Its Origins* (Berkeley: University of California Press, 1959), particularly with respect to the Typhon-Python connection. Concerning the identification of Typhoeus and Typhon, see the corresponding entry in W. H. Roscher's *Ausführliches Lexikon der griechischen und römischen Mythologie*, vol. 5 (Leipzig: Teubner, 1916–24), columns 1426 and 1442 in particular.

27. Hackforth's translation (in *Plato's Phaedrus*) seems misleading: he has ". . . or a simpler, gentler being whom heaven has blessed with a quiet, un-Typhonic nature." Robin (in *Phèdre*) has "peut-être suis-je un animal plus paisible et moins compliqué, dont la nature participe à je ne sais quelle destinée divine et qui n'est point enfumée d'orgueil." Like Robin, Ritter takes "theias" with "moiras" (*Platons Dialog Phaidros,* p. 33).

28. Sextus Empiricus alludes to this passage and *Theae.* 174b when he says "Now 'man' (if he is 'the agent') seems to me, so far as regards the statements made by the Dogmatists, to be not only non-apprehensible but also inconceivable. At least we hear the Platonic Socrates expressly confessing that he does not know whether he is a man or something else" (*Pyrroneison Hypotyposeon,* bk. 2, V, 22, trans. by R. G. Bury, in *Sextus Empiricus,* vol. 1 [London: Heinemann, 1933], p. 165).

29. The *epitethumeka* (from *epithumeo*) at 227d2–3 may echo the *epitethummenon* (from *epituphomai*) at 230a4–5.

30. Socrates' use of the Typhon image in this context contains the seed of interpretations of the Oracle that subsequently came to be identified with various schools, interpretations such as "know your measure," "know your capaci-

ties," "know your place," "know your limits," "know your faults," "know your mortality." For further discussion of these schools, see Wilkins's *"Know Thyself" in Greek and Latin Literature.*

Chapter 2: Lysias' Speech, Socrates' First Speech, and Interludes

1. "Τὸ γνῶθι σαυτὸν πᾶσίν ἐστι χρήσιμον" (Line 584 of Suppl. 1 to *Menandri Gnomai Monostichoi,* in vol. 4 of *Fragmenta Comicorum Graecorum,* 5 vols., ed. A. Meineke [Berlin: G. Reimer, 1841], p. 356).

2. Burger suggests that the speech is analogous to that which a politician addresses to a demos he wants to control. "This wooer of the *demos* must provide an assurance of his own completeness, personal disinterest, and perfect self-control, as well as a pledge of his willingness and ability to satisfy the needs and desires of those he seeks to rule" (*Plato's Phaedrus,* p. 26). I note that Lysias was a metic as well as a logographos. That is, he wrote (among other things) courtroom speeches for others but could not deliver them himself. His art thus required that he be able to put himself in someone else's position and speak in his voice, and so to understand that person as well as his auditors or jurors. Socrates incorporates the rules of such an art into the techne of rhetoric outlined later on in the *Phr.* For further discussion of Lysias and his life, see Robin, *Phèdre,* pp. xiv–xxii.

3. Cf. Rosen's remark: "In sum, [the nonlover] combines the qualities of hedonism, utilitarianism and technicism in such a way as to abstract from such human qualities as the beautiful and ugly or the noble and the base." But Rosen adds: "Like the philosopher, he disregards human individuality in his pursuit of the general or steadfast" ("The Non-Lover in Plato's *Phaedrus,*" p. 433).

4. Rosen, "The Non-Lover," pp. 435–36.

5. For a comment on these references, see Dorter, "Imagery and Philosophy in Plato's *Phaedrus,*" p. 286, and W. Fortenbaugh, "Plato's *Phaedrus* 235C3," *Classical Philology* 61 (1966): 108–09. The attribution of beauty to Sappho and wisdom to Anacreon is surely ironic. However, the problem of the relationship between beauty and wisdom becomes increasingly important from this point on. Note that Socrates refers to writing as well as speaking here (235b8, c4). The written word turns out to be the external source par excellence.

6. Cf. Aristotle, *Athenian Constitution,* chap. 7, 1. There is no reference there to the statues being life-sized or set up at Delphi; as Hackforth notes, these are Phaedrus' additions (*Plato's Phaedrus,* p. 33n2).

7. A suggestion also made by Sallis, *Being and Logos,* pp. 120–21.

8. In *The "Art" of Rhetoric,* 3:7, 11, Aristotle alludes to the "irony" of the dithyrambic invocation of Socrates' speech.

9. By interrupting himself in the course of the speech, Socrates makes it longer, even though he claims he wants to rush through it at top speed. Even

so, this speech is one of the very few that Socrates delivers in the Platonic dialogues.

10. For example, in the *Symp.*, Alcibiades says that Socrates alone can make him feel ashamed (216b). In the *Prot.*, Socrates puts Protagoras in a position where the others can make him feel ashamed for wanting to terminate the discussion (*Prot.* 348b–c). Socrates also makes Gorgias feel ashamed, as Callicles notes (*Gorg.* 482d, 494d–e). See also *Charm.* 169c.

11. J. Pieper, in *Love and Inspiration,* trans. R. and C. Winston (New York: Harcourt Brace & World, 1964), plausibly remarks that Socrates feels shame not in the face of Phaedrus but in view of what Phaedrus could be, as truly human (p. 42), an interpretation that would resolve the present difficulty.

12. Hegel repeatedly criticizes attempts to philosophize by beginning with definitions (see, for a start, the *Preface* to the *Phenomenology of Spirit*). The secondary literature on Hegel's "method," if one may so call it, is vast. An excellent statement of the "method" (at least that of the *PhS.*) and of the problems it is intended to circumvent may be found in R. Pippin's "Hegel's Phenomenological Criticism," *Man and World* 8 (1975): 296–314. For discussion of the difference between Hegel and Plato on the nature of dialectic, see my "Reflections on 'Dialectic' in Plato and Hegel," *International Philosophical Quarterly* 22 (1982): 115–30, and R. Bubner, "Dialog und Dialektik oder Plato und Hegel," in *Zur Sache der Dialektik* (Ditzingen: Reclam, 1980), pp. 124–60.

13. Both here and in the palinode, "epithumia" refers primarily to sexual desire. In the palinode and in Socrates' speech in the *Symp.*, epithumia, eros, and philia represent stages of increasingly "rational" desire. See D. Hyland, "Ἔρως, Ἐπιθυμία, and Φιλία in Plato," *Phronesis* 13 (1968): 32–46.

14. Another detail about the speech: the speaker denies that the lover's boy would be courageous in war (239d), and affirms that the lover will not stick by the boy when the cost of doing so increases very far. Thus the speaker denies the possibility of Phaedrus' "army of lovers" (*Symp.* 178e–179a). One cannot help remarking on the similarity between the concealed lover's portrait of the boy—a soft or weak person physically (239c–d) and mentally (239a)—and Phaedrus.

15. A list of the criticisms Lysias makes of eros and those Socrates makes would show that Socrates' speech includes points not made in Lysias', but also omits others.

16. Recall that it was only in the remarks made in propria persona that Socrates speaks of the concealed lover's desire to seduce the boy. Presumably one of the "corresponding good points" of the nonlover would not, then, be that he does *not* desire to seduce the boy. This leaves one wondering whether seduction of the boy is incompatible with the nonlover's amelioration of him, or whether a nonlover would simply be unconcerned with the boy from a physical standpoint.

17. In the *Apol.* (31d) the daimon restrains Socrates (for example, from becoming involved in the affairs of the city), whereas here its function seems more positive (for example, to make atonement before returning to the city). Cf. *Euthyd.* 272e, *Theae.* 151a, and *Theages* 128d. On the daimon, see Robin, *Phèdre*, p. xxxiv.

18. Socrates slightly alters Ibycus' line. For a comment on this, see D. Clay, "Socrates' Prayer to Pan," in *Hellenic Studies Presented to B. M. W. Knox*, ed. Arktouros (Berlin: de Gruyter, 1979), pp. 349–50. The men whose honor Socrates hoped to receive were undoubtedly Phaedrus and Lysias (cf. 237a10–b1). Socrates is, we recall, in a competition with Lysias. The competition continues (243d5–e2), but now it is explicitly tempered by a higher purpose, namely, that of pleasing the gods (cf. 273e, where a similar turn occurs).

19. In the *Symp.*, it is assumed at the start (177b) and by all the speakers except Socrates that eros is a god. In agreeing with this at *Phr.* 242d9, Socrates is agreeing with a widely held opinion. The qualification at 242e2, however, is more in keeping with Socrates' *Symp.* view.

20. K. Joël notes that the reference to sailors points us to Piraeus and so to Lysias ("Platos 'sokratische' Periode und der *Phaidrus*," in *Philosophische Abhandlungen*, M. Heinze gewidmet [Berlin: E. S. Mittler & Sohn, 1906], p. 88). Note also Socrates' comparison of the earlier speech with "halmuran akoen" (243d4–5).

21. On Stesichorus and his palinode, see Thompson, *The Phaedrus*, pp. 37–38 (Thompson cites the relevant texts), and see also J. A. Davison, *From Archilochus to Pindar* (New York: St. Martin's Press, 1968), chap. 8.

22. Homer, by contrast, is said to have remained blind. He is criticized implicitly here, and explicitly in the *Rep.* (especially in book 10). Socrates implies that Homer, unlike Stesichorus, created images without being able to distinguish them from originals. In the context of *Rep.* passage (586c), Socrates attacks those whose lives are ruled by the low desire for physical gratification on the basis that they are in love with *images* of true pleasure and reality instead of the things themselves. Homer is criticized, in effect, for encouraging the debasing love of the illusory. For further discussion, see my "The Ideas and the Criticism of Poetry in Plato's *Republic*, Book 10," *Journal of the History of Philosophy* 19 (1981): 135–50. The analogy between Stesichorean and Socratic palinodes, when taken together with the *Rep.* passage, points to a "political" application of the *Phr.*'s teaching about eros.

Chapter 3: The Palinode

1. *Thus Spoke Zarathustra*, pt. 1; p. 153, in *The Portable Nietzsche*, trans. Kaufmann.

2. According to 253c7–d1, the start of the myth occurred where the soul was divided into three forms, that is, at 246a3 ff.. The reference at 265c1 to the "mythical hymn" clearly adverts to the palinode's portrayal of eros, which took place only in section (2b) of the palinode.

3. The first kind of madness is said to be both a "divine dispensation" (244c3) and "from god" (d4). The second is not explicitly said to be from the gods. The third is said to derive from the Muses. At the start of the palinode, Socrates states that he wants to show that madness is a divine gift (244a7), and at 245b1 he says that the three forms of madness are sent by the gods. At 245b4–c1 he says that erotic madness is sent by the gods. Yet Socrates never says *in the apodeixis* that erotic madness is sent by the gods; on the contrary, the gods do not actively help men to recollect at all.

4. For further discussion of this difficult passage, see I. M. Linforth, "Telistic Madness in Plato, *Phaedrus* 244DE," *University of California Publications in Classical Philology* 13 (1946): 163–72.

5. R. Demos finds this passage so odd that he conjectures that "it is an insertion" ("Plato's Doctrine of the Psyche as a Self-Moving Motion," *Journal of the History of Philosophy* 6 [1968]: 134). This is a type of conjecture that is unacceptable on general hermeneutical grounds, except as a last resort (see the Introduction). But the conjecture is understandable if one reads the passage as a venture into "physics," for such a venture seems out of place here. Indeed, to some interpreters, this passage seems alien to the Platonic dialogue as such; for example, see O. Regenbogen, "Bemerkungen zur Deutung des platonischen *Phaidros*," in *Kleine Schriften* (Munich: F. Dirlmeier, 1961), p. 252.

6. This premise might be said to be true by definition, though to do so seems arbitrary; what cannot come to be or be destroyed could be ever-static.

7. I am accepting, along with Burnet, Hackforth, W. J. Verdenius ("Notes on Plato's *Phaedrus*," *Mnemosyne* 4, no. 8 [1955]: 276), and J. B. Skemp (*The Theory of Motion in Plato's Later Dialogues* [Cambridge: Cambridge University Press, 1942], p. 3n2), "aeikineton" instead of "autokineton" at 245c5. This reading is also defended by T. M. Robinson in "The Argument for Immortality in Plato's *Phaedrus*," in *Essays in Ancient Greek Philosophy*, ed. Anton and Kustas (Albany: State University of New York Press, 1971), pp. 345–53, and by F. D. Caizzi, "AEIKINHTON O AYTOKINHTON? (Plat. *Phaedr.*, 245c)," *Acme* 23 (1970): 91–97. The alternative reading is accepted by Robin, who unjustifiably declares that without it the demonstration "semble boîteuse" *Phèdre* (p. 33n3). In addition to the reasons given by the authors just mentioned, "autokineton" would lead to needless repetition in the passage, whereas the rhetoric of the passage demands (and is generally characterized by) extreme brevity. Robinson's construal of the argument differs from mine, though the last argument in my version is contained in the second and third propositions of what he calls a "subordinate proof" (p. 347). In stating one of the premises as "the aeikineton is a auto kinoun," Robinson reverses the true subject/predicate order of the proposition, which is why this third premise of his "subordinate proof" cannot validly produce (via a sorites) the conclusion he draws ("soul is immortal"). J. L. Ackrill's formulation of the "structure of the whole passage" is the same as the final syllogism in the sorites I have constructed. Ackrill uses this as evidence for his reading of "autokineiton" at 245c5, but as my schema suggests this is not necessary to preserving that

final syllogism. See his "Review of *Plato's Phaedrus* by R. Hackforth," *Mind* 62 (1953): 278.

8. This parenthetical point is supported by the text if one accepts Hackforth's and Burnet's reading of 245d3 ("οὐκ ἂν ἔτι ἀρχὴ γίγνοιτο"; see Hackforth's *Plato's Phaedrus*, p. 63n1). The alternative reading ("οὐκ ἂν ἐξ ἀρχῆς γίγνοιτο") is accepted by Robin, Verdenius ("Notes," p. 277), and G. J. De Vries, *A Commentary on the Phaedrus of Plato* (Amsterdam: Hakkert, 1969), pp. 122–23. This alternative reading seems to weaken the logic of the argument, since it in effect construes the point as a counterfactual. Robin's comment about the apparent presence here of an "ontological argument" (*Phèdre*, p. lxxviii) makes better sense in terms of Hackforth's than his own reading. In any event, the parenthetical argument in question is Socrates' only explanation as to why soul *must* be in *constant* self-motion. A soul cannot just rest and start itself moving again. Soul cannot be completely at rest and still be soul, it seems; life is incessant movement of one sort of another.

9. I am reading, with Hackforth, Robin, Verdenius ("Notes," p. 277), and De Vries (*Commentary*, p. 124), but not Burnet, "γένεσιν" instead of "γῆν εἰς ἕν" at 245e1, since, as Robin notes (*Phèdre*, p. 34n2), it better states the point at issue: that *all* movement would cease were the arche to be destroyed.

10. It might be objected that the point is that we are dealing with a counterfactual for which there is empirical disproof: since all motion *has not* stopped, it follows that the arche is indestructible. But this would show only that the arche has not *yet* been destroyed, whereas Socrates wants to make a much stronger claim, namely, that it *cannot ever* be destroyed. Support for this kind of claim seems to lie in some sort of moral imperative. See also n. 12 below.

11. Cf. Z. Diesendruck, *Struktur und Charakter*, p. 43, who calls the identification of the "arche" with soul a "dogma." Yet Diesendruck says almost nothing about the role of shame here and does not consider that the identification in question might be defensible in terms of the purpose of the palinode as a whole.

12. Gerasimos Santas has indicated to me a different construal of the role here of shame: "given what has been proved, one who said 'the ousia and logos of the soul is self-motion' would not be disgraced, i.e., he would be telling the truth." The reference to shame would thus be a sort of commentary on what has already been proven. But in my view the statement concerning shame is explicitly introduced in order to allow "soul" and "self-motion" to be connected, and no other justification for this connection is offered. With reference to Socrates' first, shameful, speech, we might say: if the soul is not self-moved, perhaps it is one of the things in us that is "acquired" rather than "natural" (cf. 237d6–9), so possessing merely "conventional" meaning, one that is not stable enough to support the palinode's ennobling thesis about eros.

13. The debate about the meaning of "psyche pasa" goes back to antiqui-
ty; see P. Frutiger, *Les mythes de Platon; Étude philosophique et littéraire* (New
York: Arno Press, 1976), pp. 131 ff. Socrates says that "psyche pasa" is
"winged" (246c1), so implying that it possesses the structure of soul that has
just been sketched, namely, the winged horses and charioteer. How could
there exist a cosmic soul possessing this structure and so possessing various
kinds of desire (symbolized by the wings and horses) under the supervision of
reason? Moreover, the horses of the gods are both good, and those of other
creatures are mixed (246a7–b1), while "all soul" qua "self-motion" is identical
in gods and men (245c2–3 and context). It would seem that the image of the
soul offered in section (2b) of the palinode cannot be an image of a world soul
and so that the "psyche pasa" of 246b6 cannot refer to a world soul. See also
Hackforth's acceptance of Frutiger's argument that the presence or absence of
the article with "pyche pasa" is indecisive so far as the collective/distributive
debate goes (*Plato's Phaedrus*, p. 64).

14. Unfortunately there is a MS problem here concerning the article. I
agree with De Vries's comments on the matter (*Commentary*, p. 128), but construe the sense of "all soul" (of "the soul entire") to pertain to what is common to all souls (instead of to a "world soul"). It cannot be the case that *each*
soul cares for "all the unsouled."

15. At *Laws* 896d–e the movement of heaven is ascribed to at least two
self-moved souls, one good and one bad. Note also the shift from "soul" to
"souls" at 898c7–8, 899b5, and the identification of "souls" with the "gods"
(899b). The good soul or souls are responsible for the periphora of the heavens
(898c); one need not necessarily ascribe the motion to a world soul.

16. A. Camus, *Le mythe de Sisyphe* (Paris: Gallimard, 1942), p. 81: "La
mort est là comme seule réalité." And p. 37: "Ce monde en lui-même n'est
pas raisonnable, c'est tout ce qu'on en peut dire." Camus's essay as a whole is
in effect an attack on Plato. For a Platonic criticism of Camus and his interpretation of the myth of Sisyphus, see my "The Myth of Sisyphus: a Reconsideration," *Philosophy in Context* 7, Suppl. Issue (1978): 45–59.

17. For a similar point in the context of Aristotle's treatment of self-
motion, see D. J. Furley, "Self-Movers," in *Essays on Aristotle's Ethics*, ed.
A. O. Rorty (Berkeley: University of California Press, 1980), p. 63.

18. I do not believe that much of the meaning of the myth's description of
love and desire is changed if one thinks of the lover-beloved relationship in
heterosexual terms. For an excellent discussion of this point, see H. L. Sinaiko,
*Love, Knowledge, and Discourse in Plato: Dialogue and Dialectic in Phaedrus, Re-
public, Parmenides* (Chicago: University of Chicago Press, 1965), p. 26n2. In
spite of the famous "pederasty in conjunction with philosophy" phrase at
249a2, at 250e and 256a–b all sexual relations are criticized (cf. 251a1,
254b1).

19. For the sake of convenience, I will abbreviate "hyperuranian beings" as
"Beings." I shall also use "Being" and "Truth" to refer to the Beings, since

Socrates uses the expressions "*οὐσία ὄντως οὖσα*" (247c7), "*τὸ ὄν*" (247d3;
also 248b4), "*τὰ ὄντα*" (or "*τὰ ὄντα ὄντως*"; 247e3, 248a5, 249e5), "*ὅ
ἐστιν ὄν ὄντως*" (247e2; see also 249c4), "*ἀλήθεια*" (249b6, 247c5–6; cf.
"*τὸ ἀληθείας πεδίον*," 248b6) synonymously. He does specify some of the
Beings by name, but, as usual, leaves the exact number of the Beings unde-
termined. In the hyperuranian "place" (247d1, 248a3) of the *Phaedrus*, "to
be" means to be true, knowable, eternally extant, without variation, as distinguished from that which characterizes "those things we now call beings"
(247e1). Unfortunately, the pleonastic phrases Socrates uses to describe Being
are difficult to translate (I occasionally use "essence," for example). Nontechnical occurrences of "*ἰδέα*" and "*εἶδος*" occur at 251a3 and b7. The "*γένος*"
at 247c8 has never been taken, so far as I know, to mean "Idea," nor
should it.

20. The subject of "*ἐστι*," *ἔοικεν*" and "*ἐοικέτω*" could be "*ἰδέα*" or
"*ψυχή*." The former is more natural since 246a3–4 draws our attention to the
"idea" as that which creates the difficulty. The problem is not just with
"soul," but with its "*ἰδέα*."

21. The "Idea" or "Form" of the soul seems referred to by E. Voegelin,
Plato (Baton Rouge: Louisiana State University Press, 1966), pp. 136–37. Robin states that "l'âme n'est pas une Idée," since the soul in the *Phr.* is composite (*Phèdre*, p. cxx; also p. cx; but cf. p. lxxviiin3); S. Rosen takes the
same approach, giving more persuasive evidence for it than Robin does,
though Rosen does not refer to the *Phr.* in this context: "ΣΩΦΡΟΣΥΝΗ
and Selbstbewusstsein," *Review of Metaphysics* 26 (1973): 626 (on p. 629 Rosen
draws the conclusion that there is no episteme of the soul). R. Demos too
states that the soul is not a form and has no form; yet he omits mention of
the "idea" at *Phr.* 246a3 and states, "To my knowledge, nowhere in the dialogues does Plato refer to the 'form' or 'idea' *of* the soul" ("Plato's Doctrine of
the Psyche as a Self-Moving Motion," p. 139). See also Jean-Marie Paisse, "La
métaphysique de l'âme humaine dans le *Phèdre* de Platon," *Bulletin de l'Association G. Budé* 31 (1972): 469–78. Paisse seems to deny that the soul has an
Idea and not just that the soul is one, but he does not examine the reference
at 246a3. P. Natorp denies that "idea" at 246a3 means "Idea," but he offers
little justification for this view (*Platos Ideenlehre; eine Einführung in den Idealismus* [Darmstadt: Wissenschaftliche Buchgesellschaft, 1961], p. 70). Hermeias,
however, does discuss the matter (*Scholia*, pp. 120 ff). One could argue on the
basis of *Rep.* 596a that since there is an Idea for every "one over many," there
must be one of the soul. I discuss that *Rep.* passage at length in my "The
Ideas and the Criticism of Poetry in Plato's *Republic*, Book 10," and show that
the passage is an intentionally wild generalization on Socrates' part. I emphasize that my present argument, however, is based on the *Phr.* only. Other dialogues (such as the *Pho.*) might well present a different picture of the matter.

22. Episteme is "not [the episteme] that is neighbor to becoming, and
which I suppose is different in the different things we now call beings, but [it

is] really the episteme of Being that really is" (247d7–e2). My other remarks here about the Beings are culled from 247c6–e4 and the talk at 250a–b and context about the images of the Beings. I am assuming that what is said about Episteme is applicable to the other Beings; for example, Justice Itself is not (with respect to its ontological character) the same as what we call "justice," and so on. That Socrates mentions Episteme and "moral Ideas" in the *Phr.* seems to reflect a major issue of the palinode, the relationship of knowledge and virtue. That the Ideas are knowable through Episteme suggests the view that knowledge is the key to virtue. A communion of Ideas seems implied here (see also 254b), but the *Phr.* sheds little light on that matter.

23. It will be helpful, at this stage, to distinguish between "Episteme" understood as what the godly souls have when they contemplate the Idea "Episteme," "episteme" understood as the result of the "method" or "techne" described in the second half of the *Phr.*, and a third sort of knowledge that one might call "gnosis" and that characterizes, in my view, "self-knowledge." As usual in Plato, however, the terminology is not used with absolute consistency. I use "gnosis" because Socrates, following the Delphic Oracle, speaks of the need "gignoskein" himself (not "epistasthai"). I am arguing, in the present study, that "gnostic" self-knowledge is not epistemic in either of the two senses just mentioned. Presumably methodological "episteme," like the "Episteme" the godly souls have when they contemplate the true thing, participates (however defectively) in the Idea "Episteme." But in the *Phr.* this matter is not considered explicitly, let alone spelled out, even though doing so would have helped significantly in bringing together the two halves of the dialogue. If gnosis participates in an Idea at all, presumably that Idea would be Phronesis (250d4).

24. If there were an Idea of the soul, then we should have to conceive, in terms of the *Phr.* myth, of the immortal souls circulating in heaven and at one point looking directly at their own essence. Whatever this might mean, it seems to me that an explanation of it would take us beyond Plato to neo-Platonism.

25. This may seem overstated, since it could be maintained that even if there is an Idea of the Soul and there is Episteme of it, it does not follow that there is Episteme of this or that soul, precisely because souls are not Ideas (I am indebted to John Malcolm for pointing this out to me). But the palinode indicates that all Ideas have images (only some of which are visual images) and that to understand the Idea is to understand that in the image which mirrors the Idea in question. If there is an Idea of the soul, then in knowing this Idea I know my soul qua soul since that is what the Idea is of (or: the Idea is what my soul "has"; it is that which makes it essentially a *soul*).

26. Socrates says there, in response to Simmias' request that he say more about the stories he has heard about many and wonderful places of the earth, stories that "persuade" (*peithein;* cf. *Phr.* 229c6, 230a2, 245c2) Socrates: "Well, Simmias, I don't think the skill of Glaucus is needed to narrate [die-

gesasthai; cf. the "diegeseos" at *Phr.* 246a5] what they are [*ha g'estin;* cf. the *hoion men esti* at *Phr.* 246a4]; although to prove them true does seem to me too difficult for the skill of Glaucus, and I myself certainly am not such as to do it, and even if I knew how to, I think the life left me, Simmias, doesn't suffice for the length of the logos. Still, nothing prevents me from telling of what I've been convinced the earth's *idea* is like, and of its regions" (trans. D. Gallop [Oxford: Clarendon Press, 1980], p. 63, slightly amended). At the conclusion of the whole "mythos" (*Pho.* 110b4, 114d7) Socrates adds that it would be wrong to assume that everything is true in exactly the form he stated it. The "idea" of the earth is not an Idea but the earth's nature, internal structure, the articulation of its parts. Socrates means pretty much the same sort of thing when in the *Phr.* he refers to the soul's "idea."

27. This point is developed at some length by M. Nussbaum's " 'This Story Isn't True': Poetry, Goodness, and Understanding in Plato's *Phaedrus*."

28. The three possibilities are *zeugous* at 246a7, *harma* at 246e5, and *ochemata* at 247b2. I omit the *sunoridos* at 246b2 as uncontroversial. For *zeugous*, "pair of horses" is preferable (Hackforth has "steeds" and Robin "attelage"), since it is in the plural and since Socrates goes on in the next sentence to talk about the horses. Moreover the *zeuge* are winged, and the organic and natural wings seem out of place on an artificial apparatus, especially given the *Phr.'s* description of the wings, their "roots," and so on. The *harma* is said to be winged, and the same point holds (Hackforth has "team" and Robin "char"). *Ochemata* is a bit more difficult, but the context makes "chariots" doubtful. Socrates says that the *ochemata* are *euenia*, that is, "obedient to the rein," a description that is suitable to the horses rather than the chariot (cf. 254c1). Thus the other souls have a hard time not because the chariots are bad but because one of the horses is disobedient. Socrates also uses at 247b2 the term *isorropos* which means "equally balanced," a term that again suggests, in the context, the two horses. If the chariot were part of the soul, it would be a very important part with a crucial function to play, and surely it would figure elsewhere in the myth; yet this is not so.

29. In a hitherto unpublished paper on the *Phaedrus,* Myles Burnyeat points out that while the Forms and soul are discussed in similar language at 250c1–4, nothing in the description of the souls matches the *hapla* which is applied to Forms, the implication being, I think, that the soul is complex. (I am grateful to the author for sharing this fine paper with me.)

30. In this I agree with J. Moline, *Plato's Theory of Understanding* (Madison: University of Wisconsin Press, 1981), pp. 57–62. Moline supplies a number of good reasons, which I will not repeat here, for the selection of a "capacity" rather than "faculty" view of the parts of the soul.

31. Socrates refers to the horses' genealogy (246a8, b3) but not to that of the charioteer or wings. Perhaps the phrase is a stereotype (see De Vries' note, *Commentary,* p. 126). In this particular context, however, the genealogical meaning (however sedimented) of the reference can remind us that horses have their origins in a natural state that differs from their harnessed state, and this

points to the problem of the soul's unity and ousia. Indeed the black horse seems closest to nature; hence it must be domesticated if the soul's nature is to perfect itself. Unbridled passion is natural but destructive. The charioteer, I add, is already a certain kind of man—one already trained and domesticated, as it were. Could the charioteer (reason) be descended from some simpler and more primitive being (for example, the merely calculative rationality of the nonlover)? In any event, the charioteer is descended, strictly speaking, from men, not from charioteers. How then did he acquire the skills of a charioteer (how did reason learn to reason)? Though this problem arises at various junctures in the myth (especially with respect to the nature of the soul in the pre-life), no solution is offered to it.

32. This point has a paradoxical air about it. The human charioteer subjugates the horses, and yet a human being *is* the charioteer *and* the horses. As S. Rosen once pointed out to me, the inclusion of a human being as a *part* of the image of a human being would seem to lead to an infinite regress; since inside the charioteer (who is the human being in this image) is the soul, one part of which is another charioteer. Similarly, see *Rep.* 588d–e and context.

33. Hackforth is correct in pointing out that "zeugous" at 246a7 *could* denote more than two horses (*Plato's Phaedrus*, p. 69n3), though this would be a possibility only for the souls of gods. Hence another structural difference between men and gods may be suggested here. However, since the only difference between the souls of men and gods that is explicitly mentioned concerns the issue of the evil horse, and since the implication seems to be that in other respects they are structurally the same, I prefer to assume that the souls of the gods also have two horses.

34. At 250c5–6 we are told that the soul is in the body as an oyster is in its shell. The shell does not just "imprison" the oyster; it also protects it from harm.

35. This phrase cannot mean "bodily part," as Hackforth has it, since the wings are part of the soul. Nevertheless, the phrase does suggest a continuity between soul and body (see De Vries's excellent note, *Commentary,* p. 130). Socrates subsequently will describe the experience of eros in physiological terms; he spiritualizes the body in order to describe the wings. All this indicates that body and soul are not irreconcilably alien to each other.

36. This point is quite in keeping with the *Symp.*'s view that eros is in-between the mortal and divine. That the gods are not philosophers (since they are not erotic) is stated at *Symp.* 204a and *Lysis* 218a. Though logos is associated in the *Phr.* with the world of incarnated souls, the myth as a whole abstracts from logos (for example, Beauty is conceived of in purely visual terms, to the exclusion of the beauty of speeches), a problem I will discuss below.

37. Possibly the daimones in the *Phr.* are souls who succeeded in seeing some of the Beings and so avoid losing their wings. For further discussion see S. Eitrem's "Götter und Daimonem; einige Bemerkungen zu Platon, *Phaidr.* 246E," *Symbolae Osloenses* 34 (1958): 39–42. See also *Rep.* 620d–e, and *Symp.* 202e–203a. The only gods explicitly mentioned in the myth are Zeus, Hera,

Ares, Apollo, and Hestia (presumably Eros is not to be counted among them).
Hestia stays home; that is, she does not see the Beings. If Hestia stands for
the earth, then the earth—to which all fallen souls are exiled—is cut off from
direct access to the Beings.

38. T. Irwin, in his "Recollection and Plato's Moral Theory," *Review of
Metaphysics* 27 (1974): 752–72, spells out the difference between what he calls
the "Socratic" and "Platonic" theories of moral knowledge and motivation.
The two positions are, I agree, represented by the first two speeches of the
Phr. and the palinode, respectively. Virtue understood as a craft allows us to
dispense with anamnesis, talk about an "ascent," dispute about the ends of
choice (this is the "Socratic" theory). In the "Platonic" view the ends are in
dispute; here "dialogue," anamnesis, and the "ascent" become important.
Irwin recognizes that the former position is criticized in the *Phr.* However,
Irwin's presuppositions about the development of views from Socrates to Plato,
and his interpretation of the *Phr.* and the other dialogues in terms of these
presuppositions, are in my opinion erroneous (see my arguments in the Introduction).

39. It is unclear in 248a4–6 whether each nongodly soul sees something of
several Beings (this, I think, is the more plausible interpretation) or *all* of
each of the Beings it does see (cf. 250a2). The issue could make a difference
as to the possibilities for recollection in this life and the judgment one deserves for one's actions. Socrates *is* clear that no human soul is utterly ignorant
of all the Beings (249b5–6, e4–5; 248a6–b1 might mislead one in this
regard) and that no soul has perfectly seen all the Beings. However, justice
shows up in the palinode as a Being and also as *Dike* (249a8); how the two are
related is unclear.

40. The problem is also noted by Diesendruck, *Struktur und Charakter,*
pp. 28–29.

41. I interpret the palinode as referring to a "first fall" of the soul, at least
within one of the ten-thousand-year cycles, since Socrates refers to the "first
genesis" (248d1–2, 252d3), the "first life" (249a5), the "second life" (249b2–
3), and so forth. The lover-beloved relationship described by the palinode
takes place within the first one-thousand-year period (see 249a, 256b). For
further discussion, see D. D. McGibbon, "The Fall of the Soul in Plato's
Phaedrus," *Classical Quarterly,* n.s. 14 (1964): 56–63, and R. S. Bluck, "The
Phaedrus and Reincarnation," *American Journal of Philology* 79 (1958): 156–64.
The repetition of ten-thousand-year cycles, I note, would seem to go on forever (there is no hint of a "day of judgment" here)—a frightful prospect.

42. Cf. A. Kojève, *Introduction à la lecture de Hegel* (Paris: Gallimard,
1947), pp. 517–28, for a fascinating discussion of the differences between the
Platonic, Christian, and Hegelian conceptions of individuality and their connection to "freedom," "history," and "finitude." As Kojève points out, if one
chooses one's life before entering into it, then the living out of that life would
resemble a comedy (p. 522n1). So far as the *Phaedrus* is concerned, there is indeed a suggestion that human life is more like a comedy than a tragedy, as

the "friendship" between Phaedrus and Socrates testifies. For Kojève, if the soul is immortal and the lives in this world are "chosen" beforehand, then man's distinctive freedom and individuality disappear, the result being that men and animals are not fundamentally different (p. 523). This would explain why Socrates says that after the first cycle of incarnation the souls of men can go into those of animals, and vice versa (249b).

43. For another effort to make sense of the list, see R. S. Brumbaugh, "Teaching Plato's *Republic* VIII and IX," *Teaching Philosophy* 3 (1980): 331–37. However difficult it may be to sort out the rationale of the whole list, it is important to keep in mind one of its central implications: there is a natural hierarchy among human beings. It is also worth emphasizing that the philosopher alone is associated with eros. The remainder of the palinode explains this association. At 250b7, c7–8, Socrates seems to identify himself as a member of the first category.

44. Socrates uses the term "ouranos" in the present passage; sometimes it means "heavens" and sometimes "universe" (the latter is clearly the sense at 245d8).

45. Cf. E. N. Lee's excellent article, "Reason and Rotation: Circular Movement as the Model of Mind (Nous) in Later Plato," in *Facets of Plato's Philosophy*, ed. W. Werkmeister, *Phronesis,* Suppl. vol. 2 (Assen: Van Gorcum, 1976), pp. 70–102. Though Lee does not say much here about the *Phr.,* the article is very helpful for the interpretation of this dialogue. Lee distinguishes between the "accomplishment" sense of "to circle" (the sense in which a point on a circle traverses, through time, the circumference of the circle) and the "activity" sense (the motion of the whole circle around its center, a motion that at any instant is complete). These are the "threshold" and "dweller" perspectives respectively of nous. In the *Phr.* the gods' activity at the banquet seems close to this activity sense of noetic circling, and the soul's efforts to participate in the feast clearly represent the accomplishment sense (hence the problem of perspective for the nongodly souls). Still, the gods are distinct from one another; they look outward, and hence their circling is not focused toward the center. Moreover, in the *Phr.* we do not get an explicit identification of nous with circular motion. Even to the gods, the Beings are visible sequentially and diachronically. Hence the "dia chronou" at 247d3 should not just be taken colloquially, though one need not ask how much time is involved here (note also the "eos" at 247d4). That the gods' noetic activity is not quite stated in terms of the dweller's perspective is also suggested by Socrates' statement that the gods "go home" after they have feasted (247e4); that is, the rotation of reason is not the home in which the gods dwell. The feasting seems to be intermittent.

46. Of the activity sense of nous, Lee says: "It is rather a model for a certain kind of relation *of* the subject *to* an object; indeed, it is the model of a relation such that in it we very nearly have an object without *any* . . . subject (any limited point-of-view upon the object). Far, then, from being the expression of any private experience or sovereign subjectivity, the model represents a

subjectivity entirely absorbed in and subordinated to the apprehension of its object, wholly reduced to an abstract, pure aboutness" (Ibid., p. 83). The circle of knowing is broken so far as the nongodly souls are concerned. Hence their vision is perspectival.

47. The only possible reference to the Good is at 246e1, though it has never been taken as such so far as I know. Socrates also refers to the "sophon" there, but "sophia" is never mentioned as an Idea. This list of the properties that nourish the wings precedes the introduction of the Beings. The list is to be taken very generally; divine values, as it were, are good for the soul. The *Phr.* seems to substitute Beauty for the Good (more on this below and in subsequent chapters).

48. Socrates says that the dianoia of a god is fed by "nous and pure episteme" (247d1–2); the two terms are closely associated. He also says that the Beings are knowable by this specific kind of Episteme appropriate to them (247c8 ff.), which makes clear that to know the Beings is to know them Epistemically, and this is done via "nous alone." As I am about to argue, this Episteme seems to be a kind of intuitive knowledge by direct acquaintance. For a similar interpretation, see G. Jäger, *"Nus" in Platons Dialogen* (Göttingen: Vandenhoeck & Ruprecht, 1967), p. 100.

49. I would like to thank John Malcolm for forcing me to confront directly this problem as to how Socrates can say both that "nous alone" *and* dianoia see the Beings. I add that in the *Symp.*, it is very clear that the vision of the Ideas is a silent noetic intuition (one that might *subsequently* give rise to logoi).

50. In his "Reason and Rotation" article, Lee argues that the "psychologistic interpretation" of the nous model is neither encouraged nor required by it (p. 83). The feelings that *might* accompany the activity of reason are subjective and contingent. In the context of the *Phr.*, however, the issue is more clouded than this. The model is both a model about the logical relationship between knower and known, and equally about the knower's consciousness of himself when knowing. I am arguing that, in the *Phr.*, the separation between the two functions of the model is abstract; in practice, the separation between the objective and the subjective is problematic.

51. For reasons that will become evident below, I am taking "κατ' εἶδος" with "συνιέναι," not "λεγόμενον." I am also accepting, along with Hackforth, Badham's emendation ("ἰόντ'" instead of "ἰὸν") since, even if λεγ. is the subject of ἰὸν, it does not make a lot of sense to characterize something that is "spoken of" as going or doing anything (surely it is a man's intellect that goes from many to one). The emendation is also accepted by L. Gil, "Notas al *Fedro*", *Emerita* 24 (1956): 323. It is not impossible to take "συναιρούμενον" as middle here, though the passive sense is simpler (it is understood, in any case, that it is a man who causes his λογισμός to do the gathering together). As Verdenius points out, the "τὸ" is not necessary in order that the participial "λεγόμενον" be used substantively ("Notes on Plato's *Phaedrus*," p. 280). See also De Vries's discussion of this passage, in his *Commentary*, pp. 145–46. I am also taking the subject of "ἐστιν" in c5 to be the

philosopher (not his dianoia) since it is the man who is "near in memory" and since the man ($\grave{\alpha}\nu\grave{\eta}\rho$) is referred to in the following sentence. The final phrase I have quoted is almost untranslatable. I note that Hackforth translates "eidos" as plural.

52. Thus the use of "$\sigma\upsilon\nu\iota\acute{\epsilon}\nu\alpha\iota$" is appropriate here, given the connotations of "hearing" and "bringing together" associated with this verb (cf. *Alc.* I, 132c10). "Logismos," moreover, is inconceivable without some linguistic structure. Verdenius justly remarks that the "legomenon" is "much the same as a logos" ("Notes," p. 280).

53. The point is not that one's ears can pick up sounds less sharply than eyes can pick up, say, colors. The work of the senses and the mind are already intertwined here, and hence "amudra organa" (250b3–4) also may refer, as Hackforth notes (following Hermeias), to our powers of reasoning (but as they function in conjunction with the senses, I add) (*Plato's Phaedrus*, pp. 94–95). As to *why* different Ideas should have different sorts of images, Socrates says nothing.

54. That the images of the "moral Forms" may be auditory has already been suggested by N. Gulley, "Plato's Theory of Recollection," *Classical Quarterly*, n.s. 4 (1954): 204. Cf. *Soph.* 234a and *Pho.* 99d–100a on discourses as images. Cf. also *Crat.* 438d ff..

55. Cf. J. Mittelstrass, "Versuch über den Sokratischen Dialog," chap. 7 of *Wissenschaft als Lebensform* (Frankfurt: Suhrkamp, 1982), p. 147: "Die Rede von einem 'anderen Ort', an dem die Seele 'geschaut' hat, was sich als Wissen in konkreten Problemlösungssituationen bildet, ist nichts anderes als metaphorischer Ausdruck einer *theoretischen,* auf die 'Objectivität' des (zumal theoretischen) Wissens bezogenen, und einer *praktischen,* auf die 'Subjektivität' der Wissensbildung und ihre autonomen Strukturen bezogenen Leistung. . . . Mit anderen Worten: das Anamnesis-Theorem ist keine Lehre von einer 'Hinterwelt' des Geistes, sondern erneut eine—mit dem 'dialektischen' Modell verträgliche—(metaphorische) Formel für den Anfang der Vernunft und die Form des Wissens. . . . Damit ist auch gezeigt, dass die Sokratische Formel vom wissenden Nicht-Wissen nicht etwa im Gegensatz zum ·Anamnesis-Theorem steht." Mittelstrass' comments accord with my own interpretation.

56. For "hypomnemata" and cognates, see 275d1, 276d3, 278a1. At 275a the term is contrasted with both "mneme" and "anamnesis." In the *Phr.*, these latter two are sometimes joined or substituted for each other; see 250a1, 252d6, 253a3, 254b5, 275a. The contrast between what is "within" the soul (accessible to anamnesis) and what is "outside" it (accessible to hypomnesis) is explicit at 275a and in the prayer that concludes the *Phr.*

57. The position I am arguing for has been worked out in a different context by A. Nehamas in "Plato on the Imperfection of the Sensible World," *American Philosophical Quarterly* 12 (1975): 105–17. On p. 116, Nehamas says "Plato, then, did think that the Forms have perfect instances in the sensible world . . ., and that they are contained in the particulars that participate in them. What is imperfect is the way in which those perfect instances are pos-

sessed by sensible objects, an imperfection which allows us to say of everything that we consider as just or beautiful or equal that it is also unjust, ugly,
or unequal. . . . [Plato's question] was the question how we can even understand each other when we say that sensible objects are equal, beautiful, good,
or large, since these words seemed to refer to exactly the same things to which
their contraries also referred; and the question how things can both be and not
be what we say they are." The problem arises for "incomplete" predicates that
are "attributive or relational"—just the sort of predicates at issue in the *Phr.*
At *Phr.* 263a–d Socrates distinguishes between these predicates, which are the
subject of great disagreement, for terms such as "iron" and "silver" about
which there is no dispute. These latter terms are "complete" and so do not, as
Nehamas argues, require the postulation of Forms. In the *Phr.* it is the "incomplete" terms that the popular rhetoricians and Eleatic dialecticians (261d)
play on, leading their audience from one of their meanings to another (even to
their opposite; 262a). The philosopher must recollect the meaning of these
same terms.

58. The best comparison of the Freudian and Platonic conceptions of desire
and love remains T. Gould's *Platonic Love* (London: Routledge & Kegan Paul,
1963).

59. For detailed discussion of the passage, see De Vries's *Commentary*, pp.
158–59, and Thompson's *The Phaedrus*, pp. 66–67. In such verses, the gods'
name is the more significant. Perhaps the duality of human and divine perspectives on Eros reflects the duality between low and high conceptions represented, in the *Phr.*, by Lysias' speech (and the black horse) and the thesis of
the palinode, respectively. *Apotheton* (252b5) may mean "secret," "esoteric," or
"known to few," the point being that the true understanding of eros as that
power which can uplift the soul is not widespread. The Lysian view is more
common among men. Given the transcendence of the limits of the world associated by the gods with eros, it is tempting to understand the hubristic quality of the second verse as arising from its meaning and not just its *ametria.*
Hermeias suggests that while the meter in the second verse is *ametron* to us,
the gods rise above all meter (*Scholia*, p. 188). More plausible is J. H. Henderson's view that "pteron in some indecent sense must be the explanation of
hubristikon in reference to the second line. Winged representations of ithy-
phallic subjects are frequent in Greek plastic art; pteron in a phallic sense
would be entirely natural, even though we have no other specific literary at-
testation" (*The Maculate Muse* [New Haven: Yale University Press, 1975], p.
128). This is certainly in keeping with the palinode's obvious use of sexual
language to express the eros of the spirit. For more along these lines, see W.
Arrowsmith, "Aristophanes' *Birds:* The Fantasy Politics of Eros," *Arion*, n.s. 1
(1973): Append. 2, 164–67. Arrowsmith also points out that "like Iris and
Hermes, Eros wears wings because he is a god who links heaven with earth"
(p. 165).

60. The natural surroundings in which Phaedrus and Socrates presently
find themselves were said to be beautiful, though even they have been popu-

lated by artifacts representative of the divine, just as in the palinode the beautiful beloveds are deified by their lovers ("agalmata," 230b8; the same word occurs as 251a6, 252d7).

61. Though Hackforth takes the description as referring to heterosexual relations (*Plato's Phaedrus,* p. 98), it can also be taken as referring to homosexual ones. The degraded lover here is said to lack "shame"; once again, we see how important the sensibility to shame is in the *Phr.* Later, this sensibility is associated with the white horse; it would seem that the degraded lover's white horse is incapacitated because the charioteer's mind is empty; the black horse then becomes dominant and unifies the soul, but according to the wrong principle.

62. There is a difficulty here. Part of the palinode implies that a beloved's beauty will not be visible to all soul types (for example, the Zeus-like will not be attracted by the beauty of someone who is not Zeus-like). Yet if the beloved's beauty is bodily and is seen before the nature of his soul becomes manifest, how could the various lovers be attracted to his beauty *because* they discern in him a certain soul type? There is a problem, in other words, in putting together the two halves (separated by the quotation from the Homeridae) of this section. Perhaps the beloved's attractiveness does portray *something* about his character, though—in the form of the beloved's gesture and way of expressing himself (sophrosyne in the sense of *Charm.* 159b and 160e).

63. On the mirror analogy, see *Alc.* I, 132b–133c. The notion of philia developed toward the conclusion of the *Phr.* seems quite close to Aristotle's notion of the friend as an alter ego (*N. Ethics,* IX, 4, 8, and *E. Ethics,* VII, 12, 1245a 28 ff.). At 1245a35–38 in the latter text, Aristotle says, "To perceive and to know a friend, therefore, is necessarily in a manner to perceive and in a manner to know oneself" (trans. Rackham [Cambridge, Harvard University Press, 1981]). The "pos anagke" conceals the complex situation being described in the *Phr.* Aristotle invokes the same point (explicitly referring to self-knowledge), as well as the mirror analogy, in the *Magna Moralia,* II, 15, 1213a10 ff.

64. Of course Socrates is playing here on the traditional characteristics of the lover-beloved relationship. These are discussed at length by K. J. Dover, *Greek Homosexuality* (Cambridge, Mass.: Harvard University Press, 1978).

65. For further discussion of the eros/philia relationship, see Hyland, "Ἔρως, Ἐπιθυμία, and Φιλία in Plato."

66. This point is also noted by H. Wolz, *Plato and Heidegger* (Lewisburg, Pa.: Bucknell University Press, 1981), pp. 274–75. My solution to the problem is quite different from his.

67. I am referring to G. Vlastos's "The Individual as an Object of Love in Plato," in *Platonic Studies,* pp. 3–34.

68. See L. A. Kosman, "Platonic Love," in *Facets of Plato's Philosophy,* ed. W. Werkmeister, *Phronesis,* Suppl. vol. 2 (Assen: Van Gorcum, 1976), pp. 53–69. For further criticisms of Vlastos's position, see A. W. Price, "Loving Persons Platonically," *Phronesis* 26 (1981): 25–34. A helpful article along sim-

ilar lines is M. Warner's "Love, Self, and Plato's *Symposium*," *Philosophical Quarterly* 29 (1979): 329–39. Warner argues that there is, in the *Symp.*, no "metaphysical self" and that this grounds the view that love of a person is love of a person's properties. This interpretation accords well with the interpretation of the *Phr.* I am offering.

69. Aristotle's thesis that the virtuous man's love for himself is not selfish because it is love of what is noble in himself is compatible with the *Phr.*'s description of the sense in which the lover's love of the beloved is self-love (*N. Ethics,* IX, 8).

70. As De Vries points out with respect to 266c1, Socrates may intend a word play in "dialektikoi" (meaning, in the play, "those who choose Zeus") (*Commentary,* p. 219).

71. For an excellent development of the point, see L. Versényi, "Eros, Irony and Ecstasy," *Thought* 37 (1962): 598–612; as well as Robin's *La théorie platonicienne de l'amour* (Paris: Presses Universitaires de France, 1964), pp. 146–49. Robin draws out nicely the analogies between the lover/beloved relationship and what he calls "Socrates' ironic maieutics."

72. In this section of the palinode, Socrates refers to Zeus, Apollo, Hera, and Ares and implies that the followers of all these gods participate in erotic madness. This seems to put them all on the same footing. I would suggest that the distinction at 256b–c between true erotic madness and the secondary sort (possessed by those who are "more ignoble and unphilosophic, yet covetous of honor") is a distinction between the Zeus-like on the one hand, and the followers of Apollo, Hera, and Ares on the other. Thus some kinds of erotic madness are better than others (a fact Socrates omits to mention in his summary of the palinode at 265d–266b). Yet the Apollo-like presumably belong to a still inferior class, namely, those possessed of prophetic madness (265b) rather than erotic madness.

73. I note that while the black horse is said to be "shaggy of ear" and "deaf" (253e4; *kophos* could mean "mute" also) and impossible to control by means of logos, he is pictured as talking to the other parts of the soul (255e6). Indeed, a certain amount of inner dialogue is generated as a result of the conflict between parts of the soul (254a6–7, c7–d5, 256a6). We hear little about conversation between lover and beloved (254d6; 255b3; though presumably the lover's "persuasion" of 253b6 is verbal). All in all, however, the ascent of the soul as pictured in the palinode is remarkably silent. The beloved, in fact, is struck speechless by the process (255d4–5; 256a1). Finally, I note that the black horse accuses his yoke fellow and the charioteer of being "cowards" when they refuse to pursue the beloved (254c8); as though lack of self-control were courageous!

74. It should also be noted that Socrates is not terribly harsh on the philotimic lovers who occasionally indulge their desires (256c–d); a Dantean inferno does not await them. In fact, a tour beneath the earth is reserved for the Lysian nonlovers (256d6–7 and context, 257a1–2). However, very little is said in the myth about punishment after death. The reason for this is that according to the palinode such punishments (as pictured in conventional reli-

gion) have restricted power to restrain the soul. True self-restraint derives from recollection, not from threats about an afterlife.

Chapter 4. Excursus: Myth in the Phaedrus *and the Unity of the Dialogue*

1. Hegel, *Lectures on the History of Philosophy*, 2:20.
2. *Met.* I, 982b18–20, trans. H. Tredennick, 2 vols. (Cambridge, Mass.: Harvard University Press, 1968).
3. For a helpful survey of the problem of Platonic myth and of the history of commentary on the subject, see K. F. Moors, *Platonic Myth; An Introductory Study* (Washington, D.C.: University Press of America, 1982). Frutiger's *Les mythes de Platon* is, of course, an indispensable work on the matter.
4. Frutiger remarks that "symbolisme, liberté de l'exposé, imprécision prudente de la pensée volontairement maintenue en deçà de la franche affirmation, tels sont, à notre avis, les trois caractères essentieles des mythes platoniciens" (*Les mythes de Platon*, p. 36). Though Socrates' first speech barely fits this description, the rest of the *Phaedrus* myths do.
5. I agree with Robin's interpretation of Phaedrus' comment (*Phèdre*, p. cxv). Phaedrus likes the sort of myths and the dinner-party interpretations thereof that appeal to the "clever" (229d4), precisely the sort of people who will not understand the myth of the palinode since they are not "wise" (245c1–2).
6. As Robin points out (*Phèdre*, p. cxvii), Socrates' playful use of etymologies is analogous to his use of myths; to the extent that both are cast in the form of a pious respect for the ancients, both must be understood as ironic (but not therefore pointless). The myths and etymologies contribute to the critique of the avant-garde, urbane, and modern stories and interpretations of which Phaedrus is so fond.
7. Frutiger, *Les mythes de Platon*, p. 233.
8. Hegel, *Lectures on the History of Philosophy*, 2:20–21.
9. This kind of immortality is distinct from the sort that characterizes the "minor ascent" (209a–e), in which emphasis is put on immortality in the sense of perdurance through time (to be achieved vicariously, as it were, through the generation of children, and so on). Eros is the longing for immortality (207a3–4). This longing is fulfilled, at the highest level, by contemplating the Ideas and giving birth to perfect virtue. Socrates' narration of Diotima's deepest teaching comes to a close with the reference to immortality, and immediately afterwards Socrates says that he is persuaded of that teaching.
10. For a different argument to the effect that myth is discourse appropriate to the soul, see K. Reinhardt's *Platons Mythen* (Bonn: F. Cohen, 1927). On p. 148, the author declares that "die Sprache der Seele ist der Mythos."
11. If "logos" at 263d3 refers to both of Socrates' speeches, then possibly there is a second suggestion there that Socrates was enthusiastic in narrating his palinode.
12. A similar point is noted by H. L. Sinaiko, *Love, Knowledge, and Discourse in Plato: Dialogue and Dialectic in Phaedrus, Republic, Parmenides*, p. 111,

who says that "it becomes apparent upon reflection, that [Socrates] could not
have done what he claimed to do—namely, tell the unqualified truth about
transcendent reality." Socrates' claim is "paradoxical and self-contradictory"
(pp. 111, 112, 113). Yet Sinaiko holds that all this "does not vitiate the fact
that [the palinode] is complete and comprehensive in a genuine sense" or that
Socrates' claim to have told the truth "is invalid and must be rejected" (p.
113). Sinaiko is on the right track here, but he does not go nearly far enough
in explaining how the self-contradiction is to be resolved and how it sheds
light on the turn from the first to the second half of the *Phr.*

13. Contra Sinaiko, ibid., p. 109*n*28. Sinaiko goes so far as to say that "if
the speech is not rhetorically effective, that is, if it fails to convince Phaedrus,
then it will be philosophically false" (p. 110).

14. For further discussion, see my "The Ideas and the Criticism of Poetry
in Plato's *Republic,* Book 10."

15. Cf. the intriguing formulation of the issue in Rosen's "Socrates as
Concealed Lover," p. 172: "We are now, incidentally, in a position to surmise
the intrinsic unity of the dramatic structure of the *Phaedrus,* which has been
invisible to so many of its readers because of their disinterest in the problem
of the non- and concealed lover. The silent psyche is the center surrounded by
speech itself and by speech about speech. Speech about speech, or a discussion
of rhetoric and dialectic, is related to the speech of the non-lover. More sharply still, speech is dependent upon non-erotic 'detachment', as well as upon
erotic madness or 'attraction.' The incoherence of the *Phaedrus,* to which I alluded a moment ago, is not a defect of its dramatic structure, but an intrinsic
aporia of Platonism, and perhaps of philosophy *per se.* The peak of speech is
silence."

16. Cf. Friedländer, *Plato,* 1:209: "Mythology is fiction mixed with truth
(*Republic* 377A). This formulation does not mean it is arbitrary, but rather
that it is deeply embedded in the nature of being and the human knowledge
of this being. . . . Thus we gain a final perspective in which the myth appears akin to irony, both revealing and concealing; and we may perhaps surmise why Socrates, the ironic man, may—indeed, must—become the inventor
of myths, why myths are infused with irony, and why, in Plato's ironic dialogues, they find a necessary place wherever a ray of transcendence (*epekeina*)
and, gradually, the plenitude of *Ideas* penetrate into this life." As Friedländer
goes on to say, by using myths that "are never to be understood *literaliter,*"
Plato "escapes the danger of a metaphysical dogmatism, just as the artistic
form of the dialogue avoids the fixity of the written word, and irony the danger of dogmatic seriousness." These points are very close to the ones I have
made in this chapter. Similarly, in his discussion of myth in *Einsicht und Leidenschaft,* Krüger argues that given Plato's critique of poetry, "Plato kann
Mythen *nie ohne Ironie erzählen*" (p. 57; Krüger cites *Phr.* 274c as evidence).
And further: "In der Tat enthält der platonische Mythos trotz seiner Aporie
eine erleuchtende Klarheit. Er zeigt, was der Logos zwar nicht erschwingt,
was er aber in Blick haben muss, um selbst mit Sinn *auf die Suche gehen* zu

können. Hier bewährt es sich, dass die recht verstandene Vernunft über sich hinausweist" (p. 62). These comments are very much in the spirit of my own interpretation of the *Phr.*

17. H. Gundert, "Enthusiasmos und Logos bei Platon," *Lexis* 2 (1949): 46: "Der Logos ist die eigentliche Bestimmung des Menschen, aber der Mensch vergisst sich in ihm ebenso wie in der mythischen Verzückung, sobald er aufhört zu fragen, und das geschieht, sobald er seinen Logos sich selbst zuschreibt, um sich im Wort des Seins zu bemächtigen. Das gilt nicht nur von der gewöhnlichen Zweckrede, sondern von der philosophischen Rede selbst, wenn sie ihr eigenes Entrücktsein als ein Faktum verkünden wurde. Ihr Logos weist enthusiastisch über sich selbst hinaus, aber nur dann, wenn er das nicht selber aussagt. Sichtbar wird ihr Enthusiasmos zwar nur in einer Aussage, die selbst enthusiastisch ist, aber wahr ist er nur in der Ironie, mit der der Logos dieser Aussage sich seinem eigenen Zugriff wieder entzieht." For a similar line of thought, see Reinhardt, *Platons Mythen*, pp. 27–37.

18. A similar conclusion is reached, by a very different route, by E. G. Ballard, *Socratic Ignorance: An Essay on Platonic Self-Knowledge* (The Hague: Nijhoff, 1965), p. 167.

Chapter 5: Rhetoric

1. Fr. 34. The translation (from Kirk and Raven's *The Presocratic Philosophers*) may well be imperfect. For a detailed discussion of this fragment, see J. Lesher, "Xenophanes' Scepticism," *Phronesis* 23 (1978): 1–21. Kirk and Raven offer another possible translation of the last phrase of the quotation: "seeming is wrought over all things."

2. Socrates makes clear that the popular or nonphilosophical politicians/rhetoricians have a sort of erotic relationship with their public. They love writing speeches because they love having admirers, and in turn the admirers love them. The politicians and their admirers seem to be simultaneously lover and beloved of each other. At first the politician acts like a lover who courts his beloved public, but then the politician becomes the darling of the public and equal to a god in their eyes.

3. I shall be using "art," and occasionally "technique," as a translation for "techne," and "artful" and "technical" for the adjective. Socrates does not use the word "techne" with absolute consistency in the *Phr.*, as 257c8 and 276e6 show (there the word has an almost nontechnical meaning, so to speak). A word such as "technique" may bear connotations often foreign to the present context, but I do not believe that I have distorted Socrates' meaning when I use it (Robin too, for example, translates "techne" at 265d1 with "techniquement"; *Phèdre*, p. 71). When in the course of this chapter I refer to, for example, the "limits of techne," it should be remembered that I am referring only to "techne" as it is discussed in the *Phr.*

4. *Phèdre*, p. xxxvii.

5. I cannot help noting that, according to the palinode, the souls of some men become incarnated in animals. As I argued in my discussion of the mat-

ter, these souls are the nonphilosophical ones; that is, they are the undernourished ones who failed to get their fill of Beauty and the other hyperuranian beings.

6. The Muses are said to be *ligeiai*, a term that reminds us of the *liguros* applied to the cicadas at 230c2.

7. It is worth noting that the Muses are children of Zeus and Mnemosyne. In the palinode Zeus is the god of the philosophers, that is, those who can remember. This observation may help explain how Socrates can say that a *philosopher* should honor the Muses. Moreover, Hesiod says (*Theogony* 79–97) that when the Muses honor "heaven nourished princes" they grant such a man the ability to speak beautifully and wisely, and so are able to persuade the people "with gentle words" when the people are misguided in the assembly. This capacity for "sweet speech" is, from the standpoint of the *Phaedrus,* the capacity for rhetoric. Also, at *Phr.* 248d the philosopher is said to be "mousikos." And at *Symp.* 216a Alcibiades compares Socrates' ability to force him to turn away from politics in order to care for himself to the harmonies of the Sirens. The Sirens are offspring of one of the Muses and of Achelous (the latter is mentioned at *Phr.* 230b7–8, 263d5).

8. Hesiod, *Theogony* 27–28, 98–103. For an interesting discussion of the Muses' two-sidedness, see P. Pucci's *Hesiod and the Language of Poetry* (Baltimore: Johns Hopkins University Press, 1977), esp. chap. 1. I note that in the *Phr.* Socrates associated the Muses with the third kind of madness, the poetic, which glorifies the countless deeds of the ancients for the sake of posterity (245a1–8). Calliope would normally be thought of as one of the Muses responsible for this kind of madness. But the poets turned out to occupy a low sixth place on the scale of human types (248e1–2), and poetic madness is inferior to erotic madness in that it does not involve recollection of the hyperuranian beings. Perhaps Socrates would therefore want to see poetry as a kind of rhetoric.

9. Nestor is the speaker of the words quoted (Odysseus spoke a moment before); he is proposing a clever way to find out which of the troops is bad and which brave, and whether it is because of magic or because of mens' cowardice and ignorance of warfare that the Greeks have failed to take Troy. The truth will be revealed by mens' deeds. At *Iliad* II.188 ff., we learn that to restrain the army's mad dash for the ships, Odysseus speaks in one way to the leaders and in another to the ordinary soldiers, thus illustrating one of Socrates' principles to the effect that good rhetoric must be suited to the souls of one's auditors (271d–272a). Perhaps when, at 261b5–7, Socrates playfully refers to Nestor's and Odysseus' manuals of oratory, written during their leisure at Troy, he is invoking not only their expertise in rhetoric, but also the complex connection between warfare and rhetoric. Consider too the reference at 260e to the Spartans.

10. Cf. *Gorg.* 454e; those who have learned have been persuaded, but there is a difference between persuasion accompanied by knowledge and that accompanied by mere belief.

11. "Excellent Cratylus, I have long been wondering at my own wisdom. I cannot trust myself. And I think that I ought to stop and ask myself, What am I saying? For there is nothing worse than self-deception—when the deceiver is always at home and always with you—it is quite terrible, and therefore I ought often to retrace my steps and endeavor to look 'fore and aft,' as the poet said" (in *Plato: The Collected Dialogues,* trans. Jowett and ed. E. Hamilton and H. Cairns [Princeton: Princeton University Press, 1969]). See also *Pho.* 91a and *Charm.* 166c7–d4, *Prot.* 348c5 ff., *Meno* 80c6–d4. On the connection between dialogue and avoidance of deception, consider also Aristotle, *On Sophistical Refutations* VII, 169a37–b3; *On the Heavens* II, 13, 294b6–13.

12. At 253c7, in the midst of the palinode, Socrates says that the soul was divided into three forms. At 263b7 he divides words into two forms, presumably using *charactera* as his guide. At 270b4 we learn that just as it is necessary for the physician to divide the nature of the body, so the rhetorician must divide the nature of the soul. At 271d4, in the midst of his third description of the art of rhetoric, Socrates refers to the need to divide souls into their denumerable forms. At 273e1–3, in the fourth description of the art, Socrates specifies that one must "divide things kat'eide." Finally, at 277b7, in the fifth description of the art, we hear about the need to cut back according to (or into) forms until reaching the uncuttable. What is cut is "each thing" (277b5) one wishes to write or speak about—another indication that the "ἕν" of 249c1 might correspond to a "whole of discourse."

13. Cf. J. L. Ackrill, "In Defence of Platonic Division," in *Ryle: A Collection of Critical Essays,* ed. Wood and Pitcher (Garden City, N.Y.: Doubleday, 1970), pp. 389–90: "That Platonic division has something to do with dividing will not be denied. But what sort of dividing Plato takes it to cover, and what sorts of terms are capable of being divided, can be determined only by consideration of all the texts. . . . Platonic division covers a variety of types of analysis and gets applied to a variety of types of term. No less than the word 'analysis' itself, which has been a modern slogan in philosophy, 'division' is dangerously imprecise but philosophically suggestive." See also M. Vanhoutte, *La méthode ontologique de Platon* (Louvain: E. Nauwelaerts, 1956), p. 82: it is impossible "de donner aux termes συναγωγή et διαίρεσις une signification bien déterminée. On les a souvent assimilés, d'après l'expression du *Phèdre,* respectivement à la dialectique ascendante et à la dialectique descendante. Mais il semble que la διαίρεσις n'est pas absente de la dialectique ascendante." Vanhoutte goes on to argue, I think correctly, that "on se rend compte que ce mouvement {dialectique} de va-et-vient forme des paliers où se situe chaque fois une intuition." R. Robinson notes that "horizein" never loses "the feel of its original connection with boundary-stones," such that "in Plato's dialogues the translations 'distinguish' and 'determine' are suitable as often or more often than 'define' " (*Plato's Earlier Dialectic* [Ithaca, N.Y.: Cornell University Press, 1941], p. 57). At least in this section of the *Phr.* Socrates tries to isolate a technical sense of the term, which he associates with collection (even though to distinguish X from Y requires division as well as collection).

14. My general approach to the method of division and collection more or less follows that of H. Cherniss: "Plato could not, then, have intended by the use of diaeresis to produce an ontological hierarchy of the world of ideas." Cherniss adds that for Plato it is "an instrument to facilitate the search for a definite idea, the distinction of that idea from other ideas, and its implications and identification, and that he did not imagine it to be a description of the 'construction' of the idea, its derivation, or its constituent elements" (*The Riddle of the Early Academy* [Berkeley: University of California Press, 1945], pp. 54–55). See also pp. 53, 41, and context. This approach is also accepted by N. Gulley, *Plato's Theory of Knowledge* (London: Methuen, 1962), pp. 111–12; K. M. Sayre, *Plato's Analytic Method* (Chicago: University of Chicago Press, 1969), p. 192 et passim; J. R. Trevaskis, "Division and Its Relation to Dialectic and Ontology in Plato," *Phronesis* 12 (1967): 128 et passim; and Ackrill, "In Defence of Platonic Division," p. 389. The view that the method of division and collection is not primarily concerned with genera and species in the Aristotelian sense, or classes and sets in the modern sense, is powerfully argued by Sayre, and by J. M. E. Moravcsik in "The Anatomy of Plato's Divisions," in *Exegesis and Argument, Phronesis,* Suppl. vol. 1 (Assen: Van Gorcum, 1973), pp. 324–48. With slight qualifications, the argument is accepted by N. White, *Plato on Knowledge and Reality* (Indianapolis: Hackett, 1976), p. 121 and notes. Moravcsik's "intensional" model of the forms fits the present section of the *Phr.* fairly well. It is certainly the case that, in the five descriptions of the method of division that occur after 266d in the *Phr.,* genera and species play little or no part. Also helpful here are F. M. Cornford's arguments against an Aristotelian interpretation of Platonic "forms" (Cornford argues against their being thought of as genera, species, classes, predicates) (*Plato's Theory of Knowledge,* 3d ed. [London: Routledge & Kegan Paul, 1949], pp. 262 ff).

15. Cf. R. Hackforth's comment in his *Plato's Philebus* (Cambridge: Cambridge University Press, 1972), p. 143: "Examination of the Divisions in the *Sophist* seems to reveal that a Collection is made at many stages of the process."

16. Cf. S. Rosen, *The Limits of Analysis* (New York: Basic Books, 1980), pp. 7–8: "The process of collection or synthesis is regularly described [by Plato] as a step in the comprehensive process of division. Unlike Kant, for whom synthesis functions in the very constitution of the concept by the transcendental ego, the Platonic dialogues do not begin with a transcendental synthesis of a concept, but rather with an opinion, or casually expressed thesis about a genus directly accessible to everyday discourse. Whereas for Kant, synthesis is the basis for analysis, in Plato the basis is opinion. . . . Platonic dialectic is itself governed by the pervasive paradigm of counting and measuring as they function in everyday life." "The curious feature of Platonic division is that it moves toward specificity by way of opinions. The sets of predicates employed at each stage of the division are treated as more or less obvious, whereas the

last step in the division, the class to be defined, is treated as the product of rigorous philosophical method. Plato does not call our attention to the fact that the use of conventional definitions can only terminate in conventional or contingent knowledge." For a similar interpretation of diairesis, see M. Nussbaum's "Poetry, Goodness, and Understanding in Plato's *Phaedrus*," pp. 111–15; for example, p. 113: "The method of division, by contrast, has no unhypothetical points, no nonempirical basis, and no stable or unrevisable elements."

17. The pedagogical utility of the art of division and collection, particularly in the *Stm.*, is established in detail by M. Miller in *The Philosopher in Plato's Statesman*. I agree with his statement that diairesis helps to suspend one's "uncritical subjection to the obvious." Miller's characterization in terms of the *Stm.* of the purpose of diairesis applies equally to the *Phaedrus*: "Finally, and perhaps most important of all, the method gives young Socrates his first experience in philosophical accountability. By distinguishing differentiation from identification and by proceeding in many small steps, thought is exposed to critical review. Intuitive judgment is broken down and made visible to reflection. In this way bifurcatory method can help to free young Socrates from the self-concealment—ignorance of ignorance, in the elder Socrates' terms—which is the essence of mere opinionatedness" (p. 26).

18. Cf. J. Moravcsik, "The Anatomy," p. 344: "Finally, one might ask: What is a natural kind? How do we find out? It is crucial for the understanding of the Method of Division that Plato gives no mechanical procedure for finding natural kinds. Plato does not think that there are any such procedures. He is not giving a discovery procedure, he is explicating the ontological configurations that obtain once we have discovered natural kinds. He does not tell us *how* to arrive at them; he tells us what things look like *when* we have arrived at them. The discovery of such kinds is as much the work of creative intellectual intuition as the discovery of the truths of mathematics." Moravcsik's point is well taken. However, I have reservations about the "natural kind" label here (though other dialogues might supply evidence for it).

19. The "τὼ λόγω" at 262d1 seems to refer, as Hackforth rightly suggests, to the three speeches in the *Phr.*, though he does not explain the implication he himself notes, namely, that the palinode would have to be thought of as a speech that misleads its audience (262d1–2; *Plato's Phaedrus*, p. 125n1). Hackforth takes 263d3 *(tou logou)* as referring to both of Socrates' speeches, now "regarded as one" (p. 127n2; so too with "logos" at 265c6 and d7). The problem with this is that Socrates' first speech did *not* begin with a definition of eros that would be suitable to *both* his speeches; hence they cannot be considered as one in the technical sense. It is as though Socrates' ambiguity here is meant to compel one to ask: are the three speeches one, two, or three, and in what sense? I take all this as a hint that the method of the second half of the *Phaedrus* is incapable of accurately grasping the results of the first half. The "heterous logous" of 264e7 must refer to Socrates' two

speeches; so too, then, with the use of the dual at 265a2–3, e3–4, 266a3. The divisions and collections of 265b ff. thus do not apply to Lysias' speech, unless it is regarded as being basically the same as Socrates' first speech.

20. Socrates makes Phaedrus read the start of Lysias' speech twice, thus emphasizing the monotonous repetitiveness of the written treatise (cf. 275d8–9). But Socrates cuts Phaedrus off at different points; and there are variations, in Burnet's and Robin's texts, between Phaedrus' two readings. See my "Plato's *Phaedrus* 230E6–231A3, 262E1–4, and 263E6–264A3," *Classical Bulletin* 55 (1979): 68–69. For some helpful comments on the particular place where Socrates interrupts Phaedrus the second time, see B. Sève, *Phèdre de Platon* (Paris: Editions Pédagogie Moderne, 1980), p. 116. I would like to thank Robert Brumbaugh for discussing with me the complex MS situation underlying the variations here.

21. The point is also noted by R. Robinson in *Plato's Earlier Dialectic,* p. 66: "The *Phaedrus* is full of remarks on method; but to what extent is it itself methodically written? It evinces a keen consciousness of rhetorical and of dialectical method; but it evinces no particular consciousness of method in the composition of the non-rhetorical parts of itself. It rather seems to imply that there should not be much method in a dialogue, since it says that a dialogue must be partly play."

22. For some helpful comments about the contrast between dialogue and methodological dialectic, see Ch. Perelman, "La méthode dialectique et le rôle de l'interlocuteur dans le dialogue," *Revue de métaphysique et de morale* 60 (1955): 26–31. At 263d Socrates claims that he cannot altogether remember, thanks to the "enthusiastic" condition he was in at the time, whether he defined love at the start of his (first) speech. He did so—hence it seems that the nymphs of Achelous and Pan son of Hermes are more artful than Lysias. How much worth, however, is there in a discourse that is produced un-self-consciously? Socrates' comment playfully points to the limits of techne, and especially to the crucial point that the use of techne, and unreflectiveness *about* the techne qua techne, are perfectly compatible. In pointing to the "monological" character of the art of division and collection, I am not denying that the art *could* be practiced in the context of a dialogue. But as so many have remarked with respect to the start of the *Soph.* and *Stm.,* the "dialogue" under these circumstances seems superfluous. The method seems to march on according to its internal mechanism.

23. The "ostensible rigor" of the techne is indicated by the "ὁδῷ" at 263b7 and the general suggestion that the division of words is exhaustive; by the demand for definition (263d, 265d4, 269b6, 277b6); by the demand for exhaustive division (all the way to the "uncuttable"; 277b7; also 271d2–7), and for a complete adding up of the results (270d6, 273e1); by the demand for "precision" (270e3, 271a5); and by the demand for completeness that is implied by the image used at 264c (also by 268d3–5, 269c3).

24. Similarly, in the *Soph.* the art of division treats the general and the

louse-catcher as belonging to the same eidos (227b). This ethical neutrality of the method is made explicit in the *Stm.* 266d. Hence the comments at *Phr.* 265b5–c3 (to the effect that erotic madness is best and so forth) have their origin outside the operation of the method; they are comments *about* the parts revealed by the method (*some* of these comments being drawn from the palinode itself). As I have already remarked, the techne under discussion resembles other technai in its neutrality with respect to its uses. The smith's shields, the mathematician's calculations, and the rhetorician's techne can all be used for better or worse.

25. Socrates did not define madness at the start of his first speech. He mentioned mania only once, at the end of the speech (241a4). Apollo and Dionysus were not mentioned in connection with the first two kinds of divine madness. Indeed, neither Aphrodite nor Dionysus were mentioned at all in the palinode. The schema does not inform us as to how the first speech misled its audience or in what sense it was composed by one knowing the truth (262d1–2). Moreover, Socrates fails to note that in his first speech eros was also referred to; eros should appear in both main branches of the division, though the two "forms" are related by contrariety. Finally, it is essential to note that nowhere in the diaireses in this section of the *Phr.* is the nonlover mentioned. Yet the nonlover is, as I have argued, important in the *Phr.*

26. In this translation I accept L. Gil's arguments to the effect that the disjunctive phrase refers not to ἐλέχθη but to the definition (this requires a change in Burnet's punctuation) ("Notas," pp. 325–27). How could the speeches be used as paradigms if there is doubt as to whether they were well or badly spoken? Both are said to exhibit techne. Moreover, Socrates says at 265c1 that the praise of eros was both *metrios* and *euphemos,* and at 266a that divine eros was justly praised in the speech, while left eros was justly condemned. This reading, in any event, makes sense of the "γοῦν" and also serves the valuable purpose of indicating that Socrates is quite aware of the fallibility of the techne of which defining is one function. "ὃ ἔστιν ὁρισθέν" I take as accusative absolute, as does Gil.

27. See Thompson's note, *The Phaedrus,* p. 108: "The functions of the ancient *mageiros* seem to have been manifold, including those of butcher and dissector, as well as those ordinarily assigned to the cook, plain or ornamental." The butcher can be responsible for slaughtering the beast. Likewise, in the *Stm.'s* image (287c), the animal is killed as it is subjected to diairesis.

28. Since it is clear that the joints are the guides for a division, the forms are not the guides, even though it would be difficult to conceive of the joints without thinking of what they join. They could be what is divided (as a leg is divided at the knee joint), the products of the division, or both. My translation is compatible with the last of these. The "eidos" of 265e4 and 266a3 clearly is what is divided. The "kat'eide" of 273e1 and 277b7 seem to mean "into forms," and the "atmetou" of 277b7 suggests that the forms have been the objects of division (cf. 253c7, where the soul was divided *into* forms).

Forms are the objects and products of divisions, at least so long as one proceeds by cutting at the joints (what is properly uncuttable may be badly cut-
table nevertheless); some parts and parts of parts are forms.

29. *Plato's Phaedrus*, p. 133*n*1. Hackforth's explanation of this is that "a
writer with more concern for exact statement than Plato had, would have
made Socrates [summarize correctly]." I discussed the inadequacies of this
kind of interpretation in my Introduction. I note that in the schema under
discussion, the left branch is not said to derive from human sickness, as we
saw in the case in the previous schema; that notion is replaced by "left eros."

30. Presumably, the form of which *aphron tēs dianoias* is a part is dianoia,
which in turn is a part of the soul. The soul supports these divisions and inhabits every one of their limbs. Perhaps the invisibility but omnipresence of
soul here is an indication of its inaccessibility to this method of analysis. The
present schema also omits to mention sophrosyne. A more complete schema,
which also takes into account forms of the two speeches unmentioned at
265d–266b, might be:

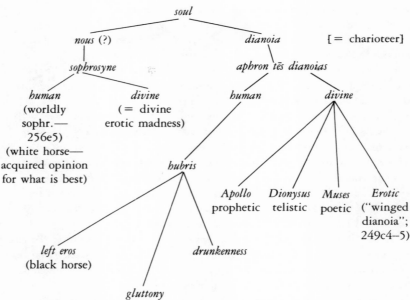

This version of the schema still suffers from a number of the defects already
discussed above. Note that erotic madness appears, illogically, under the form
of divine disturbance of the dianoia as well as under divine sophrosyne (in the
palinode the person suffering from erotic madness was capable of a kind of
self-restraint that is explicitly contrasted with mere mortal self-restraint).
Nothing in *Socrates'* diaireses shows that an erotic soul could be moderate. Of
course, to see the horses and wings as subdivisions of dianoia is not quite accurate either. I do not see how, in sum, any such schema could really capture

the teaching of Socrates' two speeches; hence I hold to the view that such schemata, while helpful in some respects, mislead in others (for example, by giving the impression that they represent and map out completely forms and their interrelations). I note, finally, that Socrates uses three words here ("aphron," "paranoia," "mania") to refer to what is presumably one idea ("madness"); why the proliferation of names?

31. Cf. M. Ostwald's Introduction to *Plato's Statesman*, trans. J. B. Skemp (Indianapolis: Bobbs-Merrill, 1979), p. xii. Ostwald distinguishes between two kinds of dialectic in the *Phaedrus*, one aiming toward the Ideas, the other to "classifying and defining concepts." Of the former, "Plato himself states in the *Phaedrus* and in his *Seventh Epistle* that it cannot be described in writing. The concept-logic, on the other hand, can be expounded in written form, and is exemplified at considerable length both in the *Sophist* and in the *Statesman*."

32. See Homer's *Od.* v.193, and context. Hermes has just been sent by the gods to instruct Calypso to release Odysseus, and she agrees. Odysseus, distrustful, makes her swear an oath to that effect; he follows in her steps only when assured that his promised sail home is not a trick. In this quotation, Socrates identifies himself with Odysseus; the dialectician-technician corresponds to the bewitching nymph Calypso. Hermes corresponds to divinely sent erotic madness (anamnesis) which sets one "free" (cf. *Phr.* 256b) to return to the piace of one's origins. Calypso thus symbolizes the powers and dangers of unchecked techne (and perhaps reminds us of the other nymph in the *Phr.*, Pharmakeia, who symbolizes in the *Phr.* the written word): techne has the power to conceal and deceive. The phrase also occurs at *Od.* ii.406; iii.30; vii.38. These occurrences seem less revealing with respect to the *Phr.*, however. See also *Od.* xvii.317; xix.436.

33. I am accepting Gil's view (which is partially based on grammatical considerations) that the "$\pi\epsilon\varphi\nu\kappa\acute{o}\vartheta'$ " should be taken with "$\delta\nu\nu\alpha\tau\grave{o}\nu$" (both of these being predicated of "$\ddot{\alpha}\lambda\lambda o\nu$") (Gil, "Notas," pp. 328–30). It is difficult to find a satisfactory construal of the "$\epsilon\grave{\iota}\varsigma$" and "$\grave{\epsilon}\pi\grave{\iota}$," however.

34. This point is also made by Trevaskis, "Division," p. 119, and is endorsed by De Vries, *Commentary*, p. 219.

35. See P. Shorey, "$\Phi\acute{\nu}\sigma\iota\varsigma$, $M\epsilon\lambda\acute{\epsilon}\tau\eta$, $'E\pi\iota\sigma\tau\acute{\eta}\mu\eta$," *Transactions of the American Philological Association* 40 (1909): 185–201, and Thompson's excellent note (*The Phaedrus*, pp. 120–21), for further commentary. As Thompson suggests, these terms are defiantly accepted here as descriptive of philosophy. One should add that Socrates may also be indirectly criticizing Pericles. Not only is it doubtful that Pericles really could define rhetoric in the required manner, Anaxagoras is criticized by Socrates in the *Pho.* and is associated in the *Apol.* (26d) with demythologizing, that is, with the kind of "boorish wisdom" rejected in the *Phr.* (229e3). Perhaps Pericles is thus tarnished by association.

36. This point is suggested by L. Sichirollo, *Dialegesthai-Dialektik* (Hildesheim: Olms, 1966), p. 48. See *Prot.* 329a–b, where Socrates compares the

inability of some speakers to engage in short exchanges to the muteness of written texts; also *Gorg.* 449b–c, 461e–462a.

37. See Sallis, *Being and Logos,* p. 172, for a helpful comment on the connection between dialectic and medicine, tragedy, and music.

38. Phaedrus' reply—that according to Hippocrates without this method one cannot even understand the nature of the body—does not solve the problem. For extensive discussion of the reference to Hippocrates, see R. Joly, "La question Hippocratique et le témoignage du *Phèdre,*" *Revue des Etudes Grecques* 74 (1961): 69–92; P. Kucharski, "La 'méthode d'Hippocrate' dans le *Phèdre,*" *Revue des 'Etudes Grecques* 52 (1939): 301–57; A. M. Frenkian, *La méthode Hippocratique dans le Phèdre de Platon* (Bucharest: Imprimerie Nationale, 1941); and A. Diès, *Autour de Platon; Essais de critique et d'histoire,* 2 vols. (Paris: Bibliothèque des Archives de Philosophie, 1927), 1:14–54. It is worth emphasizing that Socrates wants to know what Hippocrates *and* the true logos have to say (270c9–10); it is not a question of just repeating Hippocrates' doctrines. A third reading of 270c1–2 has been proposed to me by Rémi Brague, namely, that *holon* refers to the composite of soul and body (cf. 264c5, 268d5).

39. Socrates praises Phaedrus' answers at 228c9, 263d1, 266d7, 270c6, 276b1. Phaedrus frequently affirms Socrates' utterances as true, very correct, and so on.

40. For a helpful discussion of the meaning of the "eikos" and its subjective character, see Sève, *Phèdre de Platon,* pp. 144–46.

41. In the *Euthyphro,* Socrates says that if people disagree about things like additions and lengths, the matter can be quickly and peaceably resolved by recourse to a shared system of measurement, whereas topics concerning the noble and the base arouse passion because they are so intimately connected to desire and love (7b ff.). If there existed a technique to resolve disputes concerning the second set of topics, Socrates implies, we would be much better off than we are. In the *Phr.* he seems to be offering such a technique, but in such a way as to also point to its limitations.

Chapter 6: Dialogue and Writing

1. The first quotation is from *Human, All-too-Human,* 483, trans. W Kaufmann, in *The Portable Nietzsche,* p. 63. The second quotation may be found in Kaufmann's *Nietzsche,* 3d ed. (Princeton: Princeton University Press, 1968), p. 19.

2. Thompson reports (*The Phaedrus,* note to 274c–d) that Theuth was called by Egyptians "the scribe of the gods," "lord of the divine word," and "writer of truth," and was the Egyptian Hermes; Ammon is the Egyptian name of Zeus as well as the god of Thebes. In Socrates' palinode, Zeus is the god of the philosophers; a connection between Ammon and philosophy is implied here. The name "Thamus" seems to be coined by Plato (see De Vries's discussion and his reference to Herodotus II, 42). On Postgate's substitution of "Thamoun" for "theon" (274d4), see Verdenius, "Notes," p. 287. Theuth is called "daimon," and Thamus "god" and "king." Theuth is also mentioned

in *Phil.* 18b–c as a "god or god-like man." Theuth's inferior status signals the subordination of the inventor to the censor, and so of techne to telos. Possibly Theuth's concern with creation of arts that will be more useful to men than to gods also qualifies him as a daimon rather than *theos*. For further discussion of the background of the story, see J. Derrida's essay, "La pharmacie de Platon," in *La dissémination* (Paris: Seuil, 1972), pp. 95–107.

3. As Derrida points out, Socrates' description of the written word as something that rolls about indifferently from person to person suggests that writing is essentially democratic ("La pharmacie," p. 166).

4. It has been suggested that the "grammata" are meant to refer to hieroglyphics, given (among other things) the comparison of the letters with "zographia" (275d5). However, it is very unclear how much Plato knew about hieroglyphics. For a discussion of the point, see the "Excursus" of R. Buger's *Plato's Phaedrus*. It seems very doubtful, moreover, that Socrates is not referring to the alphabetic and phonetic writing that he and Phaedrus knew and that Plato used in his own writing, especially since writing is viewed here as the image of speaking. On dice, cf. *Rep.* X, 604c. Draughts are referred to in interesting ways at *Gorg.* 450d, *Rep.* VI, 487b–c (in analogy with Socrates' art of conversation). Perhaps Socrates mentions these games because they are ways in which one can lose oneself, thus forgetting the "serious" work of dialectic. For some helpful thoughts on the *order* in which Theuth discovered the arts, see Hermeias, *Scholia*, p. 255, and Brague, *Le restant*, pp. 122–23. Brague suggests that the order of Theuth's inventions caricatures the course of studies promulgated for the guardians in the *Rep.*, with the art of writing replacing dialectic. This replacement is the result, Brague indicates, of the absence of the sunlike Good (Theuth invents his arts in the absence of Thamus, the solar deity).

5. Theuth is said in the story to have invented geometry, logismos, as well as writing. It is difficult to conceive of the formulation and practice of geometry, let alone of its transmission to future students, without the possibility of its being written in some form or other. So too with "logismos." Again, we are left wondering whether they are to be included in the "grammata" here. We are not explicitly told whether Thamus permitted the introduction of these arts to men, but if he forbade all writing, he presumably intended to prohibit, or at least cripple, these other intellectual arts. Socrates does, as we shall see, relent somewhat on the prohibition of writing. It might be argued that Socrates is not really intent on prohibiting the use of writing about the nondisputable topics (which in the *Phaedrus* include, presumably, geometry and calculation), and so that he is not really concerned about the use of writing to advance knowledge in certain technical areas. But every techne must be regulated by the ends to which it is to be put, and it is the disputable knowledge of these ends that deeply worries Socrates.

6. Interpreters who agree that recollection is being referred to here include G. Rodis-Lewis, "L'Articulation des thèmes du *Phèdre*," *Revue Philosophique de la France et de l'Etranger* 165 (1975): 32; J. Klein, *Commentary*, p. 152;

and J. Derrida, "La pharmacie," p. 154 et passim. One who disagrees is W. Luther, "Die Schwäche des geschriebenen Logos," *Gymnasium* 68 (1961): 535.

7. Objections to Phaedrus' critique of writing may be found in J. Derbolav, *Platons Sprachphilosophie im Kratylos und in den Späteren Schriften* (Darmstadt: Wissenschaftliche Buchgesellschaft, 1972), p. 202, and H. Caton, "Speech and Writing as Artifacts," *Philosophy and Rhetoric* 2 (1969): 22. These authors do not, however, look at the critique in the light of the self-knowledge problematic.

8. That the spoken word is superior to the written in matters of persuasion is well known to modern tyrants as well. The author of *Mein Kampf* wrote, in a chapter entitled "The Struggle of the Early Period—the Significance of the Spoken Word" (vol. 2, chap. 6): "The chief emphasis was laid on the spoken word. And actually it alone—for general psychological reasons—is able to bring about really great changes. . . . all great, world-shaking events have been brought about, not by written matter, but by the spoken word" (p. 469). "The essential point, however, is that a piece of literature never knows into what hands it will fall, and yet must retain its definite form." The speaker, unlike the writer, can always modify his speech by seeing if his listeners "*understand* what he is saying, [and] whether, secondly, they can *follow the speech as a whole,* and to what extent, thirdly, he has *convinced* them of the *soundness* of what he has said" (pp. 470–71). In volume 1, the author declares: "Let the writer remain by his ink-well, engaging in 'theoretical' activity" (pp. 106–07; trans. R. Manheim [Boston: Houghton Mifflin Co., 1943]). These remarks about the superiority of the spoken to written word are shockingly close to some of Socrates' remarks on the issue. As I indicated in the previous chapter, it is not the case that sophists or tyrants would necessarily reject all of Socrates' prescriptions for effective rhetoric—on the contrary.

9. Since Socrates did not write, either he did not think he would reach an age old enough to worry about such things (at least, he did not permit himself to reach an age where frailty became an issue), or he had confidence in his memory. Plato portrays him throughout the dialogues as having an impossibly good memory; for example, he narrates all of the *Rep.* from memory without a pause or, so far as we know, gaps (cf. *Symp.* 180c1–3).

10. My analysis of the *Phaedrus'* critique of writing is very much in agreement with that of H. Gundert, *Der platonische Dialog* (Heidelberg: C. Winter, 1968), especially pt. 1. I agree with Gundert that "dialectic," at the end of the *Phaedrus,* is the same as "dialogue"; and that this is inseparable from knowledge of ignorance. I also agree that it is this sort of knowledge the dialectician plants and what "those who know" possess. And I agree with R. Robinson's argument (repeated a number of times in *Plato's Earlier Dialectic*) that Platonic dialectic is the process of oral question and answer. Robin too interprets the "dialectic" at the end of the *Phaedrus* as "dialogue" (*Phèdre,* p. liii).

11. The view that the *Phaedrus* is, in the final analysis, about the status of the written word (and not about self-knowledge) is argued in Burger's *Plato's*

Phaedrus. A critique of the argument may be found in my detailed discussion of the book in the *Independent Journal of Philosophy* 4 (1983): 158–60.

12. This point is reflected in the Platonic corpus as a whole, for in it we find no dialogue between two mature philosophers (Protagoras being a self-proclaimed sophist, not a philosopher). The occasion for it occurs in the *Soph.* and *Stm.*, but in one of his most dramatic touches, Plato makes Socrates sit in virtual silence before that other philosopher, the Eleatic Stranger. I will say a bit more below about the absence in Plato of a dialogue between mature philosophers. I note that if the "fruits" Socrates refers to at 277a1 are those of an orchard (a possible meaning of *kepos* at 276d1), then the reseeding of other souls in a sense is natural and unintentional; it is like the overflow of a cup. Socrates says here that the dialectician will take pleasure in watching the seeds grow (276d4–5), but the planting of new seeds seems to be done (like the farmer's cultivation of the earth) for the benefit of the planter primarily.

13. A point also made by Sève, *Phèdre,* pp. 170–71.

14. Adonis gardens grew and died in a short span of time, in commemoration of Aphrodite's brief affair with her beloved, Adonis. For an insightful comparison of the *Phaedrus'* image of the farmer with the *Theaetetus'* image of the midwife, see Brague, *Le restant,* pp. 116–17. Socrates' famous sterility (his knowledge of ignorance) is not contradicted by the productive activity or the dialectician pictured in the *Phr.* The point is not that Socrates cannot give birth to *any* discourses of his own, but that he cannot give birth to any wise and self-sufficient discourses, any speeches whose truth is beyond question. The farmer image indicates that the fruits of thought are produced only at great pain and labor, in stark contrast with the free and automatic banquet of the gods described in the palinode. The results of the farmer's work, nevertheless, are nourishing; the soul needs not just the work of dialectic but its results in order to flourish. The image also points to the necessity of a collaboration between nature and art; the soul that is left "free" to develop on its own becomes imprisoned in its desires (cf. 256b).

15. Socrates' account of dialectical pedagogy abstracts from the violence connected with it. Disabusing the student of strongly held beliefs may be painful for the student. Before sowing his seeds in the spiritual soul of his students, the father may have to clear away the weeds. To change metaphors: the father may have to drug and immobilize the student before awakening him to the true life of philosophizing (cf. *Meno* 80a–b). And a student who succeeds in becoming a dialectician may well commit a form of patricide: though he may share in his father's search, he may criticize the fruits of his father's labors. Must he not do so if he is really to be a dialectician? Indeed, by *writing* philosophy, did not Plato to that extent reject Socrates' position (as it is described in the *Phr.*) on the matter? At the same time, a father must reject his students and not be blind to their true defects and strengths (cf. the comment about Theuth at 275a1–2). All this makes the notion of a philosophical friendship very difficult. As Nietzsche's Zarathustra puts it to his dis-

ciples: "The man of knowledge must not only love his enemies, he must also
be able to hate his friends. One repays a teacher badly if one always remains
nothing but a pupil. . . . You are my believers—but what matter all believers? You had not yet sought yourselves: and you found me. . . . Now I bid
you lose me and find yourselves; and only when you have all denied me will I
return to you" (*Thus Spoke Zarathustra*, p. 190).

16. The *Charm.* translation is W. R. M. Lamb's (Cambridge, Mass.: Harvard University Press, 1964).

17. His ambiguous " 'philosopher' or something similar" phrase at 278d4–
5 presumably means that the man in question might be described not just as
a philosopher but also as a dialectician, or erosopher or lover of beauty (cf.
248d3–4). Cf. 266b7–c1 where Socrates is not sure whether he is right in
calling the one who can see the one and many a dialectician. In that instance,
however, Socrates' uncertainty was explicable (see chap. 5).

18. Phaedrus reminds Socrates that he too has a message to send to his
companion Isocrates (278e5 ff.). At the time of the composition of the *Phr.*,
it was clear that Isocrates had not obeyed Socrates' message and had not fulfilled Socrates' prophecy about him. While Socrates' message is one of hope
for Isocrates, it is a criticism of him when the message is considered as part of
a text written at a certain date. Plato holds up a sort of mirror to Isocrates
containing a picture of what Isocrates could have become. We also infer from
this that Isocrates' notion of philosophy is very different from the one Socrates
is advocating, and that the pursuit of the latter is rare even among persons
(such as Isocrates) who, as Socrates says, are potential philosophers. The potentiality is easily corrupted—a point implicit in Socrates' palinode. Detailed
discussion of the historical relationship between Plato and Isocrates may be
found in De Vries, *Commentary*, pp. 15–18, and in the literature he cites. An
interesting discussion of the relation between Isocrates' philosophy and the
Phaedrus may be found in "Isocrates the Beautiful," *Appendix* to Burger's *Plato's Phaedrus.* See also M. Brown and J. Coulter's "The Middle Speech of Plato's *Phaedrus*," *Journal of the History of Philosophy* 9 (1971): 405–23.

19. On the playfulness of Socratic dialectic, see Klein, *Commentary*, pp.
18–20. Klein mentions the playful pretense, the challenge to accept presuppositions about reality, the suggestion that this reality is really an *image* of another reality, and the inventiveness and wondering that are evoked by
Socrates' ironic dialectic. Consider also P. Plass, " 'Play' and Philosophic Detachment in Plato," *Transactions and Proceedings of the American Philological Association* 98 (1967): 358: "Inasmuch as it reflects man's position in the two
worlds, play is a species of Socratic irony, for that—at least as it is interpreted
by Plato—also arises from the tension between the two worlds [of appearance
and essence]." Note too the conjunction of play and irony at *Symp.* 216e4.
Finally, see Gadamer's *Truth and Method*, pp. 91–99, for some helpful comments on the play metaphor.

20. Friedländer makes a similar point about the development of the *Phr.*
when he characterizes the whole of its development as a case of "Plato's ironic

art." Friedländer also refers to this as an example of an "ironic shift of balance" (*Plato,* 1:150–51).

21. Cf. W. Bröcker, *Platos Gespräche* (Frankfurt: Klostermann, 1964), p. 558: "Auch der Dialog *Phaidros* selbst fällt unter das, was Plato als blosses Spiel gegen den wahren Ernst abhebt. Die Worte über das Schreibspiel sind also selbst nur Spiel und nicht letzter Ernst. Was aber dann allein Ernst sein kann, ist ein Appell Platos an die Leser seiner Schriften. Am Leser liegt es, ob diese Schriften wie verstandlose Bilder nur immer dasselbe sagen, oder ob sie auf Fragen antworten, wie ein Gesprächspartner." As my own interpretation suggests, Plato's dialogues are not mere games in the sense in which the unphilosophic writings of the poets, orators, and lawgivers are. I add that if we accept Nussbaum's suggestion that the very presence of Phaedrus in Athens is a palinode of his earlier deeds and punishment, then there are six palinodes in the *Phr.* ("Poetry, Goodness, and Understanding in Plato's *Phr.*," pp. 96–97).

22. Since I do not want the argument of this chapter to hinge on the *Second* and *Seventh Letters* (given that they might not be Plato's and especially given my desire to interpret the *Phr.* on its own merits), I am not going to analyze them in developing my interpretation of Plato's view of the written word. Any conflict between the results arrived at via the *Phr.* and those drawn from the *Letters* can then be considered in its own right. It does seem to me, however, that the lessons I draw from the *Phr.* concerning Plato's view of the written word are in keeping with the views about writing expressed in the *Seventh Letter.* Plato never has and never will write down his philosophy, for there is no way of putting it in words like other studies (VII, 341c); and indeed, in the dialogues Plato does not speak in his own name and the dialogues are not writings of the usual sort (the author of the *Seventh Letter* does not say that philosophy cannot be put into *any* words in *any* way). At 343a and 344c the author denies that insight can be adequately put into the written word and that the written word can be a truly serious activity. These views are very much like those I infer from the *Phr.* In II, 314b–c, the author seems to repeat one of Socrates' criticisms of writing ("it is impossible for what is written not to be disclosed"; this being a defect of the written word). The author of the letter claims that there is no work of Plato's own, a claim explicable by the fact that in no dialogue does Plato reveal his thoughts under his own name. On the question of Plato's "unwritten teaching," see Wieland's excellent discussion in *Platon,* pp. 38–50. The fictionalized "Socrates" of Plato's dialogues certainly cannot be identified with Plato without further ado. To the extent that Plato is not represented directly by one of his characters, and given that "Plato" says nothing in the dialogues, Plato does not disclose his true views in the dialogues. It does not follow from this either that Plato did disclose his true views through some other medium (such as the spoken word) or that the dialogues do not at all disclose his views. The author of the *Seventh Letter* denies that Plato's views can be identified in the way in which those of a writer of the usual treatise can be identified. This denial is in keeping with what I have said about Plato's dialogues.

23. I do not mean to imply that Plato invented the philosophical dialogue ex nihilo. The mimes of Sophron are usually cited as precedents, though Diogenes Laertius credits Plato with having invented the dialogue form (*Lives of Eminent Philosophers,* trans. R. D. Hicks, 2 vols. [London: W. Heinemann, 1925], 1, bk. iii, 48). There are, of course, many ways in which the dialogue form could be and has been used other than Plato's; thus my comments do not necessarily apply to the dialogue form as such. Further, I am not arguing that no one but Plato has written dialogues that possess the just mentioned characteristics.

24. Cf. Klein, *Commentary,* p. 17: "Answers can be given in a written text by the very action it presents. That is what usually happens in Platonic dialogues and what constitutes their dramatic or mimetic quality. This also confers on the dialogues the quality of completeness as against their unfinished (aporetic) character in terms of the verbal argument."

25. As Hegel notes, philosophy by nature is esoteric, thanks to the inherent difficulty of the subject matter (*Lectures on the History of Philosophy,* 2:11–12). But Plato sorts the subject matter into layers such that the surface of a dialogue normally is a generally intelligible introduction to the subject matter. My remarks are compatible with the possibility that someone who is an excellent philosopher might for reasons of his own ignore the dialogue form and treat Plato's dialogues as though they were treatises (as Aristotle does in the *Politics* discussion of the *Rep.,* and as Hegel does in his *Lectures*).

26. The audience Plato has in mind in writing his dialogues is certainly not limited to the professional or academic audience a contemporary philosopher writes for, as is suggested by A. W. Levi, "Philosophy as Literature: The Dialogue," *Philosophy and Rhetoric* 9 (1976): 19–20: "*Philosophy's literary involvement is almost directly inverse to the degree of its professionalization.* The dialogue form is clearly unsuited to a parade of scholarship or the symbolic demonstration of one's mastery of conventions of logical rigor."

27. A point made by Hyland, "Why Plato Wrote Dialogues," p. 41.

28. For Plato to *tell* us that philosophy is not about doctrines but about searching for the truth would be to fall prey to a self-referential difficulty (assuming that one can understand philosophizing only by the doing of it), as is argued by J. A. Ogilvy, "Socratic Method, Platonic Method, and Authority," *Educational Theory* 21 (1971): 7–9. As Ogilvy also notes here, by showing rather than telling his readers what he wants to say, Plato is able to suit his words to the varied natures of his readers: "The author who *tells* establishes a one-to-one relationship between himself and the Reader. Differences among readers dissolve into insignificance." Cf. also H. G. Gadamer, *Truth and Method,* p. 329: "There is no such thing as a method of learning to ask questions, of learning to see what needs to be questioned." On the sense in which dialectic is an art, Gadamer notes: "It is not an art in the sense that the Greeks speak of techne, not a craft that can be taught and by means of which we would master the knowledge of truth" (p. 330).

29. R. Robinson states that "the most hopeful place" to understand why Plato is so convinced "that the supreme method lies in oral question-and-answer" is the *Phr*. But Robinson concludes that the end of the *Phr*. by no means justifies the conviction at issue (*Plato's Earlier Dialectic*, pp. 83 ff.). After further consideration, Robinson then draws the conclusion that "it is useless to look for sufficient reasons for the Platonic doctrine that the supreme method entails question-and-answer, because there are none. The presence of this doctrine in Plato cannot be explained as a logical conclusion, but only as a historical phenomenon" (p. 86). In other words, there is no philosophical explanation of Plato's conception of philosophy; at its very heart, Platonic philosophy is based on a prereflective conviction, on persuasion without knowledge. This is a damning criticism of Plato. Robinson is led to it in part because of his defective theory of interpretation (see my Introduction).

30. As Friedländer says, with reference to Plato's handling of the dialogue form: "The dialogue is the only form of book that seems to suspend the book form itself" (*Plato*, 1:166).

31. For extended discussion of the matter, see part 2 of my "Reflections on 'Dialectic' in Plato and Hegel"; and my "Plato's Metaphilosophy," in *Platonic Investigations*, ed. D. O'Meara (Washington: Catholic University of America Press, 1985): 1–33.

32. As Ogilvy puts it: "For the *understanding* of Plato's dialogues, however difficult that may be, need not be the same as the *experiencing* of a Socratic encounter. . . . while the experience of the interlocutors almost always contains a shock of recognition and embarrassment at their *newly discovered ignorance*, the reader's unravelling of the subtleties of the relationship between the logical arguments and the experiences of the interlocutors will lead the reader, if he is lucky, to an equally shocking revelation of *new found knowledge*" ("Socratic Method," p. 6).

33. The last line of the prayer is a riddle. W. Kranz argues that "Vielmehr ist der letzte Satz voll sokratischer Ironie" ("Platonica," *Philologus* 94 [1941]: 333). For an excellent explanation of the line and of the prayer as a whole, see D. Clay's "Socrates' Prayer to Pan." Clay explains the line in terms of the palinode's description of the philosopher's brief sojourn on this earth: "The answer to this riddle is that the philosopher is a stranger, or better, a metic, in this world. His wealth is his wisdom. He can make off with none of the gold of this world, since it has no value in another" (p. 353). Friedländer too recommends reading the prayer in the light of the palinode (*Plato*, trans. H. Meyerhoff [Princeton: Princeton University Press, 1969], 3:240).

34. In the *Crat*. Socrates says that "logos signifies all things and always encloses them and ranges over them" and that Pan (who is "either logos or the brother of logos") is the "declarer of all things and the perpetual mover" (408c2–3, d3, c10). This description of Pan and logos is similar to the *Phr*.'s description of self-moved soul (cf. *Phr*. 246b6–7). The connection between Pan and logos is strengthened by the mention of Hermes at *Phr*. 263d6 and

the ironic suggestion that Pan is "more technical in the matter of words" than is Lysias.

35. Robin rightly notes that the inner/outer distinction in the prayer reminds one of Alcibiades' comparison of Socrates with the Silenus figure (*Phèdre*, p. 96).

Epilogue: The Defense of Dialogue

1. ψυχῆς ἐστι λόγος ἑαυτὸν αὔξων (fr. 115). The translation follows K. Freeman, *Ancilla to the Pre-Socratic Philosophers* (Cambridge, Mass.: Harvard University Press, 1983), p. 32. Although the evidence in favor of attributing authorship of this fragment to Heraclitus may not be overwhelming, many editors do so. The translation in Diels's *Die Fragmente der Vorsokratiker*, 7th ed. rev. W. Kranz, 3 vols. (Berlin: Weidmann, 1954), 1:176, runs: "Der Seele ist der Sinn eigen, der sich selbst mehrt."

2. See Derrida's "La pharmacie de Platon," in *La dissémination*, pp. 71–196.

3. See his *Philosophy and the Mirror of Nature* (Princeton: Princeton University Press, 1979). Rorty suggests that we engage in conversation with the aim of "picking up a new angle on things," of having an "exciting and fruitful" disagreement, and of finding a "new and more interesting way of expressing ourselves" (pp. 321, 318, 359). For Rorty one converses with the hope of reaching agreement (p. 318), but not an agreement based on the truth, or on some independent rational framework capable of settling disputes objectively. On p. 157 Rorty remarks that once we accept his notion of conversation "we shall, in short, be where the Sophists were before Plato brought his principle [that differences in certainty must correspond to differences in the objects known] to bear and invented 'philosophical thinking.' " On p. 374 Rorty argues that as a result of the "Platonic hypostatization" of the Truth philosophers "condemn themselves to a Sisyphean task." On p. 377 we learn that "for the edifying philosopher the very idea of being presented with 'all of Truth' is absurd, because the Platonic notion of Truth itself is absurd." And finally: "In my Wittgensteinian view, an intuition is never anything more or less than familiarity with a language-game, so to discover the source of our intuitions is to relive the history of the philosophical language-game we find ourselves playing" (p. 34).

4. I do not mean to suggest that Derrida and Rorty are in agreement in every respect; one cannot imagine Derrida sharing Rorty's proclivity for Dewey, for example. For Rorty's own remarks about Derrida, see his "Philosophy as a Kind of Writing: An Essay on Derrida," in *Consequences of Pragmatism* (Minneapolis: University of Minnesota Press, 1982), pp. 90–109, and "Derrida on Language, Being, and Abnormal Philosophy," *Journal of Philosophy* 57 (1977): 673–81. On p. 390 of *Philosophy* Rorty refers to his own book as an effort to "deconstruct the image of the Mirror of Nature" (see also the references to Derrida on pp. 365, 368n12, 371n17).

5. "La pharmacie," p. 196.

6. For a blunt statement of the point, see Derrida's *Eperons: Les styles de Nietzsche*, pp. 94–108. Consider also "La pharmacie," p. 108: "Le mot *pharmakon* y est pris [dans le *Phèdre*] dans une chaîne de significations. Le jeu de cette chaîne semble systématique. Mais le système n'est pas ici, simplement, celui des intentions de l'auteur connu sous le nom de Platon. Ce système n'est pas d'abord celui d'un vouloir-dire. Des communications réglées s'établissent, grâce au jeu de la langue, entre diverses fonctions du mot et, en lui, entre divers sédiments ou diverses régions de la culture. Ces communications, ces couloirs de sens, Platon peut parfois les déclarer, les éclairer en y jouant 'volontairement,' mot que nous mettons entre guillemets parce qu'il ne désigne, pour en rester dans la clôture de ces oppositions, qu'un mode de 'soumission' aux nécessités d'une 'langue' donnée."

7. For an excellent discussion of the role of questioning in Platonic dialectic, see Gadamer's *Truth and Method*, pp. 325–33. On p. 331 Gadamer says: "Dialectic as the art of conducting a conversation is also the art of seeing things in the unity of an aspect (sunoran eis hen eidos) ie it is the art of the formation of concepts as the working out of the common meaning."

8. *Philosophy*, p. 371. As Rorty also says, "edifying philosophers" (such as Dewey, Wittgenstein, and Heidegger) are essentially "reactive" and "parasitic" (*Philosophy*, pp. 366, 369, 377). See, too, *Philosophy*, pp. 180–81.

9. For an excellent explanation of this point, see V. Descombes, *Modern French Philosophy*, trans. L. Scott-Fox and J. M. Harding (Cambridge: Cambridge University Press, 1980), chap. 5. There is ruse and dissembling in Socratic and Platonic irony as well, but with the opposite intention from Derrida's.

10. *Philosophy*, p. 394. Consider also the statement on p. 377 that the conversation should continue to prevent the "dehumanization," the reference on p. 366 to "madness in the most literal and terrible sense" (also p. 349), and the "wholehearted behaviorism, naturalism, and physicalism I have been commending in earlier chapters" sentence on p. 373. For an extended criticism of the kind of position represented by Derrida and Rorty, see G. Graff's *Literature against Itself; Literary Ideas in Modern Society* (Chicago: University of Chicago Press, 1979). I have worked out the reflexive metalevel argument at length in "Plato's Metaphilosophy," in *Platonic Investigations*, ed. D. O'Meara (Washington: Catholic University of America Press, 1985), pp. 1–33.

11. Consider "La pharmacie," pp. 93, 192–94; also Rorty, *Philosophy*, p. 311: "The trouble with Platonic notions is not that they are 'wrong' but that there is not a great deal to be said about them—specifically, there is no way to 'naturalize' them or otherwise connect them to the rest of inquiry, or culture, or life."

Bibliography

The following bibliography includes, for the convenience of the reader, works on the *Phaedrus* that I have consulted but not cited. Although this is the most complete bibliography of the *Phaedrus* presently available, it is not intended to be exhaustive. For example, a number of the nineteenth- and twentieth-century German works on the *Phaedrus* (by Deuschle, Hermann, Immisch, Lukas, Steinhart, Susemihls, Usener, Vahlens, and others) are cited and discussed in Diesendruck's monograph, and I have omitted them from this list. Where a chapter of a book about Plato deals directly with the *Phaedrus*, I cite (again for the convenience of the interested reader) the chapter as well as book title.

Editions and Translations of the Phaedrus *and Other Dialogues*

Burnet, J. *Platonis Opera*. 1900–07. Reprint. Oxford: Clarendon Press, 1967–68.

Guzzo, C. *Platone, Fedro*. Naples: Loffredo, 1934. With notes and introduction by A. Guzzo.

Hackforth, R. *Plato's Phaedrus*. 1952. Reprint. Cambridge: Cambridge University Press, 1972. With introduction and commentary.

Helmbold, W. C., and W. G. Rabinowitz. *Plato's Phaedrus*. Indianapolis: Bobbs-Merrill, 1956. With introduction.

Plato. *Charmides and Other Dialogues*. Translated by W. R. M. Lamb. 1927. Reprint. Cambridge, Mass.: Harvard University Press, 1964.

———. *Phaedo*. Translated with notes by D. Gallop. Oxford: Clarendon Press, 1980.

———. *The Collected Dialogues* (including the *Letters*). Edited by E. Hamilton and H. Cairns (various translators). 1961. Reprint. Princeton: Princeton University Press, 1969.

Ritter, C. *Platons Dialog Phaidros*. 2d ed. 1914. Reprint. Leipzig: Meiner, 1922. With introduction and notes.

Robin, L. *Phèdre*. In *Platon: Oeuvres complètes*, Tome IV, 3ᶜ Partie. 1933. Reprint. Paris: Collection des Universités de France, 1970. With introduction and notes.

Thompson, W. H. *The Phaedrus of Plato, with English Notes and Dissertations.* London: Wittaker & Co., 1868.

Vicaire, P. *Platon: Phèdre.* Paris: Association Guillaume Budé, 1972. With introduction and notes.

Works Cited and Consulted

Ackrill, J. L. "In Defence of Platonic Division." In *Ryle: A Collection of Critical Essays.* Edited by O. P. Wood and G. Pitcher. Garden City: Doubleday, 1970, pp. 373–92.

———. "Review of *Plato's Phaedrus* by R. Hackforth." *Mind* 62 (1953): 277–79.

Allan, D. J. "Review of Plato's *Phaedrus* by R. Hackforth." *Philosophy* 28 (1953): 365–66.

Allen, M. J. B., trans. and ed. *Marsilio Ficino and the Phaedran Charioteer.* Berkeley: University of California Press, 1981.

Apollodorus. *The Library.* Translated by J. G. Frazer. 2 vols. 1921. Reprint. Cambridge, Mass.: Harvard University Press, 1976–79.

Aristotle. *Athenian Constitution.* Translated by H. Rackham. 1935. Reprint. Cambridge, Mass.: Harvard University Press, 1981.

———. *Eudemian Ethics.* Translated by H. Rackham. 1935. Reprint. Cambridge, Mass.: Harvard University Press, 1981.

———. *Magna Moralia.* Translated by G. C. Armstrong. 1935. Reprint. Cambridge, Mass.: Harvard University Press, 1969.

———. *Metaphysics.* Translated by H. Tredennick. 2 vols. 1933. Reprint. Cambridge, Mass.: Harvard University Press, 1968.

———. *Nicomachean Ethics.* Translated by H. Rackham. 1926. Reprint. Cambridge, Mass.: Harvard University Press, 1968.

———. *On Sophistical Refutations.* Translated by E. S. Forster. 1955. Reprint. Cambridge, Mass.: Harvard University Press, 1978.

———. *On the Heavens.* Translated by W. K. C. Guthrie. 1939. Reprint. Cambridge, Mass.: Harvard University Press, 1971.

———. *The "Art" of Rhetoric.* Translated by J. H. Freese. 1926. Reprint Cambridge, Mass.: Harvard University Press, 1982.

Arrowsmith, W. "Aristophanes' *Birds:* The Fantasy Politics of Eros." *Arion,* n.s. 1 (1973): 119–67.

Ballard, E. G. *Socratic Ignorance: An Essay on Platonic Self-Knowledge.* The Hague: Nijhoff, 1965.

Barnes, H. E. "Plato and the Psychology of Love: *Phaedrus* 252C–253C." *Classical Weekly* 40 (1946): 34–35.

Baron, C. "De l'unité de composition dans le Phèdre de Platon." *Revue des Etudes Grecques* 4 (1891): 58–62.

Beare, J. I. "The *Phaedrus:* Its Structure, the ῎ΕΡΩΣ Theme: Notes." *Hermathena* 17 (1891): 312–34.

Blass, F. "Kritische Bemerkungen zu Platons *Phaidros.*" *Hermes* 36 (1901): 580–96.

Bluck, R. S. "The *Phaedrus* and Reincarnation." *American Journal of Philology* 79 (1958): 156–64.

Boder, W. *Die sokratische Ironie in den platonischen Frühdialogen.* Amsterdam: B. R. Grüner, 1973.

Bolotin, D. "Review of T. Irwin's *Plato's Moral Theory.*" *St. John's Review* 32 (1981): 95–97.

Bonitz, H. "Zur Erklärung des Dialogs *Phädros.*" In *Platonische Studien.* 1886. Reprint. Hildesheim: G. Olms, 1968, pp. 270–92.

Booth, W. *A Rhetoric of Irony.* Chicago: University of Chicago Press, 1974.

Bourguet, E. "Sur la composition du *Phèdre.*" *Revue de métaphysique et de morale* 26 (1919): 335–51.

Brague, R. *Le restant; Supplément aux commentaires du Ménon de Platon.* Paris: Vrin, 1978.

Bröcker, W. "Phaidros." Chap. 24 of *Platos Gespräche.* Frankfurt: Klostermann, 1964, pp. 522–58.

Brown, M., and J. Coulter. "The Middle Speech of Plato's *Phaedrus.*" *Journal of the History of Philosophy* 9 (1971): 405–23.

Brownstein, O. L. "Plato's *Phaedrus:* Dialectic as the Genuine Art of Speaking." *Quarterly Journal of Speech* 51 (1965): 392–98.

Brumbaugh, R. S. "Teaching Plato's *Republic* VIII and IX." *Teaching Philosophy* 3 (1980): 331–37.

Bubner, R. "Dialog und Dialektik oder Plato und Hegel." In *Zur Sache der Dialektik.* Ditzingen: Reclam, 1980, pp. 124–60.

Burger, R. *Plato's Phaedrus: A Defense of a Philosophic Art of Writing.* University: University of Alabama Press, 1980.

Burnyeat, M. "Review of L. Strauss' *Studies in Platonic Political Philosophy.*" *New York Review of Books,* May 30, 1985, pp. 30–36.

————. "The Passion of Reason in Plato's *Phaedrus.*" Unpublished lecture.

Bury, J. B. "Questions Connected with Plato's *Phaidros.*" *Journal of Philology* 15 (1886): 80–85.

Caizzi, F. D. "ΑΕΙΚΙΝΗΤΟΝ Ο ΑΥΤΟΚΙΝΗΤΟΝ? (Plat. *Phaedr.,* 245c)." *Acme* 23 (1970): 91–97.

Camus, A. *Le mythe de Sisyphe.* Paris: Gallimard, 1942.

Carter, R. E. "Plato and Inspiration." *Journal of the History of Philosophy* 5 (1967): 111–21.

Caton, H. "Speech and Writing as Artifacts." *Philosophy and Rhetoric* 2 (1969): 19–36.

Chen, C.-H. "The *Phaedrus.*" *Studi internazionali di filosofia* 4 (1982): 77–90.

Cherniss, H. *The Riddle of the Early Academy.* Berkeley: University of California Press, 1945.

Clay, D. "Platonic Studies and the Study of Plato." *Arion,* n.s. 2 (1975): 116–32.

_____. "Socrates' Prayer to Pan." In *Hellenic Studies Presented to B. M. W. Knox.* Edited by Arktouros. Berlin: de Gruyter, 1979, pp. 345–53.

Cohen, S. M. "Plato's Method of Division." In *Patterns in Plato's Thought.* Edited by Moravcsik. Dordrecht: Reidel, 1973, pp. 181–91.

Cornford, F. M. *Plato's Theory of Knowledge.* 3d ed. 1935. Reprint. London: Routledge & Kegan Paul, 1949.

Coulter, J. A. "*Phaedrus* 279a: The Praise of Isocrates." *Greek, Roman, and Byzantine Studies* 8 (1967): 225–36.

_____. See Brown, M., and J. Coulter.

Courcelle, P. "La plaine de vérité: Platon, *Phèdre* 248b." *Museum Helveticum* 26 (1969): 199–203.

Cropsey, J. "Plato's *Phaedrus* and Plato's Socrates." In *Political Philosophy and the Issues of Politics.* Chicago: University of Chicago Press, 1977, pp. 231–51.

Dalfen, J. "Gedanken zur Lektüre platonischer Dialoge." *Zeitschrift für philosophische Forschung* 29 (1975): 169–94.

Daumas, F. "Sous le Signe du Gattilier en Fleurs." *Revue des Etudes Grecques* 74 (1961): 61–68.

Davison, J. A. *From Archilochus to Pindar.* New York: St. Martin's Press, 1968.

Demos, R. "Plato's Doctrine of the Psyche as a Self-Moving Motion." *Journal of the History of Philosophy* 6 (1968): 133–45.

_____. "What Is It That I Want?" *Ethics* 55 (1945): 182–95.

Derbolav, J. "Der Entlastungs- bzw. Entfremdungscharakter der Schrift; Kritik und Rechtfertigung der philosophischen Schriftstellerei im *Phaidros.*" In *Platons Sprachphilosophie im Kratylos und in den Späteren Schriften.* Darmstadt: Wissenschaftliche Buchgesellschaft, 1972, pp. 199–205.

Derrida, J. *Eperons: Les styles de Nietzsche.* French with facing translation by B. Harlow. Chicago: University of Chicago Press, 1979.

_____. "La pharmacie de Platon." In *La dissémination.* Paris: Seuil, 1972, pp. 69–198.

Descombes, V. *Modern French Philosophy.* Translated by L. Scott-Fox and J. M. Harding. Cambridge: Cambridge University Press, 1980.

Detel, W. "Bemerkungen zum Einleitungsteil einiger platonischer Frühdialoge." *Gymnasium* 82 (1975): 308–14.

De Vries, G. J. *A Commentary on the Phaedrus of Plato.* Amsterdam: Hakkert, 1969.

_____. "Isocrates in the *Phaedrus:* A Reply." *Mnemosyne* 24 (1971): 387–90.

_____. "Isocrates' Reaction to the *Phaedrus.*" *Mnemosyne* 6 (1953): 39–45.

Diels, H. *Die Fragmente der Vorsokratiker.* 7th ed. Revised by W. Kranz. 3 vols. 1903. Reprint. Berlin: Weidmann, 1954.

Diès, A. *Autour de Platon; Essais de critique et d'histoire.* 2 vols. Paris: Bibliothèque des Archives de Philosophie, 1927.

Diesendruck, Z. *Struktur und Charakter des platonischen Phaidros.* Wien-Leipzig: W. Braumüller, 1927.

Dimock, G. E. "'ΑΛΛΑ' in Lysias and Plato's *Phaedrus*." *American Journal of Philology* 73 (1952): 381–96.

Diogenes Laertius. *Lives of Eminent Philosophers*. Translated by R. D. Hicks. 2 vols. London: W. Heinemann, 1925.

Dionysus of Halicarnassus. "On the Style of Demosthenes." In *Dionysus of Halicarnassus, the Critical Essays*. Translated by S. Usher. 2 vols. Cambridge, Mass.: Harvard University Press, 1974, pp. 232–455.

———. *De Compositione Verborum*. Edited and translated by W. R. Roberts. London: Macmillan & Co., 1910.

Dorter, K. "Imagery and Philosophy in Plato's *Phaedrus*." *Journal of the History of Philosophy* 9 (1971): 279–88.

Dover, K. J. *Greek Homosexuality*. Cambridge, Mass.: Harvard University Press, 1978.

Dumortier, J. "L'attelage ailé du *Phèdre* (246 sqq.)." *Revue des études Grecques* 82 (1969): 346–48.

Dyson, M. "Zeus and Philosophy in the Myth of Plato's *Phaedrus*." *Classical Quarterly* 32 (1982): 307–11.

Ebert, T. *Meinung und Wissen in der Philosophie Platons*. Berlin: de Gruyter, 1974.

Edelstein, L. "Platonic Anonymity." *American Journal of Philology* 83 (1962): 1–22.

———. "The Function of the Myth in Plato's Philosophy." *Journal of the History of Ideas* 10 (1949): 463–81.

Eitrem, S. "Götter und Daimonem; einige Bemerkungen zu Platon, *Phaidr.* 246E." *Symbolae Osloenses* 34 (1958): 39–42.

Fisher, J. "Plato on Writing and Doing Philosophy." *Journal of the History of Ideas* 27 (1966): 163–72.

Fontenrose, J. *Python: A Study of Delphic Myth and Its Origins*. Berkeley: University of California Press, 1959.

Fortenbaugh, W. "Plato's *Phaedrus* 235C3." *Classical Philology* 61 (1966): 108–09.

Freeman, K. *Ancilla to the Pre-Socratic Philosophers*. 1948. Reprint. Cambridge, Mass.: Harvard University Press, 1983.

Frenkian, A. M. *La méthode Hippocratique dans le Phèdre de Platon*. Bucharest: Imprimerie Nationale, 1941.

Friedländer, P. "Phaedrus." Vol. 3, chap. 25, of *Plato*. Translated H. Meyerhoff. Princeton: Princeton University Press, 1969, pp. 219–42.

———. *Plato: An Introduction*. Vol. I of *Plato*. Translated by H. Meyerhoff. 1958. Reprint (of the 2d ed.). Princeton: Princeton University Press, 1973.

———. "Plato *Phaedrus* 245A." *Classical Philology* 36 (1941): 51–52.

Frutiger, P. *Les mythes de Platon; Étude philosophique et littéraire*. 1930. Reprint. New York: Arno Press, 1976.

Furley, D. J. "Self-Movers." In *Essays on Aristotle's Ethics*. Edited by A. O. Rorty. Berkeley: University of California Press, 1980, pp. 55–67.

Gadamer, H. G. "Correspondence concerning *Wahrheit und Methode.*"
    Independent Journal of Philosophy 2 (1978): 5–12.
————. *Dialogue and Dialectic: Eight Hermeneutical Studies on Plato.* Translated
    by P. C. Smith. New Haven: Yale University Press, 1980.
————. "Die Theorie der Dialektik im *Phaidros.*" Chap. 1, pt. 7 of *Platos
    dialektische Ethik und andere Studien zur platonischen Philosophie.* Hamburg:
    Meiner, 1968, pp. 66–72.
————. *Truth and Method.* Translated by Sheed and Ward, Ltd. New York:
    Seabury Press, 1975.
Gauss, H. "Phaidrus." Vol. 2, pt 2, chap. 6 of *Philosophischer Handkommentar
    zu den Dialogen Platos.* Bern: H. Lang & Cie, 1958, pp. 238–65.
Gil, L. "Notas al *Fedro.*" *Emerita* 24 (1956): 311–30.
Gould, J. "Klein on Ethological Mimes, for Example, the *Meno.*" *Journal of
    Philosophy* 66 (1969): 253–65.
Gould, T. *Platonic Love.* London: Routledge & Kegan Paul, 1963.
Graff, G. *Literature against Itself; Literary Ideas in Modern Society.* Chicago:
    University of Chicago Press, 1979.
Griswold, C. "Gadamer and the Interpretation of Plato." *Ancient Philosophy* 1
    (1981): 171–78.
————. "Irony and Aesthetic Language in Plato's Dialogues." In *Literature as
    Art.* Edited by D. Bolling. New York: Haven Press, 1986.
————. "Plato's Metaphilosophy." In *Platonic Investigations.* Edited by D.
    O'Meara. Washington: Catholic University of America Press, 1985, pp. 1–
    33.
————. "Plato's *Phaedrus* 230E6–231A3, 262E1–4, and 263E6–264A3."
    Classical Bulletin 55 (1979): 68–69.
————. "R. Burger's *Plato's Phaedrus: A Defense of a Philosophic Art of
    Writing*" (review). *Independent Journal of Philosophy* 4 (1983): 158–60.
————. "Reflections on 'Dialectic' in Plato and Hegel." *International
    Philosophical Quarterly* 22 (1982): 115–30.
————. "Self-knowledge and the '$\iota\delta\acute{\epsilon}\alpha$' of the Soul in Plato's *Phaedrus.*"
    Revue de métaphysique et de morale 86 (1981): 477–94.
————. "Soul, Form, and Indeterminacy in Plato's *Philebus* and *Phaedrus.*"
    Proceedings of the American Catholic Philosophical Association 55 (1981):184–94.
————. "Style and Philosophy: The Case of Plato's Dialogues." *Monist* 63
    (1980): 530–46.
————. "The Ideas and the Criticism of Poetry in Plato's *Republic,* Book 10,"
    Journal of the History of Philosophy 19 (1981): 135–50.
————. "The Myth of Sisyphus: A Reconsideration." *Philosophy in Context* 7,
    Suppl. issue (1978): 45–59.
Gulley, N. *Plato's Theory of Knowledge.* London: Methuen, 1962.
————. "Plato's Theory of Recollection." *Classical Quarterly,* n.s. 4 (1954):
    194–213.

Gundert, H. *Der platonische Dialog.* Heidelberg: C. Winter, 1968.

————. *Dialog und Dialektik; zur Struktur des platonischen Dialogs.* Amsterdam: B. R. Grüner, 1971.

————. "Enthusiasmos und Logos bei Platon." *Lexis* 2 (1949): 25–46.

Guthrie, W. K. C. "Rhetoric and Philosophy; The Unity of the *Phaedrus.*" *Paideia* (Special Plato Issue) (1976): 117–24.

Hackforth, R. *Plato's Philebus.* 1945. Reprint. Cambridge: Cambridge University Press, 1972.

Hall, R. W. "Ψυχή as Differentiated Unity in the Philosophy of Plato." *Phronesis* 8 (1963): 63–82.

Hartland-Swann, J. "Plato as Poet: A Critical Interpretation." *Philosophy* 26 (1951): pt. 1, 3–18; pt. 2, 131–41.

Haslam, M. "Plato, Sophron, and the Dramatic Dialogue." *Bulletin of Classical Studies* (University of London Institute of Classical Studies) 19 (1972): 17–38.

Hatzfeld, J. "Du nouveau sur *Phèdre.*" *Revue des études anciennes* 41 (1939): 313–18.

Hegel, G. W. F. *Lectures on the History of Philosophy.* Translated by E. S. Haldane and F. H. Simson. 3 vols. 1892. Reprint. Atlantic Highlands: Humanities Press, 1974.

————. *Phenomenology of Spirit.* Translated by A. V. Miller. Oxford: Clarendon Press, 1977.

Heidegger, M. "Platons Phaidros: Schönheit und Wahrheit in einem beglückenden Zwiespalt." In vol. 1 of *Nietzsche.* Pfullingen: Neske, 1961, pp. 218–31.

Helmbold, W. C., and W. B. Holther. "The Unity of the *Phaedrus.*" *University of California Publications in Classical Philology* 14 (1952): 387–417.

Henderson, J. H. *The Maculate Muse.* New Haven: Yale University Press, 1975.

Hermeias of Alexandria. *In Platonis Phaedrum Scholia.* Edited by P. Couvreur. 1901. Reprint. Hildesheim: G. Olms, 1971. With additions by C. Zintzen.

Hirsch, E. D. *The Aims of Interpretation.* Chicago: University of Chicago Press, 1976.

————. *Validity in Interpretation.* New Haven: Yale University Press, 1967.

Hitler, A. *Mein Kampf.* translated by R. Manheim. Boston: Houghton Mifflin Co., 1943.

Hoerber, R. G. "Love or Rhetoric in Plato's *Phaedrus.*" *Classical Bulletin* 34 (1958): 33.

Hoffmann, E. "Die literarischen Voraussetzungen des Platonverständnisses." *Zeitschrift für philosophische Forschung* 2 (1947): 465–80.

Howland, R. L. "The Attack on Isocrates in the *Phaedrus.*" *Classical Quarterly* 31 (1937): 151–59.

Huber, C. E. *Anamnesis bei Plato*. Pullach bei München: Pullacher philosophische Forschungen, 1964.

Hudson-Williams, H. L. *Three Systems of Education: Some Reflections on the Implications of Plato's Phaedrus*. Oxford: Oxford University Press, 1954.

Hyland, D. "ʼΈρως, ʼΕπιϑυμία, and Φιλία in Plato." *Phronesis* 13 (1968): 32–46.

————. "Why Plato Wrote Dialogues." *Philosophy and Rhetoric* 1 (1968): 38–50.

Irwin, T. *Plato's Moral Theory: The Early and Middle Dialogues*. Oxford: Clarendon Press, 1977.

————. "Recollection and Plato's Moral Theory." *Review of Metaphysics* 27 (1974): 752–72.

Isocrates. *Isocrates*. Translated by G. Norlin. 3 vols. London: W. Heinemann, 1928.

Jackson, B. D. "The Prayers of Socrates." *Phronesis* 16 (1971): 14–37.

Jäger, G. *"Nus" in Platons Dialogen*. Göttingen: Vandenhoeck & Ruprecht, 1967.

Joël, K. "Platos 'sokratische' Periode und der *Phaedrus*." In *Philosophische Abhandlungen*. M. Heinze gewidmet. Berlin: E. S. Mittler & Sohn, 1906, pp. 78–91.

Johnstone, H. W. *Validity and Rhetoric in Philosophical Argument*. University Park: Dialogue Press, 1978.

Joly, R. "La question Hippocratique et le témoignage du *Phèdre*." *Revue des Etudes Grecques* 74 (1961): 69–92.

Juhl, P. *Interpretation: An Essay in the Philosophy of Literary Criticism*. Princeton: Princeton University Press, 1980.

Kahn, C. H. "Did Plato Write Socratic Dialogues?" *Classical Quarterly* 31 (1981): 305–20.

Kaufmann, W. *Nietzsche*. 3d ed. Princeton: Princeton University Press, 1968.

Kelley, W. G. "Rhetoric as Seduction." *Philosophy and Rhetoric* 6 (1975): 69–80.

Kierkegaard, S. *The Concept of Irony*. Translated by L. M. Capel. New York: Harper & Row, 1965.

Kirk, G. S., and J. E. Raven. *The PreSocratic Philosophers*. 1957. Reprint. Cambridge: Cambridge University Press, 1973.

Klein, J. *A Commentary on Plato's Meno*. Chapel Hill: University of North Carolina Press, 1965.

Kojève, A. *Introduction à la lecture de Hegel*. Paris: Gallimard, 1947.

————. "Tyranny and Wisdom." Translated by M. Gold. In *On Tyranny*, by L. Strauss. Ithaca: Cornell University Press, 1963, pp. 143–88.

Koller, H. "Die dihäretische Methode." *Glotta* 39 (1961): 6–24.

Kosman, L. A. "Platonic Love." In *Facets of Plato's Philosophy*. Edited by W. Werkmeister. *Phronesis*. Suppl. vol. 2. Assen: Van Gorcum, 1976, pp. 53–69.

Kranz, W. "Platonica." *Philologus* 94 (1941): 332–36.

Krüger, G. *Einsicht und Leidenschaft; Das Wesen des platonischen Denkens.*
   Frankfurt: Klostermann, 1973.
Kucharski, P. "La 'méthode d'Hippocrate' dans le *Phèdre.*" *Revue des études
   Grecques* 52 (1939): 301–57.
————. "La rhétorique dans le *Gorgias* et le *Phèdre.*" *Revue des études Grecques*
   74 (1961): 371–406.
Lachterman, D. "Review of J. Klein's *Plato's Trilogy.*" *Nous* 13 (1979): 106–
   12.
Lafrance, Y. "Autour de Platon: Continentaux et analystes." *Dionysius* 3
   (1979): 17–37.
Lebeck, A. "The Central Myth of Plato's *Phaedrus.*" *Greek, Roman, and
   Byzantine Studies* 13 (1972): 267–90.
Lee, E. N. "Reason and Rotation: Circular Movement as the Model of Mind
   (Nous) in Later Plato." In *Facets of Plato's Philosophy.* Edited by W.
   Werkmeister. *Phronesis,* Suppl. vol. 2. Assen: Van Gorcum, 1976, pp.
   70–102.
Lesher, J. "Xenophanes' Scepticism." *Phronesis* 23 (1978): 1–21.
Lesser, H. "Style and Pedagogy in Plato and Aristotle." *Philosophy* 57 (1982):
   388–94.
Levi, A. W. "Philosophy as Literature: The Dialogue." *Philosophy and Rhetoric*
   9 (1976): 1–20.
Levinson, R. B. "Plato's *Phaedrus* and the New Criticism." *Archiv für
   Geschichte der Philosophie* 46 (1964): 293–309.
Linforth, I. M. "Telistic Madness in Plato, *Phaedrus* 244DE." *University of
   California Publications in Classical Philology* 13 (1946): 163–72.
————. "The Corybantic Rites in Plato." *University of California Publications
   in Classical Philology* 13 (1946): 121–62.
Lloyd, A. C. "Plato's Description of Division." In *Studies in Plato's
   Metaphysics.* Edited by R. E. Allen. London: Routledge & Kegan Paul,
   1965, pp. 219–30.
Luther, W. "Die Schwäche des geschriebenen Logos." *Gymnasium* 68 (1961):
   526–48.
Mansfield, H. C. "An Exchange on Strauss' Machiavelli with J. G. A.
   Pocock." *Political Theory* 3 (1975): 372–405.
McCumber, J. "Discourse and Psyche in Plato's *Phaedrus.*" *Apeiron* 16 (1982):
   27–39.
McGibbon, D. D. "The Fall of the Soul in Plato's *Phaedrus.*" *Classical
   Quarterly,* n.s. 14 (1964): 56–63.
Meineke, A., ed. *Fragmenta Comicorum Graecorum.* 5 vols. Berlin: G. Reimer,
   1841.
Merlan, P. "Form and Content in Plato's Philosophy," *Journal of the History of
   Ideas* 8 (1947): 406–30.
Meyer, H. W. "Das Verhältnis von Enthusiasmus und Philosophie bei Platon
   im Hinblick auf seinen *Phaidros.*" *Archiv für Philosophie* 6 (1956): 262–77.

Meyer, M. "Dialectic and Questioning: Socrates and Plato." *American Philosophical Quarterly* 17 (1980): 281–89.

Miller, M. H. *The Philosopher in Plato's Statesman.* The Hague: Nijhoff, 1980.

Mittelstrass, J. "Versuch über den Sokratischen Dialog." Chap. 7 of *Wissenschaft als Lebensform.* Frankfurt: Suhrkamp, 1982, pp. 138–61.

Moline, J. *Plato's Theory of Understanding.* Madison: University of Wisconsin Press, 1981.

Moore, J. D. "The Relation between Plato's *Symposium* and *Phaedrus.*" In *Patterns in Plato's Thought.* Edited by J. Moravcsik. Dordrecht: Reidel, 1973, pp. 52–71.

Moors, K. F. *Platonic Myth; An Introductory Study.* Washington, D.C.: University Press of America, 1982.

Moravcsik, J. M. E. "Plato's Method of Division." In *Patterns in Plato's Thought.* Edited by Moravcsik. Dordrecht: Reidel, 1973, pp. 158–80.

————. "The Anatomy of Plato's Divisions." In *Exegesis and Argument. Phronesis.* Suppl. vol. 1. Assen: Van Gorcum, 1973, pp. 324–48.

Motte, A. "Le pré sacré de Pan et des nymphes dans le *Phèdre* de Platon." *L'antiquité classique* 32 (1963): 460–76.

Muecke, D. C. *The Compass of Irony.* London: Methuen & Co., 1969.

Mueller, G. E. "The Unity of the *Phaedrus.*" *Classical Bulletin* 33 (March-April 1957): pt. 1, 50–53; pt. 2, 63–65.

Mulhern, J. J. "Socrates on Knowledge and Information (*Phaedrus* 274B6–277A5)." *Classica et mediaevalia* 30 (1969): 175–86.

————. "Treatises, Dialogues, and Interpretation." *Monist* 53 (1969): 631–41.

Murley, C. "Plato's *Phaedrus* and the Theocritean Pastoral." *Transactions of the American Philological Association* 71 (1940): 281–95.

Natorp, P. "Phaedrus." Chap. 3 of *Platos Ideenlehre; Eine Einführung in den Idealismus.* 2d ed. 1922. Reprint. Darmstadt: Wissenschaftliche Buchgesellschaft, 1961, pp. 53–89.

Nehamas, A. "Plato on the Imperfection of the Sensible World." *American Philosophical Quarterly* 12 (1975): 105–17.

Nietzsche, F. *Thus Spoke Zarathustra,* and *Human, All-Too-Human.* In *The Portable Nietzsche.* Translated by W. Kaufmann. 1954. Reprint. New York: Viking Press, 1974.

Nussbaum, M. C. " 'This Story Isn't True': Poetry, Goodness, and Understanding in Plato's *Phaedrus.*" In *Plato on Beauty, Wisdom, and the Arts.* Edited by J. Moravcsik and P. Temko. Totowa: Rowman & Littlefield, 1982, pp. 79–124.

Ogilvy, J. A. "Socratic Method, Platonic Method, and Authority." *Educational Theory* 21 (1971): 3–16.

Ostwald, M., ed. *Plato's Statesman.* Translated by J. B. Skemp. 1957. Reprint. Indianapolis: Bobbs-Merrill, 1979.

Paisse, J.-M. "La métaphysique de l'âme humaine dans le *Phèdre* de Platon." *Bulletin de l'association G. Budé* 31 (1972): 469–78.

Palante, G. "L'ironie: Étude psychologique." *Revue philosophique de la France et de l'étranger* 61 (1906): 147–63.

Perelman, Ch., ed. *Dialectics.* The Hague: Nijhoff, 1975.

_____. "La méthode dialectique et le rôle de l'interlocuteur dans le dialogue." *Revue de métaphysique et de morale* 60 (1955): 26–31.

Philip, A. "Récurrences thématiques et topologie dans le *Phèdre* de Platon." *Revue de métaphysique et de morale* 86 (1981): 452–76.

Philip, J. A. "Platonic Diairesis." *Transactions of the American Philological Association* 97 (1966): 335–58.

Pieper, J. *Love and Inspiration.* Translated by R. and C. Winston. New York: Harcourt, Brace & World, 1964.

_____. "Über die Wahrheit der platonischen Mythen." In *Einsichten: Gerhard Krüger zum 60. Geburtstag.* Edited by K. Oehler and R. Schaeffler. Frankfurt: Klostermann, 1962, pp. 289–96.

Pindar. *Pindar's Victory Songs.* Translated by F. J. Nisetich. Baltimore: Johns Hopkins University Press, 1980.

Pippin, R. "Hegel's Phenomenological Criticism." *Man and World* 8 (1975): 296–314.

Plass, P. "Philosophic Anonymity and Irony in the Platonic Dialogues." *American Journal of Philology* 85 (1964): 254–78.

_____. " 'Play' and Philosophic Detachment in Plato." *Transactions and Proceedings of the American Philological Association* 98 (1967): 343–64.

_____. "The Unity of the *Phaedrus.*" *Symbolae Osloenses* 43 (1969): 7–38.

Platt, A. "Notes on Plato's *Phaedrus.*" *Journal of Philology* 35 (1920): 162–64.

Pocock, J. G. A. See Mansfield, H. C.

Poser, H., ed. *Philosophie und Mythos: Ein Kolloquium.* Berlin: de Gruyter, 1979.

Price, A. W. "Loving Persons Platonically." *Phronesis* 26 (1981): 25–34.

Pucci, P. *Hesiod and the Language of Poetry.* Baltimore: Johns Hopkins University Press, 1977.

Rabinowitz, W. G. See "Editions and Translations": Helmbold, W. C., and W. G. Rabinowitz.

Raven, J. E. See Kirk, G. S., and J. E. Raven.

Regenbogen, O. "Bemerkungen zur Deutung des platonischen *Phaidros.*" In *Kleine Schriften.* Munich: F. Dirlmeier, 1961, pp. 248–69.

Reinhardt, K. *Platons Mythen.* Bonn: F. Cohen, 1927.

Robin, L. *La théorie platonicienne de l'amour.* 1933. Reprint. Paris: Presses Universitaires de France, 1964.

Robinson, R. "Plato's Consciousness of Fallacy." *Mind* 51 (1942): 97–114.

_____. *Plato's Earlier Dialectic.* Ithaca: Cornell University Press, 1941.

Robinson, T. M. *Plato's Psychology.* Toronto: University of Toronto Press, 1970.

_____. "The Argument for Immortality in Plato's *Phaedrus.*" In *Essays in Ancient Greek Philosophy.* Edited by J. Anton and G. Kustas. Albany: State University of New York Press, 1971, pp. 345–53.

Rodis-Lewis, G. "L'articulation des thèmes du *Phèdre*." *Revue Philosophique de la France et de l'Etranger* 165 (1975): 3–34.

Rorty, R. *Consequences of Pragmatism*. Minneapolis: University of Minnesota Press, 1982.

————. "Derrida on Language, Being, and Abnormal Philosophy." *Journal of Philosophy* 57 (1977): 673–81.

————. *Philosophy and the Mirror of Nature*. Princeton: Princeton University Press, 1979.

Roscher, W. H., ed. *Ausführliches Lexikon der griechischen und römischen Mythologie*. 6 vols. Leipzig: Teubner, 1886–1937.

Rosen, S. *Plato's Symposium*. New Haven: Yale University Press, 1968.

————. "Self-Consciousness and Self-Knowledge in Plato and Hegel." *Hegel-Studien* 9 (1974): 109–29.

————. "Socrates as Concealed Lover." In *Classics and the Classical Tradition, Festschrift for R. Dengler*. Edited by E. Borza and W. Carruba. University Park: Pennsylvania State University Press, 1973, pp. 163–77.

————. "ΣΩΦΡΟΣΥΝΗ and Selbstbewusstsein." *Review of Metaphysics* 26 (1973): 617–42.

————. *The Limits of Analysis*. New York: Basic Books, 1980.

————. "The Non-Lover in Plato's *Phaedrus*." *Man and World* 2 (1969): 423–37.

Rosenmeyer, T. G. "Plato's Prayer to Pan—*Phaedrus* 279b8–c3." *Hermes* 90 (1962): 34–44.

Sabine, G. H. "Review of Strauss' *Persecution and the Art of Writing*." *Ethics* 63 (1953): 220–22.

Sallis, J. *Being and Logos; The Way of Platonic Dialogue*. Pittsburgh: Duquesne University Press, 1975.

Santas, G. "Passionate Platonic Love in the *Phaedrus*." *Ancient Philosophy* 2 (1982): 105–14.

Sayre, K. M. *Plato's Analytic Method*. Chicago: University of Chicago Press, 1969.

Schaerer, R. *La question platonicienne*. 2d ed. 1938. Reprint. Paris: Vrin, 1969.

————. "Le mécanisme de l'ironie dans ses rapports avec la dialectique." *Revue de métaphysique et de morale* 48 (1941): 181–209.

Scheidweiler, F. "Zum platonischen *Phaidros*." *Hermes* 83 (1955): 120–22.

Schilling, K. "Phaidros: Die Dämonie des Lebens." In *Platon: Einführung in seine Philosophie*. Reutlingen: Gryphius, 1948, pp. 201–11.

Schleiermacher, F. E. D. *Introductions to the Dialogues of Plato*. Translated by W. Dobson. 1836. Reprint. New York: Arno Press, 1973.

Schmalzriedt, E. "Das 'Spätwerk': Der Umfahrtsmythos des *Phaidros*." Chap. 7 of *Platon: Der Schriftsteller und die Wahrheit*. Munich: R. Piper, 1969, pp. 308–89.

Seeskin, K. R. "Formalization in Platonic Scholarship." *Metaphilosophy* 9 (1978): 242–51.

————. "Platonism, Mysticism, and Madness." *Monist* 59 (1976): 574–86.

Sève, B. *Phèdre de Platon*. Paris: Éditions Pédagogie Moderne, 1980.

Sextus Empiricus. *Works*. Translated by R. G. Bury. 4 vols. London: Heinemann, 1933–49.

Shoemaker, S. *Self-Knowledge and Self-Identity*. Ithaca: Cornell University Press, 1963.

Shorey, P. "On Plato *Phaedrus* 250d." *Classical Philology* 27 (1932): 280–82.

————. "On the *Erotikos* of Lysias in Plato's *Phaedrus*." *Classical Philology* 28 (1933): 131–32.

————. "Φύσις, Μελέτη, Ἐπιστήμη." *Transactions of the American Philological Association* 40 (1909): 185–201.

————. *The Unity of Plato's Thought*. 1903. Reprint. Chicago: University of Chicago Press, 1968.

Sichirollo, L. *Dialegesthai-Dialektik*. Hildesheim: Olms, 1966.

Sicking, C. M. J. "Organische Komposition und Verwandtes." *Mnemosyne* 16 (1963): 225–42.

Sickle, J. Van. "Plat. *Phaedr*. 255d, 3–6." *Museum Criticum* 8/9 (1973–74): 198–99.

Sinaiko, H. L. *Love, Knowledge, and Discourse in Plato: Dialogue and Dialectic in Phaedrus, Republic, Parmenides*. Chicago: University of Chicago Press, 1965.

Skemp, J. B. *The Theory of Motion in Plato's Later Dialogues*. Cambridge: Cambridge University Press, 1942.

Sparshott, F. E. "Socrates and Thrasymachus." *Monist* 50 (1966): 421–59.

Sprague, R. K. "Logic and Literary Form in Plato." *Personalist* 48 (1967): 560–72.

————. "*Phaedrus* 262 D 1." *Mnemosyne* 31 (1978): 72.

————. *Plato's Use of Fallacy: A Study of the Euthydemus and Some Other Dialogues*. New York: Barnes & Noble, 1962.

Stenzel, J. *Plato's Method of Dialectic*. Translated by D. J. Allan. 1940. Reprint. New York: Arno Press, 1973.

Stewart, J. A. *The Myths of Plato*. Edited by G. R. Levy. 1905. Reprint. Carbondale: Southern Illinois University Press, 1960.

Stöcklein, P. "Über die philosophische Bedeutung von Platons Mythen." *Philologus*. Suppl. vol. 30 (1937): 1–58.

Strauss, L. "Correspondence concerning *Wahrheit und Methode*." *Independent Journal of Philosophy* 2 (1978): 5–12.

————. "On a Forgotten Kind of Writing." *Independent Journal of Philosophy* 2 (1978): 27–31.

————. *On Tyranny*. Ithaca: Cornell University Press, 1963. Includes Kojève's "Tyranny and Wisdom" and Strauss's "Restatement on Xenophon's *Hiero*."

————. *Persecution and the Art of Writing*. 1952. Reprint. Westport: Greenwood Press, 1973.

————. *The City and Man*. Chicago: University of Chicago Press, 1964.

Tarrant, D. "Plato as Dramatist." *Journal of Hellenic Studies* 75 (1955): 82–89.

Tejera, V. "Irony and Allegory in the *Phaedrus.*" *Philosophy and Rhetoric* 8 (1975): 71–87.

Tigerstedt, E. N. *Interpreting Plato.* Uppsala: Almquist & Wiksell, 1977.

Trevaskis, J. R. "Division and Its Relation to Dialectic and Ontology in Plato." *Phronesis* 12 (1967): 118–29.

Vanhoutte, M. *La méthode ontologique de Platon.* Louvain: E. Nauwelaerts, 1956.

Verdenius, W. J. "Der Begriff der Mania in Platons *Phaidros.*" *Archiv für Geschichte der Philosophie* 44 (1962): 132–50.

————. "Notes on Plato's *Phaedrus.*" *Mnemosyne* 4, no. 8 (1955): 265–89.

Vermeule, E. *Aspects of Death in Early Greek Art and Poetry.* Berkeley: University of California Press, 1979.

Versényi, L. "Eros, Irony and Ecstasy." *Thought* 37 (1962): 598–612.

Vicaire, P. *Platon: Critique littéraire.* Paris: Klincksieck, 1960.

Vlastos, G. *Platonic Studies.* 2d ed. 1973. Reprint. Princeton: Princeton University Press, 1981.

————, ed. *Plato I.* Garden City, N.Y.: Doubleday, 1971.

————. *Plato II.* 1971. Reprint. Notre Dame: Notre Dame University Press, 1978.

Voegelin, E. *Plato.* Baton Rouge: Louisiana State University Press, 1966.

Warner, M. "Love, Self, and Plato's *Symposium.*" *Philosophical Quarterly* 29 (1979): 329–39.

Weaver, R. M. "The *Phaedrus* and the Nature of Rhetoric." In *Language Is Sermonic.* Baton Rouge: Louisiana State University Press, 1970, pp. 57–83.

White, N. "The *Phaedrus:* New Problems of Language and Method." Chap. 5 of *Plato on Knowledge and Reality.* Indianapolis: Hackett, 1976, pp. 117–30.

Wieland, W. *Platon und die Formen des Wissens.* Göttingen: Vandenhoeck & Ruprecht, 1982.

Wilkins, E. G. *"Know Thyself" in Greek and Latin Literature.* 1917. Reprint. New York: Garland, 1979.

Wolz, H. *Plato and Heidegger.* Lewisburg: Bucknell University Press, 1981.

Wycherley, R. E. "The Scene of Plato's *Phaedrus.*" *Phoenix* 17 (1963): 88–98.

Wyller, E. A. *"Phaidros:* Eros und Psyche." In *Der Späte Platon.* Hamburg: Meiner, 1970, pp. 122–30.

Zaslavsky, R. "A Hitherto Unremarked Pun in the *Phaedrus.*" *Apeiron* 15 (1981): 115–16.

————. *Platonic Myth and Platonic Writing.* Washington, D.C.: University Press of America, 1981.

General Index

The General Index gives pivotal or explanatory passages for selected terms, and is not a complete listing of all occurrences of such terms in the text.

Analysis, 59–60, 163, 174, 191, 193, 198–200, 275n13, 276n16, 280n30

Anonymity: Platonic, 14, 52, 220, 222–23, 225, 247n19. *See also* Dialogue, form

Art (*techne*), 6, 20, 48, 76, 160, 169–70, 175–201 passim, 202–05, 211, 273n3, 278nn22, 23, 279n24, 281n32, 282n40, 283nn2, 5, 285n14, 288n28. *See also* Division; Method

Artifact, 232–33, 239, 249n5, 269n60

Beauty, 22, 34, 62, 64, 128, 254n5, 268–69n60, 269n62; as Idea, 35, 90, 113, 117–19, 121, 123–26, 134, 163, 218, 240–41, 263n36, 266n47, 274n5

Body, 24, 46, 61, 62, 70, 80, 115, 122, 124, 135–36, 166, 178, 184, 187, 191, 213, 228, 234, 263nn34, 35, 282n38

Character, 3–4, 42, 125–26, 171, 197, 215, 231; philosophical, 35, 118, 131,

172; type, 100, 102, 122, 130–31, 195, 199, 269n62

Chariot, 93, 262n28, 263n32

Choice: of character (soul type), 100–01, 264–65n42

Cicada, 24, 34, 141, 161, 165–68

Collection, 116, 120, 173–97 passim, 212, 275–77nn13–18

Comedy, 1, 8, 24, 29, 30, 32, 51, 67, 130, 228, 264n42

Cosmos, 3, 42, 43, 99, 101, 106, 114, 135, 149, 190, 231, 233, 239

Daimon, 71, 256n17, 263n37, 282n2

Death, 252–53n24

Definition, 50, 59–61, 162, 177, 188, 192, 196, 255n12, 277n19, 278n23, 279nn25, 26

Deliberation, 58–61 passim

Democracy, 20, 203, 253n19, 283n3

Dialectic, 22, 23, 61, 66, 130, 132, 181, 201, 204, 208–29 passim, 232, 237, 255n12, 281nn31, 32, 282n37, 286nn17, 19, 288n28; and rhetoric, 32, 116, 215; as incomplete, 106, 230, 234,

307

Index of Proper Names

Index of Greek Terms